'If there are any armchair revolutionaries left out there who still believe the IRA is some sort of liberation army fighting for freedom on behalf of the downtrodden Roman Catholics of Northern Ireland they should, at the very least, be given a hearty bang over the head with this book.' *Financial Times*

'One senior security source described the book, *Killing Rage*, as the most important exposé of terrorist methods in Ulster for more than a decade . . . [It] portrays the IRA as a fanatical, ruthless organisation whose murders are often sectarian and indiscriminate.' *Daily Telegraph*

'[It] should be compulsory reading . . . here is a thoroughly convincing portrait of the reality of Irish terrorism, which is by turns egotistical, pathetic, brainless, brilliantly cunning and ceaselessly homicidal.' *Evening Standard*

'This is a book of extreme emotional dyslexia . . . Through sheer accumulation, this catalogue of deadly banalities achieves a weird intensity.' *Guardian*

'*Killing Rage* provides a riveting insight into the mind of someone who once believed he had the right to take the life of other human beings.' *Irish News*

'This is truly the most disturbing and arguably the most important book yet published about the IRA. Disturbing because Eamon Collins holds nothing back about his days, as a terrorist . . . Important because the IRA is laid bare for what it is.' *Ulster News Letter*

'This is a disturbing book, but compelling for the insight it gives into paramilitary psychology. It has taken courage to write it and requires some strength of mind to read it.' *Irish World*

KILLING RAGE

Eamon Collins lives in Ireland with his family. He broke with the IRA after the events described in this book.

Mick McGovern was born in London in 1962. He trained as a journalist on the *Wolverhampton Express and Star*, and after working in Fleet Street joined Thames Television's *This Week*, which he left to become a writer. His work has been published in the *New Statesman* and the *Observer*.

KILLING RAGE

Eamon Collins
with
Mick McGovern

Granta Books
London

Granta Publications, 2/3 Hanover Yard, London N1 8BE

First published in Great Britain by Granta Books 1997
This edition published by Granta Books 1998

A CIP catalogue record for this book is
available from the British Library.

7 9 10 8 6

Contents

This book is dedicated to my beloved wife Bernadette and children Tiárnach, Lorcan, Sorcha and Aoife in the hope that they and their children inherit a more equal and just society.

EAMON COLLINS

INTRODUCTION

In April 1995, I appeared in a film broadcast on ITV concerning my life in the IRA.

In the film I told parts of the story. This book is the whole story. The film provoked outrage in Northern Ireland and led to questions in the House of Commons. It also seemed to unite all sides in condemnation of me. Republicans thought I should have kept my mouth shut about the dirty little deeds I had committed with others in the name of a United Ireland; unionists wondered why I was not rotting in prison for what I had done.

I decided to make the film and write this book in the light of the cease-fires. In common with most other people, I felt hesitantly optimistic that the paramilitaries had at last realized that violence was hindering, not helping, their aspirations. But I also felt that the time was right to help start a deeper process of reflection about the causes, and nature, of political violence within Northern Ireland.

This book is in part an attempt to explain why a segment of people within the Catholic population believed that the best way to redress their grievances was through violence. It is also, I believe, the most complete insider's account of the grim business of political murder written by any participant in the conflict over the last twenty-eight years. This is not meant as an arrogant boast, rather as an explanation of why I was prepared to risk the opprobrium of all by raking over my past: I had felt for some time that no one had given a complete and truthful account of even one aspect of the IRA's campaign, despite the endless books and films on the subject. Some conveyed some of the truth, but none in my opinion had touched the heart of the true horror.

Carlton Television's film, 'Confession', shocked me too. I watched the family of one of my victims, Major Ivan Toombs, talking about the impact of his murder on them. I had helped to kill the head of their family, and yet they did not utter one word of bitterness. Even off-camera, according to the production team, they expressed only concern that I was putting myself at risk from the IRA by telling the truth about what I had done.

When I set out to kill Ivan Toombs I was setting out to kill a UDR uniform. What the programme brought home was that you can never kill a uniform, you can only kill a person. I had to ignore Ivan Toombs's many human qualities in order to be able to kill him. When I saw his family on that programme, I could see that his decency survived him. Those fine people gave me hope for the future of my country. I shall carry with me until my death the knowledge of the suffering I inflicted on them – and on the relatives of my other victims. I am deeply sorry for the part I played in all of those deaths.

But my sorrow is not enough. One of the aims of this book is to move beyond sorrow or simple expressions of regret. By exposing myself to the anger of my former comrades and the families of my victims, I wanted to show that I had thought long and hard about what had happened and that it is possible to become a different person – as we all have to become different people if we are to live together in Northern Ireland without political violence.

I truly believe that only by confronting our past actions, by understanding the forces which drove us to carry them out, can we hope to create the possibility of a society in which these actions do not occur again. This book is about the IRA because that was the organization of which I was a member. The IRA was not the only group killing people in Northern Ireland. I look forward to reading similarly complete accounts from members of the loyalist paramilitaries and representatives of the Crown forces.

If I have blackened the IRA's name, I have done so with the heat of truth. I have tried to be transparently honest about my thoughts and actions during my period as a Provo. If people think I have been harsh on some of my former comrades, I hope they will also recognize that I have been equally harsh on myself. The person who emerges from these pages is not attractive; he is fanatical, full of anger and contempt, and ready to connive at the deaths of his enemies when they are unarmed and vulnerable. Ready to risk murdering enemies who turned out not to be enemies at all. During my time in the organization, I met IRA men who were brave and honourable. I met some who were the scum of the earth. I am sure I would be able to say much the same thing about my comrades if I had been in the UVF, the UDA, the UDR, the RUC or the British Army.

Of course, I know I can expect republican displeasure at this account of my life in the IRA. Three months after the film, in July 1995, a petrol bomb turned my family's car into a fireball. The car had been parked outside our house on the Barcroft Park Estate in Newry. I was not at home, but my wife and four young children were. I know who did it – he was seen running away. He is a Sinn Fein member who comes from what psychologists would call a dysfunctional family, although people on Barcroft have a more colloquial word to describe them. After throwing the bomb, he ran to the house of a woman who spies on her neighbours for the republican movement, keeping a close eye on happenings offensive to her republican morality. She thinks her association with the IRA gives her clout in the community. In one sense, of course, she is right. But she does not know that behind her back she is loathed and despised. In every Catholic community in Northern Ireland the republican movement has a network of informers like her. Republicanism gives a political legitimacy to the age-old pastime of spying on one's neighbours, turning neighbourhood vendettas into noble struggles.

They had sneaked in their act of petty vengeance against me under the blanket of nationalist anger at the release of paratrooper Lee Clegg. Our car was the only one to be burned in an estate of 300 houses. In the wake of Clegg's release, supposedly spontaneous rioting had broken out across Northern Ireland. Of course, it was spontaneous in the sense that Sinn Fein and IRA members spontaneously poured petrol into milk bottles and spontaneously hijacked cars and spontaneously burnt those cars. In Newry, a man who earned his living from his van answered his door to find representatives of the republican movement demanding his keys. They took the van, placed it across the road, and set fire to it as his terrified family watched. Across the North scores of other Catholic working-class people had their lives disrupted by the spontaneous anger of the people. There could have been no better illustration of the true nature of a movement insisting on its right to be the sole voice of the Irish nation than what took place during those few days of rioting. In the euphoria of peace, people had been able to forget for a little while that the IRA are not the liberators of Irish people. We should be grateful to the republican movement for providing such a powerful reminder of the brutality that lies at the heart of what they have to offer. And they have provided many other reminders since then: there seems to be no shortage of baseball-bat wielders ready to cripple young men for the petty crimes of the poor. Catholics on working-class estates might not like the RUC's form of justice but they are beginning to find it preferable to the IRA's.

I say these things though I do not forget the injustices imposed upon Catholics since the inception of the Northern Ireland state. Widespread anti-Catholic discrimination provided a well-spring of suppressed anger ready to be tapped by any movement which challenged the *status quo*. But the question is not 'Did Catholics suffer discrimination?' Of course they did. The important question is 'Was violence the best, and most effective, way of combatting that discrimination?' The answer to that question is: No. The Provisionals' so-called war of liberation has been a long drawn-out scourge that has failed to defend or advance the cause of Catholics in the north. The IRA's campaign helped to divert the forces which could have battled discrimination effectively. Instead, ironically, the Provos helped sustain the discrimination by helping to entrench the most reactionary unionists behind security fences built with billions of pounds of British tax-payers' money. Those unionists opposed to the very idea of equality of treatment for Catholics could hide their vicious sectarianism behind the screen of outrage kept in constant repair by IRA atrocities.

For many years after I left the IRA and had rejected the main tenets of Provoism, I clung to the belief that, at the very least, the IRA existed to defend Catholics, a last resort against the threat of loyalist assassination and pogroms, particularly in the tight communal interfaces of Belfast. After the cease-fire in 1994, but shortly before I made the television programme, I called on Seán, one of my former comrades. He was now living in Dublin and had not been involved in the IRA for more than a decade. In the late Sixties he had fought bravely to defend his particular enclave of Belfast from marauding loyalist mobs, whose activities in those days were often aided, or at least not actively discouraged, by elements of the RUC.

Seán was not enthusiastic about the cease-fire. We discussed the IRA's campaign and I said that one of the things that angered me was that we had not been able to prevent hundreds of sectarian assassinations of Catholics, particularly in north Belfast. Seán, a former OC of one of the north Belfast units, said: 'Those sectarian killings actually benefitted the IRA. They led to greater support for us in those areas. We could respond eventually by taking out leading loyalists, which proved to the people that the IRA was there protecting them.' His honesty shocked me and underlined the cynicism behind one of the most important strands of IRA propaganda. Many Catholics allowed themselves to become prisoners of the IRA for twenty-five years through a fear which the IRA did very little to assuage.

To me, the idea of a United Ireland has become an almost meaningless abstraction. To think for a moment that Catholics in the north belong automatically and naturally within an all-Ireland state is to deny reality. We have lived within a British system for seventy-five years longer than the rest of the island, but even prior to partition our co-existence with a predominantly Protestant population helped create an identity for northern Catholics distinct from that of Catholics brought up elsewhere in Ireland. The violence has isolated us from the people with whom we have most in common – northern Protestants – and deepened the gulf between us and our southern neighbours.

If I had a magic wand I might like to create a unified state on this island in which people lived harmoniously. But magic wands only exist in fairy tales. In reality there exist on this island groups of people with differing, ultimately irreconcilable, aspirations. Northern Ireland is not peculiar in this respect. The main thing we can reasonably hope for is that the various groups agree to differ without the use of violence. I am happy to see people work for the creation of a United Ireland so long as they do not resort to murder in trying to achieve their ideal. I do not want to see one more death in pursuit of this abstract concept.

I no longer believe in Utopian solutions to complicated and intractable problems. One person's Utopia usually means another person's hell. We live in a state of uncertainty, not just in Northern Ireland, but by virtue of being human. What I have tried to do over the last decade is to subject my former beliefs to ruthless scrutiny. Instead of searching for ways to confirm my beliefs, I have searched for ways to prove them false. When, after dispassionate examination, you cannot prove your beliefs false, then perhaps you are on the way to discovering some sort of truth.

Instead of looking at history in all its complicated richness, both Catholics and Protestants have tended to celebrate particular momentary episodes as signposts on the road to deliverance (to use someone else's image). I hope that Catholics will start to question more incisively the meaning for today of words uttered, for instance, in 1798 or 1916. I hope also that a similar critical debate will take place within the Protestant community, some of whose members still seem to be mentally becalmed in the seventeenth century.

Of course, there is not one cohesive Protestant community. There is a whole range of voices and beliefs, including that strand of Protestant radicalism which contributed so powerfully in earlier centuries to the development of republican ideology. The IRA campaign forced many progressive

Protestants into hiding and made the majority unite behind the most reactionary and conservative elements. One dividend of the so-called peace process is that Catholics were becoming aware of the diversity of opinion among Protestants.

One of the most enlightening aspects of my journey over the last decade has been my study of the Protestant tradition in Northern Ireland. This encounter, both in books and on the ground in hardline loyalist areas, helped to disabuse me of one of the more fatuous republican notions – the idea that once the British withdrew from Ireland the Protestants would 'see sense' and join with their fellow Catholic countrymen to shape a United Ireland. This is so much wishful thinking.

I hope that the representatives of militant republicanism and loyalism will begin to deepen their understanding of the other's ideology and culture. If they look closely enough they might see mirror-images of themselves. Both sides have learned a lot from each other during the conflict. One of the traditional media images of militant loyalism is still that of the aggressive marching band with its pipes and drums. Republicans traditionally engaged in less bombastic musical displays during marches. But during the H-Block campaign in the early 1980s a new beast emerged – the republican marching band, complete with pipes and drums, and the same limited repertoire of aggressive and intimidatory sounds possessed by their loyalist counterparts.

Wall murals provide another example of cultural hijacking. In the early days only republicans tended to paint vivid wall murals to put across propaganda and to mark out territory. These murals became so popular with television producers that before long, equally impressive murals began appearing in Protestant areas. I hope in the future that the two sides can learn more useful things from each other.

Many nationalists have been astounded by the fact that the most reasonable and compromising voices within the Protestant community since the cease-fire have often been those of the spokesmen for the loyalist paramilitaries. There have been some expressions of disgust that one of the loyalist negotiators served a life sentence for the murder of the Catholic politician Paddy Wilson who, with his Protestant girlfriend, was stabbed to death in a frenzied attack in a country lane in the seventies. His girlfriend was singled out for particularly vicious mutilation – the sort normally reserved by the UVF for Catholics: her breasts were cut off. Some people might find it outrageous that this man is negotiating with government officials. I find it reassuring and encouraging. I am far happier that he is wandering around the corridors of Stormont wearing a suit than hiding in country lanes wearing a balaclava, waiting to butcher any Protestant woman who offends his standards of tribal purity.

It is not only those who actively participated in the violence who need to examine themselves and their beliefs. I believe that everyone in Ireland should be prepared to examine critically where they stood in relation to the war. It corrupted thousands of people by making them ambivalent towards violence. Such people did not do what I did during the conflict, but they contributed to the continuation of the blood feast by quietly exulting in particular acts of violence, as they watched the television news from the safety of their sitting-rooms.

Ironically, when I was in the IRA I felt that Gerry Adams was working to 'sell out' physical-force republicanism. Indeed, I expressed these views vociferously to my comrades at the time. I realize now that Adams saw a long time before I did that the armed struggle was taking nationalists nowhere. He deserves respect for his strength of character in acting on this insight and, over the course of a decade, slowly taking the republican movement with him towards a future without violence.

Some people say that the Crown forces had to fight the IRA with one hand tied behind their backs. Although I am now deeply hostile to the IRA, and look forward to its demise, I would still say that the IRA also fought with one hand tied behind its back: in general it did not carry out the indiscriminate campaign of all-out war which it would have been capable of fighting and which, when I was a committed revolutionary, I wanted it to fight. Even the loyalist paramilitaries held back for long periods from indiscriminate excesses. Shortly before the cease-fire – with the IRA's bombing of the fish-and-chip shop in the Shankill and the loyalists' retaliatory machine-gunning of a pub in Loughinisland – I think Northern Ireland was moving towards a Bosnia-type abyss. How do you respond to the slaughter of shopfuls of people buying food or old men having a pint? Bombing a street; then a whole village: and then the bloody expulsions from cities and regions. It is to the credit of both republicans and loyalists that they walked up to the edge of the abyss, peered over, gulped, then stepped back.

I have hope for Northern Ireland. I believe the war is over, but at the same time I do not think people should expect too much from the peace. Perhaps one of the problems in Northern Ireland is that people spend too much time talking about 'the problem' and 'the solution'. Perhaps people should realize that the only *final* solution is that abyss.

I think that people have to work with the reality of a polarized society. Perhaps the way forward in the medium term is to recognize that polarization and accommodate it through separate structures of administration for the two communities: they have theirs, and we have ours, gradually enlarging the common ground in the middle.

There is a lot of pain ahead. But at least the pain can be endured in an atmosphere of relative peace. I hope that both republicans and loyalists can accept that in this divided society, with mutually irreconcilable desires, no one group can predominate.

In my own family I am happy that my kids are more interested in Batman than 'Raman, and the Addams Family, rather than Gerry Adams's republican family. However, I was a little perturbed when my seven-year-old daughter Sorcha came running to me crying recently. She had a complaint to make about her brother Lorcan, aged ten, and sister Aoife, aged six, after a disagreement over toys. She said: 'Daddy, Lorcan and Aoife said that when they grow up they're going to join the IRA and they're going to shoot me.' This incident reminded me that the cultural roots which sustained the Provos have not gone away. I received another, less amusing reminder shortly after the cease-fire when I went to the republicans' Easter March in Newry. For the first time in twenty years it was well attended, the ranks of the marchers swollen by those who now felt it was virtuous – and certainly a lot safer – to be a recognized republican. These Johnny-come-lately types are similar to those who, after Ireland's War of Independence, appeared from nowhere and claimed to have been secret activists for the IRA. And there, resplendent in their military uniforms, with their Sam Browne belts and black berets, were the IRA colour party engaging in macho posturing in memory of the noble corpses of 1916. It was a depressing day.

One day in October 1995, I felt a pain in my heart; then my left arm went limp and the tips of my fingers began tingling. I was with a friend at the time: I told him I thought I was having a heart attack. He put me in a car and drove me to Dublin's Mater Hospital which was only five minutes away. I collapsed when I got there. As the cardiac team set to work, a young nurse held my hand. I could feel myself slipping away. I said: 'I don't think I'm going to make it. Tell my wife I love her.' But I survived because I had made it to the hospital so quickly: they were able to abort the main shock wave which, the consultant said, would almost certainly have killed me.

As I floated on the fringes of consciousness I thought: 'I've done some terrible things in my life.' But worse – I had done those things in support of beliefs which I now knew to be deluded. I did not want to die knowing that nothing worthwhile had come from my actions.

My hope is that someone somewhere might learn something useful from the story of my life.

1

THE KILLING OF
IVAN TOOMBS

At the time I became one of Her Majesty's customs officers I
was about to become one of Her official enemies – a member of
the Provisional IRA.

I had not been in the Customs and Excise for two hours
when I realized that my job could merely be a means to an end.
It would provide me with a wage and allow me to buy books,
take holidays and visit friends, but I didn't see it as a 'career',
nor did I have much respect for the clerks who, in their offices
on the border, attached some importance to reinforcing the
partition of Ireland, working to legitimize this symbol of the
last relics of British colonialism.

I had a mundane clerical job. I sat behind a long counter,
facing a door through which dozens of lorry drivers entered
each day. This was the 'report seat', the public counter for
checking the importation of goods from the Republic to the
North of Ireland. I took the drivers' entry papers, made sure
that all the appropriate boxes were filled in, that the signa-
tures were in the right place, and wrote the details in an entry
book which I passed through a wooden hatch to the clerical
assistants for the final stage of the bureaucratic process.

I was the truck drivers' friend. I had spent enough years
reading about anarchism and libertarian socialism to feel solidarity with and sympathy for people who had an arduous
job and who could do without having their lives made more

difficult by petty officials. The staff, with the exception of a few of the more humanitarian and intelligent individuals, seldom liked the drivers. But drivers who were willing to clip money to the C1220 export documents or to offer goods off the back of a lorry (known as 'prog') could induce some of the old-timers to act more considerately.

Within two days of arriving at Newry customs station in December 1978 I had discovered from casual conversations with colleagues that two part-time members of the Royal Ulster Constabulary Reserve, the wife of a detective, and – best of all – Major Ivan Toombs of the Ulster Defence Regiment, all worked at the neighbouring customs office in Warrenpoint. I had stumbled on valuable information. I was not then a member of the IRA, but for all that, I decided to pass on this intelligence. I knew that by doing so I was crossing an important line, but I also knew what I was doing. The IRA was changing – influenced by radical left-wing prisoners – and I had begun to see it as a positive force for change. I was influenced by a very ultra-left kind of Marxism. I believed that the IRA could be turned into an organization which could take on the capitalist state and the agents of that state, as the Red Brigades had done in Italy. I saw the struggle in interna-tionalist terms: I believed Irish republicans should forge links with their brothers and sisters in Lebanon, in Germany, Italy, or Palestine, to help overthrow the forces who were retrenching capitalism in all the western democracies. Of course, I was one of the lucky Catholics in Northern Ireland who had had a rea-sonable education, had found a job and had been integrated into the system as a semi-loyal servant; and there were by then many thousands of Catholics who were succumbing happily to these inducements. I realized that if I joined the IRA I would be threatening my comfort and privileges, I felt I would be casting off the illusion of state protection: I would become as one with the Catholic underclass, marginalized, on the periph-ery of society, jobless and poorly educated, powerless and voiceless – at least until the IRA arrived to help them speak. I hated men like Toombs for his assumption of the right to police and harrass the people with whom I wanted to merge. I regarded Toombs and his friends as parasites, allowed to feed on the corrupt corpse of the Orange State, and kept alive by British money and the British Army. In that winter of 1978 I felt ready to cross the line. I was ready to become a Provo.

I had a direct line to the IRA through a distant relative, who was on the run in Dundalk. This man had an ambiguous relationship with the IRA. Useful to them for several years, he had quit after a nervous breakdown, no longer able to take the continuous pressure. I didn't think he had anything to be ashamed of. He had been there when the danger was at its worst, living through the chaotic years of the early seventies when IRA operations would be planned on the spur of the moment. IRA volunteers would just hijack a car, collect a couple of rifles, and take a few pot shots at the nearest army patrol. Planning, organization, and co-ordination were not familiar words in those days. Now everything had changed: a cell structure ensured that IRA members operated in small, self-sufficient units. There was now better discipline and training, and the philosophy of the movement owed more to the terrorists of the West German Baader-Meinhof group and the Red Brigades than to the IRA heroes from the misty past.

My information on Major Toombs and the other reservists helped start my career with the IRA. With it, I was like a bride bringing a dowry. My relative, whom I shall call Danny, surprised me by revealing that he knew Toombs; that he had, in fact, tried to kill him a few years previously. He and a Belfast man had lain in wait for the then UDR Captain Toombs in the garden of a house on a private estate in Newry called The Glen. The owners were away on holiday. The Belfast gunman was supposed to shoot Toombs as he drove past. My relative's job had been to prepare booby-trapped anti-personnel bombs which he had placed in the garden's thick undergrowth, where members of the Crown forces would inevitably take up positions and be shredded by the home-made shrapnel.

Toombs eventually appeared, driving his car slowly up the steep hill. The gunman was about to fire straight across the road, through Toombs's windscreen, when another car came down the hill and blocked the line of fire. Perhaps that

split-second interference saved Toombs's life. As soon as the
second car had passed, the gunman fired a round from his
Armalite rifle. But Toombs was no longer in the ideal position,
and the bullet hit the door on the driver's side, ripping off the
door handle. The 7.62mm bullet must have fragmented and
ricocheted into Toombs because the IRA men saw his face
contort with pain. However, the gunman's position, at an awk-
ward side angle, prevented him from squeezing off more
accurate shots which would certainly have killed his target.
Toombs would have died if he had panicked, braked, swerved
or crashed, but although seriously injured, he managed to drive
to the customs station two miles away. He was saved that time
by a passing car, a chrome door handle and his own courage.
Later I learned from customs men who were there that
Toombs had driven into the station yard, pushed open his
door, and fallen out of the car. As for the bombs, the army
found and defused them.

Danny was surprised to hear that Toombs had become a
UDR major, but he was excited by my information. He had
fallen from grace in the eyes of republicans as a result of his
nervous breakdown, which was seen by them as a kind of
weakness, a ploy to get out of the IRA. Now, armed with my
information, he saw a way of ingratiating himself once more –
not as a volunteer, but as an all right guy who had been useful
once upon a time and was still worthy of respect. Danny told
me he would be in touch.

Some weeks later, on a Saturday afternoon, Danny took me
to meet an IRA man called Seamus. I knew nothing about
him, but I assumed he had some sort of responsibility for the
Newry area. Bearded and reserved, he spoke to me with disturbing frankness. He seemed to suggest that I was mad to
want to join the IRA in an area like Newry. He told me a
demoralizing tale of incompetence and ineptitude. He said the
Newry IRA had an atrocious reputation and was in a chaotic
state. They had lost their independent command and battalion
status, and were run from Dundalk rather than Newry because
on their own they could not be trusted to command anything.
He pointed out that Newry IRA people, with one or two
exceptions, had always cracked under interrogation and signed

damaging confessions. They had been responsible for the loss and theft of so much irreplaceable weaponry that they were no longer trusted with weapons of their own: whenever they had an idea for an operation they had to apply for equipment, and then go through a vetting procedure to determine whether the guns were going to be put to proper use. The worst enemy of the republican movement in Newry was its reputation for attracting social misfits and petty criminals. Seamus suggested that everything touched by the IRA in Newry turned into an embarrassment or a disaster. He asked me why anyone with a decent job would want to touch them.

I had been told that the IRA never painted a rosy picture for potential recruits, in order to scare off the faint-hearted; that they liked to warn people that, at the very least, their lives would no longer be their own, and that, in all probability, they would end up on the run, in prison, or dead. But Seamus, who was obviously tired and disillusioned, seemed to be going beyond this standard warning.

I admitted I was put off risking myself for such a chaotic group, but I wanted recognition by the IRA. If Newry was a mess, I believed it could be rectified by the right people and that I was one of them. In Northern Ireland we understood that the British Army classified areas by colour according to their level of republican military activity: white, let us say, is the safest, black the most dangerous. Newry in 1978 was there-fore a grey area, and some districts were even classified white. This meant that the army felt that there was only a tiny chance of being attacked by the Newry IRA: they thought the organi-zation was decrepit. I was determined to change that, to help turn Newry into a black area. At that moment, only three min-utes' drive from Newry (which is a predominantly Catholic town), many Protestant policemen and part-time soldiers were living in the community, going to local shops without anxiety, and generally enjoying life. I wanted to replace their security with terror.

Danny was disappointed when he heard about my meeting with Seamus. He contacted another IRA man who he thought would be more receptive to what I was offering. This man was immediately alert to what I had to say. He wore a suit and had a business-like manner. Within the hour he had introduced me to two other men: the co-ordinating officer for all IRA units operating in the north, and the intelligence officer for the South Down area, who I would later nickname 'Iceman'. They came quickly to the point: was I prepared to set up Toombs and the others for assassination, and did I have any idea how best they could be killed?

I felt that I also had to move quickly to the point, and explained my reservations about joining the IRA in Newry. I needed to know that if I were to help them kill soldiers and policemen, that there would be no loose ends. Seamus's warning had been very effective. They assured me that they would use experienced men. I said I would do what I could to set them up for what I thought of as the people's justice. The intelligence officer told me I would be crucial to the success of any operation; they had no one else in a position to gain direct knowledge of the movements of these people, their routines, habits, the precautions they took. He said I had to get close to them without arousing suspicion which could even lead to a counter-operation by the RUC Special Branch. Iceman was assigned as my contact. I was asked to give him a contact number – I gave him my number at work – and we decided that when he rang he would say he was my brother John. If he wanted to see me he would invite me out for a pint. I would know it was him if he said, 'How's she going?', which he would accompany with an almost joyful laugh. It was a convivial code: in the coming years I was to hear it many times.

In my own eyes, I was an IRA man when I returned to Newry that night, even though I was not yet officially inducted into the organization. I felt important, useful, trusted; I went to work a new man. My hours spent at the report seat gave me leisure to think and fantasize about how to build an efficient terrorist organization. I began to learn the importance of building up character profiles, of gathering all kinds of intelligence – no matter how trivial or seemingly irrelevant – and how to be selective, to question people without them realizing you were looking for information. I convinced myself that the IRA had become dependent on hit-and-miss information and gossip from unreliable sources. What the organization needed was a network of sources ranging from local people, who could provide low-grade, every-day intelligence, to people inside the apparatus of the state, who could provide a lot more. I felt my job had opened up an important field of information which the republican movement could exploit. I was a clerical worker in the Imperial Civil Service. I was determined to do all I could to wreck it.

I had yet to meet Toombs. He was an idea, a force, not a person with a face; he had no humanity for me. Even in this, my apprentice period, I was learning how to depersonalize a man so that his death could not touch me.

In order to spy on your enemies in the local community with deadly intent, you need to perfect a different kind of memory. If I saw something of interest – a person, a car, a set of circumstances – I would pick a distinguishing feature, perhaps a facial scar or a cracked number plate. Soon I could order this information under specific categories: police/army/detectives. Then sub-categories: rural/urban; Bessbrook/Newry; old/young. I would turn these details over in my mind, again and again, until they were indelible. I found that the old system of rote-learning was best, as though I were memorizing the commandments, or irregular verbs, and so I got into the habit of repeating a piece of information to myself at least ten times. If I spotted a vehicle I would break down its obvious features – two-door, hatchback, colour gold. Registration number? 'B' for Bertie. Then the potential target could be code-named 'Bertie'. Over the following weeks or months any new information could be put into my mental Bertie file. And I could call up this file at any time, like a student.

Toombs and his Crown forces colleagues at Warrenpoint were not the only targets I had in mind. I visited Iceman's home covertly; if he was not in, I would put my information on paper and leave it for him: this was the only time I ever did this during my time as an IRA man. We would sit in his bedroom while his favourite Planxty record played in the background – the plaintive voice of Christy Moore covering our discussions of 'ops'. During my meetings with Iceman he had explained two golden rules to me. The first was that, regardless of whether an objective had been achieved successfully, if a volunteer were captured or killed in the process, then the operation was a failure. The second was: never underestimate your enemy, but never overestimate him either. He stressed the importance of seeking out a target's routine, finding that particular aspect of his behaviour which could open him up for assassination. No matter how security-conscious someone is, there is almost always some aspect of his behaviour which becomes habitual. Targets would hardly be human if they did not have routines.

I knew that if I wanted to learn more about Toombs I had to get near him, but not so close as to attract suspicion. Suddenly an opportunity presented itself. Someone was needed to act as a relief worker at Warrenpoint to cover for officers on sick leave or on holiday. No one else from Newry would volunteer because they feared working in an office which contained so many part-time members of the Crown forces, in the event of an IRA attack. I told my superiors that the risk didn't bother me. So I began to work at Warrenpoint every now and again, for a few weeks at a time. Each time I entered the place I was able to paint another square of the canvas.

Warrenpoint customs station was an easy-going self-contained station, not long built, with showers and a well-equipped kitchen. There were around ten members of staff, but I spent most of my time at Warrenpoint working out ways to kill only Ivan Toombs. I had little interest in any of the other people except as a means of gaining information about Major Toombs. However, one of the executive officers attracted my attention. His name was Brendan. He talked loudly and excitedly, and took great care in signing his name on official documentation in his big, bold script. He appeared even to have some knowledge of the Irish language because he gaelicized his name when he signed it: *Breandán*. I took to working late shifts with him. He was quite open in speaking to me about the H-Block protest which was gaining support at the time, in early 1979. He thought that republican prisoners were right to resist the government's attempts to remove their political status and turn them into ordinary criminals. But this was a common sentiment among Northern Catholics, so I did not immediately jump to conclusions about his real sympathies.

However, later in 1979, close to Warrenpoint customs station, an IRA bomb killed eighteen soldiers – mostly paratroopers. To my delight Brendan took satisfaction in the fact that at long last 'those murdering, aggressive, half-witted bastards' had got their just desserts for shooting dead thirteen people in Derry back in 1972. I began to suspect he was an IRA sympathizer and not just an occasional nationalist. His sister was married to a Catholic man from a particularly loyalist area in Kilkeel: Brendan told me the usual horror stories about sectarian Protestant paramilitaries and their activities, and how these went unchecked by the police.

I gave to Brendan what few of his colleagues gave him: trust and respect. Among them he was seen as a gullible fool and a miser. I found him intelligent, although lacking in common sense, and extremely shrewd and careful with money. So I took a risk one day and told him that I had a connection with the republican movement. I said I was interested in compiling information about 'Crown forces personnel' in Warrenpoint. He started giving me what he called 'snippets'. He would not give me any information on any UDR and RUC men, whom he regarded as good guys, 'nice people'. But if there was some-one he thought was 'a right bastard', then he would tell me everything he knew, with exaggerations thrown in for good measure. For my part, I detested this kind of selective repub-licanism: there were no 'good' RUC or UDR men. They were all the same targets. You did not personalize them. Brendan was very reticent about Toombs, and during my first visits to the station I hardly saw Toombs. But one day he came to where I was working and I got a good look at him. I guessed he was in his mid to late forties; a small, stocky man. His hair was sandy-coloured with the fringe brushed back. He had a fresh complexion, and was slightly toothy.

I tried desperately to find Toombs's fatal routine. I kept tabs on his times of arrival at work: they always varied. I knew where he lived, I knew his car, that he was married with several children. He did not seem to have a close friend at work. Indeed, he did not seem to have any friends: he was a loner, not out of choice, but, I suspected, out of the need to survive. He seemed to lead a truly quiet life. Once I had even travelled to a union meeting with him, but I had not been able to penetrate his shell of reserve. I listened to his Protestant colleagues discuss him and I joined in the conversation, provoking them to say things. I suggested Ivan was a self-made man, deservedly a senior officer, a pillar of the service. I had certainly stirred a witches' brew. To some of his own community he was a nobody with airs and graces who had gained promotion because he had been shot by the IRA. They did not like the way he was able to come and go as he pleased, and they sneered at his membership of a golf club.

I felt only contempt for these people who denied the man the credit he deserved. For me, the more I found out about him, the more admirable I found him. He was a man of simple tastes who behaved decently towards all, the sort of man who would have rebuked anyone who made an anti-Catholic comment. I liked him and I felt that in other circumstances we might have been friends.

I came to find out lots of little details about Ivan Toombs, but never anything I could call a routine. Without a routine, without that regular and predictable action, I was stuck. But then, after two years of bits and pieces of nothing, I struck gold. I discovered that Major Toombs had got into the generous habit of giving his staff a little treat. Every Friday he would buy them sausage rolls and make them tea and coffee, always at around the same time in the morning. At last I had tied him down to one place, only momentarily, but long enough for gunmen to get in, kill him, and get out again. The only difficulty was that the other staff would be around. But if all the other staff were in the building, then the gunmen would also be able to kill another colleague of mine at the same time – a nice middle-aged chap but, unfortunately for him, a reserve policeman (the other one had left Warrenpoint by this time). Killing him as well as Toombs would be a bonus.

Around this time Toombs, who was Brendan's senior officer, wrote a report that Brendan was not fit for promotion. As was procedure, he discussed this report with Brendan before submitting it to his superiors. Toombs said that part of the reason for the bad report was what he called Brendan's 'ablutions' on the mornings he was on early shift. I thought it typical of Ivan's strait-laced morality that he would use this Victorian-sounding word to refer to Brendan's illicit shave and shower. Brendan was extremely angry, and his thoughts turned to vengeance. Suddenly he started offering me lots of information about Toombs: he went shopping in a particular supermarket, he bought his bread in a small home bakery, he went to a particular church on a Sunday. But now I was not interested. It was too late. I had already done my homework and I did not need Brendan's help. However, I asked him if he would like to join the IRA. He said he was interested, although he kept saying: 'All I want to supply is snippets.' What he should have realized was that so many snippets make a whole, and once that whole has come together then a new process, the final process, is set in motion and moves forward to an inevitable conclusion.

I supplied the IRA with detailed drawings of the layout of Warrenpoint customs station, indicating where Toombs and the reserve policeman would be. They were to be killed in the building – in a ghastly way, a vindication of the fundamental military principle of hitting your enemy where he least expects. I wanted the IRA to act fast because I would soon be taken off relief work and sent back to Newry, where I would not be able to keep up-to-date intelligence on Toombs and his colleague. I did not trust Brendan to take over from me: his sense of self-preservation would ensure he never helped us unstintingly.

One night Toombs made a surprise visit to my area when I was working late and alone. He had expected to find another of my colleagues there with me, a young Scotsman, but I had sent him home early, offering to cover for him. The next day Toombs gave the young man a rollicking, but I felt there was more to Toombs's anger than simply the young Scot's absence. To me it seemed that Toombs had been disappointed at missing this young man's company for a few hours – a Scot, a Protestant, someone to talk to without fear of it bringing a bullet in the back – rather than me, a Catholic, a nationalist, an unknown quantity. That night Toombs had brought his daughter with him. She could not have been more than eight or nine. She had large brown eyes, fearful and nervous. I remember thinking that no child should ever be like this: it was not natural, it was not fair. I did feel a twinge of conscience, despite my utter determination and capacity to abstract myself from human feeling, because I looked at this child and I said to myself: 'I'm putting the finishing touches to your father's death.'

Just before I finished my relief work at Warrenpoint, Toombs once again came into the office when I was on my own. He asked me to come with him to board and check a Russian ship that had just docked in the town's harbour. We were welcomed by the captain, who spoke very little English. He was a middle-aged, balding man who sat there smiling through two rows of gold crowns. He gave us a few shots of very strong Russian vodka, washed down with spring water. The conversation was limited but the vodka was extremely good. The captain smoked continuously and I noticed Toombs fingering a box of matches that featured a picture of a woman in a visionary pose representing the onward march of the Soviet motherland. Toombs let it be known that he collected matchboxes from all over the world. The captain said he had a variety of matchboxes in his stores and he would let Toombs have a selection of them. We left the ship with Ivan Toombs talking – slightly intoxicated with the strong liquor – about his delight at finding so many unusual matchboxes. I felt for him at that moment and I felt angry at the people from his own community, his own tribal group, who begrudged him his senior officer's position. I had heard that after the first assassination attempt Ivan had been offered customs jobs in Britain, but he had chosen to stay in Ireland so that he could keep his command in the UDR.

And he had been born in Warrenpoint; his family had lived there for generations. This was his home, and clearly he felt it was his duty to stay. I admired this quiet unassuming man. I also felt sorry for him: sorry that he appeared to be isolated and alone, sorry that his children lived in fear, sorry that they had been brought up to be careful of whoever they met – trusting no one, weighing up every situation they walked into. His daughter's eyes told the story of that fear. Even at that time – although I hated his politics – I could see that all Ivan wanted to do was defend and protect what he saw as his land, his way of life, his community, against a subversive threat.

On the way back to the office we spoke about the new security arrangements at Newry customs station. I asked him if he thought they would be effective against attack. He said that when a group of terrorists were determined and dedicated, when they devoted their minds and energies to a task, they would succeed regardless of the level of security. At that moment I felt in a strange way that we were engaged in a similar dangerous project; we had common bonds in that we both believed our cause to be right. But that was where my sympathy stopped. I was an unpaid volunteer in the IRA, part of a secret guerrilla army with limited resources. As far as I was concerned, Toombs, and others like him, were paid for propping up a system that had institutionalized sectarian hatred for sixty years, a system with an anti-Catholic ethos, a system that operated a policy of widespread discrimination. I, and others like me, had had enough: I felt that there was no point in trying to compromise or reason with these people, particularly in a situation which had become a lot worse with the arrival of Mrs Thatcher. For me, to strike at Toombs was to strike at an ancient colonial system of élites. Killing Toombs would also be a symbol of our dogged resistance to inequality and injustice, a gesture of solidarity with the protesting prisoners in the H-Blocks who had just embarked on the first hunger strike. I was full of a heady mixture of anti-imperialism, anger, sympathy and self-importance.

I pushed hard for the operation to be carried out before I had been moved from Warrenpoint back to Newry, but without success. The intelligence officer, Iceman – who was also going to be one of the gunmen – believed it was necessary to turn one final stone. He wanted to know how the gunmen would know for sure that Toombs and his policeman colleague were in the building when they called. I suspected that Iceman wanted to use Brendan to give some sort of signal, but I knew he would not have been able to cope with the pressure. As far as I was concerned the information was up-to-date. Toombs would be there as always on Friday at eleven o'clock, preparing tea and sausage rolls.

On a frosty day in the middle of January 1981 I got a call

from Iceman. He asked me to contact Brendan: he wanted to
see us both that night in Dundalk. I had no idea why. At that
time I was involved in sketching out several operations and it
was difficult to say which he wanted to discuss. Planning for an
attack on Warrenpoint police station had reached an advanced
stage; indeed, I thought that either that attack or the bombing
of the Customs and Excise warehouse in Newry would be the
next operation. Brendan agreed to pick me up in a pub in
Newry at 7 p.m. I waited two and a half hours; he did not
turn up. I returned home believing that Brendan had realized
that he was being asked to provide more than 'snippets' to the
republican movement. He was fast becoming a nuisance and a
liability, and I was convinced he would prove of little use as an
IRA volunteer, even though he was in the process of being
officially inducted into the organization.

Brendan turned up at my house just after midnight. I have
never seen a man looking so haggard and pale: he was completely white. He said he had been unable to meet me at the
arranged time, but had eventually made his way to Dundalk.
Iceman had some news for him. Tomorrow morning at eleven
o'clock Iceman planned to enter the Warrenpoint customs station and shoot Toombs. I looked at Brendan, who was relating
this story in a state of shock and terror, and burst out laughing.
I had been smoking dope and I could not stop laughing at
Brendan's big face, his voice cracking under the weight of
dread. I laughed uncontrollably, almost hysterically, until I
realized how desperately upset Brendan was. He said over and
over: 'It's not funny. It's not funny.' I did not need him to tell
me that. He wanted me to go to Dundalk and have the operation called off. I knew this was impossible. I had no doubt that
the IRA gunmen had left Dundalk by now and had hidden
their motorcycle ready for collection the next morning.
Brendan was going to be phoned at work by Iceman as a final
check to make sure that Toombs and the other man were there.
He was not expected to do anything else.

When I had first become involved with Iceman, he told me
that there were times when he would subject me to tests of
loyalty and commitment. I felt he might only be subjecting
Brendan to such a test. Perhaps there was no operation; per-

haps Iceman just wanted to make sure that Brendan was of the right calibre for the IRA. Over the next few hours, with the help of a few stiff whiskeys, I convinced Brendan that Iceman might only be testing him, that nothing was going to happen tomorrow. Brendan came to believe me. He left my house a happier man, prepared to 'pass the test'. Part of me despised Brendan's attitude: it was not that he objected to Toombs being shot, only to the location. But when he left that night I was almost certain that the operation was going to take place the next day.

I went to work as normal. Shortly after eleven o'clock the news came through that Ivan Toombs had been shot dead.

Over the weekend I read about the assassination. I did not think much about Toombs's fate as a human being, except that he had died as the result of a perfectly-executed operation. I admit I felt real satisfaction that we had been the first IRA unit at the start of the New Year to get a kill, a good kill. I had worked for two years to bring off this operation.

I went to see Iceman during the week to hear about the assassination at first hand. He had done as I told him to do to get into the building: he stood at the security door and waved some official C10 entry papers – supplied by me – at the officer on duty. The officer then pressed the security buzzer to admit this innocent member of the public. Iceman pulled a gun on the man and took him down the corridor. The officer, whom I knew as Johnny, had told him that Toombs was not in, but Iceman put the gun to his ear and told him he would blow his head off. Johnny pointed out Toombs's office. Iceman said that when he had entered the office 'the old fucker' had tried to go for a gun concealed in his briefcase, but Iceman shot him several times. The staff had heard several bangs and as soon as the shooting stopped they had tried to run out of the building, where they were met by another gunman wearing a motorcycle helmet. He told them to get back in and lie on the floor, which they all did. Iceman said he had come very close to shooting a man who he thought fitted the description of the reserve policeman, but had changed his mind at the last second. This was fortunate because the reserve policeman was not on duty that day.

I suspected Iceman was lying about what had happened. It took me some time to piece together the full story, which I finally did when I spoke to Johnny and a friend of the other gunman. They supplied very different accounts, accounts that were authenticated much later by forensic evidence submitted at my trial. The gunmen drove their motorcycle into Warrenpoint docks from the road entrance on the Newry side. They drove past the security hut, and straight into the docks. However, before they approached the customs station, they switched off the engine, allowing the bike to glide the last twenty yards silently. They did this because the motorcycle is linked with assassination in Northern Ireland, and Toombs could quite easily have been alerted by the sound of a motorcycle engine. Johnny confirmed how he had let the two gunmen into the building, how he had been made to lie on the floor and how he had felt the metal of the gun against his ear. He remembered being terrified by the gunman's sense of purpose and coolness. Iceman told Johnny not to move. Then he entered Toombs's office.

Toombs, who was sitting behind his desk, was surprised when his killer came in and called his name. The gunman immediately took up a firing position with his arms outstretched, standing only four feet from Ivan Toombs: he pulled the trigger of his Starr Automatic pistol, but it jammed. Toombs moved quickly from his seat towards the briefcase where he kept his gun. Iceman lunged at him. They began to wrestle. My IRA comrade, although in his early twenties and about six foot two in height, found Toombs, a much older man, determined and strong. Had Toombs carried his gun in a holster or in a waistband, the outcome might have been very different. However, he did not, and part of the reason he never did so was because some of the other staff were sensitive about seeing weapons on colleagues.

Iceman called out to the other gunman who ran the twenty feet down the corridor to Toombs's office. When he threw open the door he saw Toombs and Iceman struggling on top of the desk. The gunman shouted: 'Stand back,' and Iceman let go of Toombs who must have thought his assailant was either giving up or trying to get away, because he did not hold on to him. The other gunman fired several bullets in quick succession into Toombs, who fell to the ground, dying.

The gunman instinctively left the room – just in time to stop the staff from running out of the building. He made them come back and lie on the floor. Meanwhile Iceman had managed to clear his jammed weapon and pumped several rounds into Toombs as he lay dying on the floor. The gunmen walked casually out of the building by the main door, got on their motorcycle and drove out by the pedestrian gate, which was seldom locked. They made their way to Rostrevor, a few miles away, abandoning the motorcycle in a quiet housing estate, and walked to a safe house nearby. There they stayed for a few hours until the last checkpoint had been lifted and the hunt had died down. Then they were picked up from the safe house and they returned – as the IRA usually say in their statements – safely to base.

I knew I had to check up on Brendan to make sure he was not about to crack. Iceman told me how he had called Brendan on the morning of the killing to ask if Toombs was in. Brendan had simply said: 'Yes.' I knew that the next time Brendan had heard the same voice was when Iceman walked into the customs station, holding a gun.

I arrived at Brendan's house and could see he was nervous, but there was also a part of him that was satisfied with the chat around town about the ruthlessness of the attack. Even his parents seemed to be alive with the awful excitement of the event. His father told me that it was 'the intelligence of the operation' that really struck him, and I began to think that Brendan, in his fear, might have told his parents of his role, which no doubt he had exaggerated. Everybody seemed to be basking in the sun of our success. I was just thankful that Brendan was holding up. I knew he was annoyed with me, upset at having contributed a little more than 'snippets' to this operation, but I felt he had to learn to live with his action. This was how the IRA operated: everybody was expendable (some just a little more expendable than others, of course). I had no romanticism about it, even then: I regarded the IRA as a ruthless and necessary killing-machine.

I went to Toombs's funeral. At work I contributed money

for the floral tribute. The clergyman was Robert Eames, later
to become an archbishop, and he gave a sermon. He said he had
had a meal with Toombs only a few days before his death.
During the meal they had talked about the situation in
Northern Ireland. Toombs had said – referring to either the
IRA or the nationalist community or both: 'Perhaps some day
they will realize that there are some things that are so good they
just cannot be changed.' I felt a sting of anger at a typical
Orangeman's sentiment, and thought: 'Northern Ireland is
theirs and theirs alone, so good for them; not so good if you are
a Catholic living under their heel.' After the service I joined
the procession to the graveyard. I tried to identify some more
potential targets, and I fell in behind two middle-aged gentle-
men with English accents who were wearing crombies. I heard
them discussing the IRA's operation. They were clearly army
or intelligence officers.

Brendan was also at the funeral, looking pale and drawn. I
kept a close watch on him to make sure he was continuing to
bear up: I stared at him, wanting him to know that there was an
implied threat in my stare. He could be killed just as easily as
Toombs, and I wanted him to feel that reality. Of course I felt
for Brendan's distress, and I knew we were wrong to have put
him under such pressure, but the operation was over now, and
survival required that we tighten up and leave Toombs behind.

I could still recognize his family's grief. And yet I was satisfied: satisfied that I had acted as an IRA man, as a volunteer,
and I was prepared to move on to the next operation, the next
hit, the next kill – for that was what it was all about. We had to
be as pragmatic, single-minded and ruthless as we felt the
British to be. That way they would know that they had an
equal and dangerous adversary.

It did not take long for people to get on with their lives.
With Toombs dead, customs staff in Newry were prepared to
work in Warrenpoint. The most bizarre touch was the introduction of several new security devices: they put a warning
button under a desk at the public counter and bullet-proof
glass in the hatch. If there was danger in this area, the person
at the hatch could push a button and a red light would go on in
Toombs's office! But for what? He was dead and gone. Not

even the blood stains on the carpet remained. I busied myself with other operations, and largely forgot about Toombs, but sometimes at work I would be reminded of him. I felt a respect for him: he had been a brave man. Later I asked Iceman how he felt about Toombs. He said he felt nothing. It was then that I began to think of him as icily cold and ruthless.

Some years later, long after I had left the IRA, I took a train from Belfast to Newry with a friend. An attractive young woman in her teens sat across from me. She had beautiful big eyes, short dark hair and a pleasant smile. My friend said hello. As the train arrived in Newry the girl got up to stand at the door and, captivated by her, I asked my friend who she was: 'Oh, that's Alison Toombs from Warrenpoint.'

I realized now that I had seen that face before: I recognized those eyes which once had held fear and nervousness. A terrible sadness and a wave of guilt enveloped me. I turned to my friend and said: 'I was responsible for her father's death.' My friend recoiled, looking shocked, as the train pulled into the station. I watched Alison Toombs standing at the train door. The door swung open, and she moved out into the crowd.

2

More British
than Irish

Some people say republicanism is passed on by mothers. My mother certainly taught me about Irish history.

Kathleen Cumiskey was born in Crossmaglen in 1929, the only girl in a family of nine boys. She attended a number of convent schools where she picked up a good knowledge of history, the Irish language and – what most impressed me – the piano. But I remember most clearly her love of God, the Catholic God, and her determination to instil her religious faith in her children. Not a day went by without some words of instruction from her about the Roman Catholic Church. She believed there was only one true faith, every other brand of Christianity was heresy, and one day the sinful Protestants would have to be brought back into the Catholic fold. Her pious words inspired my first ambition: I wanted to become a missionary and go to Russia to convert the godless communists.

She did not come from a republican family. Her father had no interest in politics; the harsh experience of his early life had fired him with a determination to ensure prosperity for his family. Although illiterate, he was an astute man with a good business sense. Between the two world wars he became wealthy by selling apples, fowl, fish and anything else which caught his eye. Eventually he came to own several properties and businesses, including a grocery shop. He took nothing for himself from the businesses, and lived solely on his state pension until he died in his eighties. He passed on his wealth to his sons. Like many of his generation, he was a ruthless disciplinarian. Within his family his word was law, and any contradiction was met with a horsewhip.

My mother left school after the war to work as a hairdresser in Belfast, where she experienced petty-minded discrimination by Protestants. This experience drove her home to Crossmaglen to work in her father's grocery shop, which had begun to prosper. The family business expanded into ice-cream manufacture, and they bought a van to take to public events across the north. One of her brothers, Frank, had a particularly keen eye for money-making opportunities: he decided once to drive the van to a big Orangemen's parade at Rathfriland, around thirty miles from Crossmaglen. Frank knew that the name emblazoned on the family van, 'John Cumiskey and Sons, Crossmaglen', would identify the occupants as Catholics from an area known to be disloyal to the state. But he had been reared on stories of how his father had sold apples and oranges to Protestants at dances, and so he was prepared to take a chance, believing that the Orangemen's appetite for ice-cream would be stronger than their appetite for Fenian blood. With hindsight, he should have realized that his father's tales related to the period before the partition of Ireland and the formation of Northern Ireland. Since then the more relaxed relations between the two communities (at least in the countryside) had been replaced by constant tension as the new rulers tried to create a Protestant state for a Protestant people, a bulwark against the hordes of hostile papists across, and within, the six-county state's borders.

My mother was one of the first children to grow up in the new state, and she felt a little anxious as she set off in the ice-cream van at the height of the marching season, knowing that the month of July had become a time when most of her fellow Catholics tried to keep out of sight. Everything went well during the day at Rathfriland as she served ice-cream to hundreds of Orangemen on their way to the parade, but as the day turned to evening she grew frightened, the sound of drums seeming to drive the Orangemen into a frenzy of aggression.

They decided to shift the van, but as they climbed a steep hill behind a line of slow-moving traffic, a tall, dark-haired man wearing a suit, bowler hat and orange sash tried to pull open the side door while screaming obscenities: 'Fucking papists from Crossmaglen.' My mother told me that this big, violent, loud-mouthed bastard had looked just like Ian Paisley. When he found he could not open the door, he tried to get a grip on the van in order to push it over. Several Orangemen rushed forward and tried to pull him away, saying: 'She's only a wee girl. She's only a wee girl.' But this son of Ulster persisted in his confrontation with the papist foe. He was joined in his efforts by several other men, all smelling of drink. The van had sliding windows for selling the ice-cream, and the men put their hands inside the partition to get a grip. They rocked the vehicle to and fro, their enraged flushed faces mouthing anti-Catholic invective. 'Fenian bitch. Romish cunt' – words which my mother had not encountered at her convent schools. Frank, she told me, shouted from the driver's seat: 'Hit them with the spoons!' My mother grabbed two heavy leaden spoons which had been bought from an army surplus store. She smashed the spoons down on her attackers' hands. The Orangemen shouted in pain, let go their grip and Frank accelerated away as the traffic cleared. My mother told me she stood shaking in the back of the van, holding the metal spoons dripping with blood and ice-cream. Not surprisingly, experiences like this left her wary of Orangeism, and symbolized for her the sectarianism at the heart of the Northern Ireland state. She developed a mistrust of Protestants which never left her, although she rarely expressed anger or overt bitterness towards them, and always told me that there were good Protestants as well as bad ones.

My mother could not have found a less suitable match than my father. He had no interest in religion and despised the authority of the Church. His family came from the Camlough area near Newry. They had land and did business extensively with their Protestant neighbours. My grandfather always kept a framed photograph of the reigning monarch displayed in his house, although I suspect he did so for business reasons as much as for any great reverence for the Royal Family. My father inherited the family money and, if he had looked after it,

might have become a wealthy man. He was an accomplished
cattle-dealer and a tremendous judge of livestock, but horses
were his real love. He travelled all over the country with his
brood mares. While my mother looked forward to eternal life in
the bosom of Jesus, my father expressed his concern about the
future only in terms of his desire to live until the next spring
when the new foals would arrive. My mother would often warn
him of the eternal damnation which beckoned, but he would
say: 'Fuck eternal damnation. I'll have a good time with the
devil.' His blasphemy would mortify my mother, who would
bless herself and then sprinkle Holy Water around the house.

My father laughed at death, and thought the Christian idea
of eternal life was a hilarious absurdity: 'You die and the
worms eat you and that's that.' He thought that people who
believed in life after death were going to be terribly disappointed. When he developed heart problems in later life he
refused to look after himself properly. His attitude was: 'If
you're going to die, you're going to die.' He indulged to the end
his favourite vices of alcohol and trifle. When doctors pleaded
with him to let them perform a by-pass operation he said:
'Away and fuck. You're not operating on me.' He was an angry
and unappeasable man; he even had an antagonistic relationship with his heart pain. After a bad twinge he would say out
loud: 'You nearly got me there, you bastard, but I'm still here.'

His hostility towards Catholicism was sharpened by the
damaging effect that the power of the Church had on his relationship with my mother. After she had produced two children
my father had wanted to use contraception, partly I suppose
for selfish reasons, but at least as much because he did not feel
my mother's health would benefit from producing baby after
baby. My mother told him that contraception was a sin against
God. My father said: 'Don't talk nonsense, woman. It's a sin
against no one.' So they started using a natural but – in the eyes
of the Catholic Church – banned method of birth control.
After a while my mother went to confession and told the priest
what she was allowing her husband to do. The priest told her
that she had to stop her cavorting immediately. My mother
refused to allow my father to continue committing the sin of
Onan. She soon found herself pregnant again and started to

take a new wonder-drug called Thalidomide, to ease the pains
of pregnancy. The baby was born deformed, lived a short while
and died. My mother blamed my father for causing God to
curse her, and became colder towards him.

He renewed his friendship, we later discovered, with the
woman he had loved before my mother, and continued to see
this woman until he died. After his death, my mother in her
grief told me the story about what the priest had said all those
years before. I think she realized then that the man of God had
been talking nonsense and, in his concern for her eternal soul,
had introduced a poison into her marriage.

My father was passionate and selfish; my mother was tem-
perate and selfless. My father was single-minded, with a strong
sense of independence; my mother was docile and subservient
in the face of authority, especially priestly authority. My father
did not cower in the face of any authority. His instinct was to
fight, especially if he perceived injustice in the treatment he
received. Officials from the Ministry of Agriculture could
usually expect a hard time. In the early Seventies there was an
outbreak of brucellosis among cattle in Northern Ireland.
Every few months the ministry would carry out blood tests on
herds to detect the virus. After one such visit to our farm,
they informed my father that they had detected the virus and
would have to destroy the herd, although naturally they would
compensate my father for his losses.

Two officials came out to value our cattle. Both were
Protestants. Both were dour and bureaucratic. At first my
father was friendly to them, in the hope of getting the highest
possible value for his cattle. He offered the first a cigarette but
was met with the reply: 'Non-smoker. Non-drinker.' The other
one said: 'Oh, no. I never touch them.' They indicated that
they were born-again Christians. My father muttered to me as
they moved out of earshot: 'We've got a right pair of cunts
here.' The officials came back to my father and mentioned
some prices for particular beasts. The prices seemed well
below the market rate. My father, who was holding a black-
thorn stick, started to get agitated. He was an expert on the
prices of cattle and knew that his herd was being undervalued:
he would not be able to replace the destroyed cattle at these

prices. He pointed to an expensive cow which he had only recently bought and said: 'Well, what do you say that one's worth?' They gave him an extremely low price. My father erupted: 'You're taking none of these cattle, you shower of saved bastards. You'll buy none of my cattle. Get out to fuck. There'd be no problem if I was one of your own, would there? No problem getting overvalued then.' The two officials quaked under the force of my father's bitterness. They protested, said that they wouldn't give Protestants any more than they'd give him. My father snorted: 'Would you fuck. You've been doing it all your lives, you hypocritical, corrupt bastards. Look at the head on ye, you consumptive fuckers. Youse are up biting the altar rails and praying to God every day, then you come and give a man a bad price for his cattle.' My father was waving his stick to enforce his abuse. One of the bureaucrats put up his hand and said: 'Let's have another look at your cattle.' They went away and revalued the herd; they ended up offering my father a sum close to the amount he wanted. He was seen shaking hands with them and treating them like the best of neighbours.

On another occasion a Catholic Ministry of Agriculture official played a part in refusing my father's application for a subsidy. My father took the rejection badly and dwelt on it for years. By chance, ten years later, the official ended up marrying into my mother's family. My parents went to the wedding. The happy day moved along smoothly until the evening, by which time my father had consumed a fair amount of whiskey. He walked over to the groom at the bar and started talking to him, congratulating him on his marriage. The nervous groom said: 'Thank you very much, Brian.' My father asked if he would like a drink, and the man said he'd take a malt. My father bought the drink, turned to the groom and said: 'Aye, you'll have this fucking malt, you good-for-nothing cunt.' And he threw the whiskey in the groom's face. The wedding almost turned into a riot. He had ruined my mother's day and embarrassed her in front of her family. But my father did not care: he had got his revenge.

My father's uncontrollable anger could burst out in comic exuberance, in stories that would make my mother laugh, stories rooted in the earthy reality of farming and deal-making. My mother's tales were versions of Irish history: she told us of the priests who had died to preserve our Catholic faith when the Cromwellians had hunted them down, decapitated them, and placed their heads on spikes outside towns and churches. She aroused a sense of anger in me about the wrongs done to us by the British – the atrocities, the penal laws, the theft of our estates – although she never mentioned the word 'republicanism'. For her, the fight against the British had been a fight to preserve the faith, not a fight to create a nation. She encouraged me to feel, none the less, that the injustice of partition, the division of Ireland, was yet another wrong inflicted on Catholics by Protestants. She passed on the Catholic faith in a way which passed on the idea of resistance to an enemy.

My mother instilled in me the grievances of the vanquished. She helped convince me from an early age that the Irish had been the victims of terrible cruelties inflicted by the English and their Scots planters over many centuries. This understanding developed and strengthened as I got older and read about Irish history for myself. I became hostile towards the Protestant-run state, although our family's friendship with Protestants confused my feelings. My mother took me on a pilgrimage to Drogheda at the age of ten, and I prayed silently at the shrine in the church that held the severed head of Oliver Plunkett, the bishop murdered by Cromwellians for his Catholic faith and declared a saint by the Pope – a real Irish saint. I was overwhelmed with awe when I saw the lovingly-preserved door to his prison cell. When I was eleven, I visited the National Museum in Dublin. In 'The 1916 Room' I saw the bullet-holed hat and woollen vest worn by James Connolly when he was executed by the British after the Easter Rising. I read the letters of other executed republican leaders, such as Padraig Pearse: letters to their mothers, sisters, brothers and girlfriends as they waited for their turn in front of the firing squad. I had learnt nothing about this at school and I felt angry.

I left Dublin with an exalted new sense of my country's history, and a new-found reverence for everything republican. The image of Connolly's woollen vest soiled with his blood stayed with me for a long time. In my mind Plunkett, Pearse and Connolly were all linked together. They were all martyrs for our Catholic faith, the true religion: religion and politics fused together by the blood of the martyrs. I was prepared to be a martyr, to die for this true Catholic faith.

I went to Dundalk in the Republic of Ireland for the fiftieth anniversary of the Easter Rising. I saw lines of marching men carrying banners, tricolours and symbols that spoke of a heroic Ireland, an Ireland of great deeds, courage and self-sacrifice. The ghosts of the great heroes Pearse and Connolly were invoked, their deified spirits provoking reverence. I felt those heroes of 1916 were like the priests who had died for us at Cromwellian hands. I felt my mother must be right: the struggle for our faith was not yet over. I had been staying with a cousin in Dundalk and he took me to a museum there which contained rooms full of IRA paraphernalia. I saw medals and ribbons awarded by the Old IRA, the force that fought the War of Independence between 1919 and 1921. It dawned on me that I was not just looking at a dead history of insurrection, I was looking at an alternative society, government and army.

My father did not give a stuff about Irish history, though he loathed the RUC and the B-Specials. For all that, he found in many ways that he had more in common with the local Protestant farmers than with his own Catholic tribe. He came from a family which had built up a network of trade and social relations with the Protestant community, and he cultivated those links. The people who spent most time in my family's house and whose farms we visited most regularly were Protestants. This personal knowledge of Protestants whom I liked helped to change my outlook. As I got older I began to look to Belfast and London, not Dublin. Indeed, if the troubles had not erupted in 1969, polarizing the two communities, some of my family might well have intermarried with Protestants. My father did not have the partitionist mentality. He travelled all over England and Ireland.

My father would tell his tales on Sunday mornings as he cooked us our breakfast, standing in front of the range in our huge kitchen, a blazing fire in the grate, fat sausages and bacon sizzling on the iron pan, flicking back and forward the egg-lifter as he fried eggs for any of us who wanted one. He would also fry the soda bread which my mother had baked fresh the day before. During this weekly ritual he spoke about his youth and what he had experienced. He told anecdotes about outsmarting the local police during smuggling trips. My father was not averse to a little cattle-smuggling, and on trips with him I got to know all the secret border routes.

Both of my parents loved us as children in their own distinct ways. But my father, for all his passion, could not express his feelings. My mother loved him intensely and became obsessed with him. Strife between my mother and father dominated my upbringing. To him, she was always sitting in judgement, no matter what he did. He said once that living with her was like living with the Pope. The bitterness between them only ended when he died in 1987. My father used to insult my mother in various ways. A favourite was to question her family's origin: 'Cumiskey. What sort of queer name is that. It's not Irish. Your people must have been tinkers.'

My father's gibes were motivated in part by his dislike of my mother's family. He would describe her father, John Cumiskey, in less than flattering terms. Cumiskey had beaten my mother almost until her wedding day. He believed in 'discipline', which to him meant working his children like slaves and savaging them whenever they failed to meet his exacting standards. One day the first baby in the family, Jack, had started crying interminably, as babies do. My grandfather, enraged, plucked the baby from my grandmother's arms and ran outside with it. He immersed the screaming baby in a barrel of ice-cold water outside the door. My grandmother told me that throughout his childhood little Jack never cried again. As a child of six, I went to live with these grandparents for a month when my mother was ill; later in my childhood I lived with them for several months when my parents separated temporarily. My grandfather tried to impose his traditional system of discipline upon me. My mother sent me a toy wagon with a little red man in it, but grandfather would not let me have it. I cried and pleaded for my toy. Grandfather took out a whip around which he had twisted some red insulation tape. He said: 'Here's the wee red man I'll give you.'

My uncle Jack lived in a nearby house and ran the family builders' supplies and hardware business. His experience in the barrel must have given him a taste for harsh discipline, because he also took to thrashing me for various misdemeanours. After one particularly brutal spanking I went out into the yard and used my plastic toy shovel to put four loads of sand into the petrol tank of his new Morris Oxford Estate.

In our house, battles were never forgotten. The acrimony between my parents corrupted the love they had for their children and forced us to take sides. To our simple childish minds, our mother seemed to be the wronged woman. My father did behave badly towards her, and she certainly spared no effort in detailing his bad behaviour. Inevitably, we sided with her. I would always rush to my mother's defence and I remember constant antagonism with my father. We fought verbally all the time, and he would often end up beating me. I put up with it for a long time but when I was sixteen our confrontations became truly violent. My younger brother John had bought a new pair of boots. I gave him some money so that he would let me wear them when I went out on Friday night. As I was about to leave the house, all dressed up, my father asked me what I was doing wearing John's boots. An argument started. I said a few things which annoyed him. He did not like anyone questioning his supremacy under his own roof, so he told me to go upstairs to my bedroom. He told one of the younger children to go out to the car to fetch one of his ash plants, which he kept for controlling cattle. I walked out to go upstairs. He followed me. Suddenly I turned and said: 'I'm not going up the stairs.' I stood my ground: 'Your days of beating me are over.' He punched me, and I punched him back. We started laying into each other, fighting like madmen. We must have fought for more than five minutes. I remember my mother screaming: 'Stop! Stop! Stop!' In the end we pulled away from each other. I did not go upstairs: I went out of the house and stayed away for the night. I felt desperately depressed after that incident, but the fighting did not stop. This dreadful, intermittent physical conflict finally stopped only when I left to go to university.

Even before unionism bared its teeth in the civil rights

movement's face in 1969, I knew there was something amiss in the state into which I had been born. I had known when I walked home from school at the age of eight alongside the young policeman on his way from Camlough police station to Bessbrook that the big revolver which hung from his belt in a holster was no toy. I felt it would be great to be a policeman with my own gun. As a young person growing up I began to witness the historical conflicts described by my mother being lived out, and saw them through her eyes. I remember in 1968 returning from the seaside and my parents pulling into a layby to listen to news bulletins about a man shot dead in Armagh by the B Specials. I knew that only Protestants could be B Specials. I had not had much contact with them, although I remember them shining a torch into my father's car at a checkpoint one night when I was a small child. The 'B-men' were bogeymen. In recent months I had watched on the television news their violent dispersal of Catholic people marching for civil rights. Now I felt a real sense of dread and excitement when I heard that they had taken one step further and shot a Catholic dead.

My world seemed to be turning upside-down, inside-out. I felt that whatever security I had was being threatened. Catholics were being attacked and beaten by the supposed forces of law merely for demanding the right to vote. Catholics in Camlough felt so threatened that they gathered to protect the local convent, The Good Shepherd, from possible loyalist attack. That first fatality in Armagh stunned the whole community; a feeling as basic as that of safety was slipping away.

My state of mind was not improved a little later when I went with my father to check his cattle near Bessbrook. As we went through the town we saw lines of cars parked on both sides of the street. Men in peaked caps, silver unbuckled belts and black uniforms were walking about unhurriedly. A few eyed us cautiously as we drove past. There seemed to be hundreds of them and they all carried long black rifles with polished wooden butts. They were the local B Specials. 'Look, there's Billy and Ian,' my father said quietly. I recognized people we knew: one was a farm labourer, another worked in a bacon factory, and

there were others who worked on the roads or in the nearby
mill. The bogeymen were our neighbours. They were *armed*;
we were not. The significance of this, coupled with memories of
historical disempowerment of Catholics, began to seem very
urgent. I was looking at the organization that was beating
Catholics daily on protest marches. Comrades of these very
people who were shooting Catholics dead. Fear and excitement
mingled even more intensely in my mind.

Rioting broke out in Newry in 1969. My father managed to
keep a tight rein on us, refusing even to allow us into the town
on our own. We lived only three miles away, yet we felt cut off
from the conflagration engulfing the rest of Northern Ireland.
I had been attending a nearby secondary school since 1966.
Much to my annoyance I had been placed in the 'A' stream. I
was interested only in leaving school, getting an apprenticeship
and working with my father's cattle. In that year I had even
gone with a party of schoolboys to Wales to spend a week at a
British Army Junior Soldiers' Camp. For a time I went as far as
flirting with the idea of joining the British Army. My cousin
William was in the RAF, training as a pilot: his father had been
in the Royal Ulster Constabulary, one of two Protestants who
had married my father's sisters.

Instead, in 1970, at the age of sixteen, I left school after getting five 'O' levels and went to work as a clerical officer in
London at the Ministry of Defence, after replying to an advert
in the *Belfast Telegraph*. I stayed in civil service digs near St
James's Park, run by a polite, middle-aged Englishwoman with
a blue rinse. I shared a room with a Welshman and a Scot. She
asked me what nationality I was. I said I was Irish. 'Oh,' she
replied, 'I thought we were all British.'

I travelled to work each day on the tube, fascinated by the
graffiti on the wallposters reading 'The Angry Brigade'. They
interested me: I was starting to be aware of and angry about
wealth and privilege, and I wanted to know more about radical
groups who opposed the state. I bought a Che Guevara poster
and put it up on the wall of my shared room. I was too naïve to
recognize the contradiction between my nascent sympathy for
revolutionary change and my work for the Ministry of
Defence. Each day I took the tube to Tottenham Court Road

station and walked to my office nearby, where I worked in
Technical Costs and Planning. Most of the other staff were far
older than me, but everyone was very friendly as I settled down
to a life of clerical drudgery.

At that time my hair was cropped short and I wore jeans
with braces. My Scottish room-mate told me I looked like a
'skinhead' and that some other people in the digs were frightened of me. I seemed to have a capacity to project menace, to
intimidate others unconsciously. One day I walked into the
digs' common room where several people were sitting. The
communal radio was playing a cricket Test Match between
England and some former colonials. The people were talking
among themselves, and the tedious commentary from the radio
began to irritate me. I assumed that the others in the room
were not listening to the radio as they were busy talking, so I
got up and changed the station to one that played pop music.
No one said anything but they all went silent. After ten minutes the pop music did not sound any better than the cricket so
I turned off the radio. The group looked at each other, got up
and walked out.

After a few weeks I began to feel extremely homesick. A
middle-aged male colleague took me to a pub at lunchtime and
bought me my first alcoholic drink. He tried to take my mind
off my homesickness by telling me yarns about his National
Service days in the army and how he had come to terms with
his homesickness. I appreciated his kindness. I had never experienced such friendship before, and I was touched. I liked
English people a great deal. But Northern Ireland was in the
news a lot and I could not get the conflict, the marches and the
riots out of my mind. I knew too that my mother was ill with
arthritis, and I wanted to be able to comfort her. I decided to
give up my job and return home. On the day I left, my colleagues brought in some bottles of wine.

Perhaps I should have stayed. I would have had more time
away from the pressure-cooker atmosphere of Northern
Ireland. But before I left London I went into Foyle's and
bought some revolutionary books to read on the journey home.
That same day I heard on the radio that a soldier had been
killed in an explosion at Derrybeg, just outside Newry. I got

the train to Liverpool and sailed to Belfast. My fellow passengers included hundreds of soldiers, noisy and drunken, and not much older than me. I had mixed feelings about them. They seemed alien and threatening, coming to police us as so many English armies had done, but I also felt that the Catholic community had developed a strong political voice which the British seemed to be listening to and that these squaddies were at least a response.

With the encouragement of some of my former teachers, I decided to go back to school. I won a scholarship to the grammar school in Newry, St Colman's College, to retake a few 'O' levels and to do my 'A' levels. I arrived there in September 1971, a month after the introduction of internment without trial had produced a huge wave of support for the IRA from the Catholic community. Many of the men picked up had lost all connection with the IRA; others had never had any in the first place. Some of them were tortured quite clinically, using sophisticated methods of disorientation and sleep deprivation. I remember going to an anti-internment rally near my home at Camlough, attended by a huge crowd. A recently-released internee spoke about the brutality to which he had been subjected. His ravaged appearance added force to the harrowing story he told of beatings, torture and cruelty. You could actually feel the anger in the crowd as he spoke. A local schoolteacher also spoke in the hardest republican terms: now, he said, it was a United Ireland or nothing. This was the first time I had heard such irredentist words spoken in public. His words struck a chord with me and with many in the crowd, but I feared what lurked beneath the surface of his speech. Even as a teenager something in me feared that the IRA would take advantage of justifiable outrage to plunge us into the darkest of pits. I thought then that we stood to lose the support of the progressive Protestants who had marched alongside us for our rights, forcing such people into silence. Republicanism both energized and frightened me: '*Eiróimíd Arís! Tiocfaidh Ár Lá!*' 'We will rise again; our day will come.' But I was young, and the idea of political violence began to work its way into my mind. I had a sneaking regard for the IRA, a gut sympathy. If

I had to choose between a Catholic IRA man and a representative of the Protestant state, I somehow knew on which side I
would err.

In this vacuum the total polarization of the two communities took place. I started to join with other boys on the streets
after school, taunting the soldiers and calling them murdering
bastards. But I still believed in the innate democracy of the
British system and that the British government's promises to
redress our historical grievances would work out.

I threw myself into my 'A' level studies, but at the end of
October 1971 the army shot dead three unarmed youths in
Newry. The army claimed that the boys had been about to rob
someone depositing money in a night safe at the Northern
Bank in Hill Street. But everyone felt the army was lying: the
men had been drinking and they had been holding bags of
chips when they were gunned down by soldiers hiding on the
roof of Woolworths. Stories about the shooting travelled
rapidly around town: the soldiers had used an armoured personnel carrier, or 'pig', to ferry the corpses to the local hospital.
A soldier had walked into Casualty and said to the nurses, 'We
have some meat for you,' before pulling the dead men out of
the pig and dragging them into the hospital by their legs. The
school president ordered us to remain in school on the day of
the funeral. With three friends I decided to disobey him. I
wrote sick notes for all of us.

We bunked off and ran into town, picking up stones on the
way. Newry was deserted. Every shop seemed to be closed,
except the post office and the bank near which the men had
been shot. We met up with another small group of teenagers. I
knew two of them: one was known as Domo, the other was
Raymond McCreesh, who was to die on hunger strike, as a
protesting republican prisoner, in 1981. We passed an accoun-
tants' office and I recalled a story that my father had told me
about how he had once seen a sign in their window, 'RCs need
not apply'. I told Domo. He put a stone through the window.
The first pane went with a crash and cops started to run
towards us, looking like demented penguins in their uniforms.
A barrage of stones forced the cops to retreat. We jeered.

People started looking out of the windows of the post office and the Northern Bank – another provocation: they should have closed their offices out of respect for the dead. We armed ourselves with more stones, which were piled near roadworks. Rocks shot towards the post office. The windows shattered in a tinkling crescendo. We laughed, watching the workers inside diving for cover.

Soldiers formed up at the other end of the street wearing gas-masks and holding riot shields and batons; without moving forward they allowed us to pelt them. We laughed at them just standing there, but when I went in search of more stones I realized what their plan was. Another group was moving in behind us to cut us off. We found some more stones and began to pelt the soldiers in our rear. They ran at us and I knew we would be beaten savagely if they caught us. The whole group sprinted down the street, and we had just reached the gates of Newry market when we ran into thousands of people coming from the funeral. We disappeared into the crowd which walked on slowly to meet the pursuing soldiers in their heavy gear, looking hot and furious.

Obviously people in the crowd did not know what had happened. They thought the Brits had come to insult the mourners by making their presence felt. Intoxicated with grief and anger, the crowd went wild. Paving stones were torn up and flung at the soldiers, who now had a proper riot on their hands. The soldiers fired volleys of CS gas and rubber bullets. The crowd fell left and right like a wave. People shouted in pain as rubber bullets struck their bodies. Others were vomiting from the gas. My eyes stung and I started to retch with nausea as the gas hit my lungs. Stewards from the civil rights movement used loud-hailers, telling everyone to remain calm. The riot fizzled out, and instead the crowd marched to the local UDR centre. I joined in a sit-down protest outside the gates. Finally we dispersed and made our way home. Our elation at the day's events filled the next day's school bus.

Some people reading about my involvement in that riot may feel that I was well on the way to becoming a Provo. There was certainly a pull in that direction, but it was met by a far stronger countervailing force – my confidence that we could achieve what we wanted without killing people. I could still draw a clear distinction between riot and armed insurrection. The first seemed a legitimate way to exert pressure on the system to change; the second seemed likely only to launch us into the past. I could loathe the unionist state, yet look to the British government for salvation. I could sympathize with the actions of some IRA men without agreeing with the analysis of their leaders. Many Catholic people at the time and later found themselves in this schizophrenic condition. As any psychiatrist will tell you, schizophrenia is not a Jekyll-and-Hyde state of mind, it is a mental state that involves the fragmentation of the thought processes. Many Catholics even today can offer varying degrees of sympathy to the IRA while honestly saying they do not support the organization if they personally do not carry out any physical acts of support.

My radical sympathies focused on the civil rights movement. The IRA seemed to be plunging Catholics into a cauldron in which they would be boiled to death. But I found myself questioning my ambivalence towards the IRA when paratroopers shot dead thirteen civilians in Derry in January 1972. Like almost every other Irish Catholic, I was enraged by Bloody Sunday.

By 1972 parts of Newry had been reduced to rubble by the IRA's bombing campaign, and every day I would walk past the bombed-out buildings. One target whose destruction particularly saddened me was the beautiful old Boulevard Hotel in the centre. I met one of the civil rights leaders on a visit to the town. He was a good orator, an articulate firebrand. I told him that I thought the bombings in Newry were counterproductive as they only damaged an already fragile economy. He said: 'Sometimes you've got to destroy to rebuild.'

I still believed that the British would deliver on their promises. They had suspended Stormont and seemed ready to implement the idea of 'power-sharing'. The B specials were abolished in 1970. For all my republican posturing, I still did not support the IRA's campaign, although I respected IRA men who defended their communities.

Yet for all the violence in Northern Ireland I knew that Newry was not experiencing the agony of the sectarian loyalist murders of Catholics in the traditional battleground of Belfast. Indeed, my two years at grammar school were the happiest years of my life. There seemed to be a fusion of energy and unity among Catholics, who were growing in confidence.

My final year at St Colman's began in September 1972. I was determined to get to university, but the drama on the streets distracted me. My father had tried hard to keep us off the streets since the troubles had started, but a development in our extended family gave me a chance to break free from his control at weekends: I began to spend a lot of time with my cousin Derek. Derek had been born in England to an English mother; his father was my father's brother. His parents had separated when he was very young, and his father had brought him back to Northern Ireland, where Derek was brought up by my grandmother, to the relief of his father who needed all his leisure time to chase after other women. When my grandmother died, Derek had no one to look after him, although he was still only in his mid-teens. He began to fend for himself, living a lonely and vulnerable existence in his own flat on a housing estate outside Newry.

My younger brother John and I started to spend weekends with him, partly to keep him company but also to enjoy the freedom of a weekend without adults. We ran wild, raking about the estate, making noise and annoying the neighbours. The violent political situation gave us greater opportunities for mischief. During the week I studied hard, but at the weekends I helped to build barricades and to throw stones, bottles and bricks at policemen.

Our activities attracted the attention of the IRA. A teenager called Brendan Quinn approached us one day and told us to stop causing trouble on the estate. I told him to fuck off and he backed down. A short while later as I walked alone in the dark to meet my girlfriend, a battered Mini pulled up beside me. The door was flung open and there was Brendan Quinn, blond-haired and buck-toothed: 'Get in. I want to talk to you,' he said. I told him where to put his talk. He pulled out a revolver and pointed it at me: 'Get in or I'll shoot now.' I could see in his eyes that he meant it. I got into the back and the driver – who in later years almost died on hunger strike as an

IRA prisoner – drove off. Brendan kept the gun pointed at me, and with his free hand he pulled out a pair of scissors: 'I have been authorised by the IRA to cut your hair and shoot you in the legs. We want to keep that estate quiet, to keep cops and Brits out of it so we can launch operations, but you fuckers have been making a nuisance of yourselves and drawing them in.' I apologized for my actions and said that I had no idea he was an IRA man: 'I'll see to it that the rest of the lads behave from here on in,' I said. My words seemed to satisfy him: 'Right, that's fair enough. We'll let the hare sit; we'll let the hair sit.' He shook my hand before I got out of the car, and he told me that he would have a word with the other lads just to underline the point.

I began to knuckle down to my studies. I was in my final year and I knew I wanted to get into university. The only distraction was the occasional adolescent grope in the dark with a girl. It worked: I had enough 'A' levels and was accepted to study law at Queen's University in Belfast.

I arrived in Belfast at a tense time. IRA bombs had left parts of the city in smouldering ruins; the loyalists had responded with a campaign of sectarian assassination. The loyalist killers would often have to drive through the university area to reach Catholic streets. No one felt safe, yet student life still cocooned us from the violence. Beer at 25p a pint helped a lot. I would often drink myself into a stupor and walk home indifferent to the dangers that lurked in the nearby loyalist estates. I was totally unprepared for university life. I had spent most of my life on a farm, and I lacked confidence and self-assurance. Yet I threw myself into my studies and found that I enjoyed law, even though I had to struggle to keep up with the workload.

On Christmas Eve of 1973, Brendan Quinn, the young IRA man who had once threatened to chop off my hair, was blown to pieces by his own bomb. He was seventeen. Another IRA man died with him, as did several civilians. Though I was shocked, and felt his death was a tragedy, deep down I did not really care: people seemed to be dying all the time in Northern Ireland and I had come to regard IRA men as brainless cannon-fodder. Ensconced in the Law Faculty of Queen's University, I felt removed from the environment in which people like Brendan lived. A career as a lawyer beckoned. I fantasized about becoming a criminal lawyer, defending the rights of the downtrodden. A few months at Queen's had convinced me that the law was the cornerstone of civilisation: without it we would tumble into barbarism. The IRA's campaign represented that barbarism. I was reading Dicey on constitutional law, and the progressive judgements of Lords Blackstone and Denning. Society was imperfect, yet the work of these jurists seemed to represent our civilization's striving towards perfection.

I went home for the Easter break with confidence in the future. I was becoming a bit of a prig – I even smoked a pipe to maintain my cultivated self-image. My first year at Queen's had almost ended. Soon I would sit my exams, a successful product of an imperfect system. I did not have to remind myself that my family had made their living over the centuries from trading with Britain and the colonial Protestants. Indeed, I had come to realize that I really was more British than Irish. I felt more at home in Belfast, London and Liverpool than in Dublin and I felt no shame in that knowledge.

During that weekend at home, I went for a drink with some of my former schoolfriends. We walked home together, laughing and joking. I left them at my gate and walked up the long avenue to the farm. I sucked on the last hot ashes in my pipe and went around the back of the house to the shed in which a cow was about to calve. She seemed happy enough so I left her and prepared to enter the house quietly. I would sneak into bed without waking my mother and fifteen-year-old brother John. I suspected my father would not be home yet. He had gone out to trade cattle earlier in the day, and he rarely completed his business within normal office hours. But as I got to the door I noticed my father's car stationary at the end of the avenue: it was turned half-way into the gateway, its indicators still flashing. I could see shadowy figures moving about. I knew he had been stopped by the army at a neighbour's farm earlier in the day and the 'jelly-sniffer' dog had gone mad when it smelt some spilt creosote in the boot. I knew also that my father had had an argument with another farmer earlier in the week.

My first thought was that the farmer had brought some friends with him to finish the argument. I ran down the avenue, but I had only covered half the distance when I heard rifles being cocked. An English voice shouted at me to stop or I'd be shot. I stopped and figures began to raise themselves up from crouched positions next to a thick privet hedge. 'Get your fucking hands up!' I put up my hands immediately. 'Don't you move. Don't you fucking move.' Several figures came towards me, and as they got close I noticed their red berets, the head-gear of the Parachute Regiment. 'What were you running for? Why were you trying to escape?' I told them I was only trying to find out what was happening to my father. I felt a rifle poked in my back. 'Get up against that fence, you Irish bastard.' I did as I was told. 'Get your arms out. Spread your fucking legs, you cunt.' They searched me, and found my pipe, which they threw across the field.

Two of them grabbed me, one on each shoulder, and ran me back up the avenue towards the house. I could smell drink on their breath. As we got to the turn at the top they began to beat me with their rifle butts. Others appeared and started to kick and punch me all over my body. 'Get your fucking hands on your head, you Irish cunt. Get your legs out. Get your fucking legs out.' They kicked my legs further and further apart until I fell to the ground. They spreadeagled me in the dirt. I tried to keep absolutely still, but from the corner of my eye I could see several soldiers at the front door. They kicked the door again and again until it gave way. They rushed inside and soon I heard my mother, who had been crippled with rheumatism for years, screaming from her bedroom upstairs. A soldier walked over to me and shoved his SLR rifle in my mouth, cracking my front left tooth. I could feel the cold of the steel upon my tongue as he shoved the barrel right to the back of my throat. I remember the taste of gun oil. I began to choke. 'I'd blow your brains out for tuppence, you rotten Irish cunt.' Behind me I could hear a jeep coming up the drive, closer and closer until I thought it would run me over, but it stopped, inches from where I lay. From the house I could hear my mother screaming: 'Where's my son? Where's my son? I want my son! I want my son!' The soldier pulled his rifle out of my

mouth when one of his colleagues came over from the house
and told me to get up and come inside.

They brought me into the house. John was standing in the
sitting-room, wearing a shirt and trousers. My mother stood
there in her nightdress screaming hysterically. Then they
brought in my father, looking haggard and frightened. 'Is this
the boss man?' asked one of them. 'Yes,' replied the one who
had brought in my father. The soldier in charge put his hand
on my father's shoulder and said that he was arresting him
under the relevant section of the law as a suspected terrorist.
He repeated the procedure with John and me, then they took
us outside where two jeeps were now parked. John and my
father went into the first jeep, while I got into the second.
They told me to lie on the floor as three soldiers got in on
either side of me. They began to hit me with their rifle butts on
my arms, legs, back and buttocks. I could hear my mother
screaming hysterically. One of my guards shouted, 'Fuck off
you old whore!' as the jeeps drove off. During the journey the
soldiers spat on my head continuously. I felt a hand move up
my trouser leg to pull hairs from my calf. All the time they
kicked me in my ribs on both sides of my body. One soldier
pulled me by the hair and began to bang my forehead against
the radio on the floor of the jeep. A rifle barrel was twisted
around the area of my anus, then two of them put their guns to
my head, clicked off the safety-catches and ordered me to sing
'The Sash' – the Orange Order's supremacist marching song. I
knew only one verse of the song, which I sang as best I could
with my face on the floor of a jeep. They beat time with their
rifles on my back. Then they demanded a rendition of 'God
Save the Queen', which seemed to drive them into a frenzy. I
prayed that I would survive the journey. I felt these drunken
madmen were capable of anything.

Bessbrook Barracks was only a mile away. They pulled me
out of the jeep by my hair and forced me to keep my head
down: 'Don't look up, you cunt.' They flung me against something hard and metallic. I fell down, feeling weak and
semi-conscious. I realized I was lying at the foot of an army
'pig', an armed personnel carrier. They lifted me up again by
pulling my hair and jacket and they dragged me down a lot of

steps into some sort of basement. They forced me through a door into semi-darkness. On each side of this narrow room were bunk beds full of soldiers who spat, punched and kicked as I went past: 'IRA cunt', 'Provo bastard', they shouted. Finally they pushed me into a room where I was forced to stand in a corner against the wall with my fingertips supporting the full weight of my body. I could see my brother John in the same position to my left, and my father to my right. I shall never forget the sight of my father standing there so humiliated.

Soldiers in red tracksuits took me out to a caravan. I was met by a dark-haired Englishman of strong build and swarthy complexion wearing civilian clothes. He sat down while I had to stand. He tried to convince me that my father's car had been carrying explosives. I said it was impossible, but he injected doubt into my mind: 'You're at university all week. You might not have known about the explosives.' I sat down out of exhaustion. He shouted at me to stand up. I stood only to be told to sit down. He questioned me at length, asking me about my attitude to the IRA. He mentioned the names of Belfast republicans and asked me if I knew them and I said I didn't. A forensics man came and swabbed my hands for traces of explosives. Later on an army doctor, in the presence of several of the soldiers who had assaulted me, asked me if I had any complaints. The military police photographed us and then we were put in a jeep and taken to the nearby RUC barracks, where we spent the night in a cell. The cell was bare: the bed was a wooden bench without a mattress. There was only one blanket and a filthy pillow without a pillowcase. In the late morning I was taken upstairs to what seemed to be the loft for a further interrogation, conducted this time by two RUC detectives. They sat under a huge Union flag suspended from a wooden beam. The interrogators were condescending and hostile. They did not seem to like the fact that I was a law student. They went over the same ground that the Englishman had covered the night before, but they could not catch me out on anything because there was nothing to catch me out on. For the first time since leaving school I had to ask permission to have a piss. A policeman stood behind me as I urinated. I forgot to pull the chain. 'Flush it!' he barked.

Later that afternoon the news came back from forensics: the substance in the car which had alerted the dog was indeed creosote, not explosives. My father drove us home in silence. At home we discovered that soldiers had been there all night, keeping my mother and the younger children under armed guard while they tore the house to pieces. They had pulled up the carpets, torn out all the floorboards, and drilled into the bricked-up fireplaces. One of our ceilings had collapsed. They had gone through everyone's possessions. They even intercepted the postman that morning and read all our mail. Helicopters had landed dozens of troops who carried out a meticulous search of our fields.

I returned to Queen's a different man, sombre and reserved. I was less sociable, less interested in what was going on. I continued to study and tried to put out of my mind what had happened. But my studies began to appear laughably ironic: British law, civilization, the rights of the citizen. Sometimes, as I remembered that night, I would feel the soldiers had merely made an understandable mistake in a conflict which was not of their making. Other times I would feel a surge of rage whose power would unbalance me: I would sit alone in my room and think with pleasure of blowing off the heads of those para scum.

Yet perhaps the end of the conflict was in sight. The 'Sunningdale Executive' had been set up and Catholics were to share power with unionists for the first time in the history of the state. A strike organized by the loyalist paramilitaries swiftly brought the north to a standstill while I studied for my exams. Loyalists mounted illegal checkpoints everywhere, watched over by the British Army, who seemed to collude with their intimidation. The IRA assisted loyalism by carrying out a series of atrocities. One night as I sat in my room studying by candlelight – the power workers were on strike – I heard a huge explosion: the loyalists had blown up the Rose and Crown pub, killing many Catholics. The power-sharing experiment collapsed, destroying hopes for a peaceful future. Liberal optimism that the conflict could be negotiated out of existence now looked naïve. The future seemed very bleak.

By the time I returned for the second year in October, I had begun to feel extremely depressed. My relationship with a girl from Newry had ended over the summer, causing emotional turmoil which, combined with the desperate political situation, made me feel I was stumbling around in darkness. I sought help from the student counselling service, but they could not do anything for me. My second year at Queen's became a disaster, and I deferred my exams. I had badly lost my way.

3

MOVING TOWARDS
THE PROVOS

By the time I returned to retake my second year in October 1975, I had changed my attitude towards political violence.

I still doubted whether I could support the IRA's brand of violence, but I sympathized with the Provos in a way I had never done before. The unionists' destruction of the power-sharing experiment – with the seeming collusion of the British Army – had convinced me that they were not prepared to compromise. I began to believe that the Provos had been right all along: only force would bring about justice for Catholics in this Protestant statelet. I can look back now and say that if power-sharing had worked, I would not have ended up in the IRA.

I returned without a grant because I had flunked my second year and had to survive on virtually nothing. At first I stayed in university accommodation, but the authorities eventually tired of my promise that I would somehow get a grant and threw me out. I stayed in hovels rented by various friends, surviving on porridge and pots of stew. Eventually I moved into a very cheap guest house in Botanic Avenue. I would have a hot shower in the students' union and spend the rest of the day studying in the library. I wore blue jeans, a woolly jumper, black duffle-coat, and Doc Martens (this was before they became a fashion accessory). I had long shoulder-length hair and a pair of thick hairy sideburns of which I was very proud.

I began to make friends, but still preferred my own company. I regarded myself as a maverick, an unaligned, left-wing radical. My main reservation about the IRA was that they seemed intent on getting the Brits out while leaving the middle classes in place north and south of the border. I found myself attracted to people who seemed committed to changing society in a more revolutionary way.

At about this time, a lecturer at the university offered me a room in his house. He ran it as a kind of commune, and there was a good deal of casual sex and some confusing political promiscuity: my new landlord cultivated working-class loyalist contacts, so impressed was he by their proletarian might during the Ulster Workers' Council Strike that had smashed the power-sharing Executive. Through a woman friend of his I also met for the first time a man who was a familiar figure around the campus, an ultra-left English intellectual who seemed to hold fiercely anti-imperialist views. I liked him: his fairish hair stretched down the length of his back, and for someone so quietly-spoken and mild-mannered he seemed to enjoy provoking outraged responses from liberals and unionists. During the meal he infuriated Linda, my landlord's friend, by justifying the IRA's bombing of the London Underground as a necessary part of their campaign against British and loyalist repression.

The atmosphere in our semi-commune was not exactly conducive to serious study. Our landlord made excellent hash cookies, and there was a lot of drinking and dope-smoking. I lived in a haze; I hardly ever did any work. I was considerably younger than my housemates, and in their eyes I would sometimes act in a boorish and immature fashion. The women, two graduates of middle-class Protestant background, started to behave coldly towards me. The atmosphere changed irrevocably, and I knew my days in the house were numbered.

I took my exams and went home to Camlough. When I returned in July, during the marching season, I found that my room had been given to a young gay man. I had arrived back in the middle of a party: my former housemates made me feel very unwelcome. The party had the now-usual sprinkling of loyalist paramilitaries to add a bit of counter-revolutionary chic. My main enemy in the house seemed to be one of the women. She gave me hostile glances all night, and then I heard her use the word 'papes' to her thuggish friend while she looked in my direction. Papes is a derogatory seventeenth-century word for Catholics. I did not know the context in which she used it, but her behaviour frightened me because of the loyalist heavies who were there: I suspected that any one of these paramilitaries could be taking a night off from stiffing innocent Catholics. I left the house the next morning and never returned.

I failed my exams and dropped out for a second time. Then began two years of drifting. I worked as a labourer on a building site for a year. Around the same time I lost a woman whom I had foolishly thought was the love of my life. The end of this relationship and my inability to finish my law degree led to such depression that I would do anything to absorb my time and energy. At night I read whatever would confirm my feelings of life's futility. Nothing could offer me security or certainty; in my depressed and drifting condition, society seemed irredeemably corrupt and absurd. I trawled through the anarchist writers; only their view of life had any meaning for me. My sympathy for the IRA declined: I had returned to my earlier belief that they were a reactionary right-wing movement. I regarded many of their actions as incomprehensibly barbaric, devoid of strategic long-term thinking. I became involved in a group which set up an anarchist bookshop in Belfast. Yet I wondered how the anarchists, with their emphasis on individual development, could ever develop a mass movement that would overthrow the state, which remained a vague but definite goal for me.

But in 1978 I began to turn back towards the IRA. The crucial event was the escalation of the republican prisoners' campaign against the loss of 'Special Category' political status, which they had retained since 1972. From March 1976 most republican prisoners took to wearing only blankets in their cells because they refused to accept categorization as 'ordinary criminals' by wearing regular prison clothing. An IRA prisoner called Ciaran Nugent was the first to refuse, declaring famously that the authorities would have to nail the prison

clothes to his back. In March 1978 the prisoners escalated their
campaign by refusing to wash or use the toilets; they smashed
up the furniture in their cells and smeared the walls with their
own excrement. The 'Dirty Protest' had begun. The degrada-
tion of the prisoners, who were suffering for what seemed like
a minimal symbol of dignity, inspired a vast wave of support
throughout the nationalist community in the north. This coincided with changes in the leadership of the IRA. A young,
Belfast-based leadership displaced the old southern reac-
tionaries like O'Connell and O'Bradaigh, and they started
calling for a long war of attrition against the British which
would lead to British withdrawal from Northern Ireland and
ultimately to the creation of a united socialist republic. This
was the message I wanted to hear. I was also aware of the
expansion of the RUC and the UDR – with British troops
slipping into the background – which was all part of the government's 'Ulsterization, Normalization and Criminalization'
policy. I saw the RUC as a paramilitary force, an instrument of
oppression rather than justice; and I saw the introduction of
Diplock Courts in which a judge sat without a jury as a per-
version of the law.

I was impressed by the developing H-Block campaign,
which seemed to be drawing into its net people from across the
community. Not since the civil rights campaign and the fight
against internment had there been such a groundswell of
public outrage and concern. Messages smuggled out from the
prison excited me: they preached socialist revolution and they
seemed to be generating a social movement based on community action. I felt once again that radical change was possible:
my depression and confusion seemed to lift.

While working in a bar owned by a sleazy Catholic businessman, I had another sad and abortive relationship – this
time unconsummated – with a woman called Maureen, who
was pregnant with another man's child. It ended when she
failed to turn up for a date. The next time I saw her was on her
wedding day when she fainted at the altar. I had not intended
to go – I felt it would be indiscreet – but she sent a guy to pick
me up and drive me to the church. I admired her for that gesture. I did not get her a wedding present. I was never very good

at such social niceties, at doing what others expected, not out of malice, more out of a sense of not having learned the right social habits at home. My father had taught me to pour contempt on the trivial things of life: greeting cards and presents and other celebratory gestures were at the bottom of my father's list of worldly concerns. He even taught me not to keep appointments with people unless they were to my benefit. I learned nothing about loyalty or commitment – such values did not exist in my father's universe. I often felt coldly indifferent towards other people, and had a sense of not knowing what was the right thing to do. This behaviour gave me a low sense of self-esteem which persisted right into late adolescence and cost me much happiness. So I did not really care about Maureen. The fact that she was no longer available made little difference to me.

Around this time I made a successful application for a temporary job with the Customs and Excise. I did not want the job, but it was better than being on the dole or working in a pub. Thoughts of Maureen or any other woman soon disappeared from my mind. Instead I threw myself into supporting the H-Block campaign. I would often think of my friend Raymond McCreesh from Camlough and his comrades, wrapped up in blankets, refusing to wash or slop out, smearing excrement all over their cells. Until now members of the Provisional IRA had always seemed to be mere gut republicans, an Armalite in one hand and a pair of rosary beads in the other. But the men in the H-Blocks seemed different. These were young, long-haired kids who had been hardened by their prison experience and seemed to understand their position. Stripped of everything, even of the right to have a shit in private, they had been left with nothing but their own determination to succeed. I started to visit Raymond McCreesh in Belfast's grim Crumlin Road Prison. On one occasion a fellow prisoner sitting near Raymond asked me if I had any cigarettes. I gave him several. A screw with a peaked cap walked over to me and said: 'Hey, you, you passed him something.' I said yes, I gave him a few cigarettes. He yelled at me that if I was caught doing that again I'd never be allowed back in. I had to swallow his dressing down, feeling humiliated in front of Raymond. At that moment I thought that if I had a gun I would shoot the bastard, and I left the prison an angry man.

I kept going on marches in support of the Blanket Men. A march in Armagh in 1978 was blocked by lines and lines of policeman and armoured vehicles. In my new state of angry exultation I felt I was looking at the military might of Protestantism, reinforced by the British government and now poised for victory. I felt that these Orange shock troops had to be fought and resisted: for the first time I thought about joining the IRA.

On that same march I met someone who was to become a significant influence on my movement into the IRA: the ultra-left English theoretician who I had met at a party during my time in the semi-commune at Queen's. I was surprised to see him there. I knew he was left-wing, but I had not realized that he was a member of the Revolutionary Communist Group, a far-left grouping which gave unconditional support to the Provos. He was selling the group's paper, *Hands Off Ireland*, at the march. He was a middle-class Englishman, and I would have thought he had too much to lose to risk being associated with working-class republicans. He remembered me from that evening in Belfast. He told me to come and visit him in Belfast some weekend.

One Saturday soon after that I was at a loose end, so I decided to take him up on his offer. I called at his flat, and he suggested, if I did not have anything else to do, that we go down to Dublin where a conference was being held in Liberty Hall, the building owned by the Irish Transport and General Workers Union. We travelled down by train. He bought the tickets and also paid for our overnight accommodation in a bed and breakfast. I was touched by this. The conference was on the north, and on the need to consolidate opposition among socialists to capitalism and imperialism.

I thought I had a good grasp of Marxist political theory, but the speakers lost me at an early stage. Speaker after speaker ascended the stage to offer their analyses of what was going on in the north. A Maoist appeared, followed by someone who attacked the Maoist position in favour of the orthodox communist position. He was in turn criticized by a Trotskyist who disagreed totally with both of them. The main characteristic which linked these speakers was their use of words nearly as long as other people's sentences. To me these people were fantasists because they offered no direct support for the IRA's campaign of political violence. Their connection with the 'struggle against imperialism' was purely verbal. How, I wondered, did they propose to deal with the British? I had become utterly convinced that the British government was at war with the people whom the IRA represented.

My companion created the only excitement of the afternoon when he made a point from the audience about the prisoners' struggle. Heads turned to stare at this duffle-coated Englishman and his colleague, me. Someone asked us if we were journalists. I began to turn red, but I said nothing. He said that he was a journalist from the Revolutionary Communist Group. I felt quite chuffed to think that these people might have mistaken me for a little red journalist too.

During a break for coffee, my rigorous comrade dismissed the other left-wing speakers contemptuously. He said they were quite useless. He was a quiet and reserved person but he became intensely animated as he spoke. He said that if leftists had any ideological integrity they would be organizing opposition to the capitalist state and not expressing outrage every time the Provos carried out a bombing or shooting. What were these armchair revolutionaries doing which was of any consequence? The answer, he said, was nothing: they spent their time engaging in endless criticism of the detail of the Provisionals' struggle. He asked me if I could imagine any of the other speakers – with the exception of the People's Democracy leader and former hunger striker Michael Farrell – risking death and arrest in armed struggle against the state?

During the next three months I visited this English purist at his flat near Queen's University. I found him tremendously stimulating, and I learned more from him than from any other intellectual influence in my life. He helped to convince me that the IRA was now undoubtedly an army of the people, the vanguard of a mass movement, and not just a green militarist hierarchy. We discussed such issues for hours, sometimes days, and attended H-Block marches and conferences together. He would unravel before me each and every facet of the conflict, and I came to accept the RCG's interpretation of the conflict completely. I became a republican communist. Finally, I felt, I had found some meaning in my life after years wasted in confusion and self-indulgence. And coincidentally, in December 1978, I was offered a full-time job as a customs officer.

I look back now and realize that I had also been searching for an ideology that would supplant the Catholic morality that had held me back from engaging in violence. Of course, in one sense the Catholic version of Irish history which I had picked up from my mother had predisposed me to sympathy for republicanism. Yet contradicting the unspoken message of that history, the Catholic Church throughout my childhood had taught me that violence was wrong. So now that I wanted to kill for the cause, but I discovered that my upbringing had left me with an inner revulsion against killing. I found that legitimacy for violence in the Marxism of the Revolutionary Communist Group, under patient tutelage.

I loved those marches, particularly in Belfast. Once we walked around Unity Flats in the pouring rain, holding placards and banners aloft and screaming slogans. We would come to a stop to hear speeches from leading republicans using loudhailers. I noticed some girls wearing flimsy cotton dresses in the cold rain, with worn-out sandals and cheap coats. They tried to avoid the potholes and the puddles of water as we walked the streets. Round and round we went. My family was well off compared to these people but at that moment I felt as one with them and I did not want it to be any other way. The cops sped through the flats in grey, armour-plated Land Rovers. An old woman came out dressed in a pair of slippers and an apron. She had long straggly black hair with many strands of silver-grey. She threw herself into a wailing lament for her sons. She screamed at the top of her voice about her seventeen-year-old son, who was 'on the blanket'. Her other son had been shot dead. She seemed overcome by emotion and began to sway as if she were ready to faint. The marchers had come to a halt to listen to her. Someone tried to lead her away, as if she were an embarrassment, but she stood her ground, wailing and yelling, tears streaming down her wrinkled face. Her mouth opened and closed, spit falling from her lips. I could not help noticing her teeth; the few she had left were yellow broken stumps, except for one long tooth on the left-hand side of her mouth in the bottom row. She was terrifyingly ugly.

I felt a bit embarrassed as I remembered that my educated English friend was standing beside me. But he was not embarrassed; on the contrary, he was full of admiration for this pure example of the oppressed nationalist people. The cops returned, speeding through the complex once again. Their appearance jolted the woman, who seemed to gather herself, rubbing back the tears with her bare arm, the sleeves of her cardigan rolled back. 'When my son was here,' she screamed, 'those bastards would have shit themselves going through here.' The revolutionary communists cheered and applauded her. I just felt bewildered.

It continued to rain as we left for a second march through the Short Strand area. These were narrow streets; the red, cream and white paint of the old Belfast Corporation houses was flaking. The slush and dirt of the pavement spattered my shoes as we walked through dismal streets close to the shipyard which denied a living to the area's Catholic inhabitants. I looked down and saw on the side of the road just below the kerbstone a piece of bluey red meat washed clean and shiny by the rain. I looked again and realized it was a cow's heart. I had grown up eating plenty of good meat; I felt sorry for people reduced to eating offal.

By now my duffle-coat was heavy and wet but the day had not yet finished. We went to a social club in the Short Strand. The lights were dimmed and the spotlight fixed on a young man on the stage sitting in a makeshift H-Block cell. He had long hair and a beard and was covered only by a blanket. Words from a pre-recorded tape told the audience how he had got there; melodic wailing Irish music played in the background. The story got more dramatic, building up to a climax in which he raised his fist in defiance and determination. At that time, in that place, it was a powerful piece of political theatre. His performance had the desired effect: people were moved and shaken. They applauded loudly as the lights went off and the darkness allowed the silent Blanket Man to leave the stage. It was expertly managed. This was followed by speeches from two ex-prisoners who reinforced the mood. One said: 'The prisoners think you don't care about them.' You could almost feel the guilt of the crowd; you could feel people renewing their commitment to 'the movement'.

That day was only one of many I devoted to the H-Block cause. These marches were a kind of continuing introduction to the republican movement. They made me feel guilt and shame: guilt that I was so comfortable and privileged, and shame that I was doing so little for the struggle. I was frightened of risking everything, but these events helped me to decide that only by experiencing the world of uncertainty and danger, of possible violent death and imprisonment, could I ever identify with the oppressed and rid myself of my 'bourgeois doubts' and unhappiness.

4

AN APPRENTICESHIP
IN VIOLENCE

I had spent a lot of time during my first two years in the IRA plotting to kill Ivan Toombs, but he was far from my only target during that period.

I look back on that time as my apprenticeship. I learned how to be an effective IRA member: how to gather intelligence, how to set up operations, how to avoid mistakes. Danger and doubt were part of the process of learning the ways of political violence and many things took place during that initial period which troubled me and made me question what I was doing, even though I always emerged with my commitment to the IRA strengthened.

During my first year in the IRA, I was treated with a degree of suspicion by the local chief of operations, the man I called Iceman. He was reluctant to trust me fully because of my background as a communist. Although by 1979 the IRA had, at least informally, dropped the rule that no one who supported the policies of the Soviet Union could be a member, there was a residual hostility towards communists in general. He indicated that if I wanted to be a full member of the IRA I would have to drop my apparent allegiance to the Revolutionary Communist Group. He said it was important in the meantime that I did not give any public display of my republican sympathies. I was not to attend marches; I was not to frequent republican pubs; I was not to associate with ex-prisoners or known republicans. I followed his strictures. By the end of 1979 I felt ready to become a full member of the IRA and told Iceman that I was no longer associated with the RCG. He arranged for me to start receiving my official induction into the organization – a long series of lectures and talks. I went to Dundalk at least one evening a week during the period of these lectures, which took potential recruits through the IRA's recruitment and training manual, the Green Book.

The Green Book listed the duties and responsibilities of volunteers, as well as explaining the history of the movement, the rules of military engagement, and anti-interrogation techniques. At the end of the six to eight week period you were formally sworn in to the IRA.

Toombs may have been the first person to die as a result of my actions, but his was not the first violent death I was close to while serving my apprenticeship.

The way I had entered the IRA, and the intelligence role that had been assigned to me, meant that from the start I came to know the names of many of the IRA operators in Newry while few of them knew anything about me. I would report directly to Iceman across the border with my titbits of information. In this early period he did not think it was good for me to meet too many volunteers, partly because he did not yet trust me.

In the early seventies there had been several IRA units operating from various parts of the town, but over the years, largely as a result of some hideous blunders, a more centralized structure had developed. There were now two units: one was known as the 'élite unit' and was staffed by four experienced and effective men. The other was a relatively new group of three novices, all in their early twenties.

I had been in the IRA for around six months when I met up again with Maureen, the dark-haired beauty with whom I had spent a couple of innocent nights while working as a barman, and whose wedding I had so ungraciously attended. I had gone for a drink to the pub in which I used to work when I noticed her sitting with her new husband Robert Carr and some friends. He didn't know that I knew him as one of the IRA's fledgelings. I nodded at Maureen, and her husband noticed.

He shouted over to me, calling me 'the wee barman'. Why didn't I, he said, come down sometime and have a drink with him and Maureen together instead of asking her for a drink on her own. He was probably right to give me this veiled warning. I suspect I might still have tried it on with his wife if I'd had the chance. I could see by her face that she was not completely happy with married life. I felt a certain contempt for Carr. I knew that he was in the IRA and was part of a punishment squad with a guy called Domo, who I knew vaguely, having once rioted with him in Newry as a teenager. I had heard about Carr pulling out a small automatic pistol in a nearby pub. He had shown off with it to the barman and discharged a shot into a wall in the back of the pub where the kegs were stored. Domo was even more indiscreet: that night he came over to me in the pub. He was drunk and asked me if I could do him a favour. He said he knew I was a customs officer and he wondered whether I could help the IRA to smuggle guns into the north by turning a blind eye at customs checkpoints. I could not believe that he was capable of making such an unsubtle approach. I felt these people must be typical of the idiots who had undermined the Newry IRA's effectiveness. I reported their behaviour to my ruthless superior as soon as I could.

I didn't own a car, so I had to get the bus to see him in Dundalk, walking the mile and a half from the town centre to where he lived. I had become quite friendly with him by now. This time I visited him on a frosty day: there was a crispness in the air and an echo as you walked. I felt good, full of expectations. I felt I was a living through cataclysmic events, taking on a rotten corrupt system.

He told me in his grim way how he had confronted Carr and Domo with their drunken antics. I felt a sense of relief that superior officers took breaches of discipline seriously. Iceman now told me that he wanted me to take part in the bombing of Newry customs station – the place where I worked. He said that the operation would take place that Saturday, and he asked me to borrow a car to pick him up from Dundalk, but my only role would be to drop him off in Newry. I had provided the intelligence for this, my first real operation.

I picked Iceman up on that Saturday in March 1980. I

thought how my colleagues at work would react on Monday morning when they turned up to find a blackened shell in place of the customs station. Would anyone suspect me? I drove him along the back roads with which I had become familiar as a child when I had helped my father smuggle cattle and pigs. He was on edge: Iceman did not feel as comfortable as I did with these roads. But there was hardly enough IRA activity in Newry to justify many covert ops by the army. I hoped this attack on the customs station would be the start of a process which would lead to the army reclassifying Newry as a black area.

When we got to Newry, Iceman would not let me drop him off at the safe house. He told me to stay in my car for three minutes before driving off. I discovered later that he did not want me to know the exact location of the house on the estate.

I was still living on my parents' farm outside Newry, so I drove there and waited for news. I spent the rest of the day thinking about the operation. The Active Service Unit were going to take one of my colleagues called Jim hostage in order to force him to open up the building. I knew the ASU would have to wait until at least 9 p.m., when the place closed.

At midnight the story broke: an attack had taken place on Newry customs station. Police believed that someone had been injured or killed in the incident, but they were still investigating. I listened to the news until well into the night, but there were no more details. I could not sleep. I just lay in my bed, smoking, wondering when the cops or the Brits would arrive for me.

The news said that blood stains left at the scene indicated that 'a member of the gang' had either been killed or injured in the attack. They could not say which because there was no body. I felt slightly relieved: at least my colleague Jim had not been killed. I went in to work on Monday trying to act as bewildered and curious as the rest of the workers. I listened eagerly to all the gossip. One of the women started saying: 'It was an inside job. Must have been an inside job.' I felt slightly panicky as I listened to her chattering on. I thought that if she could realize such a likelihood, then surely everybody else would. I made my way to the security box at break time. The security men would know what had happened: they were also the best gossips because they had the most boring job. They had nothing to do all day except sit in a wooden box, opening and shutting the security gates. And anyway, one of their mates had been kidnapped.

They told me everything they knew. A group of masked men had taken Jim hostage. Only the man in command had not worn a mask. They brought Jim in his own car to the customs station and forced him to open the main entrance and some of the offices. One security man said that Jim had been in the process of opening up some other buildings when a bomb went off. The IRA men had scattered fast.

I went to see the room where the incendiary bomb had gone off. The smell of burning filled the whole building and there were smoke marks all up the corridor. The smell filled my nostrils, and even to this day any similar smell triggers off a feeling of terrible nausea. I realized that someone had been practically burned alive in there. I was told that the peelers had found a pair of shoes stuck to the floor, melted. And, sure enough, I could see the burned remains of rubber stuck like glue to the floor, a dirty transparent blob. On the walls were marks of blood and flesh, which the police had neatly circled with pencil. A man had obviously been engulfed in flames and stumbled along the darkened corridor, bumping into walls as he went, until he had found his way to a window, which he had smashed and then crawled out of. I felt a terrible emptiness. Was one building worth this? I wanted to retch.

The next day, in my capacity as my colleagues' trade union representative, I had to attend a meeting of management and staff to discuss the security of the building. No one seemed suspicious about members of staff, so I left the meeting feeling very relieved. I did not contact Iceman, although I desperately wanted to know what had happened.

I spoke to one of my superiors to ask him if he thought the police would mind if I washed the blood stains off the walls, as I felt they were a ghoulish sight for staff to pass by every day. This man, who had served in the army and who had become an admirer of Ian Paisley, said he thought it would be okay: 'After all, it was someone human.' That was all he would allow this person, a slight human-ness. I felt better when I had washed the blood off the walls, almost as if I had washed away some of my own responsibility and guilt.

When Iceman had still not contacted me after several days I went to his house in Dundalk. I did not even know if he was still alive. But he was there, fit and healthy. He told me that the victim of the explosion was Robert Carr: he was now fighting for his life in a Dublin hospital with burns over most of his body. Everything had been going well. They had taken Jim down to the customs station and told him to open the premises. The unit got in and Robert Carr had gone to the main building to place his incendiary. The others were about to place incendiaries in other parts of the premises, when suddenly Domo had come running down the yard screaming: 'It's the police! It's the police!' Carr must have heard the panicked shout and dropped his bomb because there was an immediate explosion. The IRA men had scattered. I asked Iceman how he had managed to get Carr out of the building. He said that they had left Carr behind because they thought he had been incinerated; that no one could possibly have survived such an intense explosion. They had not even bothered to try to locate his body, but had simply run off. I felt perturbed to think that an injured comrade had been left in this way; it smelt of cowardice and self-preservation.

After Carr had escaped from the burning building he had somehow managed to get into the fields behind the customs station. He ripped off his burning clothes and ran naked through stony fields of bracken, damaging his wounds even more. He somehow ran three miles to a neighbour's house, where he banged on the door and then collapsed, whimpering outside like a dog. The neighbour found him on the step, burnt black, wrapped him in a blanket and brought him to Dundalk for treatment. From there he had been transferred to Dublin.

Robert Carr died of his injuries several weeks later. I sent Maureen a wreath, but it took me a little while to pluck up the courage to visit her. She told me that Carr had not been bitter about being abandoned by his comrades, although he felt that his injuries would not have been so extensive if he had received help earlier. He had kept saying to her: 'Why did they leave me?

Why did they leave me?' When Maureen visited him in hospital he still thought he had a good chance of surviving. Maureen expressed the bitterness that her husband had avoided. She had not known he was in the IRA, just as she did not know I was a member, and she poured out her anger to me at the way they had left her husband to die. She said that the IRA had offered to pay for the funeral, but she had refused to take their money. I decided to take out a three hundred pound loan from the bank to give to Maureen to pay for the funeral: I knew she did not have any money, and I told her she could pay me back whenever she liked. She accepted the money, although I knew she would not have taken it if she had known I was in the IRA. But I was not acting as an IRA man; my gesture was a personal gesture for her, not one made on behalf of the republican movement. Maureen later paid me back the money in full.

Carr had spent the day of the attack drinking in the pub. He could hold his drink, but by the evening when the team arrived for him, I suspect he was not in a condition to handle explosives. When I next saw Iceman I told him about Maureen's bitterness and also about her husband's words: 'Why did they leave me?' Iceman, typically, was unmoved. He said that the IRA had offered Maureen help but she had refused it. As for Robert Carr, he reiterated that they thought no one could have survived the explosion. He said: 'There was a huge bang and a flash, and flames were everywhere. I decided to get the unit out of the area because we thought the police were coming.' Then he added: 'Anyway, I believe he was drunk.' As far as Iceman was concerned, the subject was closed. But the events of that night had rattled me. I realized for the first time that every IRA man was expendable. This knowledge did not undermine my commitment to the organization – indeed, the momentum of the H-Block campaign had renewed my commitment – but I remember promising myself that I was not going to be so easily expendable.

In the meantime, the IRA sent in the Newry élite unit to bomb another customs building in the town. The idea was to provide a boost to morale: when things go wrong, demoralization can set in very rapidly. This time I provided the key that enabled the IRA to get in to the premises, and I was elated when they carried out the operation successfully. But this operation still came too late to prevent the collapse of the fledgeling unit, whose other members made themselves scarce.

I called down to see Maureen over a period of many months. We would just sit in her house drinking. She had become very thin, but she was still an attractive woman and I fancied her. Her long black wavy hair was beginning to lose its shine but when she lay on the floor and all that hair was thrown behind her, I felt good as I kissed her. We talked endlessly about Robert, about life, about friends and neighbours, about anything. Sometimes I brought down chickens from the farm and she roasted them. We ate them late at night, downing glasses of vodka.

We once tried sleeping together, but our relationship was doomed to remain unconsummated. I looked at her beside me and I felt a terrible sadness sweep over me. Her face was pale and thin, her eyes dark and sunken. What remained was her spirit and her courage. She told me that the nurses had tried to get her to wear a mask when she went to visit her husband in the burns unit; they had warned her that the stench of his burnt flesh might overpower her. Yet she had refused the mask. She had known when she saw him that he was not going to survive, and yet she had talked to him only about their plans for the future, about the child he had promised her. She had allowed him to hope and plan for a future she knew he would never have. Yet I felt detached from the situation. Even as I lay in bed with her, I felt as though I were a hundred miles away. I wanted to be close to her, wanted to love her, wanted to show her affection, and yet when the moment came there was no passion. This was his bed, his home, his death. I had a restless, fetid sleep, and I left early the next morning, feeling for both our sakes that it was better this way.

I visited Maureen a few more times after that night. She needed to talk endlessly about Robert. On one of these visits I told her about my involvement in the IRA and what I knew about how Robert had been abandoned. She was shocked, yet she came to terms with it fairly quickly; but of course she cooled towards me and when she went on holiday to Spain she never sent a card, and that was the end.

I had started doing regular relief work at Warrenpoint

customs station. My main target was Ivan Toombs, but there were several other people I was interested in. One was Fred, an ageing member of the RUC Reserve. Fred sometimes dropped his gun on the floor, usually during one of his afternoon naps. He was technically a target, but not one that I took too seriously. There was another reserve policeman in the office, Peter, a Catholic from Kilkeel. He told me about girlfriends he had had in republican areas, even near Crossmaglen. I could not believe that he was still alive.

Peter survived my fatal intentions because the only routine he had that gave me an opening was when we drove to Belfast for a monthly union meeting. I did not want to be sitting in a car with a policeman full of holes.

Peter got on best with Brendan, the man who would help kill Ivan Toombs. One day Peter told Brendan about a publican in Rostrevor whom the RUC suspected of IRA activities. Brendan and I visited this man's pub to warn him that he was under surveillance. Only later, when I felt extremely sure about Brendan's sympathies, did I recruit him into the IRA. Like most educated lower-middle-class Catholics, he knew that the system favoured dull mediocrities from the Protestant community in place of talented Catholics. I knew I could exploit his seething anger at the sectarian injustices he could see around him, though I didn't rate him too highly. But I wanted to have a little hold over him and another potential recruit – whom I'll call Joe – because they both had a lot of low-level intelligence information about Crown forces personnel in the Warrenpoint area. Joe, who worked as a fitter, had far more potential as a useful IRA man. I took a risk in exposing myself as an IRA man to them. I approached Brendan and told him that I wanted him to join an intelligence unit; that I needed help badly in these desperate times when men were about to die on hunger strike. Brendan arranged for me to meet his friend in a pub, and I spoke plainly to them. I told them how they could play an important role in the IRA without any of the usual risks. I felt I bluffed them into joining the IRA. My colleague in particular was very cautious, but he finally agreed to what I proposed. I wanted the two of them to provide a line into a community in which we were traditionally weak.

There was also a 'careerist' motivation on my part: I wanted them to form the nucleus of an IRA intelligence unit of which I would be the officer commanding. I had put this idea to Iceman and he had given me the go-ahead. I argued that many people were not prepared to commit themselves totally to the IRA by becoming active-service recruits, but if they were recruited as intelligence officers under army orders they would remain relatively free from the threat of death, imprisonment or exposure by informers, which were the main risks taken by more active volunteers.

A few months after the abortive attack on Newry customs station, we went for it again. We put a huge bomb in a lorry emblazoned with the name of a shoe manufacturer and parked it where it would cause maximum damage to the building. I was working there the day the bomb came in. One of my colleagues who liked to accept 'gifts' from lorry drivers spotted the shoe lorry parked below. He must have fancied a new pair of shoes because I heard him say: 'Oh! Is anyone looking after that lorry? No? I'll just go and sort the driver out.' In the meantime the IRA had phoned in a warning. My colleague's worn shoes had hardly got him to the stairs before someone came running through the office shouting: 'Bomb! Bomb! There's a bomb downstairs!' Everyone stampeded out of the office. We were able to watch from a safe distance as the lorry exploded, blowing the customs station apart. The next day the management decided that we would have to work in Portacabins while the building was being repaired. As union rep I complained, with a straight face, about the working conditions, and managed to negotiate a good deal for the staff, ensuring that we only had to work half a day for a full day's pay on the grounds that we no longer had suitable offices.

I was probably the most inefficient customs man ever to have been commissioned by the Queen. I would regularly go out in the customs patrol car and never catch a smuggler. Occasionally my bosses would question my lack of results and I would have to grab a few revenue-evaders to show I was doing something. My targets would be drivers who couldn't be bothered to wait in the queue to be processed; they would have nothing to declare and would simply drive past without stopping. There was a seventy-five pounds fine for this behaviour – the lowest fine on the scale. I became known as a 'seventy-five-pounds man'. I was also one of the only customs officers who would drive the patrol car into the republican stronghold of Crossmaglen, where people did not usually take kindly to the appearance of uniformed representatives of the Crown. After each trip I had to fill in a form stating where I had been, and after I put down 'Crossmaglen' a few times, one of my bosses congratulated me on my bravery. I said: 'I believe in making the Queen's writ run to the toughest places, sir.'

Once I was sitting at the front desk when a driver handed in a wallet that he had just found outside. I opened the wallet and saw the official identification card of a reserve policeman. My heart jumped. I was about to note down quickly the man's personal details when an older colleague sitting beside me reached over and grabbed the wallet. My colleague was a Catholic from Crossmaglen, and I knew he drank in a pub frequented by IRA men, but he had been in the British Army. He said: 'Give me that. If the wrong person got this he could do him a bit of harm.' He rang the local police station immediately. I stifled my fury: I had not even had time to look at the wallet-owner's name. If I had got a name I would have checked back through that day's documentation to get a registration number and possibly an address. The next time I saw my ice-cold comrade in Dundalk I told him what had happened. The following week my colleague came into work and I overheard him telling a friend that no one in his local pub was speaking to him. He said: 'I don't know what I've done wrong. It's awful odd.'

I also made use of the photocopier in the customs station for IRA business: I once made eight copies of the Green Book. I was a very part-time excise official.

One of my initial ambitions had been to help win back the independent status of Newry IRA – the status that had been lost in the mid-seventies when undesirables had filled the ranks. One of my first attempts to help re-establish our autonomy involved giving our unit a clear identity. When I first started working for the IRA, there was no name used consistently by

our unit when claiming responsibility for our operations.
Different people would give our unit different names: some
would say they were ringing on behalf of 'Newry IRA', others
would say 'South Down IRA', others would even say 'Dundalk
IRA'. I suggested that we should stick to one name for the
units which operated within the Newry/Warrenpoint/Rostrevor
areas. The new name I chose was the South Down Command,
which had a grander and more intimidating ring to it, even
though it referred to such a small group of men. My suggestion
was accepted and I was given the job of press officer with
responsibility for ringing the media to claim our operations.
Crossmaglen and South Armagh used the code-word 'Nancy'
when phoning journalists. I started to use the word 'Fox'
instead in order to establish notoriety for the South Down
Command among the media.

I arranged for Brendan and Joe to receive their induction
into the IRA. They started going through the Green Book.
Shortly before the killing of Toombs, when Brendan the customs man had almost completed the lectures, he kept coming
to me and distancing himself from the IRA, drawing back and
reserving his position. I had to drag every little bit of information out of him. He had become as economical with his
'snippets' as he was with everything else. Some weeks after
Toombs's death, Brendan told me that the experience had left
him feeling more dedicated to the republican cause than ever
before, but I did not really believe him. I felt he was probably
trying to reassure me that he was not going to crack. He finished his final Green Book lectures on his return from a
month's detached-duty in England: this facility existed to help
people from Northern Ireland to get over traumatic events
such as the one he was supposed to have experienced.

Soon after, Iceman tried to get Brendan to scout a bomb into
the north but he refused point-blank to have anything to do
with the operation. Brendan called in to see me at my mother's
flat one day. He told me he wished to resign from the IRA, and
he handed me a piece of paper which he said was his official
resignation letter. I almost laughed, but sure enough there was
his resignation statement in his big bold handwriting, signed,
gaelicized, sealed and delivered. Brendan's career as a soldier

for Ireland had come to an end, or so he thought. Tragically, it is not that easy to wipe the slate clean.

Around this time my family discovered that I was in the IRA. I was still living on the farm, and I had hidden some rifles and ammunition under my bed. I started to lock my door, which aroused the curiosity of a nosy younger brother. He found a duplicate key and, with a friend, had a look around when I was out. They found an arms dump. My family were horrified and ordered me to get the guns out of the house immediately. I felt my secret world had been penetrated; my inexperience induced panic and fear. I felt paranoid, as if the police were closing in on me for the murder of Toombs. I hid the weapons elsewhere, but decided to disappear for a few weeks. I had some friends in New York and I could just about afford an air ticket to see them. But after two weeks I began to feel very homesick and I decided to return and take my chances.

After the killing of Toombs, we were keen to maintain the unit's momentum and to consolidate our success in an area which had been almost unaffected by the war. As well as Warrenpoint, I had my eye on the quiet coastal village of Rostrevor, close to the mountains of Mourne. The rich had their holiday homes in this area, magnificent houses set in a few acres of land, surrounded by hedges and mature trees. The village was skirted by spectacular mountains on one side, and beautiful Carlingford Lough on the other. The village's narrow streets were lined with trees and there were many relaxed pubs where you could listen to traditional Irish music. I thought that if only we could carry out a few successful operations in this area each year, we would have achieved a lot. Indeed, only two operations a year, as long as they were successful, could ensure a constant latent fear of attack, which in turn would tie down Crown forces indefinitely with minimal risk to IRA volunteers. The bonus would be that the middle-class unionists who lived here would never be able to relax.

After my return from New York, Iceman introduced me to the leader of the élite unit, a man whom I knew briefly from a part-time job I had done several years previously. I shall call him Brian. We went drinking together in Rostrevor's pubs, and we got to know the rest of the area with its steep hills, dotted with sprawling mansions and old grey buildings. To drive along these roads was a pleasant experience, although Brian and I usually had things on our minds other than the scenic beauty. We were looking for culverts (large drains which allow water to pass under a road) in which we could plant a bomb that would take out an armoured Land Rover. We spotted such a culvert in an area called Killowen. I stopped the car and pretended to change the tyre while Brian got down to have a look. He found strong steel security covers on the culvert, which meant that the RUC had anticipated us. We abandoned the search, but I made a mental note to return to this area in the future because I knew that the UDR regularly patrolled here at weekends, and I was determined to find a way of blowing up one of their patrols.

The élite unit in Newry had been successful because Brian made it so. He led by example and in his quiet and determined way he got results. His demeanour commanded respect, obedience and loyalty from his men. They carried through some of the most violently effective operations in the north. Brian told me that he had killed his first man at seventeen. He was tall, about five foot eleven, broad-shouldered with an erect posture, his head held high on a firm thick neck. He was as strong as a bullock, and yet he had a look of innocence about him, a face that would not have led anyone to suspect him of anything. He was good company, and could retain his equanimity even in drink. He loved the IRA; it was his life. I suppose I hero-worshipped him and men like him, seeing them as reincarnations of Tom Barry and Dan Breen, the famous guerrilla leaders of the 1919–21 War of Independence.

One day he drove me past the site where his unit had blown to pieces five soldiers with a huge culvert bomb. The unit had struck the day after the death of hunger striker Raymond McCreesh, my schoolfriend from Camlough. The huge crater had been filled in, the stone walls rebuilt, and the road retarred. We got out of the car and walked along the road. Brian pointed to the field where he said the volunteers who carried out the operation had buried the bomb wire two feet underground. They ran it directly along the hedge for 400 yards. They spent many nights digging into the early hours, in order to replace each sod as they moved along, so as to hide any trace of the clay having been disturbed. They had to be so painstaking because of the army's aerial reconnaissance. The wire lies there to this day. Brian told me that the power of the explosion had disintegrated the vehicle into tiny fragments.

That evening, as he sat eating his tea at his mother's house, a news report on the television described the latest explosion. His mother looked at his muddy wellingtons, looked at his face and burst out crying. But she never said anything, never uttered a word, never passed one single remark. He went on eating as if nothing had happened.

Brian and I had started to target a Catholic policeman. On Sundays we would wait outside his church to watch him drive by; on weekdays I followed him to his girlfriend's house. After a while we had enough information to hit him any day of the week, but Iceman told us to forget about the operation. I did not find out until much later that the cop had been giving him information in exchange for immunity from IRA attack. Iceman tipped him off that we were targeting him. But soon after, Brian killed another Catholic cop who did not have the same insurance policy. He told me that the RUC man had only been a few weeks away from retirement. He had survived for so long that he must have assumed he was no longer a target and, with his pension almost in his pocket, he had started to relax. Brian said the cop had been having a quiet pint in Newry when the IRA team had entered the bar. The cop was sitting at the bar wearing a white shirt. Brian and the other gunman were dressed in leather jackets and motorcycle helmets. The policeman turned, saw the gun pointed at him and said: 'No, boys, not me.' Brian fired the first bullets into his chest, knocking him off his bar stool. Like a wounded animal, the man had tried to drag himself along the floor towards a back door. Brian had stood for an instant staring at the crawling figure, captivated momentarily by the crimson colour which had started spreading rapidly over the man's bright white shirt. Then he stepped closer and fired several more shots into him.

Brian was ruthless, but he had his own strange code of honour. I had a drink with him once before Christmas. I talked about an operation the IRA could bring off on Christmas Day when the Brits and the cops least expected it, but he replied: 'I would never kill a man on Christmas Day or anytime during that season. Christmas is a time to enjoy yourself, to take a break from life, to have a good time, to meet people, not to kill.'

Brian grew to like and trust me. His way of showing it was that he wanted to expand my role in the IRA beyond intelligence-gathering: he wanted me to become a gunman. He took me on a training exercise in a government forest in the Cooley mountains in County Louth in the Irish Republic. Below us we could see Dundalk bay. I had to fire a Garand rifle and a Browning Automatic pistol. I used the Browning to shoot the bark off trees. To hold a gun is to hold power, but even as I felt the excitement of firing live bullets, I knew that I could never use a gun on another human being. I did not mind setting up operations in which people would be shot, but I knew my limitations: I would never be a shooter. I simply did not have it in me. Brian thought differently. He said he wanted to take me on operations with him; he wanted me to be standing beside him, blasting away with my own weapon. He said: 'I've told Iceman that I think it's time, but he says you're not ready yet. I don't agree with him. I think you're ready.'

Perhaps if he had persisted in his encouragement, I would have tried to fufil his expectations and become a killer instead of a planner of deaths. But it was never to be.

5

THE RECRUITING SERGEANT

The period of the hunger strikes was the high-water mark of sympathy for militant republicanism since the formation of the Provisional IRA. Yet in Newry it also marked the lowest point of active support for the Provos.

When Bobby Sands started his hunger strike on 1 March 1981, the IRA's élite four-man unit in Newry were well-trained and trusted by the IRA; the Crown forces did not know who they were. By 19 May, they had killed the five soldiers with a landmine not far from Newry. Soon after that coup, in separate incidents, they killed an army bomb-disposal officer and Brian shot the elderly policeman in a Newry pub. But, to my astonishment, almost as soon as they had proved their effectiveness they announced their intention to disband: they felt that the IRA's commanders were compromising their security. So at the end of June 1981 I had become the only IRA man in Newry, a town that was 95 per cent Catholic, at a time when the deaths of the hunger strikers were generating a surge of support for the republican movement.

My first inkling that something extraordinary was about to take place was when Brian told me that he had demanded a meeting with the officer commanding our area. He said that his unit were worried that they were being asked to operate with IRA men who had only just arrived from Belfast. Some of these Belfast men had recently escaped from Crumlin Road

Prison, others had moved to Dundalk as a result of the testimony of the supergrass Christopher Black. All of these refugees had one thing in common: they were 'red-lights'. This was the nickname given to IRA men who were known to the Crown forces. Such people, their covers blown, could more easily be placed under surveillance: their presence in an area acted as a red light to the police and the Brits, risking those who were not suspected and who operated effectively in secret.

But there was another dimension to the élite unit's concerns. Iceman had told me some time before that earlier on in the seventies there had been a problem with a lot of the Belfast men who came to Dundalk after going on the run. A conspicuous minority had simply spent their time getting pissed, starting fights with locals, stealing other IRA men's women, running up debts all over the town and even carrying out robberies for themselves. Iceman said: 'Some of those fuckers were like occupying troops.' After several incidents damaging to the sober and austere public image of republicanism – which had led to Dundalk becoming known as El Paso – the IRA brought in a rule that all volunteers on the run had to go to Dublin: they were not allowed to hang around the border. But from 1981 the RUC's use of supergrasses – former paramilitaries who would name scores of their former colleagues, leading to mass arrests – had produced such an influx of people on the run that the IRA had to relax the rule of banishment to Dublin. The supergrass system coincided with the hunger strike and the pressure to intensify the military campaign. Many of the Belfast men started to be absorbed into local units: ours was one of them.

I was in Iceman's house when Brian and the other three members of his élite unit turned up for the meeting with the OC for South Down. I had to wait in the sitting-room while the meeting took place in the room next door. The meeting was not cordial; voices were raised several times. The élite unit operated according to the IRA's new cell structure. In theory, all IRA men were now supposed to operate in small Active Service Units (ASUs). These would comprise four or five volunteers working in a tight 'family' group. There would be a quartermaster with responsibility for weapons and explosives, an intelligence officer, and at least two operators capable of carrying out shootings and bombings. They would all work together in this self-contained unit to plan and carry out operations. In reality, the structure was not always as tight as it should have been, but the cell-structure principle was adhered to whenever feasible (although some areas, such as Crossmaglen and Tyrone, still maintained the old battalion/company structure while paying lip service to the re-organization). I found out later that the unit had told the OC that they were refusing to work with the Belfast men. Instead, they were going to 'take a holiday' while the Belfast men operated in the area. Only Brian would have been willing to carry on as before, but in any case the company he worked for was about to relocate him to Dublin, and the rest of the unit refused to risk operating outside the cell structure. In effect they had lost their nerve and gone into early retirement. From this point on, almost all IRA men who carried out operations in the Newry area actually lived across the border in Dundalk.

I did not share the others' reservations about the Belfast men. I had already met a few of them – including Angelo Fusco who had escaped from gaol just before being sentenced to life imprisonment for his part in the killing of an SAS officer – and I had been enthused by their eagerness for action. Their arrival in the area, regardless of the risks, would help turn the South Down Command into the kind of ruthless unit I longed to be part of.

This feeling was confirmed when I started operating with one of the IRA's living legends – the man I will call Seán. Seán had been one of the handful of IRA men who, between 1969 and 1970, had managed to protect the isolated Catholic Ardoyne area of Belfast. He had helped fend off loyalist mobs who were intent on burning out Catholics. He had been interned, wounded twice on active service, had a brother killed in an explosion, and had served seven and a half years of a fifteen-year sentence for blowing up the Passport Office in Belfast. While Seán had been in prison the IRA had developed a new policy with regard to former prisoners. Before the reorganization, these men had been allowed to return to their former brigades, but now this was felt to be too risky to the new cell structure.

Instead, the IRA in Belfast formed an auxiliary class of volunteers who were used to enforce 'community justice' and to protect areas, in theory, from loyalist killer gangs. They were the ones who carried out knee-cappings, the roughest form of justice imaginable, and kept the ASUs supplied with cars and safe houses. However, the hunger strike disrupted the carefully crafted reorganization. The IRA needed to intensify the military struggle and so they had to call upon the auxiliaries more and more to carry out operations. An overlap developed between the cell structure and the auxiliary structure. Ultimately, this overlap opened the whole organization up to infiltration by informers, as well as making it vulnerable to anyone who decided to turn state's evidence. Now however, in the heat of the hunger strike, necessity dictated that Seán become more active. He rose quickly to become OC of the North Belfast unit, before going on the run in Dundalk. During his years in prison he had read prolifically, and I found him ready to discuss revolutionary upheavals throughout the world. He was of medium height, with a round jolly face and a hearty laugh. He was also courageous, never expecting anyone to do anything that he would not do himself.

In the company of such tough Belfast Provos, I felt embarrassed by the local unit's behaviour. Some days after the showdown between the South Down OC and the élite unit he asked me to visit him in Dundalk. It was a Saturday. I took my girlfriend in the car with me: I told her I was just going to pop in to see a friend for ten minutes. She told me not to hang around as she wanted to do some shopping. The OC lived in a dingy bedsit near the courthouse. His room was spartan, containing only a table, two chairs, a sofa, bed, cooker and greasy lino. He sat on one of the chairs, looking extremely gloomy. He was a heavy set man, almost forty. His fair hair was balding, and he had a distinctive long Mexican moustache. He always seemed to wear the same jeans, plain shoes and open-necked shirt. He talked openly to me. He said he was very disappointed with the actions of the élite unit. He told me that even Iceman had decided to withdraw from IRA activities for a while, so he had decided to make Seán his second-in-command. He was desperate to turn the community support for the hunger strikers into gains for the IRA – into new, determined recruits.

He said to me, 'We've got practically nobody in Newry. I want you to go out and get us more people. I don't care how you do it. You're going to have to take risks. At this moment in time the IRA in Newry depends on you. Do you think you can do it?'

I felt excited and flattered, as he intended I should, and I told him I had a few people in mind. He told me to get on with it.

I left that bedsit feeling ten feet tall. My day had come: I was moving into a new area of trust and responsibility within the IRA. Part of me felt pleased that all the others had gone. The way was now open for me to show what I could do. When I returned to the car to find an angry face glaring out at me: I had forgotten that my girlfriend had been waiting for two hours. I apologized profusely and said that I would take her into Newry immediately so she could do her shopping. But I knew what I was going to do and who I was going to recruit.

Only a few months previously I had helped to prevent the emergence of a rival republican group in Newry. Now I hoped to win over the members of that group. Since the end of 1974 the Provisionals had watched uneasily as a rival group emerged within the republican movement: the Marxist revolutionaries of the Irish Republican Socialist Party (known to everyone as 'the Irps') not only offered unyielding support for the armed struggle, but also formed their own military wing, the Irish National Liberation Army (INLA). They presented themselves as being much further to the left of the Provos; and they brought themselves most spectacularly to the attention of the public by assassinating the Conservative MP Airey Neave. The IRA had watched the growth of INLA warily, but for pragmatic reasons had decided not to challenge them. In some areas there was even a degree of co-operation between them. INLA contained many former IRA men, and on occasion INLA men would move over to the IRA. But suspicion and caution were the norm for relations between the two groups.

Of the ten republicans who died on hunger strike, three were INLA. The common experience of prison led to greater co-operation on the outside – at least in appearance. Supporters of the campaign for political status joined together in H-Block committees, which aimed to create a broad front of support across the community. Behind the surface of this co-operation, Sinn Fein – in Newry at least – kept a close watch on the Irps at public meetings. They wanted to gauge the extent of support for the Irps' hard line. Sinn Fein people would report back to the IRA about what took place at the meetings. Newry did not have its own INLA unit, but we suspected that this situation would not last for long. We saw *ourselves* as the republican New Left. We were expecting a dividend from the H-Block campaign: we did not want a rival group to emerge as the voice of left-wing republicanism. Iceman suspected that the next development would be the setting up of an INLA unit in the town. He had a special hostility towards INLA and regarded many of their members as little more than criminals or political fantasists (later events would show he wasn't far wrong). In practical terms, he believed that an INLA unit would endanger our own operations; INLA attacks might bring a concentration of Crown forces into the area at times when we needed a clear run for our own attacks. And more crudely, Iceman felt that only the IRA had the right to stiff people in the cause of Irish freedom.

Iceman told me to find out who was likely to form the nucleus of the INLA unit – and to close them down before they got started. He wanted me discover who was talking to whom at the H-Block committee meetings, who was most vociferous, who was composing the impressive letters which were appearing in the local paper on behalf of the Irps. I sympathized with this hostility towards INLA although, with my Marxist background, I found myself agreeing with much of INLA's political analysis.

Before I joined the Provos I had discussed INLA with my RCG mentor from my Queen's University days. I thought that he, as a revolutionary communist, would have supported the INLA, but in fact he believed that the IRA should have wiped them out at birth. He believed that in any revolutionary conflict there should to be only one revolutionary group acting as the sole focus of the people's energy and support: rivals threatened

only to undermine the struggle and so needed to be dealt with
ruthlessly. I accepted the logic of this chillingly Stalinist analysis and so had no qualms about helping to ensure that INLA
never got off the ground in Newry, though it never came to
murder.

I had built up a list of six potential INLA men. Some of
them I knew; indeed, one of them was my cousin Mickey. I
believed that they would all make good recruits for the IRA.
They were young, active, came from 'good' family backgrounds,
and had no criminal records, so the RUC probably knew nothing about them. I had suggested to Iceman that we ought to
recruit them, but as far as he was concerned, they were irrevocably tainted by their Irps connections. Yet that Saturday, as I
left the South Down OC's flat, I knew that the former Irps
were the men for us; and Iceman could not stop me now.

After leaving the OC's bedsit I drove with my girlfriend to
Newry. I dropped her off; then I waited for her in the town
centre, near the cathedral. I spotted one of my prospective
recruits coming towards me. I had been at school with him,
although I had not had much contact with him in recent years.
I said hello and asked him if he had a few minutes to sit down
with me. I did not beat about the bush: I told him I was in the
IRA and that I was looking for recruits. He did not say anything, but listened intently. I made a sales pitch to him; and like
any good salesman I tailored my appeal to suit my prospective
customer. Since he was close to the Irps I went out of my way
to explain how the IRA had developed into a socialist organization in recent years. I told him that the IRA now stood for a
lot more than merely getting the Brits out and that we didn't
want to end partition only to maintain the existing class structure. I also underlined the importance of the changes that had
taken place locally in the Newry IRA. I said that we now had
a tight cell structure operated by disciplined volunteers committed to socialist revolution: 'Look at what we've been doing.
We killed those five Brits. We got Toombs. We stiffed that
cop. We're doing some great things, and we need people like
you to keep things at this standard.'

When I had finished he looked briefly at the ground and
then turned to me and said: 'I'm not interested in getting in

heavy, but I'm interested in helping in some way.' I said that
was fine: not everyone had to be a trigger man. I suggested that
he could help with intelligence. He had a car, so perhaps he
could do a bit of scouting for us.

'Your cousin Mickey is the one to contact. He really wants
action. He's bursting for action. I know he'd love to get into the
thick of things.'

I asked him if he knew any other people who would be suitable. He gave me eight names, including all the people from the
prospective INLA cell, and outlined what he thought would be
their most suitable roles. He thought four of them would be
'definites', and the other four 'possibles'. He said that two of
the definites were not in Newry at the moment, but the other
two – including Mickey – were. I said: 'I'd like youse all to
meet some good men in Dundalk. I'll let you make up your
mind yourselves after you've met these people. There'll be no
pressure. I won't even be there myself.' I left it to him to contact Mickey and one of the other definites. I told him to
contact me when he had a date when all three of them could go
to Dundalk. He called that evening, and I arranged the meeting. I told the OC and Seán: 'Make sure you impress them.' I
wanted these two experienced IRA men to overawe the three
Irps with their soldierly credentials.

Eight names, four definites, at least one of whom was eager
to get straight in to do the business: cousin Mickey. I had had
almost no contact with Mickey when I was growing up. His
father was my father's brother, but his mother was English. His
parents had met in England, where Mickey was born and
brought up. His family was close and loving: they got on well
together and looked out for each other. His father brought the
family back to Northern Ireland when Mickey was in his teens,
so Mickey retained a Manchester accent, supported Manchester
United, and even returned to Manchester University to study
for his degree in languages. And now he wanted to be an operator. His wish would be my command, and I knew the IRA
would be happy to facilitate him.

I never stopped looking for military targets. One of my
pastimes was to drive close to Newry police station at times

when I knew that policemen changed shifts; so that I could spot cars driving in and out of the station. Ideally, I wanted to target policemen, but as far as I was concerned anyone who worked there in any capacity was a legitimate target. One day I watched a red Datsun Cherry approach the station from the Armagh Road. The car went under the security barrier and I said to myself: 'Jesus, there's a stiff.'

I met my ex-IRSP contact, my former schoolmate, the following Saturday to discuss some of the other possibles he had mentioned. One man interested me in particular. He worked as a television engineer. My contact said: 'He gets a lot of information, this guy. He travels all over the place fixing televisions. He goes into all the Prod areas.' I could almost feel my ears twitching with excitement. I knew the opportunities for intelligence-gathering such a job could offer. I asked where I could meet this guy, and it seemed that at weekends he drank at the Maple Leaf in Canal Street. 'He's fond of a game of pool. I know he's sympathetic – he was hit with a plastic bullet once – and he's cautious. But when he's pissed he comes out with a few things. He told me recently that he'd been in a Prod house and he'd seen a policeman's uniform hanging up in the wardrobe.' He also told me that a detective called Cunningham had lived in the same street as the television man until recently when the cop had moved outside Newry, possibly up the Armagh Road. I asked if he knew anything more about Cunningham. He said: 'He drives a wee red Datsun Cherry with a black roof.' Cunningham had to be the detective I had spotted going into the police station some weeks ago: it was unlikely that there were two detectives who drove the same car and travelled into work from the Armagh Road.

That night I went to the Maple Leaf. This was my real work now, and I was revelling in it. I had told my ex-IRSP friend to let the television man know that I would be coming in for a little chat. The whiff of booze and tobacco hit me as I walked in the door. Laughter and talk filled the air. I made my way to the back extension where the pool tables were. This part of the pub was darker than the rest, the lighting directed at the tables, throwing the shadows of the players on to the walls. Wooden benches surrounded the edges of the room. I

saw my man sitting in half-darkness, sipping at his pint. He
nodded towards a ginger-haired man at one of the pool tables. I
did not waste any time: I was not here to socialize. I walked up
to my mark and said hello. He smiled and said: 'How're you?'
He was waiting his turn to play. I exchanged a few pleasantries
with him. He was about my age and seemed a good-natured
man. I stood with him for a while, watching him play, talking
to him about neutral subjects. I wanted to see what sort of a
fellow he was, how he responded to my questioning.

I let him get a few pints in him before I began talking about
the hunger strike. I asked him how he felt about it. He said he
did not like to see good men dying; he thought they were political prisoners and ought to be given political status. I said:
'And what about those cunts in the RUC and the UDR banging about full of life while those men are dying? Doesn't that
make you sick? I'm sure you must see them all. You go out to
Bessbrook and into all those Prod houses. Do you ever see anything? Do you ever see any pictures of soldiers on
mantelpieces?' He said nothing, pretending to concentrate on
his next shot, but I could see his face reddening and sweat
beginning to squeeze its way on to his forehead. He potted a
ball and moved round the table. I followed him: 'I know you
get information, and I want it. There are men dying on hunger
strike and you won't even give me a bit of fucking information.' He bent down to take another shot. I could see a slight
shake in his hand. 'That RUC shite Cunningham lived in your
street, didn't he? Where's he moved to? What do you know
about him?' The man said in a faltering voice: 'I think he's
gone up to the Armagh Road.' I was getting somewhere.
'Where on the Armagh Road? That's a big road. Is he near a
shop or a pub? What sort of house does he have? Is he married? What's his wife's name? Does she work?' He did not say
anything. He hit another shot and moved round the table again.
'Why don't you talk to me? You talk to this one. You talk to
that one. Talk to fucking me. You'll be in no danger. You just
give me a little information. You don't need to know anything
after that. No one will trace anything back to you. Just give me
the information, and leave it to me.' He took a sip from his pint
and said: 'I don't see that much.' I said: 'I know you've seen

things. People have told me you've seen things. You saw a uniform in a wardrobe, didn't you?' He looked embarrassed, his face flushed.

The room had filled with tension. Others could hear my interrogation of this now thoroughly frightened man. Balls clicked in the background. Time to ease off. I smiled at him and said: 'Relax. Don't worry about it.' I changed the subject and cracked a few jokes. As I joked I was thinking: let it breathe, let it sink in. Let him get used to the idea of what I want. Don't push him all the way yet. So, for the next half-hour, I became his best friend. I bought some drinks. I took an interest in his life. I even congratulated him on some of his shots. I returned to the subject of the hunger strike. I asked him who he thought would die next. He whispered to me: 'Look, I can't give you much.' I said: 'Don't worry. I don't want much. Just pass on wee bits here and there. I don't want you to endanger yourself. Just open your eyes a wee bit more when you're out and about. You'll see soldiers about the place. You mightn't think it's important, but it could be important to me. You might hear something in conversation: you talk to a lot of Prods. They might just drop something. All I want you to do is to open your eyes when you're out in your van.' He was by now drunkenly anxious to be my friend. He promised to let me know if he saw anything.

This was the way I gathered intelligence, and this was the way killings were prepared.

During the week I met up with Seán and the OC. I asked them how the meeting with Mickey and the others had gone. Seán said: 'That wee cousin of yours, he'll be a good 'un. That boy's bursting for action. He'll do the business. The other two were a bit nervy.' The OC said that he was going to put Mickey through the Green Book lectures immediately and send him to a training camp in the Irish Republic within a few weeks. Seán and the OC thought that the other two would be able to do intelligence work. We decided that they could work with Mickey as his back-up team, providing intelligence, although there was the danger of exposing a committed gunman to people who were less committed: they might let him down at crucial moments. My ex-schoolmate told me later that Mickey had come away from the meeting full of excitement: 'This is the real McCoy,' he had said. The third man had been less excited, but still willing.

In the meantime, I started watching for Detective Cunningham and his Datsun in earnest. I made a point of driving the streets around Newry police station before my work began at 9 a.m. As far as we knew, no policemen lived in Newry itself, but when they travelled in, they did so without any escort to protect them. I thought this was an appalling indictment of the IRA's inefficiency in Newry in recent years: they had obviously not been putting the police under concerted pressure. After several mornings spent driving round from the Armagh Road across the stone bridge past Catherine Street RUC station, I finally spotted my man. When I had first seen his car go up to the barrier at Catherine Street I had not been able to get a look at the driver or the registration number. Now, as I followed behind him, I could see that he was a heavily-built man, and I memorized his number plate – EIB 6946. Cunningham's car disappeared once again as the barrier lifted to let him through. Soon after that sighting I spotted Cunningham's car outside a Newry pub called Hales. It was a mixed pub, but mostly it was Protestants who drank there. I decided to watch out for his vehicle next weekend. That Saturday night I waited outside Hales from ten until three. He did not reappear. I drove home realizing that I would have to be very patient to catch this one.

I began meeting my ex-IRSP recruit regularly to pick up any bits and pieces of information that he had gleaned. He suggested another possible recruit called Francie. I had been at junior school with him, but had not seen him for sixteen years. I remembered him as tall and gangly, and even then bubbling with manic energy. He got a job suddenly after his 'A' levels, so he could get married: his girlfriend was pregnant. Everyone had expected him to go on to university, but instead he had ended up working as a craftsman in the public sector. He now drove an official van around the district: exactly the type of person I wanted.

One night I waited for him outside his office. Francie

emerged and rode off on a racing bicycle. I knew it was him: he still looked the same. I followed him in my car and as he got near the roundabout for Warrenpoint I flashed my lights at him and beeped my horn until he turned his head to see me driving behind him, waving madly with my right hand for him to pull over to the side for a chat. He got into my car on the hard shoulder. He recognized me immediately. He said: 'How you doing? I haven't seen you these years.' We talked casually for a few minutes, then I got to the point: 'Listen, I was talking to your man [our schoolmate who was now being so helpful to me]. He says you might be interested in helping out the IRA. I'm in the IRA. He is going to be helping me with a little bit of intelligence. I'd like you to do the same if you're prepared to do it. It wouldn't involve much. There wouldn't be any big risk. I wouldn't involve you with a lot of people.'

Francie looked at me with a mixture of excitement and disbelief. He laughed madly and said: 'Are you really in the IRA? Are you having me on? Ah, you're not, boy.' I began laughing too: 'I fucking am in the IRA.' I knew I had him. I told him to give me a time when he would be able to go to Dundalk. Francie said: 'Right, I'll do that. I'll be interested in doing that.'

He left my car laughing. He got on his bike and rode off. I started laughing again. I felt like an old-fashioned recruiting sergeant, flattering and cajoling people into joining the army. The only difference was that I could not offer these recruits the Queen's Shilling. All I could offer was imprisonment or death, the ruin of their own lives and their families.

Seán and the OC liked Francie. He seemed to be completely without ego: what he loved was finding things out. He moved on all the time to the next thing, and his restless mind soon started spotting all sorts of openings for operations. His job offered the IRA many advantages, which I was not slow to exploit. I impressed upon him the importance of 'thinking IRA' every moment of the day, especially when he was driving around in his work van which had the name of a public utility stamped all over it. It was an ideal vehicle in which to become inconspicuous: policemen and soldiers would see such vans all over the place, and so they would not give a second glance if they saw one in the same position for long periods. If they looked inside the van they would see only workmen having lunch or a tea-break. This van, this familiar and trustworthy van, could park outside police stations, people's houses, and even permanent checkpoints without setting off any mental alarms. I made Francie aware of the importance of trivia. I taught him to listen carefully to those little throwaway remarks which might contain a nugget of information. I would remind him of the credo of the Conservative Party: life is full of opportunities.

Now I had a total of four new recruits with four others who were promising. Some Newry men at last – and almost every one of them an ex-Irp. I felt I could now concentrate on my main purpose in life – finding targets and setting them up. Detective Cunningham began to obsess me: I had built up a huge amount of information about him, enough to kill him ten times over, but could not find a way of getting to him.

Towards the end of 1981, when the hunger strike was over, Iceman appeared back on the scene. So did the former leader of the élite unit, Brian. I did not care much for Iceman's reappearance, but I was delighted to see Brian again. During the time I had worked with him, we had become good friends. He seemed to be still game for action. I talked to him about Cunningham; how we knew the pub he drank in; how we knew he was in the darts team of another pub and that he went to some church or charity meeting every Sunday in Sandys Street. We knew his car. We had known all this for nearly a year, and yet we had not been able to do anything effective about it.

Within a week Brian had decided to do something. He went to visit the OC and Iceman in Dundalk. In an act of careless stupidity our OC, who was known to the Irish police as a Provo, took him out drinking. Until that Saturday night Brian had not been known to the police on either side of the border. The two happy drinkers were picked up by the Irish Special Branch, who held them for several hours. The police had been particularly interested in Brian and had spent a long time asking him how he knew the OC and what he was doing in the company of a known Provo. They released him, but now he was a suspect whose movements they would try to tag.

I got a call on Sunday morning telling me to go to Dundalk. I arrived at the safe house about eleven. Iceman, the OC and Brian were all there. I could tell that the latter two had had a hard night's drinking. Iceman, as always, was completely sober. They told me that today was going to be the day to hit Cunningham. The plan was to steal a car from a south Armagh family, who would be held prisoner for the duration of the operation. This would ensure that the car was 'clean' until we had finished with it. Brian would pick me up in the stolen car at a rendezvous on the border in the evening and then I would drive to the location of the hit. Brian would be my passenger, armed with an Armalite rifle. He would shoot Cunningham as he came out of church. We were also taking a grenade in case we came up against any police patrols; and I was given a Luger pistol equipped with a silencer. After the shooting I would be responsible for dumping the car, hiding the weapons and, most importantly, ensuring that we both escaped.

That evening, I arrived at the border at the arranged time. I sat for quite a while, but no one came. It was getting late; Cunningham was due out of church in a few minutes. Something had to have gone wrong. I drove off and raced back to Newry just in time to see Cunningham coming out of church. I watched him stand by his car talking to a friend for a few minutes. I imagined what would have happened if Brian had been with me. We would have driven up to him and cut him to pieces in a fusillade of high-velocity bullets. Instead, I watched him get into his car and drive off.

Later that night I drove to Dundalk to find out what had gone wrong. The OC told me that the Special Branch had followed Brian to a rendezvous with Iceman, who was going to hand over the weapons for the job after retrieving them from an arms dump. Iceman had caught sight of the watching police. Brian made a run for it with the weapons in the hijacked car. The police decided to give chase to him rather than Iceman, who managed to escape. Brian had shot off towards the border, hoping to get to the safety of Her Majesty's jurisdiction. He got close to the border, but he was not a skilled driver and he crashed the car at speed, almost killing himself.

He had raised a rifle towards the approaching Irish police officers, but had thought better of it and surrendered.

The following week I was at work when one of my colleagues, Bob, came up to me as I sat at my desk, processing shipping documents. He was a senior officer, filling in for the late Ivan Toombs. He was an affable chap, and I had been taking an interest in him because I had been told that his son was a policeman. He startled me by saying: 'Wasn't that your friend who got arrested last Sunday outside Dundalk?' Bob had met Brian a few times when he had come to visit me at work. Now Bob was holding a copy of a newspaper with a story about my friend the Provo. I knew I had to handle the moment carefully. I let the conversation flow in what I hoped was a natural way. I looked at the article and expressed surprise. I said that I had known Brian as an acquaintance from years back. Yes, he had dropped in to see me a few times since I had bumped into him by accident in Warrenpoint where he also worked, but we were never friends.

Bob said: 'He was caught with quite an arsenal. It seems that Armalite had been used in as many as thirty murders right across the north.'

'My God,' I said.

I said no more. I did not want to overdo my act. Bob walked off. I felt that if he had really suspected me he would not have discussed the arrest with me in the first place. Indeed for me – in terms of the safety of my position in the Customs and Excise – the débâcle was quite helpful: Brian would be linked to the murder of Toombs, and any lingering suspicion about the involvement of customs staff would lift.

As Christmas approached, I began to reflect on my time to date in the IRA. I had cut my teeth. I was no longer in awe of those who carried guns or planted bombs. Now I felt I was one of the boys. I even had an MI Carbine with a loaded magazine lying in a brown nylon zip-bag under my bed in my new flat in Newry. What bothered me most that Christmas was that we had lost one of our best volunteers. I thought of him as I put the family Christmas tree – which I had taken from the forest at Camlough – into a huge bucket of clay: it seemed a wilder tree than the ones you could buy in the shops. Its branches stuck out and jagged you badly if you touched it. I was now living with a girl I had met some time previously. Her name was Bernadette and we were getting married in January. I had wanted Brian there as the best man but he was sitting in Portlaoise prison on a number of very serious charges. I vowed then that I would avenge his capture by making sure that we killed Detective Cunningham. I did not care how long it took to get him, but he was good as dead. This was my contribution to the Christmas spirit as the year 1981 ended.

6

END OF A FAIRY TALE

I married Bernie in January 1982. Within days of arriving home from my honeymoon Seán called me to Dundalk.

He said that an order had come through from general head-quarters, the ruling executive council of the IRA, for all units to prepare for a week of co-ordinated attacks on commercial targets in the north. Although all IRA units have a large degree of autonomy in choosing the operational who-what-when-and-where, they must always give precedence to orders from GHQ even if that means abandoning other operations that are ready to go.

Seán told me that he wanted us to go for a good economic target in Warrenpoint. He thought that a hotel would be best. I agreed with him: the IRA had already obliterated every hotel in Newry, and though Warrenpoint was a ten-minute drive from Newry, it could have been in another country, so untroubled was it by the war going on around it. The people there seemed to be cocooned and relatively prosperous. Middle-class Catholics and Protestants lived in harmony, united – as I would have put it from my Marxist perspective – by their class inter-ests in maintaining their high standard of living. The Catholics were in a majority, yet the IRA hardly ever attracted recruits from the town. I loathed the tranquillity of this little seaside town: Warrenpoint was to me a little sugar-plum fairy on the top of a rotten unionist cake. The town symbolized 'normal-ization' and what a British Home Secretary had once defined as 'an acceptable level of violence'. Its plump citizens enjoyed a good night-life with pleasant pubs, coffee-houses and restaurants. It was a safe haven for the Crown forces: a lot of policemen and soldiers lived there, enjoying a good relationship with their Catholic neighbours. The place had become the focus of all my anger. I was going to enjoy bringing Warrenpoint's fairy tale existence to an end.

I chose the Crown Hotel in the main square. I had been there several times myself after evenings spent practising with the Cloughmore Male Voice Choir, of which I was a member. I enjoyed singing and was a first tenor, but I had joined the choir largely as a cover for IRA intelligence-gathering. There were a lot of Protestants in the choir, whose members tended to come from in and around Warrenpoint, and I thought I might be able to pick up bits and pieces of information, particularly about senior Crown forces personnel who lived in the town. Even the pleasure of music was subordinated to my gleeful revelry in planning mayhem. We would often travel around the countryside giving recitals in Protestant churches: I would scour the audience looking for policemen. The churches often amazed me with their displays of flags and military regalia, celebrating the colonial history of the Protestant people, glorifying the battles that had established their rule. I would emerge after such recitals feeling even more justified in what I was doing for the IRA. Once I even appeared with the choir on an Ulster Television show with Gloria Hunniford as presenter.

I knew the RUC had a famous choir and my ambition was to join it, if they admitted civilians. I made enquiries but I was told that you had to be a member of the police to join. After my weekly rehearsals I would go for a drink with the choir and on several occasions I spotted policemen drinking in the Crown. It was a beautiful hotel, elegant, stylish, with character and a sense of history. The bar was made from timbers taken from the last wooden ship to have been made in Warrenpoint docks. The hotel was owned by a Catholic family. Indeed, the owner's father had been a nationalist MP, and the bar was full of memorabilia from his father's time and before: artefacts and newspaper cuttings from Warrenpoint's social and industrial past. The magnificent fireplace was always full of burning logs. For me the Crown, snug and ivy-covered, symbolized the collaboration of constitutional nationalists with the unionist enemy. To knock it out would be to knock out a big part of Warrenpoint's social life. And it didn't even have security cameras.

I planned the operation for a day on which I did not have to start work until the early afternoon. I wanted to be able to bomb the hotel and still have time to get home for my lunch before going into work. My role was to act as scout for the volunteers driving the car carrying the bomb. I would drive ahead of them, at a distance of about 300 yards; if I saw a police or army patrol I would tap my brake lights three times in quick succession, so giving my colleagues a chance either to turn off the road or slowly to turn the car around without raising suspicion at the checkpoint. Once the bomb had been planted I would scout the team, which was going to include my cousin Mickey, back out of the town, dropping two of them off at a safe house in Rostrevor, then leading Mickey and one of the others into the mountains where they would dump their own car and get into mine. Then I would drive Mickey back to Newry and leave the other man at the Dundalk bus-stop. I would scout the other men from the Rostrevor safe house to Dundalk later in the evening.

On the day of the operation, I arrived at the rendezvous in a hotel car-park just across the border. I saw the IRA team's silver estate car. Apart from Mickey, I knew two of the others vaguely from Dundalk. As soon as I knew they had seen me I drove off with them following. We arrived at the hotel, and I waited while they took the bombs inside. They were 'keg bombs'. A keg is a large metal cylinder used by farmers to take milk to the creamery for processing. These kegs contained at least a hundred pounds of nitrogen fertiliser with ten pounds of gelignite in the centre. The fertiliser would have been ground down to make it more explosive. The other ingredients would have been sugar, diesel oil, and a drop of nitroglycerine. I heard later that the IRA volunteers, almost as soon as they walked through the door, had been confronted by the hotel's

owner, dressed in tweeds and twills, and protesting vociferously at this attack on an historic nationalist building. One of
the team pointed an Armalite at the old gentleman and said:
'Get on the fucking floor, you old cunt.' The others carried in
the bombs and primed them.

I watched in my mirror as the team walked quietly out of
the hotel and got into their car. I led them out of the town and
we drove to Rostrevor, where two of the men got out and
walked to the safe house. Then I drove on into the mountains,
through stony valleys, into an area crisscrossed with streams. I
pulled into a yard near a huge hayshed. A farmer drove past in
a tractor, waving. He must have assumed we had pulled in to let
him pass. Mickey and the other man dumped their car and
jumped in beside me. I set off for Newry. I loved this landscape and whenever I came here I felt an emotional pull to the
past. Tall pine trees stood guard beside abandoned stone
houses where labourers and small farmers had reared large
families for generations, until they had been driven out to fill
the factories, armies and servants' quarters of the industrial
nations. These abandoned ruins dotted a landscape that had
once been densely populated. I felt that we in the IRA were the
offspring of their humiliation: at that time I regarded myself
and my comrades as history's vengeful children, come to exact
the price for a society built on injustice. I believed that in our
actions we gave form to the stifled rage of our ancestors. I felt
I was part of an organization designed to make unionists feel
the killing rage of generations past and present. It certainly
reflected my own rage and frustration. I talked to the others
about history and oppression, and the car filled with passionate agreement, helping to divert our minds from the worrying
prospect of a checkpoint around the next corner. I drove along
the back roads into Newry. The police and army usually kept
regular checks on the main roads, but they tended to be more
wary of the by-roads, which offered such good camouflage for
an ambush. However, they still posed a risk: there was always
the possibility of meeting a patrol of soldiers who had been
dropped into the area by helicopter. Also, you could never rule
out the possibility that you were being watched by an army
surveillance team, dug in for weeks to watch suspicious people

and vehicles, although these clandestine operations were often spotted by the locals eventually.

I dropped two men at the safe house in Rostrevor, and the other man at the bus-stop in Newry where he could pick up the bus to Dundalk. I left Mickey in town. I drove to my mother's flat to give her a bit of company before I went to work. As I made a pot of tea and put butter on slices of home-made wheaten bread, I waited for the news on the radio. I did not have to wait long: 'The Crown Hotel . . . bomb placed by armed men . . . hotel ablaze . . . damage extensive.' I decided to treat myself to a soft-boiled egg to celebrate, then I went to work.

I had not been at work for an hour when I got a call from Dundalk. I was told that the men at the safe house wanted to be brought out: they did not like the idea of sitting around until the evening, and they wanted me to come for them. I felt very annoyed. This was a dangerous departure from the plan, and I refused.

After a tea-break, I drove to Warrenpoint to view the hotel. There was a police car parked outside the devastated building. All that remained was a pile of rubble and smoking timbers. The sky drizzled rain, and little wisps of smoke occasionally rose from the smouldering ruins. Signs had been put up saying: 'Unsafe Building'. Fairy tale Warrenpoint suddenly looked depressed: its brightness seemed to have faded to a dull grey.

After I finished work I went to the safe house. The woman who answered the door told me that the men had gone. I could not believe what I was hearing. 'They got a taxi? Got a fucking taxi? This is a disaster. No one should need to get a taxi,' I said. They had left some weapons at another house; I decided to take them to Dundalk that night. Before transporting the weapons, which included an Armalite, I drove to the border to check that the roads were clear. They were, and I sped back to pick up the gear. Only a few miles from the border I drove up behind a car whose occupants I did not notice until I got close. They were policemen, three of them, driving an unmarked, unarmoured Chrysler. I kept my cool and stayed behind them, stopping carefully at each set of traffic lights.

When I got to Dundalk I was given a roasting by Seán, but

I felt that I had not done anything wrong. I discovered that the man who had been putting on the pressure to be taken back to Dundalk was the older, heavy-set man whom I had correctly identified as being from Belfast. Everyone called him 'Hardbap'. I did not realize then that this was my introduction to a man whom I would come to loathe.

On the news that night I was delighted to witness the impact that the bomb had made on the town. A local Catholic politician was interviewed. He said that the bomb had torn the heart out of Warrenpoint. I was pleased to listen to him confirming my analysis. Then the hotel owner came on. He claimed that the IRA team had rifled the hotel's till and stuffed their pockets with money before leaving. I thought he was talking nonsense: I could not believe that the team would have done something like that in the middle of an operation. When I next saw Mickey I told him what the hotel owner had said. Mickey looked a little embarrassed. He said: 'It's true. Hardbap robbed the tills.'

'The thieving fuck,' I said. I felt that Hardbap's behaviour had taken the shine off the operation and made the IRA look like common criminals. He had been able to pay for the taxi to Dundalk with the money he had robbed. My romantic image of the IRA soldier was receiving its first hard knock.

7

'LEGITIMATE TARGET'

The television repairman whom I had bullied into becoming an informant held his pool cue in one hand and smiled at me.

'I might have something for you,' he said. He picked up a cube of chalk which sat near one of the pool table's pockets and stroked the top of his cue with it, then gave the tip a little blow. He leaned over the table to line up his next shot. He was determined to draw out his dramatic moment.

He lowered his voice, so that I had to move forward to hear him. 'There's this guy who's in the UDR. His name's Hanna. Norman Hanna.'

'Aye, is that so?' I said. 'Tell me about him.'

'He's married to the daughter of Crozier, the landlord of the pub in Water Street.'

I knew the pub; I had even drunk in it a few times with customs officers. It was a mixed pub, although mostly Protestants went there. I had been interested in it for some time because I knew a few cops drank there.

'How do you know Hanna is in the UDR?'

'Everyone knows he's in the UDR. Anyway, I seen him at a checkpoint a few weeks ago.'

I was delighted: I could smell a definite hit. 'You're a good man. Everybody knows he's in the UDR? Well, there you go. Everybody knows, but the IRA don't know. That's why you're invaluable. We need people to tell us little bits of information that "everybody" knows.'

I asked him if he knew anything more about Hanna. The repairman said he was thin, about five foot eight or nine, and he drove a metallic brown Chrysler. I bought him a drink and left the pub. People talk and people die.

I did not waste any time. I made a point of going past Crozier's pub at every opportunity to try to get a look at Hanna and to follow him home or to the place where he worked.

Before long I spotted Hanna's car parked outside Crozier's pub. I drove to a nearby newsagent and bought a magazine and a newspaper. I parked the car close to the pub and sat there reading, eating sweets and smoking. I had the window down. It was a bad wet day and it was beginning to get dark. A cop car drove past but showed no interest in me. I waited and waited, but there was no sign of Hanna. I was just about to go when my patience was rewarded. A slightly-built man in his early thirties came out of the pub and walked up to the car. The rain was falling so heavily that it almost obscured my target. I could see that he had dark hair, a sallow complexion and a heavy moustache. The wind blew open his raincoat and I noticed a shirt and tie underneath. I thought he looked more like a civil servant than a soldier, but so had Toombs, and he had been a UDR major. He opened the car door and got in. This casual action surprised me: why had he not checked under his car for a bomb? Hanna drove off. I took down his registration number, but I decided not to follow him that night. I had made a good start. I had a definite description – a face to put to the information – and the guy seemed careless about his own security.

I spent the next few weeks, in between doing other bits and pieces for the IRA, trying to spot his car again outside the pub. One morning I struck lucky. It was just before 9 a.m. and his car stood close to the pub. The town was busy. There was traffic everywhere. I had not been waiting long when Hanna came out and got into his car. Again, he did not check under the wheels: we could have put a booby-trap bomb under there. He drove off. I followed him, pushing and nudging my way through the traffic. I accelerated down North Street and came out on the New Road. I could see Hanna's car several hundred yards in front of me. I had him in my sight, but I kept my distance. I had to allow for his caution, even though to date he had behaved no differently from any ordinary civilian. I watched him slow down and indicate to the right. He turned into the Vehicle Testing Centre, where you went for your MOT or sat your driving test. I watched him park and get out. He was carrying a lunchbox. Now I knew where he worked.

I stopped at a public phone box and rang my cousin Mickey. I knew he was close to finishing his Green Book lectures and I knew I could trust him to carry out a bit of intelligence work for me. I arranged to meet him during his lunch break. Mickey worked in the housing executive, the large organization responsible for public housing in Northern Ireland. He had access to every single housing file in the huge Newry and Mourne district. Not only would I get information on potential targets, but I would also have intelligence on the intimate details of their lives; for instance, whether they were separated, in debt, or had difficulties with their neighbours. I could build up detailed personal profiles of future victims.

I met Mickey and asked him to check whether there was a file on Norman Hanna. Mickey nodded eagerly: 'No problem.' I knew his enthusiasm was impressing the commanders in Dundalk. He seemed positively to enjoy being involved in political violence, although at the moment he had more eagerness than experience. He had already identified a part-time RUC man who worked as a maintenance officer with the housing executive. This was grade A information to us and Seán was very pleased, as he told me himself when I met him in Dundalk a few days later. I told Seán about Hanna and that Mickey was checking out his details at the housing executive. I had arranged the meeting with Seán because I wanted him to get my two ex-Irp legmen involved in putting Hanna under surveillance. Seán agreed and set the two of them to work. Over the next few months, they kept tabs on Hanna to establish his routines. They reported back to me that he always seemed to go to work at the same time in the morning; he even parked his car in the same place most of the time. Neither of them ever saw him in his UDR uniform or watched him driving into a UDR base, but that did not worry me too much. After all, the television repairman had seen Hanna at a checkpoint only recently.

'This guy's a gift,' I thought. Mickey added to the good news by informing me that Hanna did have a file at the housing executive. The file confirmed he was in the UDR. I told Seán in Dundalk: he told me to arrange the kill. He said that Mickey would be the gunman.

I told Mickey to follow Hanna for himself one morning. Mickey did as he was told and reported back to me. He said that Hanna followed his usual routine. For the first time a doubt entered my mind. I said to Mickey: 'I can't believe this guy. He's a pretty careless UDR man. He never checks under his car; he always follows the same routine. You could set your watch by him. Is he on a suicide mission or what?'

Mickey told me not to worry. He assured me that the official housing executive card listed him as a UDR soldier. I felt more reassured, but something still did not seem right. I was holding a man's life in my hands and I did not want to make a mistake. IRA policy (officially, at least) was that once people left the Crown forces – regardless of what they had done while they were members – then they were no longer targets. If Hanna was no longer a member of the UDR he was not a legitimate target.

But everything had checked out, and I was under pressure to carry out the op as soon as possible. I had several meetings with Seán in which we discussed the best way to kill Hanna. We decided that Mickey would shoot him as he arrived for work one morning. Mickey would be driven to the scene on a motorbike by another IRA man. I could not think of anyone in Newry who would be able to do that job. Seán told me not to worry about finding a bike man: he would find someone in Dundalk or south Armagh, and he already had a bike, which had been stolen recently in Dundalk and given new plates.

I chose the day for the hit, and briefed Mickey fully about what he was expected to do. Then, on the evening before we struck, I took Mickey with me to Dundalk for a final planning meeting with Seán. It had already been agreed that I should leave Mickey in Dundalk that night and return to Newry; I would drive back to the border in the morning

around eight-thirty in order to scout Mickey and his accomplice into Newry. The plan was for them to wait in a side road
near the MOT station until they saw Hanna's car drive past.
Then they would follow him, and Mickey would shoot him as
he got out of his car to go into work.

Mickey and I arrived in Dundalk and drove to a meeting
house for IRA men. By now Mickey had been to an IRA training camp where he had learned how to use basic small arms
and rifles. But he had never before seen the gun produced by
Seán in the back bedroom. It was a Browning 9mm Automatic
pistol. Seán said: 'This is the gun you're using.' Seán, who
was wearing a pair of red rubber gloves, held the gun out in
front of him with the casual air of the professional. He pulled
the top part of the gun back a little bit: 'That's one bullet up
the spout.' Then he pulled the top part back the whole way:
'That's fourteen bullets ready to go. You can just pump them
off one after the other.' Then he pressed a button on the side
and the magazine popped out. Seán held up the magazine and
I could see the bullets held in place by a spring, packed tight
for release, their fat little brass bodies each tipped with a head
of grey lead. He clicked the magazine back in to the butt. Then
he pulled back the top metal casing of the gun to expose the
narrow silver metal cylindrical barrel. He slid the casing past
the narrow oval ejection slit at the side where the empty shells
would be emitted. 'Once you pull this right back you can fire
until she empties.' I heard it snap forward into place as it was
released and the firing-pin levered backwards, fully cocked, to
fire again: 'Safety-catch on. Safety-catch off. Make sure the
safety-catch is on at all times when you're not using it.'

I looked at Mickey: his face coloured with eagerness and
excitement as Seán handed him the weapon. He smiled a
hideous boyish smile as he felt the Browning; he stared at it,
touched it, and looked at it from all angles. 'Right,' said Seán,
'let's see you doing it.' Mickey's features composed themselves
into serious soldierly lines as he followed Seán's orders: 'Cock
it. One up the spout. Safety-catch on. Safety-catch off. Eject
the magazine. Put it back in again.' Mickey took to the weapon
easily and did everything smoothly. 'Good man,' said Seán.
'Are you happy with that?'

Mickey smiled eagerly: 'Yeah!' Seán told him to do it all again. And again. He said: 'There's a fair kick-back on this. Make sure you hold it with both hands. Show me your firing pose.' Mickey clasped the handle with both gloved hands and stood in the classic pose of the modern gunman, legs apart, arms pointed straight ahead. The metal of the gun extended beyond the end of his flesh, yet seemed to become almost one with the flesh. Mickey's eyes were alive with excitement. He pointed the gun at the bed and for a moment his eyes seemed to fill with hate. I could see that in his mind the bed had been transubstantiated into the flesh and blood of a living target. For an intense moment I too could see the human being who would soon be dead. Seán said: 'It's gas-operated. This is some weapon. There's some power there.' Mickey came out of his trance and smiled again: 'Yeah!'

I told Mickey that I would see him in the morning at the rendezvous. I had already agreed to have the bike rider collected after the hit. He would be taken to my flat in Canal Street from where he would be taken back across the border later in the evening. Mickey would go on to work at the housing executive, keeping the gun in his pocket. I would meet him at lunch-time to pick up the weapon. Everything was ready: I said my goodbyes and returned to Newry.

That night I could not sleep. I twisted and turned in my bed, looking in vain for a comfortable position. I always felt nervous before an operation but that night I kept getting flashes of doubt as well. Hanna seemed to be too easy a target: what if he had left the UDR? Perhaps that was why he was so careless. I fought hard against those doubts: we had checked him out as best we could. An official file confirmed he was in the UDR and an informant had seen him with his own eyes at a checkpoint.

That first attempt on Hanna's life turned out to be a fiasco. He didn't turn up, and Mickey carelessly dumped the bike and crash helmets in a side street, advertising an IRA operation for any RUC man with eyes. I had to pick up the helmets, and berated Mickey when I collected the team's guns from him. As I drove back to my own flat I still felt uneasy: Mickey's behaviour had shaken my confidence in him. Of course, he had only

behaved that way because of his inexperience, but perhaps
Hanna had been targeted as a result of that same inexperience.
I decided that we would have to carry out further checks on
Hanna before we rearranged the operation.

I asked Mickey to have another look at Hanna's housing
file. I said that this man was just not looking like a UDR man;
he didn't seem to be concerned about danger, laying himself
wide open to attack. I asked Mickey to check his record again
and to read it all, and get back to me.

Mickey came round to see me the next day. I asked him if he
had read Hanna's file thoroughly. Mickey said he had, and that
it said he was in the UDR. 'But it does say in one part that he
left the UDR six years ago.'

'What! Six years ago! Then he's not a fucking target!'

Mickey shook his head: 'The records are lying. He was seen
at a checkpoint only the other week.' I could see that Mickey
was determined to go ahead with the operation at any cost. I
told him to go to Dundalk and to tell Seán what he had discovered in the files. I thought that Seán would cancel the
assassination.

But I was wrong. Mickey called around to see me again after
speaking to Seán. He said: 'It's all right. It's going ahead. The
bike is getting scouted in the day after tomorrow. You don't
need to do anything, apart from getting the bike rider back
across the border after the op.'

I felt queasy. I said: 'But what about the housing file? Did
you tell him what it said?' Mickey said that Seán was satisfied
that Hanna had been seen at a checkpoint recently. I could not
say any more. Perhaps Hanna really was in the UDR; perhaps
Seán had information that I did not have. Perhaps other people
had seen him at a checkpoint. Yet there were grounds for reasonable doubt. I shrugged my shoulders: this was not a court of
law; there were no abstract legal niceties to get Hanna off the
hook. The IRA had found him guilty of being a legitimate
target, and we had passed a sentence of death, to be carried out
at our leisure.

Mickey turned to walk out the door. He suggested that we
meet near an electrical transformer in the town.

That night I tried to push out of my mind the idea that we

were about to make a terrible mistake. But for all my efforts I could not eradicate my doubts. I had seen the man with my own eyes and he did not behave like a soldier. The following night I went to pick up the guns. It was a particularly dirty night. The wind blew hard and the rain bit into my skin. I entered the open hallway to the flats in Greenfield Park. The stairway was empty. I walked through to the coal-house out the back. I took the keys from my pocket and opened the coal-house door quickly, looking around to see if there was anyone watching me, and pushed back the coal to find the shoulder bag. I lifted it up and could feel the weight of the Browning and the Smith and Wesson. I went back though the hallway of the flats, then walked down the few concrete steps to the street outside. The night had become pitch black; even the light of the occasional street lamp could not penetrate it. I thought about Mickey as I walked towards the transformer: what was he becoming? And what had I become?

I got to the transformer. It stood there solid and square, its electrical current giving off a steady hum, hardly audible in the wind. Barbed wire topped the railings which surrounded it; red and yellow DANGER chevrons loomed up at me. Mickey stepped out from the side of the transformer. He came towards me with his left arm outstretched. He wanted the bag. In his eyes I could see that same excitement I had seen in Dundalk when he had felt the Browning for the first time. I realized how desperately impatient he was for his first kill. But I was not in such a great hurry. I did not take the bag off my shoulder. Mickey came up close. 'Mickey, the card said he left the UDR six years ago.' Mickey said nothing. 'Mickey, you know what the card said.' My words exasperated him: 'Jesus Christ, he was seen at a checkpoint a few weeks ago.' He reached out for the bag; his fingers wrapped themselves around the strap; he pulled it, but I would not let go. I looked straight into his eyes. Part of me admired the determination I could see there, the readiness to kill, the desire for action. And yet I could also see an ambitious young warrior desperate to be blooded, desperate to prove himself, desperate to fulfil the needs of his own ego. I came close to pulling the strap out of Mickey's fingers and walking away. Mickey must have read my thoughts because he said with firmness: 'He was in full uniform at the checkpoint. I'm sure of it. It's definite: he's a UDR soldier. Other people have seen him.' I did not take my gaze from Mickey's eyes, but I could say no more. I let the bag go; I let the handle slip from my right hand. Hanna's fate was sealed. Mickey shouldered the bag, then turned quickly and walked off.

I walked back home with a heaviness of heart I had never felt before in connection with the IRA. In my mind's eye I could see Hanna: he was finishing his supper, he was playing with his child, he was cuddling his wife, he was preparing his clothes for work the next day.

Mickey would become a trigger man, an operator, a member of the élite band of IRA 'stiffers'. Tonight he would sleep close to his guns: they were his passport into another country. In that new mental landscape he would be roaming with the killers.

I spent another night without sleep. I knew that I was on the verge of an event which I would regret for the rest of my life. Yet I too could not turn back. My own pride, my own refusal to be seen as a waverer, determined me to continue with my own role in Hanna's killing. At that point I rational-ized it by telling myself I had other lives to consider – the lives of Mickey and the bike boy. A ruthless pragmatism took over: there was no room for prevarication and uncertainty. I had made my decision when I let that bag slip out of my grasp. In the choice between the man who was perhaps in the UDR and the solidarity of the organization, there could be only one winner.

I knew that Hanna would be punctual. Just after nine-thirty word started going around the office that someone had been shot in Newry, although as yet there was no official news. I went out on patrol in the customs' Vauxhall Cavalier. I had a colleague with me, a Scotsman who spent a lot of his time talking about how much he loved the Queen. We drove around Newry, but my attention was not on the job. As we drove down one road near the centre we passed a police patrol which had stopped a motorbike rider: they seemed to be giving him a thorough check. I turned on the car radio for the eleven o'clock news: 'A man has been shot dead outside the government

Vehicle Testing Centre where he worked in Newry . . . A gunman shot him several times at close range before escaping on a motorbike driven by another man . . . The victim has been named as Norman Hanna . . . Police say he was a former member of the UDR. He left the regiment six years ago . . .' My colleague said: 'The fucking bastards. The fucking bastards. I knew that man. I've drunk with him in Crozier's. He's married to Crozier's daughter. Those fucking murdering bastards.' I did not have to feign my own shock.

My weakness had killed Hanna. He had been drowning in our self-righteous rhetoric and I had not thrown him a line. I was more guilty than Mickey of Hanna's death.

At lunch-time I went home. I had arranged for the bike boy to be taken to my flat by a sympathizer. I knew my wife would be at work. I walked into my sitting-room and nodded a greeting to the bike boy, who was very young indeed. He was sitting in my armchair. There was no colour in his face and he sat there shaking, as if he had just been let out of a fridge. I gave him a cigarette, but his hands were shaking so violently that he could hardly put it in his mouth. I went into the kitchen and made him some soup. I brought it out to him and said: 'That man was not in the UDR. He left six years ago.' The boy looked at me: 'Oh, Jesus.' I told him that it was not his responsibility. I said that he had done his job well and he should be pleased with himself.

I was about to ask the boy to tell me what had happened, but without prompting he began to blurt out what he had seen. His words came out in barely-formed sentences: 'Your man got shot . . . he got shot too . . .'

'What? Who got shot?' I asked.

'Your man, the fella shooting with the gun. He got shot when he went to put the gun back in his pocket. A shot went off and the bullet ricocheted off the pavement and hit him above the eye. It just grazed him.'

'Is he all right?'

'Aye, he went to work after I was taken here.'

'What about the man who is dead? What happened to him?' The bike boy swallowed. I thought for a moment that he was going to cry, but he composed himself: 'He arrived in his car, but his wife and child were in the car too. He got out of the car and we followed him. Then the fella started shooting. He must have put about eight bullets in him. There was blood everywhere and he dropped his lunchbox. He fell to the ground.'

The boy turned his head away from me and looked at the carpet. He said: 'His wife started screaming and crying, and the wee girl was jumping up and down in the back of the car screaming, "Daddy, daddy, daddy".'

'Listen,' I said, 'forget about it. Put it out of your mind.'

I gave him a newspaper and a packet of cigarettes, then turned on the television. I told him to try and relax, to have a bath and wash his hair. He might have picked up some cordite particles.

I had arranged to meet Mickey to pick up the guns that lunch-time at the flats near where he worked. I parked my car beside a phone box and waited. I saw him walking towards me, briskly. I could not see the shoulder bag. He got into my car.

Mickey told me that he had walked into work straight after killing Hanna, carrying the guns in the pockets of his duffle coat, hung the coat up on its usual peg, and worked normally until lunch-time. Then he had walked home and hid the guns in his bedroom before coming to meet me. I arranged to collect them later that night. I looked at his forehead. Just above his right eye was a graze where the burning bullet had passed: it had not even broken the skin. I said nothing about the operation. I felt too sick about it. And it was not yet over: I had to get the young lad and the weapons safely back to base. I could not find a way of letting Mickey feel my anger, and I had no time.

That night I drove to a point on the border in south Armagh with the bike boy beside me. He had recovered somewhat, but he was still shaken. I stopped when we got to a yellow cross in the road which indicated the point at which Queen Elizabeth's domain ended and the Irish Republic began. The rain was beating down hard. The bike boy got out of the car and ran across the border. My headlights illuminated him for a few seconds, until he disappeared into the night. I turned my car around and drove home. Old crumbling forts dotted the landscape. These old ruins always fired my imagination. But that night I wanted to remind myself that being in the IRA still meant being part of the noble tradition of resistance to the invaders, despite what we had just done. I told myself that in any war mistakes are made, and do not undermine the validity of the struggle. Rationalizations hardly touched the sense of bleakness that had overcome me.

I stopped off at Mickey's and he gave me the guns in another bag. I took them to my flat. I sat in my bedroom and emptied the contents of the bag on to my bed. I stared at the Browning. I took out the gun's magazine and emptied the bullets on to the bed. There were five of them. They had hollow indentations along their sides: dumdums. They were designed to cause devastating injury on impact. I picked up the Browning and smelt the gunpowder in the barrel. This was the weapon that had just killed an innocent man in front of his wife and daughter. The bag also contained Mickey's Manchester United scarf, which he had been wearing when he shot Hanna. I looked at it. To my horror I saw that the scarf was spattered with tiny flecks of blood, hundreds of little pin-pricks, like the fine spray from a hose. I carefully picked up the scarf and took it over to my open coal fire. I placed it on the fire and watched it burn, slowly at first, then intensely, and then it was gone. I put the guns back in the bag and hid them. I would have to take them to Dundalk another time.

The next day I rang up a local journalist and claimed responsibility for the operation on behalf of the South Down Command. I kept the statement terse. I said that the Active Service Unit had set out to attack a UDR man. I did not apologize for our mistake.

I contacted Mickey and the ex-Irps and told them to meet me at my flat on Saturday evening. I made sure my wife was out visiting her mother: we were under orders not to let our wives know anything about our activities. This rule, although frequently breached, was for our safety and for theirs: what they did not know they could not talk about – to their friends, to their family or, under interrogation, to the police.

The boys arrived together. I did not say hello, or engage in the usual banter. They sat quietly in my front room. I asked what they thought of the operation. They all shrugged their

shoulders and looked at each other. One of the scouts said:
'What d'you mean?'

'I mean, what do you think of it, Hanna being shot?'

The other ex-Irp said: 'Well, it's done. That's what we were
asked to do, and now he's shot.'

I said: 'I'll come to the point right away. I'll tell you what
I've spent the last four or five days thinking about. I think it
was fucking awful, a total, unmitigated fucking disaster.'

Mickey looked almost amused. There was a half smile on his
face. He said: 'Why was it a disaster?'

I became angrier. I asked him who he thought he had shot
the other day? 'I'll tell you what you shot, you shot a man in
front of his wife and child; you shot a man who wasn't in fuck
all.'

The second Irp chipped in that it was a mistake, that he had
a brother who was in the UDR, that's what they were hearing
now.

'A brother? A fucking brother? I never heard of his brother
before. Even if he has got a brother in the UDR, why weren't
we shooting this brother instead of shooting him? You were all
asked to find out whether this man was in the UDR, and you
didn't do it.'

Mickey said: 'He was in the UDR once.'

I ranted at him that this man had died because he was once
in the UDR, that he had shot an innocent civilian dead, that
there was only one thing I wanted to know from them and that
was whether he was in the UDR; and they couldn't even get
that right.

One of the boys said: 'It was that television repairman that
said he seen him at the checkpoint.'

I looked at him and wanted to know what he was saying. On
the slimmest bit of evidence from that pool-playing pisshead
we go and stiff a man. Hearsay.

Mickey spat words at me defiantly; that that was not how
the brass in Dundalk felt about it.

His words stopped me momentarily. Mickey had obviously
been up to Dundalk in the last few days, seeking congratula-
tions on his first hit: 'The brass in Dundalk. What did they say
about it?'

Mickey smiled: 'They said it was a good hit.'

For a moment I imagined Mickey being patted on the back by the commanders in Dundalk, 'Welcome to the IRA stiffers club, Mickey. You're now one of us.' I could not quite believe that they would have regarded it as a 'good hit'. Perhaps they had not wanted to demoralize the eager young warrior. How would he have had the confidence to carry out the next hit and the next hit and the next hit? Or perhaps they did regard it as a good hit. I could imagine them saying: 'Hanna's carried a gun for the UDR once. He was a cunt once. Once a cunt, always a cunt.'

I told Mickey as quietly as I could that I wasn't in Dundalk, I was in Newry, and I had to be involved in that hit, and that it was not ever going to happen again, that I was not going on hearsay any more.

I knew I was using my anger to give myself a respite from my guilt. They did not say anything, but just sat there looking pale. I felt disgusted with myself, ashamed of myself. And I knew that one reason I let it go ahead was because I knew how much Mickey wanted to do it.

I remember saying to him, then, something like this: that it wouldn't have mattered if he was out of the UDR for six years or twenty-six years because he was dead for one reason only, and that one reason was to give him the first notch on his revolver. 'You just wanted your first kill to impress people. Isn't that right, Mickey? And you got it. And I fucking let you. And that's what pisses me off: I let you.'

I stood up and walked over to the front door and told them to fuck off. I opened the door. The three were silent. They stood up and filed out into the night.

That night, for the first time, I could not be reassured by any grand or angry political scheme. Was this what it was all about? Robert Carr practically burned alive, deserted, abandoned, screaming in agony in the darkness; Ivan Toombs riddled with bullets in his office; and now Norman Hanna shot dead in front of his wife and child. Where were we going? Where was I going?

I lay in bed that night next to my young wife. She was sleeping peacefully. I thought of Hanna's wife sleeping alone. I felt

pressed down in my bed by the dead man's weight. I could not
sleep. I stared at the ceiling and the lightbulb. I tried to read
the faint greyish writing on its base, but I could not. In the
street I could hear late-night drinkers returning home rau-
cously. I felt an extraordinary pain that would not go away.
Every now and again I would fall off to sleep, but would wake
again after what seemed a few minutes. In my sleep I moved in
darkness, but the darkness seemed to have a form; like the
mouth of a beast. I was inside the beast. Awake, the images in
my mind were worse. I could see Mickey shooting him; see the
lunchbox dropping to the ground, see Mickey's English football scarf catching the arc of blood that sprayed the air. I had
never felt so empty. I had chosen this way and I could not turn
back. I remember touching my wife, kissing her hair and
crying silently. I was crying for Hanna, perhaps, for his wife
and child, but also mostly for myself, for what I had become.

8

NONE TAKE PITY

The killing of Norman Hanna could, even should have undermined my support for the IRA, and yet I kept going.

Depression gripped me but it also carried me along. I
thought of Hanna often, and each time his image entered my
mind I felt a stab of pain and guilt. But in the turbulence of my
mind at that time there were two conflicting ideas: first, theo-
retically, politically and emotionally I supported the IRA's
armed struggle and, second, at some human level I regarded
Hanna's killing as a foul act. Yet if Hanna's death was wrong,
did that make the IRA wrong? I still refused to accept such a
conclusion. Catholics had, after all, died in their thousands
over the centuries for the nationalist cause; ten men had just
died on hunger strike for the same cause; I had given more
than three years of my life to the struggle. Could we all be
wrong? I look back now and realize that I resolved the ensuing
mental crisis by hardening my heart towards those I perceived
as enemies. I fought to curb what I saw as my 'weakness',
namely, my readiness to see my victims as ordinary human
beings and their deaths as deserving of sympathy. I busied
myself with work for the IRA, and gradually the images of
the dying Hanna began to clear from my mind. I told myself to
be strong, that the cause was more important than any individual. Over the next eighteen months I struggled to suppress
my instinct for compassion; and I renewed my dedication to

the Republican Army. Each subsequent death mattered less to me than the previous one. I became even more committed to turning Newry from a grey area into a black area.

Within a week of Hanna's death, I played a peripheral role in another unjustifiable killing. I was asked to help scout a car over the border. It contained a bomb. I knew only that it was aimed at an 'economic' target. My commanders told me that they needed me to act as scout for a part of the car bomb's journey. I arranged to do the job during my lunch-break. I met up with the red Volkswagen Golf containing the bomb: Hardbap was the driver. I noticed he had a passenger, a woman in her mid-twenties. I was immediately alert and resentful: I was in a customs patrol car, wearing my uniform, and I was being exposed to someone I did not know, but there was nothing I could do but drive. I drove quickly along the agreed route and then turned back to Newry, letting someone else scout the bomb the rest of the way. Later that afternoon I heard on the news that an eleven-year-old boy had been killed by a bomb in the town of Banbridge. The police said they had received a brief warning but the bomb had gone off while they were still trying to clear the area. The boy had been standing in the interior of a shop when a piece of shrapnel had come through the window and embedded itself in his head. The bomb had also caused a lot of destruction to the town centre. I was shocked by the death of the child, although I did not feel as personally and intimately responsible as I had done for Hanna's death.

I went to Dundalk to find out what had gone wrong. I called at Seán's house and heard his wife describing Hardbap as 'a bastard' for what he had done. Apparently, Hardbap had planted the bomb and then driven to the border some twenty miles away before phoning a warning. His excuse was that he had got caught in traffic and then when he found a phone in the Irish Republic that he could not get through to the right number. In the end he had phoned the Irish police and had left it to them to transmit his warning to the RUC. I thought his excuse was pathetic: he had an hour between the planting of the bomb and the explosion. The drive to the border should not have taken more than thirty minutes, but somehow he had managed to leave the police with only a few minutes in which to clear the area. The warning could easily have been phoned from somewhere else nearer Banbridge, yet Hardbap had delayed until he had got clean across the border. It was a miracle that more people had not been killed.

I met Hardbap in a pub that evening. The loss of the child's life did not seem to worry him. He blamed the Crown forces for the death: 'I did give the warning. I definitely gave the warning. Those bastards must have let it go off so that we'd look bad.' By the end of the evening it seemed to me that his greatest concern was that the incident might affect his chances of promotion within the IRA. He need not have worried: the IRA did not dwell on such incidents. The rationalization was very familiar: 'A child has been killed. It was an accident. Accidents happen in war. In all the operations we have carried out, we have never deliberately targeted civilians. So if we kill civilians, the public knows that it was not meant to happen. Even the police and army know we are dependable in the sort of targets we choose, even though they will naturally seek to glean propaganda value from our mistakes.' At that time, I would have accepted that general explanation, yet I still felt angry at the child's unnecessary death.

Shortly before I had begun to target Hanna, I had also found another potential hit. My ex-Irp, who had proved so incompetent over Norman Hanna's real status, surprised me by telling me about a policeman who lived in Newry. I had thought that Newry-dwelling policemen were an extinct species, but my source assured me that an RUC inspector called Albert White lived undisturbed not far from his own home. He said White was ageing now, but definitely still in the police. I asked him how he knew. He told me that he watched him going to the police station almost every day, although White was careful and changed his route often. It was the same White who had been severely injured by the IRA at a church-yard near Jonesboro, south Armagh, in 1973; he had also been wounded in 1962 at the very end of the IRA's disastrous 'border campaign'. I asked my source to point White out to me in the street.

I met my informant half an hour before the time White usually left the police station. We walked slowly along the most likely route he would take, talking and waiting. I was determined to see him for myself: I would be satisfied with no one's description but my own. Eventually, he came along the street, a man in his late fifties or early sixties, tallish, his greying hair still with wisps of its original red colour. He was wearing a tie and a long blue raincoat. He walked confidently with his hands in his pockets, looking intently through black-rimmed glasses. His face was keen and hawkish. He had been a policeman for many years and had walked throughout this town without ever being hindered. I could not understand why the IRA had allowed him to live in the midst of a Catholic population, unless he was of some use to us, but that could not have been the case because I would already have been told not to touch him.

My source knew that White lived somewhere on or around the Rathfriland Road and that his wife drove a blue Saab. He had converted to Catholicism and he went to mass late on Sundays at Newry cathedral. I discovered later that his two sons had been to my old grammar school. I decided to see whether I could spot him coming from mass. I hoped to follow him home. That Sunday I parked my car in a housing estate near the cathedral and walked down just as people dribbled out at the end of the service. It was a cold day. Snow had fallen and I walked carefully down a steep footpath along Sandys Street. I met White and his wife walking up towards me. I had my hands in my duffle-coat pockets. I wanted to get a good close-up look at him. I was looking for distinguishing features. Were his glasses black-rimmed or silver-rimmed? I walked towards him, looking at him intently. White must have noticed my stare because as I passed him he said: 'Hello.' I said hello back. I thought: 'This is where we'll kill him.'

I got back to my car so that I could try to follow the Whites if they walked home, as I suspected they would. I drove up the Rathfriland Road, past the old hospital and turned left. I could not see the Whites anywhere. But I drove on, looking into the entrances of the private houses on my left. As I continued along the main road, I looked down the side roads which I passed. And there they were, arm in arm, sauntering down Dora Avenue. They had to live in that street because it was a cul-de-sac: there was nowhere else they could walk to. I drove on to the next crossroads and turned the car slowly to go back the way I had just come. I turned into Dora Avenue. I could not see them anymore. I drove to the end, and there, sitting outside number twenty, was the blue Saab. I'm sure I smiled: White was as good as dead. I memorized the registration number and drove home.

I kept tabs on White whenever possible. His wife seemed to pick him up from work every day in their car. She would meet him at different places at different times. I decided initially that the best time to hit him would be when his wife picked him up, but I soon realized how unpredictable he was. However, the fact that he took such precautions confirmed his role as an important operator within the Newry police apparatus. His elusiveness kept him alive for longer than I had planned; and soon he became merely one of several planned targets. This was the nature of the business of political violence: a constant ferment of ideas for operations.

Another operation supplanted the killing of this Catholic RUC man as a priority: the destruction of the huge Customs and Excise bonded warehouse. The warehouse was a prime target: I had taken an interest in it from my first days in the customs service. I had assembled a lot of information about it, and I knew that the building housed huge vats of liquor, which were in the final stages of being distilled into rum and vodka. At this stage of the distillation process the liquor was as inflammable as aircraft fuel.

The first operation against the warehouse was unsuccessful. The IRA team were able to breach the building's security effectively, and to switch off the expensive laser-beam alarm system for detecting intruders. They had drained all the vats of their contents and planted the bomb. It failed to detonate. I arrived at the building soon afterwards and heard the army's bomb disposal people say that the whole industrial estate would have gone up in a fireball if the bomb had gone off. We refused to give up, and arranged another attempt to take place in June 1982.

The date to put the bomb in the warehouse turned out to be a beautiful summer's day. I was going to help the team to plant

the bomb during my lunch-break, an hour so often given over
to schemes of destruction. In the morning I had suggested to
my work colleagues that I take the customs car out on a border
patrol to look for smugglers. This had enabled me to check all
the roads in the area for Crown forces. For some reason all the
main roads, and even most of the side roads, were saturated
with police and soldiers, wearing flak jackets with their sleeves
rolled up. It seemed to be a major operation: the soldiers were
wearing backpacks and looked like they were preparing for a
long haul. Had they been alerted to a pending operation, or was
the Queen flying in to boost morale in the bunkers? I knew that
if the bombing went ahead we were going to be putting ourselves at risk. The whole border area as far as Crossmaglen was
swarming with British Army patrols, but I found a suitable
route along narrow roads through which I could scout the team
to their target.

At lunch-time, I drove to the rendezvous with the IRA
team, in the car-park of a hotel near Dundalk. Seán met me.
He was wearing gloves. He told me that there were two bombs:
one in a Toyota Hiace van contained almost 700 pounds of
explosives and was destined for the warehouse; the other had
been built into the dashboard of a brown Mark 4 Cortina,
which would be used as the getaway car. It would be abandoned with the aim of attracting a nosy bomb-disposal squad
officer or policeman. If the glove compartment was opened, an
electrical circuit would be completed which would detonate
ten pounds of high explosives. Another unit had used a similar
trick some time earlier. A bomb disposal officer had cut out the
windscreen of the suspicious car in order to avoid opening the
doors; then he had leaned in and opened the glove compartment. The ensuing explosion had thrown him far down the
road, killing him instantly. I would be waiting at a pre-arranged
location to pick up the whole team as they abandoned the
Cortina. Then I would take them to the safe house, and drive
back to work.

I explained to Seán about the numerous checkpoints. He
said: 'But is there a way in?' I said there was, but it would be
difficult and dangerous. His only reply was: 'Let's go.' He gave
me one final instruction. He said that if a covert army patrol

did jump out at us, I was to ram them in order to give the rest of the team a chance to escape. 'Thanks very much,' I thought. Seán himself would not be accompanying us. Hardbap was the driver of the Toyota van, a young volunteer was to drive the Cortina. My cousin Mickey was his passenger.

We set off in a convoy, with me leading the way. The Cortina was right behind me, and the Toyota van was behind that. We crossed the border, avoiding one checkpoint, and climbed steeply up a hill. Down below I could see soldiers spread out, stopping a long line of cars.

We came out behind a major checkpoint and drove on the main road for at least three miles. I could see another big checkpoint at a bridge about a mile ahead, so I took a right turn and we continued along a narrow road. The road took us out just behind the big checkpoint at the bridge: soldiers were no more than a few feet from us. We drove on to the warehouse, about four miles down the road, where I left them and made off at speed to the pick-up point.

I had chosen a spot which gave me a bird's eye view of the warehouse and the roundabout which the team would have to drive round to get to me. I heard the warehouse's alarm go off, a high-pitched scream. I watched the Cortina race through the industrial estate trying to get to the roundabout as quickly as possible. Just at that moment, behind me on the hill, I could hear another car coming down fast. I turned my head just in time to see a maroon Volkswagen Passat containing four police-men shoot past me on its way to the warehouse. The policemen, with their green shirts and dark flak jackets, looked tense and ready for action; the butts of their rifles rested on their laps, the barrels were pointing upwards. Were we being set up? I looked down towards the roundabout: my lads hit it just as the police turned off. They had zoomed past each other. I jumped in my car as the Cortina with its three occupants came roaring towards me. They abandoned their own car and got into mine. I moved off at speed, my swiftness aided by the shock of seeing the heavily-armed peelers.

I dropped them off at the safe house and said I would see them later. I stopped off at a phone box and rang my boss at the Customs. I was breathless and sweaty. When I got through

I explained that I had just taken my mother to the doctor's and was running a bit late. I said I would be at work soon, although I warned him that there were traffic hold-ups in town at the moment. He said there was no hurry. I drove through the town. Police were stopping cars everywhere. I came to a junction where a policeman signalled me to stop. I opened my window and held out my identity card. He did not even bother to look at it as he had seen my customs uniform: 'Go ahead, sir.' The police must have thought they had trapped the IRA gang.

I arrived at work and walked into an excited atmosphere. Really, they assured me, the IRA had put a bomb in the warehouse only fifteen minutes ago, leaving one hour to clear the area. My boss told me that if the bomb went off I would probably have to work that night, keeping an eye on the warehouse to prevent looting. We sat about the office looking at newspapers. I kept an eye on my watch and, within a few minutes of the allotted hour, there was a thunderous roar as the bomb exploded.

I spent the rest of the week on duty at the warehouse. The place had been devastated; millions of pounds worth of damage had been caused. On my first night on duty every wino and drunk from miles around had descended in the hope of picking up a bottle from the wreckage. We did not try too hard to stop people. Indeed, a few customs officers joined in the plundering, filling the boots of their patrol cars with vodka, whisky, brandy and gin. Van loads of spirits were allowed to leave the premises night and day. I even managed to pick up a few cases of wine myself. I spoke to one of the warehouse staff who had been on duty when the IRA team arrived to plant the bomb. He said that one IRA man, a heavy lad with a big mouth – this had to be Hardbap – had run into the shed screaming and shouting and waving his rifle as if he were John Wayne, telling everyone to hit the deck. The staff member had actually said to the gunman: 'Take it easy, son. No call to get excited. You can plant your bomb. We won't give you any hassle.'

Hardbap was not typical of the Belfast IRA men who had taken refuge in Dundalk. Several of these 'refugees' – most of

them on the run as a result of the supergrass Christopher
Black – had started to play an increasing role within the South
Down Command. Seán was their leader. Just before we moved
on White, Seán decided to squeeze in another killing. Mickey
had supplied me with information about one of his colleagues
at the housing executive, a part-time RUC reservist called
Sammy Hamilton. He always parked his car next to the offices.
Seán appointed himself as the gunman. He walked up to
Hamilton as he parked his car, and before Hamilton realized
what was happening, Seán had taken out a pistol and fired at
point-blank range through the window, hitting his victim in the
face, chest and neck. Then the back doors of a Hiace van
parked nearby burst open. A plank of wood shot out, and a
man drove a motorbike down the plank. Seán jumped on the
back, and the two roared off.

That night I had had to drive Seán back to Dundalk. Before
setting off with him, I had checked that the route was clear, but
by the time we crossed the border the Irish security forces had
set up a checkpoint. Seán was carrying two handguns, including the one he had used in the hit. As we approached the
checkpoint Seán said: 'Let me out. I'm going to walk past.
You drive through and pick me up on the other side.' He casually strolled past the police and army, who did not regard
pedestrians as a threat, and I picked him up on the other side.
Amazingly, Hamilton survived this attack, although seriously
injured.

I have to admit that these Belfast men energized me. A man
I shall call Declan also became involved in our operations. He
was from the Ardoyne, the son of a Protestant father who had
converted to Catholicism after marrying a Catholic. Declan
was a tough, stocky, bullet-headed man with a very deep voice.
When he was drunk, he always sang 'Born Free'. He had the
build of a heavyweight fighter. Sometimes he would talk about
his brother, who had been shot dead by the IRA as an informer.
He could get upset about this, especially when he remembered
the signs of torture that the family said they had found on the
body. The IRA claimed that the burns on the body had been
caused by the discharge of the weapon that killed him, but
Declan was convinced they were cigarette burns. The rest of

the family had cut their links with the republican movement after this murder, but Declan decided to remain in the IRA. However, he would often talk to me about his pain and loss: he felt that his brother should have been shown mercy in the way that other, less deserving characters had been shown mercy in the past. Sometimes, when drunk, he would say: 'Why didn't they give our kid an amnesty? They gave that other bastard an amnesty, why not our kid?' His grief disturbed Seán and Hardbap. They were embarrassed by it, and would say nothing in response. They tried to ignore it, hoping it would be washed away with more alcohol.

I discussed with Declan the plan to assassinate Albert White. In the months since I had first started to target him, I had discovered that he was no longer a policeman. He had retired from active police duties in 1974 as a result of injuries he sustained in the IRA's attack on him in 1973. Now he was the civilian office manager of the criminal investigation department at Newry police station. But in our eyes his job still made him a target. Anyone who helped the British war machine in any way by any act of collaboration was a target. The fact that he still lived in Newry reflected only the past weakness of the Newry IRA. I felt that he should have been killed years ago instead of being allowed to survive in the heart of our community. He would never have survived, for instance, if he had been living in south Armagh. The IRA in south Armagh were extremely successful, not merely because they had many veteran volunteers who operated in a community with a strong history of resistance. There was something else which helped them gain that commitment: they ruled their area with a rod of iron. They deliberately struck terror into the hearts of the people with their ruthlessness. As I became hardened in my commitment to the IRA, I came to feel that the IRA throughout Ireland should have regarded the behaviour of the South Armagh Brigade as the model for their behaviour. Given my increasing commitment to this ruthless logic, I was not going to treat White benignly just because he was a partial invalid who had converted to Roman Catholicism. And this was the logic of the kind of war we were fighting.

Once we almost got White in Dundalk: he was sitting in his

car while his wife went shopping, a few hundred yards from an
IRA safe house. She returned and they drove off while we
were still looking for a gun. But I knew I was getting closer.
His luck could not last forever. I decided to go for him at the
most dependable killing place: outside his own house. Soldiers
and policemen are always most vulnerable at home, because
regardless of how they vary their routine this will always be
their end point. Their homes are even more vulnerable if they
are not living in a Protestant area. White lived in an area which
had once been a 'safe' Protestant area, but most Protestants had
moved out and been replaced by Catholics.

Mickey was to be the gunman, with Declan as his back-up.
After Hanna, I had not wanted to work with Mickey or his
sidekicks again, but in the three months since Hanna's killing
I had had no choice. Indeed, if anything, I had grown to like
Mickey. We began to spend a lot of time together. I found him
intelligent and humorous: at least he laughed a lot, and he was
very eager to please. Although he was my cousin, I had hardly
known anything about him before he had joined the IRA. As a
student he had become a militant socialist, and he grew to
loathe Ulster's unionists for being an exploitative capitalist
class. However, his hatred of unionists disguised his gut sectarianism. He worked in a mixed Catholic and Protestant
environment at the housing executive. One time he heard one
of the Protestants talking loudly to his colleagues about the
1641 massacre in Portadown when Catholics had thrown scores
of Protestants into the river and drowned them. 'They killed
an awful lot of them but they didn't manage to kill them all,'
said Mickey's Protestant colleague. Mickey looked up from his
work and grunted: 'Pity.'

The football World Cup of 1982 was creating the usual
excitement at this time. The whole community, including the
police and army, seemed to be staying at home to watch the big
games. I planned the operation for the day when the dazzling
Brazilian team were playing. The kick-off would take place
soon after the end of normal office hours, and I calculated that
Albert White would want to get home to see the match.
Mickey, armed with his Browning, would shoot White as he
arrived home. Declan would be there to back Mickey up with

his .38, if necessary. The getaway driver would be the young
volunteer from the warehouse bombing. The day arrived and
the team took up positions near White's house.

I was told later that White had arrived home promptly, as if
he were working to our schedule. As usual, his wife had driven
him in their blue Saab. As they parked the car, our car pulled
up in front of them. Mickey jumped out and fired three shots
through White's windscreen, which all missed. White opened
the passenger door and tried to get to his house. Mickey ran
around and stood in front of him, wearing a wig and dark
glasses, with his Browning extended. White made feeble mum-
bling cries and tried weakly to fend Mickey off with his
umbrella, waving it left and right, as if he were parrying a
fencing opponent. Mickey fired bullet after bullet into the old
man, and White fell to the ground, dead. So Mickey now had
his second kill.

Mrs White watched her husband being killed and, although
distressed and in shock, ran to his body and pulled out his
gun. She chased after Mickey who had run with Declan to the
getaway car, its engine revving. But her weeping convulsed her
and she was unable to get off a shot. Mickey saw her with the
gun in her hand and prepared to shoot her but he told me later
he respected her bravery, and spared her life. The car sped off,
but on a back road two miles from the scene it crashed. The
three men jumped out of the car and legged it for more than a
mile to a housing estate where Mickey had friends.

The next day I met up with Mickey and Declan. Mickey
was saying: 'That dangerous old bitch ran after me with a gun.
She was crying, you know, screaming, "You bastards! You bastards!"' He was also outraged at what the papers were saying:
they claimed that the gunman had smiled at Mrs White after
he had shot her husband. He said: 'It's the usual old tabloid
shite. The lying bastards. It's just propaganda.'

I read in the paper about Albert White's funeral. The
requiem mass was held at St Mary's Roman Catholic Church
in Newry. My second cousin, the Reverend Ray Collins, said
mass. I had not seen him in years; I knew he was extremely
critical of the IRA. My former headmaster, the then Father
Brooks, now the Bishop of Dromore, preached in the cathedral

about the evil in our midst. I noted that the burial had taken place at Monkshill cemetery on the outskirts of the town. I waited a few days and went to visit White's graveside. Not to pay my respects, but to read the messages on his wreaths to see whether his RUC colleagues had left any useful personal details. I knew that they would not be so stupid, but as an IRA intelligence officer I had to live in hope of such unlikely windfalls. I stood beside the grave and looked down at the wreaths, all neatly placed across the freshly-dug clay. I read the messages. However, there was nothing that I could follow up: I blessed myself for all that, and said a little prayer for White's soul. God knows who heard it.

1982 brought no more 'successes' of this kind, only abortive operations. As the year ended, I realized more and more that in the IRA the next operation was the one that counted, not the one before, and that it didn't matter what you had done in the past: if you stepped out of line that was what you were judged on.

The former OC of our area, who had supervised the killing of Hanna and other operations, had asked me earlier in the year to bring the MI Carbine rifle that lived under my bed to Dundalk. I was not sure why he needed it, but I assumed he wanted to put it in a proper arms dump. I put the rifle in a bag and pushed it down between the front seats of my car. I set off on a dark night and as I approached Dundalk I was stopped by the Irish police. An old sergeant asked me for identification. I reached across to the glove compartment for my licence. To my horror, the rifle had shifted slightly in the bag and now the barrel was protruding by about four inches. What could I do? I knew that any sudden movement might draw the sergeant's attention to the bag, but fortunately he was not using his torch. I stayed cool and handed him the licence. He examined it, handed it back, and told me to go on.

The OC was pleased to see me, and seemed strangely grateful for the rifle, as if I were doing him a personal favour by bringing it. I did not know when I handed him the weapon that I was playing a part in a chain of events which, before the year was over, would lead to him being sentenced to death by the

IRA. I knew he was fond of his drink, but I had not realized that he had crossed the boundaries of social drinking. He found that his small income could not finance his binges, so in an act of madness he used the rifle to rob a bread-van. Then later, desperate for money, he committed an even greater act of madness: he approached Dominic McGlinchey, the chief of staff of the rival Irish National Liberation Army, with an offer to sell him IRA weapons. McGlinchey, a ruthless and fearless operator whom the tabloids dubbed 'Mad Dog', told the IRA about his offer. The IRA interrogated the OC for several days. Although he was a senior commander, the IRA decided that, according to Green Book regulations, his crime merited the death penalty.

His captors blindfolded him and tied his hands behind his back. They took him to a wooded area near the border where they planned to shoot him, but as he walked with his executioners he broke free and ran through the dense forest, with his blindfold still on. He hid himself and lay there all night while they searched for him. The next morning he managed to push off the blindfold and after several hours managed to find his way to a Garda station where he confessed to a knee-capping that he had carried out in the Republic some time before. He received a prison sentence, and after his release went to live in an obscure part of the Republic.

It took me some time to piece together his story, because the IRA did not like people to nose around too much into security matters. I felt sad for him, and shocked, too, by his fall from grace. He, as much as anyone else, had helped to put us on the verge of turning our area into a black area for the Crown forces, but our war left no room for pity, even among ourselves.

9

SMOKING GUNS

The end of 1982 left the South Down Command feeling demoralized. Its morale was boosted soon after the New Year holiday of 1983.

Before Christmas I had been called to Dundalk by Seán, to be briefed about a pending operation. Seán told me that he had received reliable information about a member of the Ulster Defence Regiment who took his elderly father to the post office in Rostrevor on Tuesdays to pick up his pension. Seán said we should kill the UDR man outside the post office, and he wanted me to reconnoitre the scene of the planned assassination as soon as possible. As soon as Seán finished his briefing, I drove straight to where we were going to kill the target, although once again I felt uneasy. How could I be sure that the information was reliable?

At the post office in Rostrevor, everything seemed normal and familiar. I walked inside to buy some stamps. The usual routine: a female clerk worked quietly behind a closed-in counter at the back, a scene you could have found in any village post office in the country. In the few minutes I was there I took in everything that needed to be taken in. Out on the street, I took a good look at the other shops nearby. I was putting myself in the position of the gunman, memorizing every detail, imagining the potential target as the gunman would see it. I could not bring him here on this scouting mission. To do so might compromise him by putting him at risk of being recognized when he carried out the killing.

According to my briefing in Dundalk, there were never any police in the area on a Tuesday. I drove over to the nearby village square and parked my car. I thought that the enclosed nature of the square, which had a few trees dotted about the place, might impair the view of the post office, but I could still see it perfectly. The gunman and his getaway driver could park here ten minutes before the target arrived. Yet everything seemed just too easy. I drove past the post office one final time. I timed the journey from there to the point down the hill where you joined the main road out of the area. It took only forty seconds. I returned to Dundalk and said that I could see no real difficulty about doing the hit in the near future. I left it to Seán to decide who would be the trigger man and when he would act.

A few days into the New Year, I returned to Rostrevor on another matter. On my way back home I passed a silver Ford Escort being driven towards Rostrevor. I did not recognize the driver but I did recognize his front-seat passenger: it was my cousin Mickey. I assumed the driver was one of the Belfast men now living in Dundalk. Their presence told me that the hit was going to take place the next day. I did not think about the operation until I heard the news on the radio at work the following afternoon. The newscaster said that just after 11 a.m. two policemen had been shot dead, and one seriously injured, in Rostrevor. What had happened to the UDR man?

Two policemen dead, one seriously injured: I imagined that several Belfast men must have been involved with Mickey, all of them blasting away with rifles. That morning I found out that I had passed some important exams for an Open University course I had started in the autumn of 1982. So the day had provided me with a double delight and I felt on a real high. Around nine-thirty that night I got a call from Seán. He said very little save to tell me to 'go and talk to the big fella with glasses'. This was the eccentric Francie, the bicycling enthusiast I had recruited some time before. I did not realize that the commanders in Dundalk did not have a clue about what had happened that morning in Rostrevor, and they were as keen as I was to find out.

It was a bitter winter night. I drove from my house in Newry deep into the heart of south Armagh, on the road to Crossmaglen. I drove through the slush of icy snow on a mountain route, along narrow, winding roads on an ever-increasing gradient.

I parked the car and walked along the narrow path between two rows of bungalows until I came to Francie's back door. I rapped firmly but quietly on the door. Francie's daughter – a tall, bespectacled eleven-year-old – answered. 'Is your daddy in?' I asked. She turned and went to get him. I could see into the house. There was a small hall, about four feet wide, and beyond I could see into the sitting-room where her father sat in an armchair pulled right up to the fire. I noticed there were only a few pieces of coal left in the grate. Francie had married at seventeen and was saving to build his own house. He was sitting there with a blanket wrapped around him and one of his feet in a basin of water. His wife sat next to him in the other armchair, holding his hand. His daughter came back and said: 'He'll be with you in a minute.' I realized I was not going to be invited in for tea. I told her to ask him to meet me at the end of the path, in my car. When I was standing at the door I had seen him talk to his wife with a tense look on his face. I had seen that look before, and I knew the situation in which it appeared: the IRA man gets involved in a very serious operation and suddenly his wife is awakened to the reality of what he has become. Some wives wanted to run away, others wanted an immediate divorce; some tried to get their husbands out of the IRA, a few felt proud of what their men had done.

I watched the big fellow as he hurried towards me. I remembered his face as boyish-looking, but tonight he had a look of fear and shock about him. He got into the car. I passed the usual pleasantries quickly and asked him if he knew what was going on, as I had been told to contact him. I expected that there were Belfast men to pick up and get out of the area. 'No,' he said, 'there were no Belfast men. Only me and Mickey.' I felt an almost physical tingling. 'What do you mean, "only me and Mickey"? There's two peelers dead and one seriously

injured. And what the fuck were you doing with that blanket
round you, sitting at the fire with your foot in a basin? Have
you 'flu in your foot or something?'

'No, I got shot.'

I felt almost dizzy, but all I could do was ask him how he had
got shot.

He told me, 'The policeman lying on the ground shot me –
the one Mickey had the gunfight with after he shot dead the
other two.'

I felt faint. Francie took me through what had happened
that day. He said he had travelled down to Warrenpoint in his
own car, as instructed. He had parked the car behind the silver
Ford Escort. Then he got into the Escort and drove to a working-class housing estate in the town where he picked up
Mickey. The plan was to drive to Rostrevor and to wait near
the post office for the UDR man to arrive. Mickey would then
jump out, shoot the UDR man, and jump back in the car.
Francie would drive to Warrenpoint where he would abandon
the hot car and pick up his own. Then he would leave Mickey
at the nearby safe house and drive home. However, just before
eleven, as they were waiting for the UDR man, an orange
Mitsubishi had driven in behind them. It contained three uniformed policemen – two in the front, one in the back. It was
not the usual unmarked police patrol car with bullet-proof
glass and armour plating, but an ordinary saloon car with no
extra protection. Had it been the former, then Mickey and
Francie would have had to surrender or been shot dead. But
even with the unprotected car, if the policeman in the back had
got out and covered his colleagues with his Ruger rifle, then the
IRA men would have had to give up, because they were armed
only with one pistol and one revolver. But only one RUC man
got out of the car and walked towards the IRA car. He had his
hat off and was using it to cover the gun which he was holding
at waist-level near his belt-buckle. So the police suspected
something, but obviously not an IRA operation. Perhaps they
thought there was going to be an 'ordinary' robbery.

When Francie saw the police he had wanted to surrender,
but according to him Mickey sat calmly, staring straight ahead,
with a copy of the *Irish News* covering the Browning pistol on

his lap. He had the pistol fully cocked, with the safety-catch off and his finger on the trigger. The policeman approached Francie's window. He remembered him saying, 'Wait a minute. Let's see what they want. Keep calm.' Francie said he wound down his own window and said to the policeman, 'Do you want to see my licence?' He had a .38 Smith and Wesson revolver lying between the seat and the door on his right-hand side, but he was too nervous to use it. Anyway, he didn't know how.

He was just about to hand his licence to the policeman when he turned around to see Mickey getting out of the car. The policeman began to say, 'Hey, you, wait a minute,' or, 'Where do you think you're going?' or words like that, when he saw Mickey lean outstretched across the roof of the car and fire at the policeman, both hands clasped around the gun. The policeman was hit and he fell to the ground. Mickey raced to the police car and started firing. Francie saw the windscreen collapse and blood splash from the policeman's face – the one who was sitting at the steering-wheel. The other policeman at the back moved to get out because the back door was opening, but Mickey stood on the pavement and again, holding both hands on the weapon, fired several shots into him. Francie heard shots coming from the other side, and it was the first policeman firing at Mickey, who screamed, 'Turn the car, turn the car,' and Francie did, with Mickey now in a shoot-out with the policeman who was using the IRA car for cover as Mickey fired at him from behind the front passenger wing of the police car.

As Francie began to turn the car around he could see the injured policeman lying in the road and aiming shots at the car. He felt a burning sharp pain in his right foot. Mickey jumped in, still firing at the policeman, and they drove to Warrenpoint, where they dumped the Escort and picked up Francie's own car. He ended by saying that Mickey was now in the safe house.

Francie had been shot in the toe. The impact of the bullet had left a hole in his sock and a tear in his trainer. He buried the sock under heather on Camlough Mountain, tied a stone to the trainer and threw it into Camlough Lake. We talked at length about Mickey's quick reactions, his coolness under pressure, and, most importantly, his ability to kill. We were both proud and amazed. We had already started to compare him to legendary IRA men like Sean Treacey and Cathal Brugha, who had fought the British between 1916 and 1921. Mickey, we felt in our euphoria, would go down in history with men like these. We did not think then of the devastation caused to the families of the dead policemen.

I was glad Francie had survived. I said goodnight to him. But the operation was not over yet. Mickey was in a house in Warrenpoint, sitting there with two guns. It was my responsibility to get him out and safely across the border. I drove home and immediately rang a man whom I wanted to act as scout for me, driving ahead to check the roads were clear. This man must have heard about the operation on the news because he sounded very scared when I rang.

I asked him if he could do us a favour with the car. He said: 'The wife's got the car.' I asked him what time his wife was likely to return. He began stuttering: 'I . . . I . . . I don't know. I don't know.' I knew he was lying. Apart from being an IRA volunteer, he was also supposedly a close personal friend of Mickey. I could have ordered him to get a car somewhere else but I could not be bothered. Another IRA man had once told me knowingly: 'Once they start using "the wife" excuse, you know they're no fucking use.' I put the phone down and felt alone. I was the only IRA man in Newry. I had had to get used to that reality. I told myself I did not need people like him. I was prepared to exploit whatever usefulness they had, but they were so cowardly that they had become a liability. No sooner had I put the phone down than it rang again. It was a contact in Warrenpoint. He told me that checkpoints in the area had been cleared in the last thirty minutes and I could go and pick up my friend.

I set off for Warrenpoint without a scout. When I arrived I found the housing estate and drove slowly down the road looking for the right number. It had begun to rain, and I could hardly see out of the windows. Then I saw a figure running towards me. It was Mickey. He opened the door quickly and jumped in. He said he had left the guns in the house. I drove off. Mickey and I exchanged few words until we got back to my house. He told me that he had spent most of the day sitting with the guns in the upstairs bedroom of the safe house. A UDR patrol had come into the street quite soon after he had arrived. He had been expecting them to come in, but they had merely enquired of the occupier, who had been mending a fence in his garden at the time, whether he had seen any suspicious people or activity in the area after 11 a.m. He said he had not, and the patrol had moved on in its fruitless follow-up operation, after the discovery of the getaway car nearby. Mickey said he had been ready to shoot his way out if they had entered the house. I believed him.

Mickey's version of events was more graphic than Francie's. He was high on death, and exulted in the details of the gun-fight and the killings. He had leaned across the car, trying for a head-shot, but the policeman moved and took the bullet in the shoulder near the neck. Mickey had fired at the young cop in the car through the windscreen and hit him in the face, and then several more times after the screen had disintegrated, watching his body bounce as the rounds hit him. The third policeman stumbled out of the car and fell to the ground, where Mickey gleefully described him whimpering and crying as he fired into his side along the split in the flak jacket, and then he had fired again at his first victim who was shooting at him from the ground.

When he reached the safe house he called Seán and said: 'I've passed all my exams.'

I was sleeping the next morning when my former school-mate and another of the ex-Irps were arrested. The Special Branch asked them if they knew of a customs man who was in the IRA. I found out later the same day that the second man's wife had left her home shortly after they had been arrested and had travelled across town to Barcroft Park trying to find my house. She knocked on several doors asking if they knew where Eamon Collins, 'the customs officer', lived. She had been followed by the police who sat in a patrol car watching to see where she would take them. Luckily for me, no one she spoke to knew me. I was not from Newry town and had only been on the estate for a year. But if she had used my wife's maiden name then everyone would have known who she was

talking about, and the police would have been led directly to
my house and to the two smoking guns under my bed. I was
annoyed and shocked, but I had been pleased to discover loyalty in other people who had warned me about what had
happened. I was not prepared to panic but I knew I had to get
rid of the guns fast and also to take myself 'off-side' (that is,
over the border) while the arrested men were being interrogated, in case one of them gave the police my name. I took the
guns out of the house, suspended them on a cord and put them
through the small vent at the back of a blocked-up, disused
garage. I retrieved them that evening and drove to an arms
dump high in the mountains, where I handed them to the
grizzled IRA veteran who ran it. Then I drove to Dundalk.

Seán arranged for me to stay in the home of an IRA sympathizer, a huge man who worked at a meat-processing factory
near Dundalk. The house was filthy and the sheets smelt of
stale urine. The owner kept two rabbits in the back garden
which he called 'Provo' and 'Bullet'. In the evening, I realized
how he had come to be so fat: he brought home three cooked
chickens which he placed on the table. Then he proceeded to
tear into them with his bare hands. He said to me: 'Help yourself, man.' I told him I was not hungry. The next day I pleaded
with Seán to find me somewhere else to stay until the other
men were released (I had already phoned the customs with an
excuse for my absence).

Seán found me another safe house. I took advantage of my
stay in Dundalk to look up a friend who had once been in
the IRA. I knew he had worked part-time at the same meat-
processing factory where the fat man had worked, so I told
him about my encounter with his former colleague. 'Jesus,' he
said, 'I don't think I'd have liked to stay in the same house as
that fucker. You know, I think it was him that did the business
on Nairac.'

Captain Robert Nairac was the SAS man who had been
abducted by republicans from a pub in south Armagh while he
was on an undercover operation in May 1977. The IRA had
admitted executing him after interrogating him, but they had
never handed over his body. I asked my friend what he meant.
He said: 'Well, you know that meat-processing factory was full

of Provos. We all used to get a bit of work there when we were on the run.' He said that the management used to take on a lot of casual short-term labour when they had big export orders. They did not know they were employing IRA men. When Nairac was abducted he was taken to a field just down the road from the factory. After shooting him they didn't know what to do with the body. It was getting light so they didn't want to bury him. One of the guys had a brainwave – put him through the meat mincer at the factory. 'So that's where he ended up. I heard they just treated him like any other carcass.'

I could hardly believe what I was hearing. Even then, fresh from complicity in a couple of killings, I did not think it was right to deny Nairac's relatives a body. I said: 'What do you mean, "like any other carcass"?' He almost whispered: 'They scalped him, cut out his innards, then turned him into meat and bone-meal. I think they must have burnt the scalp and the giblets.' My friend said he had not witnessed this himself, but he had heard about it from another Provo working at the factory. Apparently the body had first been dumped temporarily into a pit close to the factory; then the next day, during a slack period, when hardly anyone was around, the body had been brought in for disposal.

Some years later, I met someone who had been sitting in his car in the car-park of the pub in Drumintee on the night of Nairac's abduction. This man, who was not connected with the republican movement, said that he had watched as Nairac was severely beaten. He told me that the beating was so ferocious that he felt that no one could have survived it. He said that he saw the abductors pick up Nairac's limp body and put it in a car. I realized then that the Provos had butchered Nairac's body because they had not wanted people to know about the appalling injuries he had sustained. Of course, the irony was that the abduction of Nairac had not been officially sanctioned by the IRA; all but one of the men who snatched him were simply IRA sympathizers who had been drinking in the pub. The only IRA man in the group was a raw recruit. The IRA would have liked to have interrogated someone like Nairac for weeks; they might even have used their prize as a bargaining-counter. Instead, by the time the IRA at a senior level came to hear about Nairac's capture, the unfortunate SAS officer was little more than a bloody mess lying in a field.

The two men were released from custody after a few days. Both were later dismissed from the IRA in disgrace, as a result of suspicions about what they had done while in custody: they were suspected of having talked. I felt that the IRA had treated them rather harshly, but the decision to dismiss the two of them had come from the IRA's security branch who had debriefed both of them after their police interrogation. The security branch is made up of the IRA's bogeymen, the faceless internal police, and is known as the 'Nutting Squad' because they are the ones who put a hood over the heads of informers before 'nutting' them with a shot in the head and leaving their bodies at border crossings. IRA members feared the security branch more than they feared any enemy unit and, at that time, I felt this was necessary to deter informers. I was still all for ruthless discipline, the iron hand of the revolutionary organization keeping its members united.

I returned home at the end of the week, realizing how close I had come to being caught. I was now more cautious, but the peelers were already halfway to finding me: they knew there was an IRA man in Barcroft Park, and they suspected he was a customs officer. And there were not many of us to choose from.

The following week, Francie came to see me at my house. He was upset; he had been criticized by some of the Belfast IRA men. They had jeered at him, saying he should have been able to use the Smith and Wesson to shoot the policeman who had asked for his driver's licence. They made him feel guilty: the injured policeman had probably been able to identify Mickey. They were, of course (even in terms of their own macho standards), being extremely unfair to Francie: he had never attended an IRA training camp or even handled a gun before. I thought he had behaved extremely bravely in driving the car away while under fire. When Francie called, I had a handgun in the house. I unloaded it and handed it to Francie. He stood at the top of the stairs, this tall, gawky man, pointing the gun and pulling the trigger, which clicked harmlessly as the hammer found only empty chambers. It was like watching a child play cops and robbers, except that Francie said: 'This is what I should have done. This is how I should have shot him.'

Years later, I discovered that the information which had led to the operation in the first place was inaccurate. The man who brought his father to Rostrevor post office on Tuesdays was not in the UDR.

10

PROFICIENCY

Mickey's feat at Rostrevor meant that we moved into the new
year with renewed enthusiasm.

However, the Irish police threw a little cold water over
Mickey's celebrations. Almost all IRA members have a 'honeymoon' period when they first join the organization, during
which they are invisible to the police and army. A few days
after the Rostrevor shootings the Irish police stopped Mickey
at a checkpoint when he was in a car with Hardbap. Until this
time, Mickey, although he had now killed four people, had not
been suspected of involvement with the IRA. But Hardbap
was a known IRA man, a red light, and to be seen in the company of such a man was as good as stamping IRA on your
forehead. Mickey's honeymoon was over: he knew that he
would soon be getting an early-morning call from the peelers.
He decided to move immediately to Dundalk.

He moved into a flat while I was still kicking my heels
about the town, waiting to see whether the arrested men
would be released from custody. I went to visit him, but I had
not been there long when the doorbell rang. Mickey
answered the door and I heard a Special Branch man introduce himself. He had several colleagues with him. I thought
that my own honeymoon was also about to come to a sudden
end. Mickey told them he was alone in the flat and, if they
did not mind, he was about to take a bath. I was sure they

were going to push past him into the flat, but instead they obediently left.

Once the two hapless ex-Irps had been released without charge, I returned to Newry. I had the compensation of a newly-acquired status within the IRA. I had not panicked after the arrests and had not dumped the weapons, but instead had brought them safely to Dundalk. I felt I had won the respect of the Belfast men. Indeed, several of them now refused to operate in Newry unless I was going to be responsible for taking them in and out. The IRA now began to trust me with their best operators. Perhaps this was pride before the fall because I suspected I was coming close to the end of my own honeymoon. I knew the police were on my trail, but I believed I could survive for a good while yet, if I was careful. And pride had at least partly driven aside the feelings of disgust and revulsion at the human cost of our botched operations.

I pressed on with my efforts to bring the war to the so-called safe areas of South Down outside Newry. I had kept up contact with the man called Joe who was still an active informant. He was an excellent source of information about what was happening in the Warrenpoint area. With his new wife, he was renting a flat close to the site of the bombed-out Crown Hotel in the square. I went to visit him, to see whether he had anything of interest to pass on. I was delighted with what he had to tell me. From his flat, he had an excellent view of Warrenpoint police station. He said that he had noticed that on Saturday and Sunday mornings, before noon, one policeman, sometimes two, left the station and crossed the road to a sweet-shop to buy sweets and buns, presumably for their tea-break. He thought that we would be able to attack the police as they came in or went out of the shop. He suggested that Sunday was the best day because the station did not have its full complement of officers on that day; also Sunday seemed to make the police more relaxed, and thus more vulnerable to attack. The fact that there would be fewer policemen on duty also meant greater security for the IRA team, because there would be fewer officers to man checkpoints across the area in the wake of an attack. By exploiting an apparently insignificant human weakness (in this case a sweet tooth), we would hit the police both physically and, even more important, psychologically. They would realize that the IRA could find vulnerability in the most humdrum of activities.

I wasted no time in selling the op to Seán. I arranged for Joe to go to Dundalk to explain his idea to Seán in person. Once I had set the wheels in motion, I did not want to have anything more to do with it. Seán agreed with me and said he would give me a rest. However, it was not to be. Only a few days after his promise, Seán rang me at home. If anyone else had phoned me I would have told them where to go, but I respected him and knew that he would not have phoned unless he really did need me. I went to a public phone box and rang the number he gave me. He told me that the op was going ahead on the coming Sunday, but they would not be able to get a car with clean registration plates at such short notice. He wanted me to arrange for a taxi as a getaway car. Belfast men had a strange fondness for using taxis on operations, presumably because there were so many of them on the road in their home city. Seán outlined where the taxi could pick up the IRA men and where it could be hijacked. I told him I would phone him back in ten minutes.

I phoned directory enquiries and asked for the number of the Newry taxi rank. I phoned the number I was given, and I heard the voice of a middle-aged man on the other end. I changed my accent to a southern Irish one and asked whether it would be possible to book a taxi for ten on Sunday morning. I said that a friend and I needed to be taken across the border to Carlingford. The taxi-driver was eager for business. I explained the importance of leaving Newry for ten. And I insisted that his passengers came to him, excusing this strange arrangement by confiding in him that we were meeting married women and did not want to alert their families. I rang Seán back immediately. I gave him the taxi-driver's details and left him to pass them on to the volunteers who needed the car.

Some time after the operation, I spoke to one of the volunteers involved. He was in his late twenties and came originally from the Rostrevor area. This man told me that he and another volunteer had gone to the taxi-driver's house that Sunday morning. The driver chatted amiably, then, just before they crossed the border, my informant stuck a finger in the driver's back and said: 'This is the IRA. We're commandeering your car.' They hijacked the taxi just before they crossed into the Republic of Ireland because they wanted the offence to be committed in the north, so that the Gardai would not become involved in the investigation. The driver had been very frightened but he did what he was told and drove into the mountains. He was taken to a rendezvous where two other IRA men were waiting with the weapons. They took the driver out and perched him on a rock, leaving a man to guard him until the operation was over. The other two volunteers got into the taxi. One of them was the getaway driver, the other was going to act as armed back-up in the attack. This volunteer was in his early twenties; he was from Dundalk and I had met him a few times there. He was little more than a moronic thug and I thought he should not have been allowed to join the IRA: I suspected he had joined solely because of his love of violence. I had heard a story about him slashing someone's face and throat in a drunken brawl.

One man, the one who told me about what happened next, was armed with an Italian Beretta submachine-gun, the other carried a .38 and a grenade. They drove straight to Warrenpoint. The town was quiet, as usual. They parked in the square, out of sight of the police station and close to the sweetshop. Joe had agreed to give a signal when the policeman emerged from the station. Joe said he would close his livingroom curtains to alert the ASU. But Joe chickened out at the last moment: he did not give the signal when a single policeman came out of the station at the usual time. Unfortunately for the policeman, one of the team still managed to spot him as he came back out of the shop holding his bag of purchases. The gunman jumped out of the car and ran to the policeman as he was about to cross the road. The first volunteer pulled out the Beretta from underneath his coat and in that split second the policeman saw what was about to happen. He dropped the bag and was about to run when he was hit with a burst from the submachine-gun. The man who fired the gun told me: 'The impact just lifted him clean off his feet and carried him up the street like a paper bag.' The getaway car pulled up swiftly beside the ASU. A policeman opened fire from the station. The second gunman threw his grenade and fired a few shots from his .38. Then he too ran to the car, claiming later that he had administered a *coup de grâce* to the dying police-man. ('Yeah, I put one in the hoor's head,' he told me. I did not know whether to believe him.) The ASU escaped and got safely back across the border. The policeman was dead when his colleagues got to him.

We moved on to the next operation. There were several possi-bilities circulating in my brain. In the four years I had been in the IRA I had developed a network of intelligence sources and my hard work was beginning to reap a devastating dividend. I felt that I was moving towards a state of terrifying efficiency as an IRA operator; I was getting better all the time. I had no illu-sions about the nature of my work: I never lost sight of the awfulness of what I was doing, yet I felt this savagery was the necessary price of our struggle to create a more just society. We were involved in a war of attrition and even then I knew that my participation in that war had changed me: I knew I no longer existed as a normal human being. Every aspect of my life was dedicated to the purpose of death. I knew that a change had taken place within me but at the time I felt I had changed *for the better*: I was becoming a true revolutionary. I had almost rid myself of any sympathy for my victims, and fought hard to suppress any feelings of compassion for my enemies. I kept telling myself that compassion for the oppres-sor was a debilitating legacy of the bourgeois morality of my upbringing.

I received information from one of my sources about a part-time Royal Ulster Constabulary reservist. He had a full-time job delivering bread, and he drove a distinctive red and white van, emblazoned with the words, 'Mother's Pride'. I was told that he was a dark-haired man in his thirties named Fred Morton, and that he had a daily bread run in the Rathfriland area, after collecting his supplies at 6 a.m. from a huge con-tainer lorry in the car-park of a cash and carry on the outskirts of Newry. My informant did not know where he lived, so I decided that my first job would be to get a precise address for him. Since the hunger strike, Sinn Fein had been developing an explicit strategy of combining revolutionary violence and the ballot box. Our participation in local and national elections meant that each of our offices was entitled to have a copy of the electoral register, listing all voters and their addresses. In Newry Sinn Fein's office I consulted their electoral register. 'Morton, Frederick', constituent number 969, lived at 163 Tandragee Road in the Tullyhappy ward of Newry and Mourne District. One Sunday I drove out to the Tandragee Road, but it was a rural area and the dwellings were well spaced out and often did not have street numbers. However, by spotting a couple of numbers, I was able to narrow down Morton's location to half a dozen houses spread over half a mile. I returned later and drove up and down past the houses at a time when I though all God-fearing Protestants would be at church. And then I saw the red and white Mother's Pride van tucked in beside its owner's little homestead. The poor man might as well have hung out a neon sign saying, 'Kill me'. I drove home, but I still needed to get both the registration number and a clear look at the driver, so the next morning I made sure I was at the junction of the Armagh Road which I knew he would use to travel to his bread pick-up point in Newry.

I posed as a jogger. I borrowed a pair of black tracksuit bottoms, and a light blue sweatshirt. I had not jogged in years but I left my house at 5.30 a.m. and cut across the disused railway sidings near my home. I jogged through the Meadow Estate and then into St Colman's Estate. I got on to the Armagh Road. I was beginning to slow down when I saw my target. Out of a light mist came the Mother's Pride van. As it came close I noted the registration number and then I looked up at the driver. He had a weather-beaten, craggy face. He seemed almost familiar. He was wearing a heavy black overcoat. I thought it looked like the overcoat worn by former B Specials. I exulted to myself that this was a bonus, to find a former B-man who was still a target. He wore a woolly dark monkey hat on his head and sat bolt upright in the cab. He was sixty, if a day. So much for him being in his thirties. He drove past, and I knew I had everything needed to kill him.

I reported my findings back to Seán. Within a few days I was showing the getaway driver Morton's route. I told him that Morton would have to slow down as he came to the end of the Armagh Road in order to turn at the junction into the Newry-Portadown Road. I suggested that would be the best moment to shoot him.

Within a week Morton had been shot dead. A Belfast volunteer, on the run in Dundalk, was the gunman. He used a Heckler and Koch G3 high-velocity rifle. On the morning of 15 March 1983 the ASU had driven behind Morton as he went down the Armagh Road, then as he slowed at the junction the IRA car had overtaken the van on the outside and the trigger-man had blasted Morton several times at close range. Morton died instantly. His van went out of control and crashed down an embankment before coming to a halt at the end of a field. The man who fired said he had hit Morton in the face. He described Morton's head exploding.

There was only one hitch in the operation: the ASU could not find the safe house so they ended up knocking on my door to ask for directions. I went into work for 10 a.m. and went out soon afterwards on a border patrol. I checked that the roads were clear of checkpoints and then, at lunch, I drove to the safe house. The ASU got into their car and I scouted them across the border. I felt elated at the success of the operation, proud of my proficiency. The next day I saw a photograph of Morton in the newspaper. He was wearing his policeman's uniform, and I realized why I had thought his face was familiar. A few months prior to the operation, I had dropped in some vehicle documents to Bessbrook police station. I recognized Morton as the elderly sergeant who had dealt with me. He had seemed a nice old chap. But I could feel no sadness at his death.

Looking back now, I can see that Morton's death was in fact a sort of turning-point. Although as a planner of death I continued to become more ruthless and efficient over the next two years – almost until my final arrest – psychologically I was at the peak of my resilience and conviction as an IRA man, in the sense that I had still no doubt that what I was doing was right. I thought coldly about Morton's killing; when I reflected on it at all, it was only in terms of a successful operation. I believed

I had rid myself of any remaining psychological tension about what I was doing, and I had achieved this state gradually over the preceding four years by ruthlessly suppressing any doubts. As Morton was buried, I congratulated myself on my hardness: I had embraced the logic of revolutionary necessity and had, so I thought, allowed it to supplant the old values that would have made me question the means I was using to pursue what I regarded as the IRA's justifiable ends. I realize now that in fact that psychological tension had not disappeared, only become more acute and inaccessible, and those doubts had only retreated into a little bunker in my mind. Over the next two years those doubts slowly began to re-emerge, fighting, although first I had to descend into the darkest pit of ruthless amorality.

11

FIFTY/FIFTY

If all of the IRA's planned operations had been successful, then large parts of the north would have been turned into no-go areas for the Crown forces. But from my own experience I would estimate that no more than 50 per cent of our plans worked out as we intended. There were many reasons for the low success rate, including failure of nerve on the part of volunteers, interception by Crown forces, sheer incompetence, betrayal by informers, and simple bad luck.

One failed operation will serve to illustrate all the others.

For a few years, I had been nursing the idea of taking out an Ulster Defence Regiment armoured Land Rover in the Killowen area, near Rostrevor. I had first discussed the idea with Brian before his arrest: we had even driven around the area looking for a suitable culvert in which to place a bomb. The IRA always approached attacks on the UDR with a special enthusiasm and within the wider nationalist (that is, beyond the specifically republican) community, the killing of members of the UDR was always more popular than the killing of policemen. The origins of the UDR lay in the hated B Specials who had been nominally disbanded but effectively re-established in the form of the UDR. We regarded them as a Protestant militia – little more than loyalist paramilitaries in uniform. Indeed, there had been court cases in which UDR members were shown to have colluded with, or become actively involved in, Protestant paramilitary death squads. The sectarian attitude and aggressiveness of many UDR men on the streets meant that even non-republican Catholics hated them and cried no tears when the IRA hit back at them with bullets and bombs. Of course, in one sense, the IRA ought to have been grateful to the UDR because they helped create a large pool of sympathizers for us. Although our most frequent targets were local Protestants in uniform, I saw only the uniform, not the religion. I was strongly opposed to sectarianism, but I rarely reflected on the fact that many on the other side saw only the religion, not the uniform, and so regarded our campaign as sectarian.

So I felt that to take out a UDR patrol around here would hurt the enemy, enhance our reputation among Catholics, and increase our profile in an otherwise quiet area. I knew that the UDR regularly came up from Ballykinlar army base to patrol Annalong and Kilkeel before making their way to Rostrevor and Warrenpoint. In the spring of 1983 I went to call on Joe, who was renovating a house in the area: he was bound to have some knowledge of the movements of these patrols. Joe confirmed some of the rumours I had heard and he said that Saturday night would be the best night to catch a patrol. They appeared to go into Warrenpoint just after eleven, just in time to meet people coming from pubs and clubs.

Joe had a good tactical eye which could spot the most unusual opportunities for attacks, but he had one lethal limitation: a weak stomach. He did not lack courage, but his nerves snapped at crucial moments. I was aware of this and it did not bother me because I never saw the need to push him unnecessarily. I arranged for Joe to meet with Seán in Dundalk to discuss the attack on the UDR patrol. I had warned Seán before about Joe's strengths and weaknesses, and I hoped he would not expect Joe to attempt things he could not do.

I waited for news of the attack, but several weeks passed without incident. Then Seán phoned and asked me to go to Dundalk. He was not happy: he said that Joe had let the unit down. The plan had been for the IRA team to detonate the bomb from across Carlingford Lough in the Republic of Ireland. However, it would be difficult to do this at such a distance in a hilly area. So Seán had asked Joe to meet up with the vehicle further down the road, follow it in his own car, and then contact the bomb team by CB radio as the Land Rover approached the bomb. Seán told me that Joe had failed to make contact on two separate occasions. On the first, a flock of sheep had descended on Seán and the IRA team as they waited for Joe's call. Seán decided to steal a sheep to eat later and, leaving one man by the CB radio, ordered the team to catch a sheep. During the chase, Seán sprained his ankle while the others hurt their backs after falling over rocks. The Irish police added to this night of humiliating farce by arresting the team: the limping volunteers had bumped into a routine patrol as they made their way back to their car. They had been taken to Omeath Garda station where they were held for several hours, during which time they read *Republican News*, harangued the guards, and were eventually released without charge. Joe had given Seán an apparently plausible excuse for his failure to get in contact, so the operation was rearranged for the next weekend. Yet again, Joe failed to use his CB radio. The IRA team had abandoned the operation but on their way back to base they again ran into a Garda patrol. This time the IRA men were in a car: they shot off at speed into the mountains, followed by the police. One of the IRA team fired several shots from an Armalite over the roof of the patrol car, but the police continued the chase. The IRA gunman then aimed a shot directly at the centre of the windscreen and shattered it. The Garda car braked to a halt and reversed down the mountain at speed. The unintended consequence of the gunman's marksmanship was a disturbance to Gerry Adams's holiday: unknown to us, the Sinn Fein leader was on holiday in the Omeath area, close to where the chase occurred. The enraged Irish police decided to raid Adams's holiday cottage in revenge for the loss of their colleagues' windscreen. Adams had not been pleased when Uzi-wielding detectives disrupted his solitude, and the result was that our unit received an order from Belfast to stay clear of the Omeath area: not even a bullet was to be allowed within several miles of Gerry's cottage. We decided to ignore the order, at least until we had blown up this UDR patrol.

Seán asked me to pay a visit to Joe to find out why he had

failed yet again. I sympathized with Joe as soon as he told me what had been expected of him. Seán had wanted him to follow the UDR patrol right up to the point of explosion. Joe said that he could not face the idea of driving through the carnage that would have followed, the disintegrated Land Rover, the burning and mutilated bodies. I was amazed at what Seán had expected him to do. He had foolishly believed that Joe would be steady to the end, despite what I had told him about his limitations.

We realized that the only way to carry out the operation was by detonating the bomb from an elevated position close to the target, but not too close, as the two volunteers would need to be protected from flying shrapnel. I drove to the area to find the ideal position: a scraggy, stony hill adjoining one of the Mourne mountains. The bomb team would have a clear view of the surrounding area and any approaching vehicles; and there was a back route down the hill which would enable them to escape. I asked only one more thing of Joe. I wanted him to help me scout the bomb in when the day came. The bomb team would consist of two volunteers. They would have a motorbike on which they would escape to the safe house a few miles away, once they had detonated the bomb. I would be responsible for getting them out of the safe house and back to Dundalk, once the heat had died down.

We used a hijacked Mitsubishi Colt Lancer in which to place the bomb. The car had been under wraps for some time. The back seat had been taken out and the springs had been strengthened in order to carry up to 1000 pounds of 'co-op mix' explosive. Each hundred pounds of nitrobenzene fertilizer would have a ten pounds charge of high-explosive gelignite. The IRA engineers had found a problem with the radio signal: the receiver was not picking up what the transmitter was sending out. I was asked to buy a whiplash carbon fibre aerial to see if that would sort out the problem. I bought the aerial from a car accessory shop in Newry, and it did the trick. Tests had already been carried out to ensure that the radio signal would be able to penetrate the army's protective radio-wave shield which surrounded every police station, army base, and military vehicle and blocked signals between sophisticated radio

devices. (There was a constant battle of wits between British
Army and IRA specialists. Once an IRA radio-bomb had failed
to detonate, the army could retrieve the weapon and identify
the radio code on the receiver, thus neutralizing all bombs
using the same signal. When this occurred the IRA could
spend more than a year trying to find a new signal which would
break through the shield.)

I was given the job of finding a 'clean' Mitsubishi Colt
Lancer, preferably in the area of the intended detonation, so
that it would not attract suspicion if it was checked out. I
found a suitable car, memorized the registration number, and
then phoned a car accessory store to order the new plates from
an IRA sympathizer. I never met this man; he never saw me. I
gave him the code and he made the plates. Someone else would
pick them up. Once the car had been fitted with the false plates,
the bomb had been packed, and the radio signal had been
checked, everything was ready. The feeling was that there
would be six fewer UDR bigots on the streets once this little
package was delivered. I planned to scout the bomb from
across the border around 5 p.m. on Friday, which was always a
good time to move weaponry – RUC men would be getting
ready for a night out.

I had hoped to get off early from work on the Friday in
order to make the rendezvous with the bomb team, but an
impromptu party was held in the afternoon to celebrate a colleague's promotion, and I did not leave the office until four
thirty. Even then I could not refuse another colleague's request
for a lift down the road to Warrenpoint: he must have wondered why I was driving so fast. I dropped him off and then
drove at breakneck speed to the border. The roads were clear of
checkpoints, but that could have changed by the time we had
returned. I was in a customs car, wearing my uniform, as I
arrived just on time for the rendezvous in a pub car-park on the
southern side of the border. I could not see the bomb team and
I started to feel conspicuous. I decided to park the car in a
side road near the pub, from where I could see the car-park. No
sooner had I parked than one of the team drove past, followed
by another on his Kawasaki motorbike. They must have
assumed I had missed the rendezvous and they were too fired

up to wait. I started up and followed, flashing my lights and honking the horn wildly. They noticed me and pulled in. I turned a corner and headed downhill, just in time to see a Garda sergeant placing a STOP sign in the middle of the road as several Irish Army soldiers jumped out of a jeep. The sergeant looked at me. I smiled and gave him a courtesy salute. He saluted back – a movement which prevented him from stopping the two volunteers who drove past him quickly in my wake. I was grateful for the politeness of the Irish police.

I saw Joe sitting in his parked car as we crossed into the north, and I flashed my headlights at him. I thought he would follow us, positioning himself behind me, but I looked in my rear-view mirror and he was nowhere to be seen. I felt a great sense of relief as we entered the private driveway of the abandoned mansion we were using as a hideout: there was a disused shed in the grounds. A row of magnificent broad-leafed trees in full bloom hid us from view. I left the team to settle themselves down for the night.

The next day was warm and beautiful. I finished work just after four. There was nothing to do now but wait. I went shopping with my wife and child, but I could not take my mind off the operation. It was always like this: I would try to get on with the normal things of life but I would spend my time continually thinking about violent operations. Going for a drink, playing with the kids, visiting the relatives, preparing Sunday lunch, going for a drive in the country, reading the newspapers – I liked to do all these normal things which ordinary people did, but the enjoyment of such normality was impossible. I could pretend, but I could never be relaxed or absorbed by normal activities, because thoughts of the IRA were always at the front of my mind, nagging me, putting me on edge, torturing me with images of what might go wrong. No sooner had one operation passed, than I would move on to the next one and the next one. Usually, I would have several on the go at the same time.

This constant pressure seeped gradually, like a poison-gas, into every corner of my mind. I had come to ditch almost everything and everybody not connected in some way to the IRA. It had become my whole life and I was beginning to ask myself what sort of life I had. I went through the motions of enjoying myself, but how could I live happily when I spent most of my time in the company of people whose business was death? And I was one of them. Always looking for people to kill, finding people to do the killing, constantly exposing myself to danger, more and more danger. There was no respite. Yet I lived life with a weird intensity. I felt myself to be part of a large family whose members had powerful emotional links to each other. The idea of turning my back on the IRA had become as repugnant to me as turning my back on my own children. As soon as I left this intense environment I found myself missing my comrades: the dangers and risks we shared brought us close. We respected each other and in our own eyes we were a few ragged-arsed lads taking on the might of the Orange state. I had become addicted to the struggle: operations became my fix. But I often asked myself: when will my final fix arrive? The one that will kill me, put me in prison, or break me?

I washed and shaved, played with my baby son, and stayed close to the phone. I put my son in his cot and watched him as he lay there asleep. I hoped he would never have to do what I was doing. The clock said 11 p.m. The boys would be moving the bomb into position now. I put on the radio, and waited to hear the news which would surely come within the hour. It was a quiet night. Outside in the street I could hear taxis driving up and down. I looked out the window and watched people dressed up for a Saturday night on the town. I needed to get out for some fresh air so I took a quick walk around the estate. It was peaceful. Two teenagers talked behind the disused garages; a kid kicked a ball up against a fence; a woman stood, arms folded, with slippered feet, talking in whispered tones to her neighbour. This was a normal working-class estate, long-established and respectable; many residents had bought their own houses. A delivery boy walked past me carrying plastic bags smelling of Chinese food.

I went back inside. The clock said eleven-twenty. Still nothing. The bomb should have gone off by now. Maybe the UDR had been late, maybe there was no patrol that night, maybe the bomb had failed to explode, maybe a hundred other things.

Only one thing was certain: by tomorrow I would have to go back to the detonation area and do what needed to be done, regardless of what had happened. I listened to the midnight news. The reports were sketchy and delivered in a staccato style; it was Saturday night so they had not sent any reporters out and were dependent for their information on statements from the Army and police. But there had been an attempt to blow up a patrol of Royal Marine Commandos near Rostrevor. The soldiers had dismounted from their Land Rover to examine a suspicious vehicle when the bomb's detonator exploded. However, the bomb itself had not gone off, and no one was injured. The area had been sealed off and a follow-up search was underway.

Royal Marine Commandos: we had been close to taking out a whole patrol of élite troops! I could do nothing for the moment but wait. Hopefully the motorbike had started and the bomb team had got back to their shed safely. I would pick them up in the morning. It rained heavily all night, torrential summer rain. In the morning I got a coded call from a sympathizer near the safe house. He said 'the big guy' had made it back from 'the mountain weekend', but the other guy had not yet turned up. Their motorbike had failed to start. I felt sick. There was a man lost in the mountains, which were being combed by hundreds of troops. They would have found the abandoned motorbike and knew that the IRA unit had gone to ground in the area. One of the men was originally from the area, so he had been able to find a way through, but the young man on the run came from Belfast. I would have to wait until they stopped searching. That night I got another call from the local sympathizer. He wanted me to get the volunteer who had escaped out. He told me that the troops had now narrowed their concentric search pattern to a smaller ring and had left the Rostrevor area to concentrate directly on the mountain and Killowen. This was good news: I thought it meant that the search would end soon. I said I would pick up our man early in the morning, but for safety I left him there another day. All this time it rained steadily. I feared for the man hiding out on the mountain: there was no news on the radio that the army had caught anyone, but I wondered how he could survive in such conditions.

Early on Tuesday morning, at around six, I drove towards Rostrevor. The rain seemed to have washed everything clean. I drove up to the mansion. The house to the left had red ivy growing up its grey walls; the magnificent landscaped lawns were dotted with wrought-iron summer seats, painted white. It would have been a perfect setting for a 1930s English upper-class murder drama. Just as I stopped near the shed a bedraggled figure stepped out from behind the old granite archway nearby. He walked towards me wearing an olive-green combat jacket. He carried a Beretta submachine-gun held on his shoulder by a khaki strap. A black woollen hat covered most of his gingery-blond hair; he had a moustache with the thick stubble of three days' growth.

I told him to get in the car and lie down on the floor in the back. He said that he would use the Beretta if we were stopped by the police. I drove him to my house in Newry, made him breakfast and we discussed the events of the last few days. He said that at first everything had seemed to go as planned. The ASU had retired to the firing position up the hill along with the bike. He said he could hardly believe his luck when two armoured Land Rovers came along and stopped close to the bomb car. Around a dozen soldiers had got out and were swarming around the vehicle when they sent the radio signal to detonate the bomb. There had been a bang which had merely rocked the car; a fire had started which sent up a cloud of smoke. The soldiers dived to the ground immediately, but several of them had got a grip on themselves within seconds and rushed across the road. Then they raced up the hill towards what they had correctly identified as the firing point. They would have heard the coughing and spluttering of the motorbike as it failed to start. They would also have heard the sound of the two men running for their lives through the bracken, expecting to be shot dead at any moment. After a short distance my breakfast guest had run out of breath and stopped. He was a smoker. He told his comrade to save himself; and told him in which direction to run. When he had got his breath back he staggered through a forested area until he eventually arrived at the hideout shed, where he had collapsed, exhausted, breathless and in shock.

I left him at the house and went to work. I kept thinking of the lad from Belfast still lost in mountainous terrain. I could not even be sure that he was still alive: he had been without food and exposed to the elements for several days. At lunchtime I drove into the area to look for him. There were no checkpoints. I scanned fields to the left and right of me, but there was no sign of him. That evening I drove the first man to Dundalk. When I returned home that night I got a call from the wary local informant near Rostrevor. He said that my 'wee friend' had turned up. I felt a tremendous sense of relief. I asked the contact whether he would be able to drive the wee friend to Newry, but he refused point blank. He had already done far more than he had bargained for. Disappointed and annoyed, I decided to make the pick-up myself that night. I found the Belfast man looking remarkably well, considering his experience. I drove him down to my house and we discussed his adventure over a cup of tea. He said that when the bike had refused to start, they had been able to hear the Marines panting as they fanned out and ran up the hill. He did not realize that he was running in a circle and had started to panic. He had actually managed to run the complete circumference of the mountain – a good run by the standards of any athlete. It had taken him several hours, and several times he almost ran into groups of soldiers. He said he had almost died of shock when he found himself back at the firing point. He was able to watch the disposal teams working on the bomb on the road below. Once again he heard soldiers approaching him so he had crawled into a thorny thicket where he had crouched down, hardly daring to move or breathe. Very slowly he had managed to pull the Browning from his coat pocket and, with a fear exaggerated by the slightest sound, he had cocked the weapon fully – which took him a long time. He said that the soldiers were so close that he could have reached out and touched them. He had the pistol in one hand and a grenade in the other: he was prepared to fight his way out because he felt that surrender would have meant summary execution.

He sat in that thicket in the pouring rain for a night and a day. Eventually the soldiers eased off and left the area, but they had maintained checkpoints on the road. Hunger eventually made him leave the thicket. He managed to move from the thickly-forested area to the back entrances of some beautiful summer houses owned by wealthy people from the city. One house seemed to be unoccupied; he spent the night in an old potting-shed. The next day he buried the Browning, grenades and his combat jacket in a rockery. The roads now seemed clear and he made his way to the safe house.

I got him back to Dundalk safely. Then the next day, using his description, I found the rockery of the house where he had buried the weapons and I took them back to base. We had come close to bringing off an attack which would have gone down in the history of the IRA's campaign as one of the most significant strikes against the British Army.

The failure of this attack on the Royal Marines in May 1983 marked the start of a period of almost a year in which none of our bombs worked. Over the course of that year we must have planted at least a dozen bombs in and around Newry, but they all failed to explode. The IRA's engineers would repeatedly test every aspect of the devices before they were sent in – the batteries, the wires, the timers, the detonators, the explosives – but still nothing would go off. Declan said to me at one point: 'Jesus, what the fuck's going on? Newry should be a car-park by now.' Once the engineers decided that there was nothing wrong with the bombs, the IRA began to suspect that there was a British agent in our ranks who was tampering with them. Everyone became a suspect, and various ruses were used to try to smoke him out. Everyone in turn found themselves not being included in certain operations to see what would happen in their absence. Only the trusted of the trusted would be sent on bombing missions. Volunteers from south Armagh were used to plant some of the bombs: twice they tried a new device encased in steel which they put into little two-wheel shopping trolleys. Then female volunteers placed the trolleys in a supermarket. But still the bombs failed to explode. The IRA concluded that the army's bomb disposal people must have developed an effective new way of neutralizing bombs very quickly. It was suspected that the IRA's standard twenty-minute warning was giving the Brits enough time to chemically 'freeze' the bombs, which they would then dismantle later. We had a healthy respect for their ingenuity. So the IRA's engineers changed all the bombs' timers and detonators; they also put on new anti-handling devices; then the volunteers on the ground started cutting back on the length of warning time given to clear an area.

Finally the bombs started to explode as planned.

12

STRANGE TIMES

By the summer of 1983, I had become a person who could, with barely a flicker of disquiet, contemplate the killing of any enemy of the republican movement. Even now I can hardly comprehend the mental state I was in.

I had insulated myself so well from feelings of compassion that the doubts that were eventually to undermine my confidence in the rightness of our campaign first surfaced in response to fears for my own safety, and not as a result of stabs of conscience.

Seán had taken over as OC of the area after the previous incumbent's disgrace. He soon became the best OC, from the IRA's viewpoint, that the area had ever had. I admired the fact that he would never ask anyone to do anything that he would not do himself. In this respect, at least, he was an exemplary soldier; but his conduct in his personal life led to a court martial – and his ignominious expulsion from the IRA.

In the nationalist community, in republican circles anyway, IRA men have considerable status, and for those Provos who look for sexual advantages from it, there is no shortage of women willing to give more than the time of day to IRA volunteers. Seán, although married, started playing around. I thought badly of him for this. Commanders were expected to display exemplary behaviour in both their professional and personal lives. There were, in any case, simple pragmatic reasons why IRA leaders had to try to be purer than pure: illicit affairs caused anger among local people, among our supporters but also among those who perhaps might come over to us. Mickey and Hardbap annoyed me by seeming to encourage Seán's flings. I warned them that Seán might jeopardize the position of the whole unit; at the very least, he himself might end up being compromised.

Rarely a weekend passed in Dundalk without some sort of party for republicans. There were many Belfast families living in the area. They all knew each other and sought solace and support from each other. One summer's day, some of them held a party which turned into a fairly raucous affair. It had started as an afternoon barbecue but it went on into the evening and then well into the night. Seán was there, drinking heavily. When he got pretty full he tended to withdraw for a few hours to sleep off the effects. He went into the living-room and lay down on the sofa, dozing. Soon afterwards, an attractive married woman who had been taking tranquillizers for a nervous condition, was helped by her friends into the room. She was obviously feeling the effects of the booze and the tablets. Seán woke up and saw the woman on the floor, close to him.

What happened next led to Seán being accused of rape. He was brought before an IRA court, which heard two versions of what had taken place. The woman claimed that Seán had pounced on her while she was sleeping: he had forced himself upon her, and when her friends – who knew she had been drinking and wanted to check that she was all right – had come back into the room in the middle of the act, she had screamed for assistance. Seán had a different story. He said that the woman had flirted with him and made plain her willingness to have sex. The woman's angry husband had demanded justice and threatened to kill Seán himself if the IRA did not discipline him. A court martial was convened. The IRA believed the woman's story and, despite Seán's record, they dismissed him in disgrace.

Ironically, Seán would probably have had a better chance of acquittal if he had been tried in a British court. Instead, he had faced trial by his peers, who included such paragons of virtue

as Hardbap. Whatever the truth of the charge – and such was
my respect for Seán as an IRA man I could not disbelieve
him – in military terms, the removal of Seán was a disaster.

As I thought of Seán in exile in Dublin, I remembered an
incident from a few months previously, when he had shown
that strange combination of ruthlessness and decency which
marked him out. At that time, before the latest series of
killings, there was still a tiny space in my heart for compassion
towards my enemies. I had witnessed the birth of my first
child at Daisy Hill Hospital, an extraordinary and breath-
taking experience which had filled me with love and admiration
for my wife. Bernie had been determined to ensure that the
birth was as natural as possible, so she had refused pain-killing
medication. During the week she spent in hospital before and
after the birth, Seán had contacted me with information about
a part-time UDR sergeant whose wife was apparently then
giving birth in the same hospital. His name was Ferguson.
According to Seán, he drove a yellow Mark 3 Ford Cortina
Estate. I did not like the idea of killing a man while his wife
was having a child. I told Seán about my reservations. He
assured me that the man would not be killed anywhere near the
hospital, but he insisted I take advantage of my visits to Bernie
in order to confirm and clarify the intelligence about Ferguson.
That night, as I drove into the hospital car-park I saw
Ferguson's car. I went in to visit my wife. She had already
given birth and was convalescing. She had made friends with
the woman in the bed opposite: an older woman who had just
given birth to her sixth child. My wife told me that this woman
had been very kind and supportive to her: 'She's a lovely
woman, that Mrs Ferguson.' I looked over at Mrs Ferguson
and smiled. Her husband was sitting by her bed, a heavy,
broad-shouldered man who looked more like a ruddy-faced
farmer than a soldier. His lank silver hair was brushed to the
side. Protestants did not normally have large families, but
the Fergusons were from Kilkeel, where they did things
differently. I remembered that the UDR in Kilkeel had a particularly bad reputation with the local Catholic population. I
told my wife that Mr Ferguson was in the UDR. She told me
that she already knew: Mrs Ferguson had confided in her. I

told Bernie that Seán had asked me to set him up for assassination. My wife went pale and said: 'You can't do that. You
can't deprive this woman of her husband. She's just had a
baby. How will she take care of her baby? She'll be too distraught to do anything. You mustn't do it.' I remembered the
image of my own son being born, and I realized that I could
not face having Ferguson shot. The thought of Mrs Ferguson
in the ward, going into convulsions with her grief at the death
of her husband, frightened me. But, on top of my own reservations, my wife made me promise that I would not set him up.
Yet that night, as I walked back through the car-park, I experienced temptation. Ferguson was a gift: we could have killed
him easily with a bomb under his car. Even shooting him
would not require much effort: a two-man team, perhaps. But
I thought once again of his good wife, that homely woman
who had been so kind to my young wife. I decided that I would
have no part in any operation against Ferguson. On my next
visit to the hospital, I arrived in time to see the Fergusons
leaving. Mrs Ferguson had been discharged. Bernie and I
waved goodbye to the couple as they left the ward, with Mrs
Ferguson leading the way, full of life and motherly enthusiasm.
I watched from the window as they got into their car. I noticed
that Ferguson did not even bother checking under it. What a
foolish man. He had carried his wife's belongings as she had
carried the new-born baby. I thought, 'Good luck to them
both.' I met Seán that weekend to discuss a number of operations. After we had exhausted all the other items on the agenda,
Seán asked me about Ferguson. I told him that the opportunity
to kill him had gone: his wife had left the hospital. I said it
would have been easy to hit him, with either bomb or bullet,
but I told Seán that I had decided not to pursue the operation.
Seán did not castigate me or make an issue out of my scruples.
He just shrugged his shoulders and changed the subject.

An even greater blow than Seán's disgrace was Hardbap's
appointment as OC. By now I had worked with him on several
operations; he had distinguished himself only by his ineptitude. When he was merely one volunteer among many, I could
tolerate his continued existence in our unit. Yet now he
was supposed to be a leader. By the autumn of 1983 a new

recklessness and sloppiness had entered the South Down
Command: people who should never have been recruited or
whose usefulness was questionable were being included in IRA
schemes. An operation designed to wipe out an army foot
patrol in the village of Bessbrook brought home to me how
incompetent we could be.

I had long cherished the ambition of bringing mayhem to
Bessbrook. The village was little more than a huge military
base containing the busiest heliport in Europe, as well as a home
for the SAS. The SAS captain, Robert Nairac, had operated out
of here before his death. I thought it was incredible that the
IRA had never made a sustained attack on the barracks in the
way they had launched continuous attacks on the barracks at
Crossmaglen. I wanted to change life in Bessbrook just as I had
helped bring terror to Newry, Warrenpoint and Rostrevor.

Perhaps one of the reasons why the IRA had left Bessbrook
relatively unscathed was because there was a question mark
over which unit had responsibility for the area. In the past, the
South Armagh Brigade had tended to carry out attacks there.
But the South Down Command had in recent years expanded
its role and was now carrying out operations in areas which
were not strictly within its geographical demarcation lines.
These demarcations struck me as irrelevant, but I recommended an approach to south Armagh to tell them we were
planning an attack. Indeed, I wanted them to help us.

My job in the customs gave me opportunities to drive
around Bessbrook inconspicuously. I had spotted unmarked
Sherpa vans leaving the barracks containing soldiers in plain
clothes, obviously involved in covert SAS operations. My dear-
est ambition at this time was to wipe out an SAS unit in transit
to or from a covert mission. I would try to get out at night in
the customs patrol car as often as possible. When on patrol I
would try to stop vans, particularly Sherpa vans, whenever I
found them, especially if they were driving through back roads
in quiet country areas. One time, late at night, I gave chase to
a van; I followed it for miles through country roads, flashing
my lights to get it to stop. Finally, the van pulled to a halt. I got
out and walked to the driver's window. The driver's face was
tense: I could tell that the adrenaline of fear had been pumping

through him. He had turned towards me in a way which indicated that he had a gun in his hand below the window, pointing straight at me. I suspected that there were probably another five rifles pointed at me in the back of the van. I asked him for identification. He said: 'Military' and showed me his army ID card. I said: 'Oh, sorry for stopping you. Have a nice night.' After that incident the army made a complaint to the Customs and Excise and a memo came round saying: 'Could all customs officers please ensure that they wear their hats when stopping vans at night.'

I scoured the area for potential targets, but it was Francie who finally spotted a good opportunity for an attack on Bessbrook. One day he had gone into the village on his rounds to work on a house near the main street. From a back bedroom he had been able to watch patrols of soldiers regularly leaving the military barracks to walk up the street to the old police station. The house offered a good view of the area. Francie noticed that the soldiers always passed a particular telegraph pole on their way to the police station. A radio-controlled bomb could be detonated from the window, despite the fact that the pole was some distance away. There were no obstacles between the window and the pole to interrupt the radio signal. I hoped that South Armagh Brigade could provide the necessary technology.

In fact, they had not been having much success with their radio-controlled bombs of late. The Brits had managed to capture a radio-controlled device left on a tractor and, as a result, they had been able to identify the IRA's new code, which had been designed to break through the army's protective technological umbrella. Thus the army had been able to strengthen even further their protective shield. However, after months of hard work, the IRA had come up with a new radio signal that could break through the army's protective shield and set off a bomb. Now the South Armagh Brigade were offering us this new device for the Bessbrook operation.

On the day chosen for the operation, I was to use my car to scout in a blue van containing two volunteers whose job would be to take over the surveillance house. These would be the button men who would detonate the bomb. Once the bomb had gone off, they were to sit tight until it was safe for someone to go in to scout them out. Hardbap was arranging for someone else to place the bomb near the telegraph pole, which also happened to be near a small Presbyterian church. I did not know who was going to drive the vehicle with the bomb. All I knew was that he would be driving a silver-coloured Ford Escort. Someone else was acting as scout for the bomb driver, who would be driven out of the area in the scout's car as soon as he had parked the bomb. He would then be taken to my house and I would be responsible for getting him back to Dundalk. We knew what time the bomb was due to arrive in Bessbrook, and I planned to lead the button men to the target house some fifteen minutes later.

The bomb had already been primed in south Armagh, so the driver did not have to do anything to it, apart from pick it up from the arms dump. The bomb was in a two-foot bullet-shaped cylinder, resembling a torpedo. It contained around thirty pounds of explosives with another thirty pounds of sharp, jagged shrapnel, including nails, bolts and the scrap ends of steel and iron.

I drove into south Armagh, around four miles from Crossmaglen, to meet up with the button men in the blue van. I waited outside a village pub and in a few minutes the van arrived, flashed its lights at me, and we drove off. I had been told by the south Armagh unit that along the route I would pass people at various points who would give me the 'all clear' signal. I was pleasantly shocked by the number of people waving us on, flashing their lights, and saluting us throughout the whole ten-mile journey. There were people digging at the side of roads, people cutting bushes, people parked in cars at crossroads: I did not know any of these people, but they obviously recognized my car.

It was astonishing to observe at least five or six local people – farmers, labourers – turning out to ensure that no threat was posed to us along the route. It was the most impressive sight I had ever seen, one which I was never to see again. It was little wonder that south Armagh was an area apart. The IRA's success was built on the support of many ordinary people weighing in behind the IRA's volunteers.

The van with the button man arrived safely in Bessbrook, and I left the men to get on with taking over the house. I drove home, had my lunch and changed into my customs uniform for work. Before I left the house there was a knock on the door. I opened it and was faced by a tall young man, perhaps in his late teens, wearing a combat jacket. This was the bomb driver. I let him in and he told me his name. I was a little unnerved to hear his English accent. There was something a little strange about him: he did not seem to be quite all there, but I put this down to nerves. After all, he was very young, and this job was obviously one of his first. I wondered why Hardbap had chosen such an obvious novice for such an important job. I was also a little worried by his green combat jacket. IRA volunteers operating in rural areas, wanting to blend in with the hedges, fields and trees, could wear such jackets, but they were not the gear for towns and villages. You had to blend in with the local population: you had to look like a mechanic, or a postman, or a bank clerk, not Fidel Castro. Again, I put it down to his inexperience. I left the ruddy-faced young Fidel sitting uncomfortably on my settee as I went to work. I told him that I would take him to Dundalk later.

Since 1978, my work at the customs had become an extension of my work for the IRA. My colleagues knew I was a republican and some of them now suspected that I was associated with the IRA. But it was one thing to suspect someone, and quite another to be sure. So long as my colleagues could not confirm definitely that I was involved in the IRA, their minds were full of uncertainty and doubt. I tried to ensure that I maintained the uncertainty in their minds. In particular, I was careful about what I said. I followed the old maxim: 'Nobody knows anything apart from what you tell them yourself.'

Later on in the afternoon, I took a break and went home. There was a strange car outside my house. I walked into the living-room to find the man who had driven the van into Bessbrook talking to Fidel. I knew something had gone wrong. 'What are you doing here?' I asked. He said: 'We took over the wrong house. We can't see the bomb car from the back room. The car outside belongs to the woman of the house we've taken over. She lent it to me to come here. They're very friendly, very sympathetic.' He said he had left the other button man behind at the house, along with the van. I told him to go back and take over the right house. The people in the wrong house were clearly not going to shop him: they were obviously sympathizers. This he refused to do. Before I had the chance to do much about it he had called a senior IRA man, Brendan Burns, on the phone. I picked up the phone and spoke to Burns, who was the IRA's most experienced bomb maker. (Burns was to die, blown up by his own explosives, near Crossmaglen in February 1988.) He instructed me to send in Fidel to retrieve the bomb. He said that the device must not under any circumstances be allowed to fall into the hands of the Brits, otherwise they would crack the new code, ruling out sophisticated IRA operations for at least another year. By now the bomb had been sitting outside the church for almost three hours. Burns insisted that we abandon the operation: he reiterated that he wanted me to send in young Fidel to retrieve the bomb and bring it back to south Armagh.

I asked Fidel if he had the car's ignition keys. He said no: the car had been started by crossing two wires where the ignition switch had been ripped out. I told him that he might have to go in and drive the bomb out. Fidel said: 'No, I don't want to. The only thing I was asked to do was to drive the car in. I'm not prepared to do any more.' I was amazed at his reply, but I put it down to nerves. I said to him: 'Look, you are an IRA volunteer, and operations don't necessarily stop at one stage. You have got to be able to react to a change in circumstances.'

'But I'm not an IRA volunteer,' said Fidel. I went silent. Fidel said again: 'I'm not an IRA volunteer.' I looked at him and thought, 'What the fuck is going on here? This must be someone's idea of a bad joke.' I turned to the other man and beckoned him out into the hallway. I said: 'Who or what is this guy, and how did he get into this?' He explained that IRA men regularly drank in a pub that Fidel frequented in Dundalk. Fidel's family had lived in England for years (explaining Fidel's English accent), but had returned to Dundalk. Young Fidel had seen IRA men in and about the pub and had spent many hours listening to their wondrous tales of guerrilla warfare.

Fidel who, to put it politely, was not exactly an intellectual, had started pestering our new OC to give him a gun: he wanted to get into the thick of things; he wanted to play cowboys and indians too. I asked the van driver why Fidel had not been put through the normal recruitment procedures like everyone else. The reply was blunt: 'Because he's a fucking nut. He's over the top. He's completely crazy.' At the arms dump, when he'd gone to collect the bomb, he had told these masked south Armagh men that he'd seen an IRA man who'd been shot in the face six times with a Browning Automatic and had survived. Then he had started showing them the Browning he was carrying.

The embarrassed volunteer explained that our OC was stuck. He needed someone to drive the car in, and Fidel had agreed to do it if Hardbap gave him a gun. So Hardbap gave him the gun.

I walked back into the living-room and asked Fidel for his gun. He gave me his look of crazed innocence. He looked hurt and upset: I was taking away his toy. I gave the gun to the real volunteer and told him to keep it on him, to make sure that it was not cocked and that its safety-catch was on, but most importantly to keep it out of Fidel's sight. I told the IRA volunteer to come with me back to Bessbrook: we were going to see if we could find another detonation point. I drove through Bessbrook, past the bomb car, and noticed that there were two policemen sitting in an armour-plated car only sixty yards from the bomb. My first thought was that they were treating the vehicle as suspicious and were keeping an eye on it. I drove out of Bessbrook, but drove back an hour later. The police were still there. I got Francie and Teddy – another former Irp who had come into the IRA after I had recruited his friends – to check the car alternately at half-hour intervals. The police stayed where they were. I informed Burns about what was happening, but he seemed to think that the police presence was irrelevant. He claimed that several of his contacts had been sent in to the area and they had not seen anything suspicious. He insisted again that I send Fidel back in to retrieve the bomb. I approached the young fellow again and explained the situation. He did not like the idea, and I did not blame him: he might have been crazy, but he could see the risks involved. Yet now I had my orders. I told Fidel that it did not matter that he was not an IRA volunteer. He was not known to the police, and he could hot-wire the car and bring it out safely.

Then I had another idea. I rang Burns again and asked him if he would be satisfied if we merely blew up the device to ensure that it did not fall into enemy hands. He said he would be. I decided that I could now dispense with Fidel's services and arranged for him to be taken back to Dundalk, along with the other button man who had stayed in the wrong house, being fêted by the occupants, throughout this miserable saga.

Later on that night, we detonated the bomb from a safe distance, once we had established that there were no civilians around. After the operation, I had a chance to examine the radio transmitter which had sent the signal to the bomb. It was a small, gold-coloured, oblong box, about eight inches by four inches. On the top there were three switches, like household light switches, and three lights – one green and two red. The middle switch lit up the green light: this would turn on the bomb. The other two switches, which lit up the red lights, had to be flicked at the same time in order to detonate the bomb. This oblong box was connected by a wire to another device which had an aerial from which the radio signal was sent. It looked very finished, very professional.

People in Bessbrook had been in bed, or preparing for bed, when we detonated the bomb. No one was injured, although a few people did suffer shock. The two cops in the patrol car must have got a bit of a shock. The roof and front of the church were badly damaged, which I was sorry to see. This was interpreted as a sectarian act, but the damage was unintentional. In my mind we were committed to fighting a non-sectarian military campaign based on principles developed by one of our founding fathers, the Protestant Wolfe Tone, during the 1798 rebellion. It had not yet impinged on my mind that non-sectarian intentions can have very strange effects. I felt that, by not ordering Fidel to retrieve the bomb, I had probably saved his life. I hoped I would never meet him again. But to my horror the IRA began to use Fidel on other operations. A sense of impending disaster hung over him like a shroud.

At first I tried to stifle my doubts about Hardbap. I just got on with the job, but he kept setting up dangerous and sloppy operations. I began to think that there was only one certainty about my future: I would end up dead or in prison, as probably would most of the unit, save for Hardbap himself, who no longer went on operations, preferring instead to choreograph his dance of incompetence from the safety of Dundalk.

In the meantime, on 25 September 1983, thirty-eight IRA prisoners broke out of the Maze in the biggest escape in the history of British prisons. Their coup was a tremendous boost for the whole republican movement, and our unit took a keen interest in it. We knew that several of the men had made it to rural parts and were hiding, half-starved, in ditches and bogs, frightened to approach local people in case they were not sympathetic. I tried to go out on patrol in the customs car as often as possible, hoping that I might catch sight of an escapee. Then I heard that two of them had made it to the Rostrevor area. They were hiding out in the house of a family with republican sympathies. We heard that some members of the family were complaining openly to their non-republican friends about the length of time the escapees were staying in their house. Our absentee OC arranged for an IRA team to go and pick up the escapees and take them to a safe house in Newry. However, the wife of a now-disgraced republican stalwart spotted the team, with the escapers, on their way to the safe house. This woman, who was drunk, had been thrown out of Sinn Fein after some money for the H-Block campaign went missing. Not only did she follow the team to the safe house but she followed them in. The IRA team could only stand openmouthed as she pushed her way through the door, introduced herself to the escapees, and congratulated them heartily on their success. After the team had expressed less than wholehearted delight at her grand entrance, she went to the Dundalk home of a senior IRA commander and told him how she had managed to 'save' two escapees. The IRA man got her to tell him the address of the safe house and – presumably thinking that the South Down Command could not be entrusted with the care of a library book, let alone the safety of escapees – got word to the IRA's élite south Armagh unit which promptly sent down a team of their volunteers to 'rescue' the escapees. These men, armed to the teeth with machine-guns, assault rifles, grenades and rocket launchers, arrived at the Newry safe house and took charge of the escapees. The Newry team had not even had the sense to move them immediately after their security had been compromised. This pantomime represented the nadir of the local unit.

A virus of incompetence had taken a grip on our unit. I was consumed with a feeling of impending doom. There was fear, yes, but also something deeper. For the first time in my IRA career I began to ask myself not only whether I personally should continue to be a member of the IRA, but also whether the armed struggle itself was worth continuing. Should cowards, opportunists and half-wits have the right to decide who should live or die in the cause of Irish freedom? I began to ask myself how such an organization could ever take power, set up an alternative government structure, and win the hearts of the people. If all we had to offer was bumbling thuggishness and occasional military effectiveness, and if we could only attract the naïve or the brutal, how could we appeal to the mass of Irish people in the late twentieth century?

In those first months of doubt, I stilled the implications of my thoughts by remembering the words and actions of the ten dead hunger strikers. Men like Bobby Sands and my school-friend Raymond McCreesh. However, even on my most optimistic days, I could not ignore the signs of the incipient collapse of the South Down Command: we were beginning to sustain weird personalities, not a movement. Even looking beyond my own unit, I felt that although the movement bequeathed to us by the hunger strikers would sustain itself for some time yet, it was no longer a true revolutionary movement. Of course, I was still judging it at least partly by the ultra-Leninist standards I had absorbed in Belfast, but when I observed the electoral antics of Sinn Fein I became depressed. The republican movement seemed to be turning itself into an institution made up of élite groups posturing for power. I tried to stop myself dwelling on these negative thoughts: I felt as if I had no choice but to continue. I was impelled forward by the dynamics of the choice I had made some years before. It was as

if I had boarded a fast train without brakes; I knew it was
going to hit the crash barriers at some point, but I could not
get off and, if I did not think too deeply about my predicament, I could continue at times to revel in the insane rush of
the journey.

The IRA had become my life. I lived and breathed it. I
could see that we seemed to be a million miles from our goal of
a united Irish socialist republic, yet we had fought the British
almost to a standstill. The erection of border forts and permanent checkpoints left in tatters the British claims of
'normalization'. Then more doubts: the British might have
failed, but so had we. I had always known that the IRA could
only win the war if the people in the Republic of Ireland
became involved in the struggle. I realised that if the hunger
strike had failed to secure this kind of mass mobilization in the
south, which was obviously the case, then nothing was likely to
secure it. However, the fact that I was starting to acknowledge
that we could never hope for the victory to which we aspired
did not mean that I wanted to abandon the campaign immediately. I oscillated wildly. I felt there were still many gains which
could be achieved by political violence. Yet on bad days I
would be overcome with a sense of the futility of our campaign. Logic, when I allowed myself to use it, told me that we
could never win. But my emotional wishful thinking about the
IRA usually overrode my logic, and kept me on the moving
train.

I trained another young recruit. We let off two blast incendiaries in Newry town. Yet even as I continued to create new
candidates for disaster, my sense of the futility of what I was
doing began to grow. My negative thoughts were certainly first
engendered by Hardbap's elevation and his vicious incompetence, but they deepened for other reasons too. I was seriously
alarmed by my cousin Mickey's degeneration. He seemed to
have lost any sense of the wider perspective, and was just
obsessively absorbed by the details of the next killing. He
hadn't the slightest interest in a long-term strategy for victory.
He was hardly alone in this regard – and that was the problem:
no one seemed to be coming up with any clear analyses of
where the movement was going and what the next step should

be. I knew it was not enough to be sustained by the actions of the hunger strikers. Of course we had benefitted from their deaths, but the response of the IRA, particularly in Belfast, indicated to me a frightening level of confusion. Listening to people slavishly parroting every platitude which fell from the lips of Gerry Adams or Danny Morrison did not inspire me with confidence. The hunger strikers had helped to generate widespread electoral support. Momentarily (by which I mean an historical moment of several years) they had created a strong political base which gave the republican movement credibility and legitimacy in the eyes of the world. Not since the early days of the present phase of the conflict had such a mass movement been mobilized. Yet our leadership clearly did not know how to respond to it.

To me the clearest evidence of this paucity of understanding was the widely-reported declaration of Danny Morrison about how the republican movement would take power in Ireland with an Armalite in one hand and a ballot box in the other. This was supposedly the new beginning. Morrison was right to think of it as a new beginning: it was the beginning of the end of the armed struggle. Despite all the rhetoric, and the continuing violence, the political wing of the republican movement was in the ascendant – the very development that my mentor in the Revolutionary Communist Group had warned against years ago. There could, logically, be no marriage of democratic politics and armed struggle. Part of me could accept these political developments, but I also just wanted the leadership to be honest with the foot-soldiers about the future of the campaign.

These larger doubts would then be buttressed by my encounters with Hardbap. Every time I looked at him I began to feel I was looking at the face of defeat. Yet I could not follow through the implications of my doubts: I could not leave the IRA. Even though I was coming to realize the futility of our campaign, I devoted myself to planning operation after operation with a ruthless determination – the sort of determination possessed only by those trying to distance themselves from reality. And emotionally I was dead to the moral consequences of what we were doing – the enormous anger of revolutionary violence now detached from any political strategy.

I found that I wanted to spend more time with my young son. Life, in the shape of this child, became more and more of a contrast to our obsession with death. A serious conflict began to develop between the demands of maintaining some sort of family, keeping my job in the customs, and being on call twenty-four hours a day for the IRA. I could no longer sleep properly at night.

I realize now that the foundations of my future collapse had been firmly laid.

13

HARDENED TO DEATH

Even while I was in this contradictory and unstable state, something happened which sent a surge of excitement through me. I was standing on a street corner in Newry when a green Chrysler Alpine drove past. I looked at the driver: it was Detective Cunningham, the cop with nine lives, the man whom I had sworn to kill in revenge for Brian's imprisonment. I was sure it was him. I would have recognized his face and build anywhere. But he had a new car. I memorized the registration number.

I saw the car again, and again – each time close to an RUC station, once at Bessbrook, once at Warrenpoint. One time I even saw it inside the barrier of Newry RUC Barracks. Then I had the sighting which I thought would seal Cunningham's fate: I saw his car outside Hughes's betting-shop in Monaghan Street, Newry. I decided to concentrate my attention on the betting-shop. I checked the newspapers for details of important racing events. Any spare moment I got, I would wait outside Hughes's. Cunningham did not disappoint me. He turned up regularly for his little flutter.

In the meantime, I had told Hardbap about Cunningham. He asked me whether I was sure that this man was in the RUC. I said: 'Of course I'm sure. What do you think he's doing in RUC stations? Putting up lightbulbs?' I was so sure of his identity that I did not even bother checking out his car registration on the vehicle computer at work. We decided to shoot Detective Cunningham at the betting-shop the next week. This was such an important operation for us that I decided to take a week's sick leave in order to complete the planning.

My cousin Mickey was going to use his favourite Browning Automatic to carry out the hit. Another volunteer would provide back-up with a Kalashnikov AK-47, while another would be waiting to drive them away. The getaway car would rendezvous with my car and I would drive Mickey and the other gunman back to my house. The getaway driver would then dump the car on a nearby housing estate and I would go and pick him up as well. I would also have the job of establishing that Cunningham was actually at the betting-shop.

On the day of the operation, Mickey found that the Browning was jamming. It was too late to get another weapon, so I told Mickey that he would have to go for one head shot. If an emergency arose, then Mickey's back-up would have to use the AK-47. Throughout the morning I travelled down to the betting-shop at fifteen-minute intervals in order to spot Cunningham's car. But he was not there. I began to feel that he might have escaped our form of justice once again, but I told myself to be patient. The newspapers showed there were several big race meetings after two o'clock. I cooked lunch for the team, and I left the house again at five past two. I drove to the betting-shop, and there was Cunningham's car.

I spun the car around and drove back. I hurried the team out of the house. The idea was that they would wait in their car in a street close to the bookies while I drove past one last time to check that Cunningham was still inside. If he was, I would scratch my head as I drove by. The car was indeed still there. I kept on driving, then I scratched my head, and I saw the team move off.

A few minutes later their car screeched to a halt beside mine, and Mickey and the other gunman jumped in. The other car raced off. I looked over and saw that a group of young boys had been watching as the switch-over was made. I stared at them. They stared back. They were young but they were not stupid: I knew they understood what they had just seen. I drove off as fast as I could and dropped off my passengers close to my

house. Then I went a different route to pick up the getaway
driver. Unfortunately he had parked right beside a bread-van
from which the driver was serving a customer. The getaway
driver came running towards me. The two men at the bread-
van looked at us; they were still looking as I drove off. We had
been seen clearly by two groups of people. The getaway car
would be found; the army would blow it up for fear of booby
traps, and people's memories would be jogged. I dropped the
getaway driver at another location and drove back to Newry. I
was surprised to find a long tail-back of traffic as I entered the
town. The tail-back was caused by the army stopping cars. So
the RUC were admitting that Newry could no longer be controlled solely by them: they needed the Brits to back them up.
The army's presence was an indication that Newry had become
a black area, a dangerous area where the Queen's writ did not
run. It was a moment of bleak satisfaction. A soldier checked
my licence and I was let through.

Later that day we listened to the radio news about the killing
at Hughes's betting shop: Mickey had shot dead an innocent
Catholic called Sean McShane. I had identified the wrong
man.

The news shocked Mickey deeply. The man had been standing at the counter, filling out a docket; Mickey had walked up
to him and put the gun to his head and pulled the trigger. Now
he put his head in his hands: 'We've killed an innocent man.
For fuck's sake, Eamon, how did you target him? I've shot an
innocent man.' He continued these recriminations for some
time, until I got tired of his whining and moaning. He had not
been so worried about Hanna, the alleged UDR man whom he
had shot dead in front of his wife and child. Had Mickey
beaten his breast in sorrow when we had found out that Hanna
had left the UDR six years before? Had Hanna's previous
UDR career made his death a more justifiable mistake? Did the
fact that Hanna was a Protestant make his death more acceptable? Did the fact that McShane was a Catholic make his death
more reprehensible? I had grown sick of such hypocrisy.

McShane was dead and, on that day in October 1983, I
could not have cared less. I felt numb, as if I had lost the capacity for feeling. I think that even if the whole crowd in Hughes's

had been wiped out I would not have cared. I looked at these IRA men as they sat down for their meal. Mickey was silent. I had two things on my mind: my Open University exams next week, and the Active Service Unit in my living-room. I felt uneasy about the people who had seen us that afternoon, the schoolkids and the two men by the bread-van. What if they had reported my car's number? The news had said that McShane was a very popular man around town, well known in Gaelic Athletic Association circles. These sort of mistakes caused Catholics to open their mouths to the police about little things they might have seen. Apparently McShane sold car accessories for a living. Perhaps that was why I had seen him at police stations: he must have been selling car accessories to all those coppers with their racy little Fords. I remember thinking that if that's what he'd been up to, then he deserved to die. For such crimes we were willing to kill people. I focused instead on what I was going to do with the ASU in my living-room. I had become such a fanatical operator.

I had also seemed to develop a sixth sense about danger: I had a feeling that something was going to happen that night, so I decided to get them out of the house. I went to a neighbour and asked him if he would let the ASU stay overnight. He had helped me in a small way before but only on condition that I would never ask his help again. He reminded me of this when I called. He was a widower with six children and I knew he had enough on his plate. But I was desperate. I practically begged him to let the ASU stay in his house. He agreed finally, provided that they did not let the children see their weapons and that I would never, ever, ask him for anything again. I agreed to both conditions. Around 11.30 p.m., when I was sure his children had gone to bed, I brought the ASU round to his house.

At 4 a.m. the police raided me. Several armoured Land Rovers descended on my house. I had been dozing when they banged on my front door in a way which meant my visitors could only be policemen. I did not feel anything, not even fear: part of me had anticipated their arrival. I put on some clothes, went downstairs and opened my door. There were several of them, all heavily armed. They pushed their way into the house while one of them said: 'Eamon Collins, we are arresting you under Section 11 of the Prevention of Terrorism Act.' While they began searching the house I was taken outside to an unmarked red police car. I was put in the back and two police-men got in, one on either side of me. The driver turned the car round and drove to Gough Barracks in Armagh City. On the journey no one said anything to me, although one of them offered me a cigarette, which I refused. At the barracks I was placed in a cell.

Two teams of detectives interrogated me throughout the day. One team was made up of two middle-aged men who were humorous and quite placid. They told me that they had heard a lot about me. One of them said: 'You're smaller than we thought. We were expecting someone six foot six, four foot broad, with steel teeth, the stories we've heard about you.' The other team comprised two detectives in their early thirties. They accused me of murder, calling me an evil man. They rolled up their sleeves and came in close several times. One particular detective constantly made derogatory remarks about Catholics who, he said, were the same the world over: you had only to look at the squalor in South American countries to see the poverty and filth that Catholics were associated with. They implied that I could end up dead and let me know of a number of crimes which they suspected me of having been involved in. One policeman referred to the Crown Hotel bombing and how afterwards I had taken the mountain route with Mickey in the car. I was startled by what they knew. They mentioned Toombs and Hanna, and said they knew I had been involved in both murders. I maintained silence throughout. I just hoped the Active Service Unit was safe. He said how much he would have loved to have caught Mickey and me travelling round the mountain roads in my old Renault, how he would have loved to have seen us filled full of holes with a good rifle. He seemed to revel in this description, his eyes bulging wide, his cheeks taking on a pink glow. They kept saying, 'Talk to us. Come on, let us hear your voice. Just once. Come on, Eamon. Talk about football, whatever you like.'

I kept silent, with my arms folded. I was stunned by the information they had. They even knew about how depressed I had been after Hanna's death. Someone had been talking.

They knew I was involved in the killing of the two policemen in Rostrevor, and they knew that Mickey had killed them. They kept calling me a bastard and asked how someone like me, with a good job and a decent standard of living, could get involved with such a bunch of gangsters. They took me into a bigger room with a telephone and told me to phone my wife: 'Go on, phone your wife and say hello.' One RUC man kept threatening to beat me up. Finally I spoke: 'Fuck off.' This incensed him even more. 'You wouldn't say that to me in uniform. Some customs man you are, fucking IRA man.' Then they took me into a smaller interrogation cell, where the two middle-aged detectives introduced themselves to me and said they were from the Special Branch. They took me out for fingerprinting. As a detective took hold of my right index finger he tapped it several times and said: 'This is your trigger finger, Eamon.' I almost laughed. They might have been the enemy, but these two at least were likeable bastards. They said they were interested in helping me. They said the other two detectives were not so sympathetic, that they wanted to put me away for 'the big M' (murder). They, on the other hand, knew I was a terrorist but they were willing to grant me immunity from prosecution for anything I had done.

'Did you leave anything around for forensics to find, Eamon? Maybe a bloodstained jacket or scarf. If you did, we'll have it, and we'll have you charged with murder.' They were pleasant one moment and angry the next, shouting and making threats. They had succeeded in rattling me. I had given Mickey my padded white Wrangler jacket. He had been wearing it when he shot McShane. I worried that I had left it in the house, or had I given it to Mickey to take with him in the zip-bag with the AK-47? This played on my mind all day: if they had found it, then I would certainly be charged with McShane's murder. There was no doubt of that. I tried to keep my cool.

One detective played the role of my 'saviour'. He held out immunity for me. He even understood my reasons for being in the IRA. He recognized that there would be a United Ireland at some time in the future, that was inevitable, but it would not be achieved through violence. He said that he even bought his clothes in a Catholic-owned store. He pushed a sheet of paper towards me and said it was a written guarantee of immunity: 'Take it, Eamon, take it. Take it back to your cell, Eamon. Give it to your solicitor. It's your guarantee. But it is only available for so long. Tomorrow at midday we are going to withdraw it and you are going to be charged with murder.' His tall, grey-haired colleague asked: 'What about the murder of Sean McShane yesterday, Eamon? What do you know about that? An innocent man going about his own business in a bookie's shop, shot through the head. His life ended by you cunts. A man's life gone, destroyed, finished. Have you any conscience about it? You were involved in it. And what about that cousin of yours, Mickey? He went on the run because he was seen in a car with an IRA man in Dundalk. Funny reason for going on the run. Your cousin has killed a few people, hasn't he Eamon?'

I sat there, impassive, looking at the table but listening. I should not have been listening. I should have been trying to fill my mind with other thoughts, about music, history, anything to divert my mind from the line of questioning. But it was very hard to go against my natural human response and adopt the stance which the IRA, in their anti-interrogation lectures, teach their recruits to adopt. The IRA instruct you to pick a spot on the wall or on the table, to concentrate on it, and to try to ignore what your interrogators are saying. If you cannot find a spot to concentrate on, then think of a burning flame, concentrate on the image in your mind, watch the flame flicker. I tried to do this but the interrogators knew what I was doing: 'Is it the dot on the wall, Eamon, or the spot on the table or the flickering flame?' They passed their hands across my eyes, checking to see if I was in a trance. One interrogator got up and went outside. Another talked at length about Mickey. He began to swing back and forward on his chair close to the wall. He said: 'You know, at night I have nightmares about that murdering cousin of yours. I dream about him all the time and I wake up to find I'm strangling my wife, thinking it's that bastard Mickey.' He leaned back too far and fell back against the wall, hitting his back and neck. I almost laughed but I managed to keep myself in check. I was trying to show no emotion in front of these people. The interrogations continued, with a break for lunch and tea, until around midnight. During the last interrogation the swarthy detective said: 'You did all right today. You never opened your mouth, like a true IRA man. You are an IRA man, aren't you, Eamon?' They took me to my cell and I thought about what they had said. I still could not remember whether I had given the bloodstained jacket to Mickey.

I felt relieved that I had moved the ASU out of my house and prevented what would have been a total disaster. I knew that Mickey would not have surrendered: he had too much to lose. Policemen would have been shot dead as they arrived at the front door. There would have been slaughter. If any of us had survived, we would have been charged at the very least with the murder of Sean McShane: we had the murder weapons and a jacket spattered with McShane's blood.

I did not think about McShane at all. The only other worry on my mind, apart from the bloodstained jacket, concerned my Open University exams. I had become hardened to death. How else could I have survived so long? I remembered how in the past I used to spend hours examining my conscience after every killing. But now a stiff was just a stiff. I had grown tired of emotionalism, and was bereft of humanitarian feelings. And I was able to convince myself that the enemy did not get emotional about killing republicans. They had killed children with plastic bullets, sponsored loyalist death-squads and tortured vulnerable Catholics. Why should I wreck my mind with feelings of guilt when the enemy never seemed to flinch from committing the most barbarous acts? No, I was now hardened to death, and I preferred it that way. At least now I could meet my enemies on their own terms and beat them.

The light stayed on in my cell all night, preventing sleep. The sheet and pillow case were made of tissue paper. I had a shower the next morning. Then the interrogations continued as before, with the usual barrage of insults, aggression and blackmail. Towards the end of the first interrogation, the aggressive detectives suddenly softened towards me.

'Eamon,' said one cop, 'I bet you could turn the Newry and Dundalk IRA inside out and upside down. How would you

like to become a supergrass? Just imagine it – living somewhere in absolute luxury, sitting with a big glass of brandy.
VSOP, perhaps. You know, Eamon, Very Sore On Pocket. A
lovely blazing fire, with logs crackling and a big hunting dog
lying stretched out across the hearth. How does it sound, huh?
What do you think? It's all there if you want it, just start talking to us, that's all.' I remained silent. 'Ah, fuck it,' said the
detective, 'Eamon would probably pull a gun and shoot the
poor doggie. Come on, back to your cell.'

During the next interrogation I was asked again and again to
accept the immunity or be charged with murder. A detective
put his hand on his watch and said: 'One minute to twelve,
Eamon. Thirty seconds, twenty seconds, ten seconds. Time's
up. Come on, Eamon, take your immunity, take it.' He pushed
the document towards me and I grabbed it and ripped it up.

I stayed silent and was taken back to my cell. After lunch, I
was interrogated aggressively by the other team. One detective
said: 'If this was Beirut we would just take you out into that
yard and shoot you. You're not going to walk out of here, but
if you do then someday you'll get what's coming to you. We
mean to get you, you murdering little bastard. You don't come
from Newry. You're from Camlough and your mother's from
Crossmaglen. You're a murderer from south Armagh. We
don't give a fuck what goes on out in the bogs and mountains of
south Armagh, or who you Provos kill out there in your gaelic
shitholes, but you're not going to bring it into Newry,
Warrenpoint and Rostrevor like you've done; you're not going
to bring it into civilization. No, your terror campaign has come
to an end and we're going to stop you.'

I was interrogated several more times during the day. After
tea, the older team took me into a small interrogation cell.
The detective said that even though I had not taken the
immunity I was offered, he had been able to secure my release.
He had worked hard for me, he said. He said his boss had
given the OK and they were letting me out tonight. He told
me to take this card he was giving me, and that it had a phone
number on the back. All I had to do was to ring it and ask for
him by name. They would be prepared to meet me in
Banbridge, outside of Newry, or anywhere I liked. We could

even go for a drink or meal together, well away from anywhere I'd be noticed. And I wouldn't have to do much: just let them know who the suspicious characters were around Newry, if I saw something happening that we might be interested in.

I took the card. I was interested to know what was going on. Back in my cell, I looked at the card. A Sinn Fein Advice Centre had issued it in support of the leading south Armagh republican, Jim McAllister – one of the few Sinn Fein politicians I admired at the time. The RUC seemed to have a thing about Jim McAllister because during one of my interrogations one man had tried to imitate McAllister's south Armagh brogue, saying: 'The oppressed nationalist people.' McAllister represented the voice of militant and intransigent republicanism: he saw the armed struggle as a central element in the republican movement's strategy. I saw him as an intelligent and uncompromising man, and the loyalists obviously feared him. I looked again at the card: there were several Sinn Fein numbers on it, as well as a number which had the detectives' first names written beside it. I started to tear it up, but then I changed my mind and decided to keep it. I thought the IRA might be interested to have a look at it.

No sooner had I put the pieces in the back pocket of my jeans than I was taken down for a further interrogation by the younger team. After an hour of aggressive questioning I was taken back to my cell. The older team of detectives saw me last. They told me that I was going to be released and that they hoped I would be in touch with them soon. I spent another few hours in my cell before finally being released around 10.50 p.m. I had been held for two days. Later, although I didn't feel I'd been too mistreated in custody, I wrote a four-page letter to my doctor and the well-known Dungannon priest Father Faul, complaining about my treatment.

I returned home. My baby boy was sleeping peacefully in his cot. I looked at him. Six months old. What would the future hold for him? I stroked his head. I thought about my interrogators and their comments on my life-span. I knew what the Crown forces were capable of; I knew that if they set out to kill me they would eventually achieve their goal. My son's little chest expanded and contracted as he breathed. How would he fare in life without his father? What sort of a future was I offering him? I felt tired, and for the first time I began to feel old. That night I could not help thinking how nice it would be to live an ordinary family life without all this. But I felt nothing about McShane. Indeed, I seemed to feel very little for anyone. I just did not seem to care any more. Something was happening to me, and I was not yet sure what it was. I asked myself where my conscience had gone. I was supposed to have – I believed I had – devoted the last few years of my life to fighting for a more just social system, yet here I was incapable of feeling the slightest bit sorry for an innocent man whom I had helped to kill. I was suddenly nauseated by my lack of feeling for other human beings. There seemed to be a void inside me where my conscience had been. Was it over for me? Had I lost my nerve? This was surely just exhaustion. I would feel better when I had got my exams out of the way. Then I thought again about the whole sorry mess. I traced my finger gently over my son's face. Was I preparing him too for the sacrificial altar of republicanism? I wanted to live. I wanted my child to live. I wanted to be normal again. I wanted my child to have a normal upbringing. I knew I was at a turning point. At the very least the police were going to make my life a misery from here on. With hindsight, I realize that from that night I began mentally to slide downhill, to crumble, but I could not face up to what was happening; I could certainly not confide my doubts in my colleagues. To them I presented a hard front: Eamon Collins was ready for business as usual.

I read in the *Irish News* that the IRA had suspended the volunteer responsible for the McShane operation and had launched an enquiry. I realized that I had to accept this IRA discipline. Hardbap contacted me to say that I had to come to Dundalk to discuss my interrogation and the McShane operation with the security people.

In Dundalk I was taken to a safe house and put in a room whose windows had been draped with a dark curtain. I sat on a chair facing a darkened wall, while in the background two men from the IRA's internal security squad began to question me. They wanted to hear the details of all my interrogations and what I had said in them. One of them had a deep gruff voice. They went through these interrogations a few times, and I could hear someone giggling in the background when I relayed the comments that the Special Branch man had made about waking up after a nightmare about Mickey only to find himself strangling his wife. At the end of this debriefing they said they were satisfied that I had not talked, but advised me against saying anything at all during interrogations, even the words 'fuck off'. They said that classic interrogation techniques had been used on me. My police interrogators had not been interested in convicting me of anything, they wanted only to secure intelligence; which was why they had released me early, a gesture calculated to see if I would respond. A different security officer began to question me about the McShane killing. Why had I decided he was a target? I covered every aspect, from the time I had first discovered Cunningham's identity several years before. I said the careless and disastrous lapse was explained by exhaustion. I was told that I had put two and two together and come up with five, and as a result an innocent man had lost his life. The security officer said that this had resulted in bad publicity for the IRA: the movement had been placed in a bad light. He was right: I had let the movement down. I did not tell them about my loss of feeling for others, how I was losing any spark of decency or humanity. I can look back now and see that I was very far gone. My indifference to McShane's death was an indication of how far I had slipped down the slope to inhumanity. I did not say any of this because even I did not fully realize what was happening. I was a man who had lost almost all of his principles. Mickey had shown more concern over McShane than me. I had lambasted Mickey over Hanna's death some years previously, but now I had become worse than Mickey: I had become a cold, killing automaton.

The security officer told me that I was still suspended. He asked one final question: was there any chance of me 'going down the Damascus road'? I realized that what he wanted to know was whether, in my guilt over the killing of an innocent man, I would turn to God to repent my sins, perhaps even confessing to the police in an effort to clear my conscience. I said: 'No. There's no possibility of that, no possibility at all.'

Death had become my way of life, my everyday mission, my business, my reason for being. I had become skilled at my trade and I would continue to practise it. After the IRA interrogation, I steeled myself to fight my doubts about what I was doing.

14

UNDER PRESSURE

My suspension did not affect my work for the IRA.

I continued intelligence and other back-up work for operations throughout this period. After a month, I was called to Dundalk to hear whether my 'suspension' had been lifted. A leading south Armagh IRA man – one of the so-called 'generals' – had been brought in to give me the results of the IRA's enquiry into the McShane killing. I knew that he was a member of the IRA's ruling army council so what he said had been sanctioned by the upper echelons of the republican movement. He told me that the enquiry had completely exonerated me: I was reinstated in the IRA and was free to return to my unit. I had messed up badly, and killed an innocent Catholic, yet my only punishment was a slap on the wrist, a suspension in name only. The army council representative asked me how I now felt about the incident. I told him I was not dwelling on it. I knew an innocent man had died, and I could not excuse that, but I just wanted to get on with what I had been recruited to do. He accepted my noble sentiments and shook my hand. I tried to give an impression of relief and gratitude, but inside I felt empty. I could not have cared less about my exoneration. I cared only about the waves of negativity that kept sweeping over me whenever I thought about the IRA's campaign. I could hardly bear to listen to the radio anymore in case some war news came on.

I was in this state of mind when my unit bombed a tyre depot in Newry, causing major damage. I used my father's house to hide the volunteers who carried out this operation. I was not happy when one of them told me he had used a small cul-de-sac near my own house to dump the getaway car: I knew the police would soon be knocking on my door again. There was no reason why the car could not have been dumped outside the town and burned. He added to my displeasure by informing me that he had left an AK-47 magazine in the car. The gun and magazine belonged to south Armagh IRA who expected volunteers to account for every bullet used.

I retrieved it the next morning, using my car while Francie blocked the entrance to the cul-de-sac with his van. Just as I was about to drive off I noticed an old man looking straight at me. I shouted at him: 'What are you looking at, you nosy old cunt?' The old man turned away.

The annual customs dinner-dance was taking place that night. I had organized the event and had been given the day off to tie up the final details. A work colleague called for me around 2 p.m. We had arranged to go to a nearby forest to cut down a Christmas tree and some holly which we would use to brighten up the customs station. I enjoyed being out in the open with my bow-saw, doing something ordinary. I had begun to cling on to every moment of normality in my life, trying to delay the arrival of the next moment of madness. My colleague dropped me back to the entrance of my estate. It was already dark. I walked briskly towards my front door.

I had got within fifty yards of my gate before I noticed the police surrounding the house. You could have heard my heart thumping as my blood accelerated through it. There was an armoured Land Rover and a patrol car. A policeman stood facing me, holding his rifle. I hoped he would not identify me in the dark as I took a sudden turn into a path only yards from my house. The cop was looking straight at me, but he did not challenge me. I walked down the path and came out near where I normally parked my car. There were another two armoured Land Rovers with more police standing by them. 'Fucking hell,' I thought, 'how many do they need to deal with one man?' I wondered what had brought them to my house. Had the old man I had insulted that morning rung them with my registration number? Did they know I had collected the magazine, and had they raided my house thinking I would still have it on me? My legs turned to rubber but I walked on. I knew my house was empty: my sister was looking after my baby son while my wife was having her hair done for the dinner-dance. I hoped she would not mind that we would not now be going. Perhaps it was just as well. I had not been looking forward to it. I knew the deputy collector of Cushley was going to be there. He had a brother who was a senior member of the RUC, so I was sure that all my bosses at work now knew I was in the IRA, however much they pretended to the contrary.

I decided to go to my most recent recruit's house, the young man called Teddy, and hoped desperately that he was in. He was not yet a suspect, but I did not think this status would last for much longer now that Hardbap had got a grip on the South Down Command. The thought of spending up to seven more days in Gough Barracks listening to the RUC interrogators revolted me. Panic gripped me as I walked. I had become the victim of my own worst fears about imprisonment and torture. Teddy's mother answered the door. She said he was not in, but I almost pushed my way past her as I asked whether I could wait for him. She was a shy, friendly woman who smoked cigarettes nervously. I felt guilty. What was I doing bringing down trouble upon the heads of these people? Teddy returned home, and I breathed more easily. He was a relatively inexperienced recruit but he was brave and he inspired confidence. I explained the situation to him and he arranged for me to stay the night in his sister's bedroom.

This young man was a skilled carpenter; but the sea was his real love. He had been a sailor and wanted to go back to his ships. In his own way, he was a sensitive man. Despite everything, there were decent men in the IRA, hard as it may be for some people to imagine this. It would be easy if the IRA were made up only of corrupt brutes. In the IRA family this young man was like my favourite younger brother.

That night I thought about my future, and I decided to go to Dundalk, perhaps indefinitely. I felt as though I had come to

the end of my time in the north and prepared myself for a life
on the run. The next day Teddy drove me to the border. I had
the AK-47 magazine in my pocket.

I went to stay at Seán's old house, which had now become an
unofficial hostel for IRA men on the run. My wife and child
joined me for Christmas Day of 1983. She was upset at what
was happening and felt that her world was collapsing. I told her
that I thought I would have to live in Dundalk permanently.
Hardbap had been surprisingly friendly to me. He had told me
that he wanted me to take over as full-time intelligence officer
for the Dundalk/Newry area. Hardbap had even arranged to
pay me wages – an extra £10 to £20 a week on top of what I
could get from the dole office. But I had not yet resigned from
the customs. I was merely on extended sick leave. My IRA
wages would only represent a tiny amount of the salary I
earned at the customs, although the idea of being a full-time
IRA man had a strange appeal for me. During the few days
spent resting in Dundalk, I had begun to think that perhaps
my confused state had resulted from overwork: I had been
holding down two full-time jobs at once – my job in the IRA
and my job in the customs. At least if I took up his offer I
might have a little more time to myself and my family. But
after talking to some more experienced IRA men, I decided
that I would return to Newry to brass it out. The cops did not
really have anything on me, so I would take the chance.

I returned home to Newry and I soon discovered that the
one thing the police had got was the manpower to put me
under constant pressure. They had promised me that they
would make my life a misery, and they kept their promise. I
began to receive intimidating phone calls at all hours of the day
and night, threatening death: 'We're going to get you, you
Provo cunt. We're going to fill you with holes.' They began to
raid my house again and again – at breakfast, at lunch, at tea-
time, even when I was not there. They would go through all
my personal possessions, although they never caused any
damage or made abusive remarks. The skill of some of the
searchers impressed me: they could take out and put back
ninety-six Pampers nappies without destroying the packaging.
They sneered at my expensive chess set with its hand-made

wooden pieces ('Working class revolutionary, my arse'). They would go through all my books ('Jesus, look at all the books he's got'). One searcher found eight copies of a Revolutionary Communist Group book about the IRA ('Is them for all your wee friends?') and all my photos ('You take an awful lot of photos of scenery, Eamon'). One time they came across a photo of a Wessex helicopter landing in a field. ('Is that scenery, Eamon?' I said it was a historical record.) If I went shopping, the police would ring the shop while I was inside and tell the manager that there was an IRA man on the premises. Members of staff would then follow me around until I left. Outside I would find smirking members of the RUC. I could not go into town without being stopped and searched. A policeman would always cover me, his rifle pointed straight at my head. One time I put out my hand to get my licence back. The policeman held on to it for a few seconds as I tried to take it off him. He was saying: 'We're getting close, Eamon. We're getting near.' I knew he was right.

Once I lent my car, for an innocent purpose, to a non-IRA friend. They stopped him on the motorway outside Banbridge. He told me later: 'The police do not like you. They threw the seats into the road and the spare wheel into the field. I'm not driving your car again.' Everywhere I went, there would be three or four police cars shadowing me. They tried not to give me a moment's rest. This was psychological warfare, aimed at breaking me down. A man walking his dog in fields overlooking my house had sensed the presence of an army undercover team. I suspected they were keeping me under surveillance. Every time I left my home I would turn towards the fields and wave. Around this time, a teenager told me that the police had asked him to keep an eye on my movements. He said that they had shown him a photo of me. I asked him if it was a photo that had been taken in the police station. He said: 'No. It was a long-distance one. You were standing by your car and waving.' I had been having a problem with sleeping for some months; now I could hardly shut my eyes even to doze. I went to the doctor for sleeping tablets. I heard later that people thought at times that I looked as though I had been sleeping rough. The police's pressure combined with my own growing doubts was starting to destabilize me, but I never showed my IRA colleagues that I was beginning to crack.

I had annoyed Hardbap by returning home. He knew I would have made a good intelligence officer. He felt that my wife had the power to wrap me around her little finger and he feared that if she were ever arrested with me I might be extremely vulnerable. For the first time, he had been closer to the truth than he imagined. I knew that I would not be able to bear the thought of my wife suffering in any way.

Throughout those months of early 1984 I was still able to elude the police surveillance and continue with my work for the IRA. I fought against my doubts by intensifying my commitment to the organization. And at Easter 1984 I received an unexpected accolade. I was asked to give the IRA's oration at the annual commemoration service of the Easter Rising at Crossmaglen Cemetery in south Armagh. Although an honour, it would put me at risk of being pulled by an army snatch squad as I would (illegally) be wearing a mask. I travelled down to Crossmaglen on the Saturday night. I had been told to sit in a particular bar where a woman would meet me. She would ask if I was 'Peter'. I would say yes, and she would take me to where I was going to spend the night. Everything went according to plan. The woman who met me was middle-aged and matronly. She handed over an envelope containing the army council's Easter statement, and also the statement from the South Armagh Brigade. I followed her out of the bar and she handed me over to a sprightly elderly woman called Mary who, she explained, would put me up for the night. Mary scouted me up Crossmaglen's North Street, walking several paces in front of me. She took me into her house and made me comfortable. I spent most of the evening reading through the IRA statements, practising my speeches.

The next morning we all congregated at the Rangers Football Club hall. I watched the Provo colour party form, and I got an unexpected shock. I recognized one of the colour party: he was the boy who had driven the bike for the operation to kill Norman Hanna. My memory of the awfulness of that killing suddenly hit me with tremendous force, perhaps

because it reminded me of the time when I still had a conscience. I caught the bike boy's eyes. He recognized me, but
turned his head away. He looked older and harder. I wondered
what other sights he had seen since that awful day. I did not say
anything to him. I waited until the colour party had formed.
They carried the nine-county Ulster flag as well as the Irish
tricolour. We marched along the streets, through housing
estates and into the graveyard. I used the confessional of a
nearby church to change into the clothes that Mary had put in
a bag for me. The bag contained a combat jacket, white mili-
tary-style belt and a black hood. I was wearing my black
customs trousers – the only black pair I owned. When I had
dressed I walked outside into the crowd. I went to my position,
which was almost in a hollow with the local people surrounding me to act as a shield against the police and army. When I
finished my oration I gave a clenched-fist salute. As the crowd
clapped and cheered, I slipped away: my meeting with the bike
boy had turned the honour into ashes. I changed in the confessional and left the graveyard unhindered.

After Easter, a bizarre event alarmed me. A number of
masked men had entered a community centre in Newry and
read out a statement warning people against antisocial activities. I discovered that the leader of these vigilantes was a man
nicknamed Mooch. He had recently come out of prison after
serving time for IRA offences and had soon become Hardbap's
chief sidekick. From what I heard, he was little more than an
impressionable fool. I regarded him as part of the discredited
'old guard' of the Newry IRA, although he tried unsuccess-
fully to shake off the stigma. In custody he had signed
statements implicating himself, a stain on his reputation which
he seemed determined to expunge. He was still in the IRA but
he had not sought official permission for his foray into the
community centre. I thought this sort of behaviour was disastrous for the republican movement: we were hardly likely to
gain support from people who thought they were being bullied
by low-lifes.

Around this time, at the end of May 1984, the South Down
Command received another blow. Teddy had been caught by
the Irish security forces with an Armalite rifle in his car. It

looked as if he was about to be sent down for a long time, but amazingly he came up against a very humane judge who released him after Teddy told a sob story about how he had to marry his pregnant girlfriend. Teddy's surprising release led some people in the IRA to suspect that he might have been compromised by the southern Special Branch, that in return for his freedom he had agreed to work for them. I thought the idea ludicrous, but there was a new paranoia afoot in the IRA as a result of the supergrass trials. Everyone suspected everyone else. The IRA had strengthened and expanded the role of its security unit to combat the efforts of the renewed British counter-insurgency campaign, of which one arm was the supergrass system. The IRA had become convinced that there were moles buried deep within their ranks and they were determined to root them out. Each unit was responsible for tightening up its own security: one new rule was that when volunteers met each other, if there were new members present, they had to wear masks. We would therefore sit around a table with ski masks on our heads, only our eyes and mouths visible.

But the inadequacies of the new security arrangements became apparent in the case of the IRA member Brian McNally. This young man had recently driven a motorbike for a gunman in an attack on a UDR soldier, who survived the attack.

McNally had been arrested by the police and interrogated in Gough Barracks, before being released. After his release he was called to Dundalk for debriefing. McNally told an incredible story about the brutal treatment he had received at the hands of the RUC. He gave details of a horrendous catalogue of assaults and abuse, but he claimed he had not broken under torture. Hardbap took him at his word and even contacted *Republican News* so that the details of McNally's treatment could be given a wider audience, even though he knew that the IRA's own security unit needed to debrief McNally. As press officer for the South Down Command, I had been in regular contact with the paper. So the *Republican News* journalists called at my house for tea before going to the Sinn Fein Advice Centre to interview McNally. They gave the story impressive coverage in the paper. But no sooner had it been published than officers from the IRA's security unit debriefed McNally. Under their interrogation, McNally admitted that he had lied. The Special Branch had actually broken him in Gough Barracks and he had admitted his role in a number of operations. He secured his release by agreeing to work for the police, who were obviously desperate to find a way into our unit. McNally's role in the IRA had been minimal and so the damage he had caused was slight, even though he had endangered the few volunteers he knew personally.

To my surprise, the security unit showed him mercy. He was given an amnesty and dismissed in disgrace from the IRA. They had not even forced him to go and live in the south. I suppose the decision to treat him leniently was based on the fact that he had not actually started to work as an informer: he was merely a vulnerable young man who had broken under interrogation and been coerced into agreeing to work for the police, and had been discovered before he had had the chance to help them.

Some weeks later, at the end of July 1984, I went to England to spend a week at a summer school at York University as part of my Open University degree. One day I picked up a copy of the *Guardian* as I was following the miners' strike. I noticed a small story tucked away in a corner: 'IRA shoot informer. Family claims he was tortured.' I read the few column inches quickly. The story said that someone called Brian McNally had been shot dead as an informer; his body had been dumped at the border. There were signs of torture on the body, according to McNally's family.

He had been given an amnesty. I had been able to forget the IRA for a short period but now all my worst thoughts came flooding back. I wondered yet again what I was doing in the movement. I had never had a romantic vision of the IRA, but neither had I imagined the sordid depths to which they might sink. I felt sure that Hardbap had had something to do with this killing. I had felt nothing at all when McShane had died as a direct result of my actions, no guilt, only coldness and indifference. But I felt real anger over McNally: it was a stirring in the void.

A few days after I returned from York, I went to see my

cousin Mickey in Dundalk. A colleague at work had told me that he had spoken to McNally's mother. She had said there were visible signs of bruising all over his face and body – the clear marks of torture. I felt revolted and shocked. I was determined to find out the truth. To torture people was to behave like the cruel and despotic colonels of Latin America. If we tortured people we gave up all right to call ourselves soldiers of the people. To remain part of an organization that accepted torture would be final proof for me that I had stripped myself of any shred of dignity and decency. I had to find out what had happened.

I spoke to Mickey at length. He strongly denied the accusations of torture. He said that the marks found on McNally's face had probably appeared as a result of him falling to the ground after being shot. Mickey was embarrassed by my questioning. He tried to reassure me: 'He was a bad cunt. He tried to have me and Hardbap shot dead.' I could not quite understand what Mickey was saying. This man had been dismissed from the IRA. How could he end up getting shot for trying to set up IRA men? Mickey told me that he had been stuck for information in the Warrenpoint/Rostrevor area and he had decided to approach McNally again to see if he could provide some, even though he was no longer a member of the IRA: 'How could it have hurt? He would have been at very little risk to himself.' Of course, Mickey had missed the point. McNally had been dismissed because he was a weak and vulnerable person and so he should not have been approached again under any circumstances.

My cousin went on to explain that he had phoned McNally and asked him to come up to Dundalk; Mickey had outlined what he could do and McNally had agreed. A few weeks later he had come up to Dundalk all excited, saying he had a great plan for an operation. He said an unmarked police car went past a certain spot on a regular basis. It would be easy to hit and the IRA could come down and use his house to launch the attack. It sounded good, Mickey said. Hardbap and he and one other were going to be the gunmen in the operation. But when Brian went home after the last meeting, Mickey began to smell a rat. As he put it, he went to see 'someone else' to talk about this and 'the other man' told him to coax Brian up again as soon as possible.

I listened to Mickey but he had said nothing to convince me that McNally had deserved to die. The 'other man' to whom Mickey had confided his fears should have told Mickey that he was wrong to have contacted McNally in the first place. When McNally again came to Dundalk he was placed under arrest by the IRA. They walked into the room where he was talking to Mickey and seized him. Mickey said that McNally had confessed almost immediately. He admitted that the detectives who had broken him in Gough Barracks had stopped his van in the street, arrested him and taken him to Warrenpoint police station where he admitted that Mickey had been in contact with him again. They had suggested to McNally that he help them set up an elaborate operation to catch Mickey. They gave him the idea for the unmarked police car and told him to pass it on. I felt terribly sorry for poor McNally who by then must have felt himself drowning in a sea of danger. He was not very intelligent and I doubted whether he could have ever worked out a way to extricate himself from his peril. The police who had threatened and manipulated this vulnerable young man were no less reprehensible than the people who murdered him. McNally was merely a pawn. The IRA should have realized that he was easy prey for whoever decided to use him. I felt the IRA could easily have expelled him from the north and then patted themselves on the back in *Republican News* for their decency.

Instead, Mickey told me, McNally was offered the customary last request before his brains were blown out. He asked if he could write a letter to his mother. But he was so easily manipulated that he allowed the IRA to dictate a large portion of it. I could see the propaganda plan of his executioners: McNally would exonerate them of his own murder. Mickey quoted what McNally had written. I realized he had been present during those final hours: I found myself hoping that Mickey had been telling me the story of McNally's interrogation second-hand. Disgust engulfed me as I listened to Mickey quote McNally's letter. I can't remember the exact words but I remember clichéd phrases of abject apology for setting up his brave comrades, to whom in his last moments on earth he was now reconciled. The final sentence went something like: 'Goodbye, Mother, your loving son, Brian. May the Lord have mercy on my soul.' I shall never forget that last sentence. Mickey said it with a smile on his face, as if he wanted me to congratulate him for catching an informer. May the Lord have mercy on my soul.

I was beginning to feel physically sick, desperately afflicted by all this horror. I was losing my nerve, losing my way, and still I could not stop; could not get off the speeding train, and now I was allowing myself to be propelled from one disaster to the next. McNally's last words would not leave my mind.

I did not say anything more to Mickey. I couldn't share my feelings with him, or with anyone. I had felt a stirring of my conscience again, yet I had lived without a conscience for so long that its reappearance only frightened me. Later on that week, another IRA man asked me about McNally. I said: 'Ah, fuck him. He was a tout.'

15

THE ARMALITE AND THE
BALLOT BOX

Wider political developments began to affect me while these terrible events were taking place. In my state of growing disillusionment with the IRA, I could not have anticipated the effect that the growth of Sinn Fein was to have in pushing me further into despair.

In the wake of the H-Block campaign and the hunger strike in the late seventies and early eighties, for the first time since 1969, the Provisionals had begun to develop a grass-roots political organization aimed seriously at winning seats in elections.

Sinn Fein had always been there, but not in the form that it now began to take. The hunger strike had helped the party to grow in confidence and strength throughout Ireland – though it was still extremely weak in the south. I had always taken such politics with a pinch of salt. Until recently Sinn Fein had been little more than a sort of Rotary Club for retired IRA men or people who had not had the guts to join the IRA in the first place.

Since the twenties, Sinn Fein had not existed independently of the IRA in any real sense, but now suddenly the party, like an invalid learning to walk after years of lying bedridden, was striding around the north. The IRA were like the invalid's former carers: in one sense they were amazed and gratified by the transformation in their charge's abilities, but in another

sense they were worried and concerned at where he might go
and what bad company he might fall into. Some of the invalid's
carers had preferred him as a dependent. At least then they
could control him. I was certainly one of those IRA men.

I had entered the IRA with a political perspective rather different from that held by most other recruits. Although I had
never joined the Revolutionary Communist Group, I had,
under the influence of my strange English mentor, come to
sympathize with its political analysis. It is one of the ironies of
my story that the Marxist analysis which had helped to bolster
my decision to join the Provos was later to play an important
part in undermining my faith in the organization. It would
take me several more years to realize that that Marxist analysis
was itself deeply flawed. My RCG friend had always stressed
that the Provos would never succeed in forcing the British to
withdraw unless people in the south of Ireland became
involved in large numbers in the struggle, creating a mass revolutionary movement north and south of the border. At the
time I joined the IRA I thought that the Provos, through the
Dirty Protest and the hunger strike, were helping to build such
a movement. The RCG identified two dangers in the growth of
such a mass movement. First, if Sinn Fein developed real
political muscle in terms of electoral support, then republicans could be sidetracked into constitutional politics, which
for them was a contemptible collaborationist activity. A movement in this direction would gradually undermine support for
the armed struggle: political violence was seen to be crucial in
the building and maintenance of revolutionary consciousness
among the masses. Second, my ultra-leftist friend warned
against the danger of concentrating power within the republican movement in Belfast. No one area should have a monopoly
in dictating the future development of the struggle. Whenever
power became concentrated, it fell typically into the hands of
an élite within the dominant group. This élite would then be
capable of calling off the struggle if the establishment could
sufficiently flatter their egos and buy them off with the power
and position available within constitutional politics.

The hunger strike was called off in October 1981 after ten
men had died. As I've already explained, it seemed obvious to

me that the political wing of the republican movement was now in the ascendant, moving us stealthily towards constitutional politics. The people responsible for this new direction formed a narrow Belfast-based group of personalities – the triumvirate of Gerry Adams, Danny Morrison, and Joe Austin (with Tom Hartley as Gerry Adams's bag-carrier). I hoped at first that my analysis was wrong, but the development of the republican movement seemed to prove that I was right, and it seemed to prove the foresight of my Marxist friends.

I was extremely wary of the way in which Sinn Fein was developing, and I made my views known whenever the subject came up in discussions with members of the South Down Command.

I would explain my analysis in the following way: Sinn Fein had started its life independent of the IRA. The two only came together after Britain decided to grant the Irish limited self-rule within the empire, by allowing them to form their own parliament, the Dàil. In the first post-war, all-Ireland general election of 1919 to decide the composition of the Dàil, Sinn Fein won 76 out of the 109 seats. The British suspended this parliament and effectively declared war on the Irish people. In the aftermath of the 1919 suspension, Sinn Fein became almost as one with the IRA – two wings of the same mass republican movement. Political violence with mass support led to the granting of independence to twenty-six of Ireland's thirty-two counties and the formation of the 'Irish Free State', now the Republic of Ireland. The largest part of the republican movement accepted the partition of Ireland, albeit as a step towards an eventual United Ireland. A significant minority rejected the partition and the result was civil war in the new state. A rump IRA fought their former comrades in the new Free State Army, and the IRA lost. But IRA members continued to carry the memory of the moment when Ireland's nationhood had been expressed in the election for the first and second Dàils. The new Dàil of the Free State could not have the same legitimacy because Irish people in the six counties of the north could not vote to send their representatives to it. So, in the eyes of true republicans, the last legitimate Dàil – and the Dàil from which they drew their legitimacy – was the

second one. Any subsequent Dàil was a bastard pretender. The
legitimacy that the IRA claimed to have as a result of the 'frus-
trated 1919 Dàil' created another cornerstone of republican
politics: abstentionism. The republican movement abstained
from participation in both the government of the new Irish
Free State and the government of Stormont in the north –
both created by the 1921 Government of Ireland Act. This was
republican orthodoxy.

All IRA men knew that constitutional nationalism was the
most potent political force in Irish society. They also knew that
the IRA did not, could not, engage in constitutional politics.
The IRA's distinctive role was to uphold the physical-force
tradition in Irish history. The other essential element of this
strand of republicanism was the belief that only violence would
get the British out of Ireland. For the Provisional republican
movement to dabble in constitutional politics would be to risk
undermining its very reason for being. Violence defined us.
The history of Irish republicanism showed that those times
when believers in physical force became involved, for whatever
reason, in constitutional politics were the times when the physical-force tradition came close to being extinguished. It had
never mattered to physical-force republicans that they were in
a minority because they could always cheer themselves with
the knowledge that they held aloft the true flame of Irish freedom: they could see through the sham of bourgeois democracy;
and they were sure they embodied the pure spirit of the Irish
nation. The IRA would trace their roots back through the 1916
Easter Rising, the Irish Republican Brotherhood, the Fenians,
Wolfe Tone and beyond, far beyond, to the earliest times when
Irish people had used violence to resist the invaders. We had a
whole mythology of resistance through violence. I would even
tell my IRA comrades that the people who espoused political
violence were Ireland's warrior class, the true aristocracy,
regardless of their birth. Did aristocrats ever care a fig for
bourgeois democracy?

To me, there was a relationship between physical-force
nationalism and constitutional nationalism, but there was a
paradox at the heart of this relationship. The Fenians and the
Irish Republican Brotherhood of the nineteenth century had

been tiny illegal groups, outlawed secret societies, yet they were not completely antagonistic to constitutional politics. The paradox was that they depended on constitutional politicians to articulate the issues for them. They needed a bigger political body than themselves to act as a unifying agency for the demands of nationalism, and they latched on to the mass movement provided by the constitutional nationalist, Charles Parnell. Although the constitutional nationalists opposed the physical-force argument, the former drew much of their strength from the latent threat of political violence provided by the Fenians. They helped to boost Parnell's power and influence, even though they opposed the compromises he was willing to make with the Crown. Physical-force nationalists, despite being a minority, somehow represented the conscience of the dead, the exiled and the enslaved. For me, they brought to life that damaged part of the Irish psyche which would neither forgive nor forget the suffering inflicted on Ireland by the English and their Scottish planters.

Sinn Fein had played no part in the genesis of the civil rights movement against the discrimination built into the Orange State. The IRA had been there, but only in the sense of jumping on a bandwagon which others had started rolling. When the civil rights movement emerged, the IRA leadership embraced a vague Stalinist theory of Irish development. I regarded it as a form of pseudo-Marxist fantasy. The civil rights movement jogged them into activity because they realized that they were in danger of being sidelined by a genuine mass movement that had emerged almost despite traditional Irish republicanism. The civil rights movement of course had more in common with constitutional nationalism than with the physical-force tradition. So the old Official IRA – led by those who were soon to form the Provisional IRA – tried successfully to subvert the movement and turn it into an inadvertent ally of physical-force republicanism. This was hardly surprising: anyone with any knowledge of the IRA's history would have been able to predict how they would try to use such a movement. Some people still believe naïvely that the IRA played no part in turning peaceful marches into full-scale riots. Of course, the IRA were assisted by the over-reaction of the police

and loyalists, but the violence of the latter merely comple-
mented the violent intentions of the former. Indeed, as the
police and loyalists began to put greater and greater pressure
on the citizens' defence committees set up by concerned people
to protect Catholic areas, so the IRA's influence grew in leaps
and bounds.

The Provisionals claimed to inherit the legitimacy of the
first Dàil – and they could produce veteran members of that
body to sanction the inheritance. I had watched such veterans
ascend the stage at H-Block rallies and had listened to their old
voices asserting the right of the Provisionals to continue the
unfinished fight for a free and independent Ireland. These H-
Block rallies contained the beginnings of the Sinn Fein
political machine.

Under the umbrella of the H-Block committees there developed a broad front which mingled a myriad left-wing, liberal
and humanitarian organizations. The hunger strike so affected
the social conscience of the Irish people that they elected
Bobby Sands as a member of the British parliament and two
other hunger strikers as members of the Irish Dàil. Sands
received 60,000 votes; 100,000 people attended his funeral.
The dead hunger strikers gave the republican movement a taste
of the irresistible lure of electoral politics and an impressive
political apparatus which could be used to refine the taste, and
to keep tasting.

Since 1977, the leadership of the republican movement
had been in the hands of Adams, Austin and Morrison. The
hunger strikers had done what the men of the Easter Rising
had done: they had known that their deaths would not defeat
the British immediately, but they had anticipated that their
sacrifice would help create a mass movement of Irish resistance. In another sense they helped to renew the legitimacy of
the IRA campaign: the IRA no longer had to hark back constantly to 1916 or 1919 to reaffirm the legitimacy of their
struggle. The hunger strikers provided them with a whole
new iconography of martyrs to exploit. Ironically, what provoked the H-Block protests and the hunger strike – the
ending of political status for republican and loyalist prisoners – had occurred at a time of great weakness for the IRA.

Had political status been maintained, the war might have fizzled out between 1982 and 1984. Instead, the British gave the republican movement a tremendous boost.

Of course, I was delighted in many ways with Sinn Fein's new-found electoral support. What disturbed me was what the IRA was trying to do with this support. In 1984, IRA volunteers all over Ireland had to meet to discuss the next step of this process – the ending of abstentionism in the south. Should Sinn Fein members enter the Dàil and local councils? We met in small groups to debate this matter. I was opposed to dropping this hallowed symbol of the physical-force tradition, but my views were in the minority. I could not see what we would gain from participation. The Official IRA (which later became the Workers' Party after it had renounced the armed struggle) had gone along this route, and where had it got them? A few councillors and a few members of the Irish Dàil. Even if they were able to influence policy in a minority government, this was a million miles away from my goal of a socialist republic. I said I thought it was the beginning of the end of the armed struggle. As far as I could see, it meant that our leaders felt the armed struggle was defeated. And why, if that were the case, could they not come out and say so? Of course, the Belfast triumvirate tried to give the impression that they had learned from the Workers' Party's mistakes by keeping the Armalite as well as the ballot box, but surely this would merely become a paddle for them as they raced the rapids of electoral politics.

I returned from that meeting with my comrades in the South Down Command feeling extremely depressed. I asked myself what was the point in continuing with the war? Why not call it off now?

Such had been the level of support for the republican movement during the H-Block campaign and the hunger strike that the Irish government and the main constitutional nationalist party in the north, the Social Democratic and Labour Party (SDLP), had begun their own political initiative to promote a peaceful solution to the conflict. They had worked together for more than a year on the Forum Report, whose findings were published amid pomp and ceremony at the Irish Parliament in Dublin on 3 May 1984. On that day, while there were photocalls outside Leinster House, the IRA blew up three telephone engineers by putting a bomb under their car in Newry. One of them died. It turned out that they were members of the Territorial Army, which for some reason exempted them from targeting by the IRA.

Hardbap told me to tell the press that the men were in fact gathering intelligence for the loyalists. But there was no evidence of this, and in my state of disillusionment and anger all I felt was that they were as good a target as any of the others. If we were going to kill, why make petty distinctions? Why should we differentiate between the UDR and the Territorials? We saw little to choose between them and the UDA or the UVF. So I made a statement to the press saying that this was the South Down Command's riposte to the Forum Report selling out the Irish people.

Hardbap was furious and scared. I had changed army policy. He threatened me with dire consequences, but what this was really about was control, and about walking a thin line between politics and total war.

Sinn Fein were going to be participating in the European elections in June and Danny Morrison was hoping to be elected as an MEP. All IRA units received an order from general headquarters to 'take a holiday' during the period of the election. Did Sinn Fein really think that they might eat substantially into the vote for the SDLP? As far as I was concerned, people who believed this had not read their history books. Sinn Fein had won seats in both the British and Irish parliaments in the past, but the times when their electoral support had increased beyond the dependable bedrock had been rare and transitory: this additional support had always dissipated in a relatively short period. It seemed obvious to me that if republicans received a low share of the vote in an election, then they would leave themselves open to the criticism that they did not have a mandate from the Irish people for continuing their war. Of course, in one sense the IRA had never worried about the lack of such a mandate before. But at least they had sensibly tended to avoid electoral situations in which the lack of such a mandate would be illustrated. In that sense this traditional attitude of republicans towards 'the people' coincided with my own rigid Marxist-Leninist view of 'the people'. I realize now that for me 'the people' were an abstraction. Effectively, any of 'the people' who refused to support the Provisional republican movement ceased to be regarded as people whose views mattered. Perhaps the real danger of constitutional politics, from the RCG's point of view, was that republicans would start listening to the people as a whole – the people who in their 'false consciousness' consistently voted overwhelmingly for non-violent nationalism.

In other elections since the hunger strike, republicans had thrown stones at John Hume, insulted the human rights campaigner Father Denis Faul, and even orchestrated street attacks on the legendary (albeit unorthodox) republican Bernadette McAliskey. They exhibited a peculiar combination of stupidity and arrogance. Our movement was now behaving as if it occupied the highest moral plateau; we were acting as if Gerry Adams had received a new set of commandments from the Lord – and anyone who questioned our divine right to rule the Catholic ghettos and rural backwaters was liable to be stoned. Encouraged by our Belfast leaders, we were engaging in gutter politics. And for what? For what turned out to be a 13 per cent share of the vote in the June 1984 European elections. I knew this figure would only be used against us in the future.

Republicans outside of Belfast had begun to suspect that had it not been for the influence of the Derry republican leader Martin McGuinness, the armed struggle would have been called off long ago. It now seemed to me that if the republican movement were diverting people's time, energy and money into bourgeois democracy, then the military campaign ought to be called off. The twin strategy of the ballot box and the Armalite did not work; you could have one or the other, not both.

I was convinced that the IRA was only continuing to exist through the strength of the new cell-structure and the pockets of popular support among a few local communities in the north. These two factors meant that the IRA could sustain a limited number of operations of limited consequence indefinitely. So the 'long war' would continue, but its continuation did not make for victory or anything approaching victory. I

knew that the political leadership knew this. I knew also that
foot-soldiers like Hardbap did not: but these foot-soldiers did
not care. They would continue to fight the war because by
doing so they gave themselves power, status and influence
which they could never have achieved otherwise. They now
disgusted me.

Yet despite all of this, I remained a soldier. I could not leave
the movement to which I had become wedded. I stayed in the
hope that changes could be made, that the impetus from the
hunger strike could still create a mass movement north and
south of the border, which could be channelled into a renewed
military campaign that would destroy the Orange State. I
thought that the brutal and ruthless volunteers of south
Armagh might show us the way forward by stopping the rot
that had set in. But in my heart I knew this was an impossibil-
ity. I knew that the IRA's so-called 'long war' was built on
foundations of sand which would eventually be washed away,
but it had taken me many years to convince myself that I was
right to join the Provos; it was going to take a long time to convince myself I was wrong. People do not cease to be
revolutionaries as the result of overnight conversions. In any
case, even though I was almost sure by the middle of 1984
that we could not win the war, I helped to maintain my flagging commitment to the armed struggle by telling myself that
we still needed political violence to secure the best deal for
nationalists in the eventual political compromise: we needed
the loyalists to realize that we would continue to secure nationalist areas from attack and we also needed to secure the release
of our prisoners.

16

THE SICKLY SMELL
OF SUCCESS

After hearing about the execution of Brian McNally, I felt relieved to breathe fresh air after leaving Mickey's house in Dundalk.

He had categorically denied that McNally had been tortured before his execution, and I wanted to believe him. But the horror of that stupid boy's death still filled my mind. I felt sick as his last words repeated themselves over and over in my mind: may the Lord have mercy on my soul.

I had an appointment with Hardbap. It was a summer's day and the sun dazzled me as I threaded my way through the traffic. Hardbap was waiting for me. I could barely respond to his pleasantries. He told me that he was going to take me to meet some of 'the boys from south Armagh'. An intelligence officer from north Armagh had also requested a meeting, but he would arrange that for another day. I assumed that these meetings concerned information about Crown forces targets outside south Down which I had accumulated by putting through the vehicle licensing computer the registration numbers of cars seen going into police stations.

I could not manage even a grunt of enthusiasm over my new-found popularity. I nodded at Hardbap, who smiled and then adopted the manner of a superior rewarding a diligent employee. He said there was one other meeting that he was going to take me to that day: 'You've been chosen to become a part of the security unit.'

It took a few seconds for his words to register. The security unit, the IRA's internal police, the Nutting Squad which had just killed McNally. Hardbap noticed the look of disbelief on my face. He must have thought I was merely registering the shock of an unexpected promotion. I felt as if some supernatural force were mocking me. The IRA wanted me to be part of the Nutting Squad; wanted me to join them in dealing with future McNallys. Hardbap said that I and another south Down volunteer, the man known as Mooch, had been chosen: we would be part of the main unit but would also effectively form our own security unit for the Dundalk/south Armagh/ south Down areas.

I said: 'Right.'

Hardbap took me to another terraced house a short distance away. He took me straight upstairs to an empty room. The floors were bare. It looked like someone had just moved in. There were people already in the room. I recognized one of them: he was known as Scap and I knew he was a security officer. He was a dark-haired man in his early thirties. He had been the one who had asked me after the McShane incident whether I was likely to 'take the Damascus road'.

I was introduced to Mooch for the first time. This was the clown who had raided the community centre in Newry and read out a statement warning people against antisocial activities. Now he was Hardbap's sidekick.

But the room was dominated by an older man. John Joe Magee looked as if he were in his fifties. He was well built and had the air of someone who had been physically formidable in his youth, although he had now gone to fat. He stood while everyone else sat on the bare floorboards. We fell silent and waited for him to speak.

He lit a cigarette from a packet of Benson and Hedges and started to talk. He had a deep voice with a Belfast accent. I had heard that voice before: he had been the masked security officer who had debriefed me after my interrogation in Gough Barracks. I had been impressed by his thoroughness.

He said: 'You two people have been taken here today

because you've been picked to join security. I have no doubt
that both of you know about the function of security because
both of you have met security officers before. I'm head of
security and this is my deputy.' He pointed to Scap. 'Although
I know you have some knowledge about the security unit, I am
going to cover it again in more detail.'

He took a drag from his cigarette and launched into a lecture
on the British system of supergrasses: how they tinkered with
it, adjusted it, until they got it just right. Then they launched
it with a colossal bang, and everybody felt its effects. It had
devastated the ranks of the IRA. Experienced men suddenly
broke under interrogation. He spoke of needing to know why,
at a certain point in their lives, men suddenly cracked.
Sometimes it was just a case of people saying, 'John Joe, I just
couldn't handle it anymore. I'd just been through it so many
times. I'd just had enough.'

Magee had been pacing about slightly as he talked. He was
a man who was used to commanding attention. He told us that
we were to be part of a new northern command security structure. We would have to vet new recruits. They would not be
allowed to join unless they'd been vetted by us. We would have
to debrief IRA people who came out of interrogation centres,
before they talked to anyone else.

He was an impressive man, fluent and articulate. If I
detected a weakness, it was his enjoyment of hearing the sound
of his own voice. He continued: 'Another part of your work
will be making sure that all volunteers in your area are adher-
ing strictly to the Green Book rules, that there is no breach of
discipline. You will be part of any enquiry into breaches of discipline that could involve suspension or court martial. Lastly,
as a consequence of this work, you could find yourself discovering informers. In many cases, informers get an amnesty, but
in cases where death is the sentence recommended by the court
of enquiry, a member of the army council makes the final decision. At some stage down the road you could find yourself
executing touts.'

His words stabbed me. After McNally, I could really feel
what they meant. And yet I was still hypnotised by John Joe's
performance: 'You will still continue with your own duties

within the IRA, in addition to your security duties. Don't forget that we are all part of the northern command staff, so if you agree to join you will be a northern command officer, but you will still have to operate through your own OC. However, you won't discuss with anybody outside our circle the work you are involved in while you are acting as a security officer. It is totally secret, and must be kept so. You two people have been chosen because you're first-rate volunteers. What do you think? Are you happy to join us?'

For years, my ambition had been to rise within the IRA to a position of influence in the command structure. Magee was offering me a job as a northern command staff officer: he wanted me to become part of the trusted élite. I have to admit that, despite my feelings about McNally, I was flattered. I had no doubt why I had been chosen: John Joe and Scap must have thought, particularly after the McShane incident, that I was especially ruthless. They would not have chosen me if they had not believed that, in time, I would be capable of shooting touts, former comrades perhaps, human beings with their hands tied behind their backs pleading for mercy.

Perhaps, I told myself, if I joined security, then I could help make sure people like McNally did not end up getting shot. My ego took over. The kindest thing I can say about myself is that I did not have the inner strength to turn round and say no. How could I refuse? After all, McNally was undoubtedly a tout. I told myself that we were IRA soldiers fighting a dirty war, using methods which should not be part of a civilized society. But I could still convince myself that we were using those methods because we wanted to create a more civilized society.

'Yes, I'm happy to join.' I said. Mooch said something similar. John Joe said he was pleased to have us.

I left the house with Hardbap and Mooch. I felt dazed. I was trying to pump myself full of enthusiasm for the step I had just taken, but any excitement that rose within me disappeared almost instantly into the emptiness. Hardbap said that he wanted to have a quick operational meeting with me, Mooch and Francie, who was waiting for us at another house. I sat in the living-room, feeling depressed. I did not want to be there.

I could not bear to plan any more bombings and killings. But I listened to what Hardbap had to say. He said he was desperate for a good operation, as several recent ones had failed.

Francie suggested an operation. He said that the old creamery in Newry, which was only around a hundred yards from the police station, was being redeveloped. He thought it would be possible to drive a lorry packed with mortars into the site, park it close to the high stone wall which hid the site from the street, and set off a salvo. Mortars had that range and, if we were very lucky, we might be able to kill some policemen. However, mortars were inaccurate and posed a threat to civilians. I thought they were more trouble than they were worth. Hardbap expressed a mild interest in the idea, but he swiftly moved on to other matters, although later all of us would have cause to remember this casual conversation. Francie left, and I got talking to Mooch. He told me he had become involved in organizing Sinn Fein. As far as I could see, the local Sinn Fein Advice Centre was little more than a rest home for ex-prisoners who had nothing else to offer and a meeting point for rabble to rip off a few pounds of paper money and mess about with other men's wives. And I did not like Mooch. He talked as if, while he was in prison, the movement had stood still waiting for his reappearance. He talked about the problems that Sinn Fein had in Newry, and I made various suggestions which Hardbap greeted enthusiastically. This made me suspicious. I thought for one awful moment that Hardbap might have been trying to get me involved in running the centre. The reasoning behind his behaviour became clearer later in the afternoon when he took me to meet the boys from south Armagh.

The people I met were the south Armagh OC, and another even more senior IRA man who would have had overall responsibility for co-ordinating the whole of the republican movement in south Armagh. He was a high-ranking activist, close to the army council. The OC was quite young, in his early twenties, but his reputation as a soldier went before him. He was an uncomplicated, impressive, ruthless man. The other officer was a brusque, no-nonsense type, but he had great shrewdness and was capable of judging any situation swiftly and making an informed decision. I learned later that he had responsibility for the movement of all IRA arms, munitions and explosives in the whole of Northern Ireland – a very powerful position, a sort of Quartermaster General, and he would have a final say over who got what arms. He had a hooked nose, black hair and a beard. He was stocky, almost barrelchested, and spoke with deliberation and authority in a slow rural brogue. He was the leader of an area which was the last word in IRA effectiveness, and he looked the part. They had brought with them a man for whom I had the greatest respect, a south Armagh Sinn Fein politician. He did not have the military experience of the other man but I respected him for his ability to deflect some of the shine from the Belfast triumvirate. He was a man who realized that Sinn Fein had a limited role to play in the armed struggle to remove the Brits.

The Quartermaster officer told me that they had arranged this meeting because they had noted my total opposition to the growing role of Sinn Fein, and they agreed with my analysis. Sinn Fein in their view was the IRA's Achilles heel: it should have been covered up with the first signs of the current dangerous developments. They said that the fact that Sinn Fein had been allowed to grow showed that the current leadership was, at best, inept and, at worst, on the verge of ending the military campaign, albeit by stealth. They said that the present leadership obviously felt that the easiest way of ending the war was by using Sinn Fein: the best resources of the republican movement would be directed into Sinn Fein, thus slowly neutralizing the IRA. These south Armagh men said that the IRA was taking a back seat for the first time in the modern history of the physical-force republican movement. My south Armagh hosts wanted me to help them stop the rot.

The senior man said that he wanted me to join Newry Sinn Fein immediately. The politician said that I would be put on the list of Sinn Fein candidates to fight the next council elections. They wanted me to take over Newry Sinn Fein and run it as an extension of the IRA. My taking over Sinn Fein in Newry would be part of a strategy involving people across the north to prevent Sinn Fein from developing independently: the needs of the IRA came first and Sinn Fein had to exist for the convenience of the IRA. I expressed concern about becoming a glorified social worker. I said there was surely still the danger of me being identified with the state through my negotiation with state departments on behalf of my 'clients', the ordinary people of Newry. I wanted to be reassured that there was a clear overall strategy of revolutionary subversion.

They tried to put my mind at rest, saying that my job would be to take over the local Sinn Fein branch and to organize, run and develop it in the way that I would organize, run and develop any other IRA unit. The IRA and Sinn Fein had to become one and the same. My job would be to further the aims of the IRA. I would use my role in Sinn Fein to spot potential IRA recruits, to penetrate deeper into the community, to gather intelligence by using Sinn Fein's links with other community groups and state bodies, and to make contact with people who in time would allow their homes to be used as IRA safe houses. I would be expected to attend local and regional Sinn Fein meetings.

What I had just been told was nothing less than an IRA strategy to turn Sinn Fein once more into a puppet organization.

Once again a flicker of egotistical satisfaction surfaced from my depression and disillusionment. I felt flattered but I was hardly keen. Once again I had to tell myself that this was the very strategy that I had once discussed with my RCG friend: politics as the supporting arm of a campaign of all-out revolutionary war. On this strange day everything I had always wanted was being offered to me. I felt like a person who had won the pools on the day his terminal cancer was diagnosed. But I told the south Armagh men that I would be willing to do as they suggested.

I drove back to Newry that night. Some routine phrases, like cheerleaders in my mind, tried hard to lift my morale and, for brief moments, succeeded. But over the next few days I settled into depression. I felt as if I were beginning to suffer from multiple personality syndrome. One minute I could be an efficient IRA man, opposed to any developments that might end the war, the next I just wanted the war to end, just craved to become normal again. And the minute after I would feel nothing, absolutely nothing, as if I were some sort of automaton. The pressure of the last few months had left me incapable of sleeping. I knew I was losing my nerve and that I was on the verge of mental and physical collapse: this was the only explanation for the weakness and fear I felt every day. I started to plan what I was going to do in Sinn Fein, but then revulsion would overcome me as I thought about the republican movement. Yet I still kept going. I had to keep going.

Within days, I had begun to work for Sinn Fein and surprisingly my gloom seemed to lift. I began to think that I was coming out of my depression, but before the end of the week an incident occurred which crushed me. On 9 August, the anniversary of the introduction of internment, Brendan Watters, an enthusiastic but inexperienced IRA volunteer, was blown up by a home-made grenade close to my home in Barcroft Park. Some time before this incident Hardbap had shown me the grenade which was to kill Watters. This indigenous product of Irish industry was a grey metal cylinder, around seven inches long and two inches in diameter. IRA engineers had obviously perfected it with factory machines. Hardbap unscrewed the top to show me the explosives inside, in a little bag. On the side of the cylinder was a lever. You held the grenade to your ear and pressed the lever: if you did not hear a click, then you were not to use the grenade as it was defective. If you heard a click, you had to press the lever twice more to prime the grenade. Then you attached a small square battery to the plastic battery-holder, also on the side of the grenade. At this point you had approximately five seconds in which to throw the weapon. I found out later that Watters had volunteered to throw it at a police Land Rover. When his day came, something went wrong. The device exploded in his pocket as he ran with it. I felt he should never have been allowed near the badly-designed grenade, but I knew he had wanted to prove himself to Hardbap.

I attended Watters's funeral as a Sinn Fein representative. Gerry Adams had come up from Belfast and he had brought some other leading republican figures with him. The lines of RUC men outside the dead volunteer's house in Derrybeg daunted yet angered me. I took several photos of Watters's father standing next to the IRA colour party. The night before, I had attended the wake as an IRA representative, helping to form the guard of honour around the coffin in the house. I had felt uncomfortable as I stood there in my combat uniform, a mask and beret on my head, a dead man beside me. I looked at the body of this 24-year-old and I thought: what a waste, what a total waste. I felt I was taking part in a piece of cheap theatre for the benefit of the gullible masses; a publicity stunt for the kids on the street who would be enticed to die next. Hardbap and Mickey had stayed up all night, getting drunk and crying into their glasses. Crocodile tears, I thought. Watters should never have been given the grenade. A typical Hardbap operation. He stayed safe while dupes died. They called Watters, and volunteers like him, heroes. But he was not. He had merely died as a result of his own stupidity and the technological inadequacy of his weapon. What was heroic about that?

We walked through the streets of Newry in the funeral procession, taking measured, dignified steps and wearing black armbands in honour of the dead volunteer.

We arrived at St Mary's Cemetery to be confronted by lines of grey armoured Land Rovers parked along the side of the road. Scores of policemen, tense and ready for action, stood beside them. The procession slowed almost to a halt as it moved through the narrow entrance-gates. This bottle-neck had the effect of compacting the crowd together in one solid mass. Spontaneously, the people began to stamp their feet, the sound reverberating through the silence. A crowd had done this many years before when Newry buried three unarmed men who had been shot dead by the army in Hill Street. The effect was eerie, a reminder of suppressed anger, and it sent a chill through all present.

Suddenly a bearded man with dark wavy hair rushed through the crowd: 'Stop, stop,' he said quietly but firmly. 'This is not helping our cause. This is the type of behaviour that the RUC want to witness.' The man was Francis Molloy, a leading Sinn Fein activist from Dungannon in County Tyrone. His words caused the stamping to falter, and the rhythmic, ominous beat began to die down. I did not want the sound to die: these people had a right to express themselves. Indeed, such stamping was the only way they had to show their anger in the face of the formidable military presence. I walked forward and said: 'Don't listen to him. Bang your feet if you want. Don't listen to him. Show the RUC you're not afraid. Show solidarity with the dead volunteer!' Immediately, the dying beat kicked into life. The sound of hundreds of crashing boots vibrated through the mass, and I knew I was right. The RUC presence reminded me of why I had joined the IRA and why I continued to be a member: we were reminding the RUC that we were a distinct and separate people, existing at one end of an extreme whose other end was occupied by them and their military force. We were reminding them that these extremes would never come together: our culture and identity would never be assimilated in the corrupt state of which they were the protectors.

Molloy rushed back towards Gerry Adams to tell him what was happening. Adams had already succeeded in calming a confrontation between a group of RUC men and some mourners prior to the funeral mass, a mile from where Watters was now being buried. Adams's ability to read dangerous situations and to move in fast to resolve them was in one sense admirable. But I thought that Newry needed a violent confrontation. Pictures of the RUC men wielding shields and batons, wading into men and women, would have been flashed around the world before the peelers could have got back to their barracks for a tea-break. Surely the republican movement could only benefit from such an outcome, if we were still committed to the armed struggle? Why was Adams trying to defuse situations which offered such potential? His behaviour only made sense if the war was over. I think it was at this funeral that I realized, with depressing clarity, that the war *was* over. Adams was behaving in this way because he knew that this was true: he could see that there was no point in inflicting too much more unnecessary suffering on the people. We were all taking part in a charade, wearing our costumes for the occasion, our white shirts, black ties and black armbands. I knew that Watters's death had been a waste, that he would soon become nothing but another name to add to the list of casualties. Of course, each year he would receive a second's recognition from the republican movement for his supreme sacrifice, but that was all. Life, any life, was better than this, and yet we were continuing to embrace death recklessly. The war was over; the only problem was that no one could call it off.

I was living a lie, pretending to a commitment, because I still wanted to live, and I knew that Watters had wanted to live, but his naïvety and stupidity had killed him. Here they were, burying a volunteer whose death had sprung from an act of political violence, which in turn had sprung from a militaristic ideology which these republican mourners supposedly supported. Militarism must have its uniforms, ranks and the marching of disciplined men. The funeral of an IRA volunteer is the time when the secret military organization walks publicly with the community upon whose support it depends. Without the community we were irrelevant. We carried the guns and planted the bombs, but the community fed us, hid us, opened their homes to us, turned a blind eye to our operations, even though that community support had dwindled over the years. Part of me wanted the community to say: 'We need you, as you need us.' Perhaps I hoped the stamping sound would help me to deny the truth that had already crept up on me.

I felt angry, yet satisfied, as I walked behind Watters's coffin which was now being carried towards the freshly-dug grave. I began to descend the steps into the graveyard, and I did not notice who was behind me. I heard a voice say: 'Everything went well today, Gerry. Not a bad turnout . . .' I felt my blood boil: not a bad turnout? Everything went well, Gerry? What did they think this was? A boy had died, his body practically torn apart, and these people were discussing his funeral as if it were a football match. 'No,' said the distinctive voice of Gerry Adams, 'it went quite well. No serious incident, apart from this man here.' Then he put his hand on my shoulder. I turned around slowly. I said: 'What incident was that?'

'That incident when you encouraged the crowd to stomp their feet after they had been asked to stop,' said Adams.

'There was nothing wrong with that. They were showing their support for a dead volunteer.'

Adams shook his head: 'To me it smacks of militarism and fascism. I –'

I did not give him a chance to say another word. I rounded

on him and said between clenched teeth: 'That's like some-thing the Sticks would come out with!' Adams's hand slipped from my shoulder. He looked shocked. I had hit him with the accusation that his competitors within the Provisional republi-can movement had been levelling at him since he first became the movement's most charismatic figure since Padraig Pearse and Michael Collins. There was no greater insult that one Provo could level at another than to accuse him of following in the footsteps of the Official IRA (later the Workers' Party), who had abandoned violence and embraced parliamentarism. I walked away, furious, and no more was said between us.*

Jim McAllister of south Armagh gave the oration at Watters's graveside. The coffin was lowered into the grave. It was as if this death had been inevitable. Watters had become an admirer of Hardbap early in his IRA career, after entering into that circuit of drinking and socializing. His childish heroic fantasies had led him to beg Hardbap to give him a grenade to throw at a Land Rover. He saw the grenade as his passport into the ranks of the warriors. No amount of roses, dirges and orations could change the fact that he had died for nothing.

After the funeral, I busied myself with the additional responsibilities I now had in Sinn Fein as well as the IRA. Perhaps rationally I accepted that the war was over, yet emo-tionally, and practically, I could not respond to this truth. I tried to counter my doubts by telling myself that every IRA volunteer experienced doubts, especially volunteers who had been active for a long period. I did not talk to anyone about my feelings, not even to my wife, and certainly not to a single other IRA volunteer. I did everything in my power to maintain that façade of hard dedication.

---

* Official IRA members and supporters became known as 'stickies' or 'sticks' after they produced paper Easter lilies for the annual 1916 commemorations with an adhesive backing; their Provisional IRA rivals used a pin to attach the Easter lilies to their lapels.

17

MEETING THE PEOPLE

I joined Newry Sinn Fein within days of my meeting with the men from south Armagh.

I began immediately to take a leading role, which caused some resentment: people did not like the idea of someone trying to dictate the pace of the organization when he had only been in the building half an hour.

I soon found an opportunity to win credibility. I helped organize a concert at Newry town hall by the folk singer Christy Moore, and ensured that it was not advertised as a Sinn Fein event, which meant that more people turned up. Their last attempt had died from lack of support. The star even got paid and we made a healthy profit. I held a raffle at the event, launching myself on the Newry public. As a prize, I threw in my own framed poster of Bobby Sands (made by supporters in Iran).

I rose fast. I trampled over several old stalwarts in order to further the ambitions of the IRA. Practically nothing could go ahead unless I had given it my stamp of approval. Most Sinn Fein members realized quite quickly that an IRA man was running the show, and no one objected.

The Sinn Fein Advice Centre was in a condemned house due for demolition. We needed a lot of money to turn it into a respectable place to which local people would feel comfortable going. I went to see a local republican businessman to see whether he would be willing to give us an interest-free loan. He was not in a generous mood, although he agreed to buy a one pound raffle ticket. However, later the same week he contacted me with a proposition. He said that he wanted the IRA to blow up one of his hotels in Warrenpoint. I did not ask why, but I assumed the hotel was ailing financially and he needed the insurance money. He said that if the IRA blew up this hotel then he would give Sinn Fein ten thousand pounds towards the new advice centre. Unfortunately, the businessman was killed in a car accident before I could put the operation into effect. Since the 1970s the IRA in Newry, and presumably throughout the north, had blown up a lot of businesses with the collusion of their owners. Sometimes the businesses were in decaying premises, or they were in financial difficulties. Part of the compensation paid by the government for these attacks had ended up in the pocket of the IRA. A lot of businessmen in Newry had been put on the path to wealth by IRA bombs. These hypocrites were often the sort of people who would not support the IRA, but I could see why it was in the interests of the IRA to take advantage of their greed.

When Sinn Fein first took over the building for its centre there was no furniture, but I had managed to remedy our lack with the help of Her Majesty's Customs. I raided the stores of Newry Customs House and took away some mobile partitions, a fan heater, desks, swivel chairs, and filing-cabinets, piling my booty into a patrol car. By this stage I was making no attempt to disguise my republican sympathies at work. Indeed, I had even started to sell republican newspapers, Christmas cards, diaries and draw-tickets in the customs station. I was reckless, and provoking fate became a way of resolving the contradictions in my head.

One of my tasks was to boost the sales of *Republican News*. The newspapers were delivered weekly from Belfast, and I distributed them to my sellers, and then called for the money from those too lazy to hand it in for the Tuesday returns. This task also led to many arguments with the has-beens and wasters. I had to push for the dismissal of several of these characters, an act of mercy for many of them as it freed them to spend more time in the pub, although perhaps they had less money to spend once there. Within a few months we were selling 500 copies of the paper. Each paper made us 5p; the rest was sent to Belfast.

Dealing with the grievances people brought me began to absorb more and more of my time. Nothing was too trivial: disputes between neighbours, complaints about rowdy teenagers, badly-fitting doors, rising damp. One woman brought me round to her house to tell me about a problem she was having with a store from which she had bought a sofa and armchairs. The suite had fallen to pieces but the shop was refusing to honour the guarantee. I said she could tell the store that a Sinn Fein advice worker would be helping her to compile the case for the small claims court. The store acted swiftly to deal with her complaint.

After a while, one aspect of my encounters with people and their complaints began to depress me. I realized that a lot of people, often not even republicans, would seek the help of Sinn Fein in order to draw on the threat of IRA muscle – so they hoped – in solving their disputes. At times I felt as if people were treating me as a Mafia godfather. One former work colleague asked me if I could sort out his son-in-law. Apparently the latter was beating up his wife, my former colleague's daughter. I said that it was none of Sinn Fein's business. Then my former colleague said: 'Yes, it is. That man is never out of the police station. I'm sure he's an informer.' I said that he was making a very serious allegation. I said that if the IRA were to investigate it and find it to be groundless then they would come looking for the person who made the allegation. Unfortunately, the allegation that so-and-so was an informer (was 'never out of the police station') became one that I heard regularly from people who wanted extreme violence done to their neighbours, often for very petty reasons, such as damage to bushes, dents in cars, loud music. Once I understood someone's motivation, I could usually disregard their allegations. During my time in Sinn Fein I never caused violence to be inflicted upon anyone as a result of domestic disputes.

Meanwhile, however, contradictions began to emerge between Sinn Fein's new role and the armed struggle.

One day I got a call from Hardbap who demanded that I go immediately to Dundalk. When I arrived, he told me that he wanted me to arrange two operations. First, I had to find a target for a bomb which south Armagh wanted to get rid of. Second, he wanted me to find a black Ford Granada diesel car, ideally with a white roof.

The bomb had been lying in a culvert for a considerable period of time for use against an army or police patrol. I did not take long to decide the venue for the explosion. I would sandwich the bomb between the arts centre and Newry town hall, causing maximum damage to the two buildings, both of which had recently been renovated at great cost. I chose this target because I felt that both buildings had become the preserve of an unrepresentative group of aspiring middle-class Catholics. As far as I was then concerned, the arts centre was run by mediocrities who catered only for minority tastes. From my communist revolutionary perspective I felt they saw culture merely as a means to boost their own status and class position. I even looked forward to hearing them decrying cultural vandalism. I began to plan the operation, but Hardbap rang me again and told me that he had decided on a different course of action. Another target had been chosen for the bomb.

At lunch-time on 14 September 1984 a huge bomb exploded in Railway Avenue, breaking hundreds of windows and sending a shower of rubble and shrapnel over a wide area of nationalist Newry. People were terrified; women and children ran screaming down the street, their faces covered in blood. Seventy-one people were injured, several seriously, but by some miracle no one was killed. The IRA had attacked the Catholic population: I had no doubt that Hardbap's team had dumped that ageing south Armagh bomb. He had used, I later discovered, volunteers from out of town who did not know the area. They had got the streets mixed up and had abandoned the bomb in a panic, unable to phone a warning until it was too late for the police to clear the area. The bomb reminded me of what my work for the republican movement really meant.

Was this the republican movement's new dual strategy: the IRA would blow out your windows and Sinn Fein would mend them for you (or at least pressurize the housing executive to do so)? The armed struggle was contradicting, not enhancing, the political struggle, and vice versa. Those in the IRA who thought that the two struggles could run side by side were wrong; and actions like this bombing were, in terms of their new strategy, acts of political suicide.

In the meantime I had found Hardbap the car he wanted, though I wondered what use a slow diesel car could be. I had it hijacked at gunpoint and taken to the south. Then someone told me that Hardbap wanted the car for a buyer in the republic: this was a private deal to raise some cash for himself. I knew that Hardbap would not have done this off his own bat – he had the example of the previous OC who had almost been executed by the IRA, partly because he had been accused of carrying out 'owners' (that is, thefts for personal gain). Other IRA men had to be involved, probably at a fairly senior level, because I knew Hardbap would not have taken the risk on his own. When I confronted him about it, he behaved evasively, telling me I did not need to know what the car was for.

My disillusionment with the republican movement began to accelerate. I began to ask myself: is this an organization that thinks it can do whatever it likes to people and get away with it? But there was still no easy way out. People will say: why did you not just resign? But it is extremely hard to admit that what you have spent the last six years of your life doing, straining every nerve and suppressing every normal human emotion, is wrong. It is easier, for a while at least, to make one last effort to force yourself to believe that what you are doing might somehow still be right.

Others were more aware of my disillusionment than I was myself. My confrontation with Gerry Adams at Watters's funeral had not been forgotten. In November, I rang a senior Belfast Sinn Fein figure, Tom Hartley, and arranged an appointment with him at the Falls Road headquarters. I needed to talk to him about something to do with sales of *Republican News*. I walked into the centre and realized that people were waiting for me, in a very hostile atmosphere. The first person I saw sitting at his desk was the Sinn Fein publicity director,

Danny Morrison, later sentenced for his role in abducting an alleged informer. He looked up at me with an air of authority and said: 'Did you call Gerry Adams a Stick?' There were other people in the room and I could see that they had all stopped work in order to listen. Morrison almost spat at me: 'You called Gerry Adams a *Stick* at Brendan Watters's funeral, didn't you?' I felt uncomfortable but I denied calling our president a stick. I muttered that I had merely said that he had made one statement which I had felt was something like the Sticks would come out with. Morrison began to talk slowly and deliberately, his teeth almost clenched. He told me that Gerry Adams was not a Stick, had never been a Stick, and would never be a Stick. He explained at elaborate length Gerry Adams's republican bona fides. I had obviously touched a very raw nerve. At that moment Adams himself walked in to the office, smoking his famous pipe. He did not glance at me and went over to a filing-cabinet from which he took some papers. Then he walked out of the room. I said to Morrison: 'Look, there's Gerry. I'm willing to apologize to him personally. I did not really mean to suggest in any way that he was a Stick.' Morrison looked at me and repeated. 'You called Gerry Adams a Stick.' The atmosphere was extremely tense. I said: 'No, I didn't.' Tom Hartley, who had been hovering in the background, came over to me. He said: 'I've got a wee bone to pick with you. Come into my office.' I went into his office and could feel Morrison's eyes glaring at my back. Hartley bolted the door of his cubicle. I began to feel even more intimidated and uncomfortable. He said: 'You did call Gerry Adams a Stick.' Hartley then said, very coldly: 'Perhaps you need to reconsider your position within the republican movement.' I denied again vehemently what I was being accused of. Hartley appeared mollified. He looked at me for a few seconds and then he changed the subject. We discussed newspaper sales in a desultory way for ten minutes and then I left the building. I was glad to emerge again into the open air, but I suspected that I had not yet heard the last word on the subject.

18

THE NUTTING SQUAD

My promotion to the security unit had given me an initial glow of satisfaction.

I tried to allow the swelling of my ego to overshadow the horror of what I was involved in. My 'promotion' became a crutch to support myself in the collapse of my belief in the armed struggle. But so advanced was the process of mental deterioration that I could no longer quite believe my own desperate attempt at self-deception. I knew I was staring at my own defeat. Yet my vanity gave me the strength to continue acting out for a little while longer a role that was no longer mine.

My first experience of the work of the security unit was the debriefing of a young man who had operated with Brian McNally. He had been arrested and interrogated in Gough Barracks before being released. Before he came in for his debriefing, a heavy dark cloth was placed over the window to darken the room. The volunteer was taken in and told to sit on a chair facing the wall, with his back to us. There were no other chairs. I sat on the floor with Mooch.

John Joe Magee spoke quietly and politely. His voice was impassive. He said: 'Don't be alarmed at the darkened room, son. That is to protect you as well as me. This debriefing is what happens to everyone who has been in an interrogation centre. It doesn't matter who you are. I've been through it myself. Do you understand that?'

'I do,' said the volunteer, with a hint of nervous tension in his voice.

'Good. Relax. Feel at ease. There's nothing to fear. Right, all I want you to do is to begin at the beginning from when you were arrested. Take your time, son.'

The volunteer started to talk in detail about everything that had happened to him in Gough Barracks. John Joe helped the flow of the narrative by asking short and precise questions. He wanted to know how many interrogations he had had and what sort of things had been said. He listened patiently to the answers. He never rushed the volunteer with questions. The young man admitted that he had talked to his interrogators but he swore that he had not told them anything about his IRA work. John Joe asked him why he had spoken. The volunteer said: 'I thought I could explain my way out of it by giving them excuses.'

'Aye,' said John Joe, 'and you could just as easily have talked your way into prison.'

Mooch mimed the gesture of shooting a revolver. What was he saying? That because this young volunteer had spoken to his interrogators he should be shot? The egotistical glow of importance I had experienced earlier disappeared. I looked at Mooch and wondered how someone like him could be given the power of life and death over people. I had not yet reached the point when I would ask the same question of myself, of all of us. The special irony in Mooch's case was that he had just come out of prison for a sentence he had received after breaking under interrogation and signing statements implicating himself.

John Joe had told us earlier in the day that we would know from the flow of someone's story whether he was telling the truth. A good consistent flow, without hesitations, contradictions or gaps tended to indicate that the subject was telling the truth.

John Joe continued to probe. He asked the volunteer whether the police had said anything that had surprised him. The volunteer said: 'They tried to make me feel angry about the shooting of McNally.'

John Joe asked how they had done that. The volunteer said: 'One of them said, "Your mate Brian McNally was shot dead by the Provos and that cunt Danny Morrison was seen from an army surveillance post crossing the border at four in the morning with stubble on his face. He was after being up and involved in the stiff of your mate McNally. He came up from Belfast to give the OK. Good old Danny. The Lord Chief Justice himself."'

Magee did not say anything. He continued with more questions, all of which the volunteer answered satisfactorily. Magee finished the debriefing by repeating that he was wrong to have talked to the police, but that he believed that he had not given anything away, so as far as security was concerned he was clean.

After this session in Dundalk, Hardbap again took me to see the south Armagh 'general'. This man told me that Magee and Scap were fine men but he wanted his own security officers because he was tired of depending on people from Belfast. He said there were parts of the south Down region outside of Newry which were rotten with informers and he could not authorize the passing on of guns, explosives and vehicles to those areas. He said that Belfast security people often lacked the special knowledge of border areas which he felt was needed to eradicate touts. I knew the subtext of what the south Armagh man was saying: he thought the security unit was under the control of the Belfast IRA, and he did not like the power over his area that such control gave Belfast. On the surface the security unit had no regional bias and acted in the interests of the IRA as a whole, but he knew who really pulled the strings. I could see that a power struggle was taking place within the republican movement. Apart from his attitude to the security unit, his fears illustrated the nature of the tension between Belfast and areas such as south Armagh. He saw that the republican movement's power was becoming concentrated in Belfast among aspiring politicians who were stealthily moving towards a political compromise and abandonment of the armed struggle.

I did not tell this man that I knew the subtext of what he was saying. In one sense I agreed with south Armagh's analysis of the direction in which the republican movement was moving. Indeed, part of me regarded my recruitment into the security unit as a way of getting to the heart of the Belfast

organization in order to subvert the growing power of the
Gerry Adams group. My plan, in moments when I could beat
back the growing sense of self-doubt, was that by appearing to
align myself with Magee and Scap I would in a short time get
to know everyone who was anyone in Belfast, and begin to
influence Belfast IRA men, helping them to see what was really
taking place in the movement, and building up a base of support within Belfast.

However, this was a fantasy, because I was doubting more
and more both my own commitment to the armed struggle
and the validity of the struggle itself. I was not sure that I
cared anymore about anything – except my own survival. I
was beginning to feel like an empty shell, as if it were not me
who was living my life. I told the south Armagh IRA leader
that of course I was interested in becoming a more specialized
security officer for our border area in the future, but that at the
moment I needed to do the bidding of Scap and John Joe.

For eight hours a day I was owned by the customs; for the
rest of my time I was owned by the republican movement. I
continued to work without a break. I worked for Sinn Fein, for
the security unit and for the local unit of the IRA. I helped out
on a number of operations. One day I sat with Teddy in my
kitchen, looking out of the window at an army patrol walking
past. Teddy pointed to the patrol leader and said: 'We could
take his head off from here with a good rifle.' I looked away. I
did not want to listen to war talk. I felt a sense of nausea and I
asked to myself: 'What difference is it going to make, shooting
that soldier?' But I did not say that to Teddy. I could not talk
to anyone about what was taking place in my mind. I maintained a front of impenetrable hardness, frightened that if any
crack appeared on the outside then total inner collapse would
follow.

Over the next few months I got to know John Joe and Scap
quite well. Scap was small and barrel-chested, with classic
Mediterranean looks – olive-skinned with tight black curly
hair. He was the son of an Italian immigrant. John Joe was
freckled, puffy-faced, with bags under his eyes. He had wisps
of greying hair on a balding head. He walked slowly, ham-
pered by his weight, but he still exuded the brash confidence of

the retired NCO, his soldierly air enhanced by his clipped military moustache. I came to learn that his military knowledge had been developed during service in the British Army – the Special Boat Squadron of the Royal Marines, no less. He had put it to good effect in the service of the IRA. In his early days as a Provo he had even got one of his former officers to stand up in court and vouch for his good character. John Joe had worked on his good character over the years; indeed so good was his character that he had risen swiftly to become the head of the Nutting Squad. He was a sort of chief executioner and witchfinder general rolled into one, and he loved his job.

One time I sat in a house with them to await the arrival of some men who had just been released from police custody. The woman of the house had made us tea. John Joe and Scap started reminiscing about past experiences. I asked them whether I would personally be expected to shoot informers. Scap, his mouth full, said that when the time arrived I would have to do it. I asked whether they always told people that they were going to be shot. Scap said it depended on the circumstances. He turned to John Joe and started joking about one informer who had confessed after being offered an amnesty. Scap told the man that he would take him home, reassuring him that he had nothing to worry about. Scap had told him to keep the blindfold on for security reasons as they walked away from the car.

'It was funny,' he said, 'watching the bastard stumbling and falling, asking me as he felt his way along railings and walls, "Is this my house now?" and I'd say, "No, not yet, walk on some more . . ."'

'. . . and then you shot the fucker in the back of the head,' said John Joe, and both of them burst out laughing.

I could see the man stumbling as he made his way slowly along. The most perverse part was that the poor bastard thought he was going home. And I was now part of this. I did not have the courage to say: 'I can't go through with this. I haven't got the stomach for it.' Part of me hoped that my self-doubt would pass, because part of me admired John Joe and Scap. I could even envy their ruthless certainty that what they were doing was right.

Scap told me that we had a lot of work to do that day. We were going to debrief several former prisoners who had recently formed a punishment squad in Newry, and had just been lifted by the police, detained for a couple of days, then released. We were also going to be vetting a few budding recruits.

John Joe vetted the punishment squad and said they were clean. For the next few hours, Scap interviewed a succession of five potential recruits from Newry and the surrounding area. I sat watching with Mooch. They were taken into the darkened room one by one. Scap asked all of them the same questions: had they had any prior connection with the republican movement? Did they attend republican marches, events or funerals? Did they drink in well-known republican pubs? Had they ever sung rebel songs publicly? Were they known in their areas as IRA supporters? Had they ever been arrested? If so, what was the outcome of that arrest? Did they have a criminal record? If so, what for? If they answered yes to any question, then Scap would ask follow-up questions: when, where and with whom did they attend this march, event or funeral? Had they to their knowledge been photographed by the Crown forces then or at any time since? Were they stopped and searched regularly by the Crown forces?

The most significant question was: why did they want to join the IRA? The same simple reasons cropped up all the time: the Brits were killing our people; the army, police and legal system were biased against Catholics; they felt as Catholics that they were discriminated against generally in society and nothing was ever done about it. Almost always they expressed personal experiences of harassment and intimidation from the Crown forces. In the simplicity of their answers these young men expressed their total alienation from the state.

After telling them that they had been successfully vetted, Scap said that they all had to steer clear of everything republican. They were to show no sympathy for the IRA, keep away from republican events and avoid the company of known republicans. Scap said they had taken the first step on the road to becoming volunteers and they were ready to take the next step – the Green Book lectures.

During the next few weeks, I met up with Scap who told me
that there was an informer in the Dundalk area, and that he
wanted me to find a safe house in Newry where we could vet
recruits from now on. He told me not to tell Hardbap, although
he said I was allowed to tell Mooch, who had found another
three prospective recruits from Banbridge. These three would
be the first ones to be vetted in Newry.

One of my informants, the television engineer, had recently
passed on one of his snippets. He had been driving on the
Armagh Road late one evening and had seen a man coming out
from behind a hedge and getting into a car which had swiftly
driven off. He identified the man from his distinctive, tall,
gaunt and bearded look. He was the father of a dead IRA volunteer. My source had taken the registration number of the car.
I had put it through the vehicle-licensing computer: it was a
police car. Scap said: 'This could be embarrassing.' I said: 'I
know. Maybe he's only passing off low-grade shite gossip from
the streets.' I knew the man myself. I knew also that Hardbap
spoke to him regularly on the phone. I told Scap that I had
already passed on the news to Hardbap. Scap said: 'Listen,
contact him and tell him you want to go for a drink with him
some night in Dundalk with Hardbap.'

I told Mooch about the plans for a Newry safe house for the
security unit. He seemed anxious when I told him that we had
orders not to tell Hardbap about the plan. There was a colour-
ing of personal hatred to the games that were being played. I
knew that Scap and Hardbap loathed each other. Even before I
had joined security I had heard that one night after a drinking
session in Dundalk, Scap had tried to run Hardbap over in his
car.

The next day I met up with Scap. He took me to Belfast's
Lenadoon Estate. We drove past acres of box-shaped blocks of
flats, dire monuments to the utility architecture of the sixties.
Republican graffiti decorated the space between windows and
doors. Scap told me that the man we were about to interview
had come forward through an intermediary (his brother-in-
law, an IRA man) to admit that he had worked for the RUC's
Special Branch. He wanted to take advantage of the IRA's

public offer of an amnesty to anyone who admitted working for the police. Scap said they had already interviewed him once but they had called him back to clear up 'a few minor matters'.

We walked into a block of flats and Scap knocked on a door. A man in his early thirties answered. He invited us in and said he was about to go out. John Joe Magee was in the kitchen. We waited as we heard the informer being taken into the bedroom, whose windows had already been covered. The three of us entered the room. The man sat on a chair with his back to us. He seemed to be in his late forties. He was wearing heavy boots and an overcoat. He had a wiry black beard and on his head was a monkey hat. He sat with his shoulders slightly hunched. John Joe spoke first: he told the man not to be worried because he had been given an amnesty which was a cast-iron guarantee. However, he said with great emphasis, the amnesty could be undermined if it was discovered that he had not told us everything about his dealings with the peelers.

'I told you everything. I held nothing back,' said the man excitedly, in a high-pitched voice.

John Joe said: 'Well, I don't think you told us everything about that rifle that you saw your brother-in-law hide in the pub where you worked. The police found that rifle and you bear the responsibility.'

'I didn't tell the Branch anything about it. I swear I didn't. Please, you've got to believe me. I didn't know that rifle was kept there and I didn't tell the Branch man about it, I swear.'

The man began to sway backwards and forwards in his chair, like a child. Scap beckoned to me to go forward and begin questioning the man. I thought that Scap should have briefed me a bit more first about the ground they had already covered with the informer. I did not want to go over the same things. As I moved forward, John Joe stepped back into the darkness. I walked right up to the man. I wanted him to feel my presence, close. I wanted to add to the frightening atmosphere. I wanted to impress John Joe and Scap.

I said: 'So you worked for Special Branch, giving them information on IRA men, but you never gave them the golden opportunity to seize a rifle. And yet the rifle was found and you say, amazingly, that you had nothing to do with it.'

'That's the truth I'm telling you. I wouldn't lie. Why should I lie?'

I said: 'Why should you lie? I'll tell you why: because you don't want us to know the real harm you've done the IRA in south Down, because you're trying to play down your role. Now I would call that a pretty good reason for lying.'

'Well, I can tell you, boss, I'm not lying. I went to the IRA of my own free will to clear up a few things, and that's what I did.'

I paused for a moment and changed my position. John Joe asked him why he had started informing in the first place.

The man said: 'Well, as I told that other man who questioned me last week, I was angry when I heard my wife was going out with someone else and the IRA had done nothing about it. So I got drunk one night and rang the police in Newcastle and that was the start of it all.' He named the detective with whom he had first made contact and he detailed the money he had been paid for keeping a watch on the movements of suspects.

I moved in again with a technique I had learnt from the RUC during my own interrogation. I moved right up close, literally breathing down his neck. I wanted him to feel a strong, intimidating physical presence.

I said: 'You gave up the rifle, didn't you? What better way to hit back at your wife than by informing on where her brother keeps his rifle.'

'I didn't. I swear I didn't.' Again he began to move backwards and forwards in his chair, rubbing his woolly hat continuously with his big calloused hands. I could see that he was feeling the pressure, see sweat breaking out on his neck. 'I didn't tell them about that rifle. Honest to God, I didn't.'

I shouted: 'Well, how the fuck did they get it, then? How did they know to go directly to where it was hidden? How come? How come?'

'I don't know. I told that other man over and over that I didn't do it. I didn't do it.'

I moved back from him and paused again. I quietened my voice and said: 'All right then, you didn't do it. So why didn't you do it? You were a paid informer. Here was a good oppor-

tunity to get back at that bitch who left you and let you down
and who was screwing around with someone else. So why
didn't you take the opportunity? Why? Why?' I had moved
right up to his neck again. He had started exuding a pungent
smell. He continued to deny everything. I felt I was working on
someone who had already been terrified half to death. I started
to feel sorry for this wretched man and sick at myself. We were
not going to get anything more out of him. I was terrorizing
him to impress John Joe and Scap, perhaps even to impress
myself. I was using this piece of sick theatre to prove to myself
that I was still a committed IRA man capable of acting with
ruthless dedication for the struggle. I imagined McNally sitting
like this man, terrified and sweating, before they shot him.

The interrogation continued for another two hours. Finally
John Joe decided that it was going nowhere and he brought the
inquisition to an end. The informer was allowed to go. He was
going to live.

I still refused to face up to the reality of my disillusionment. I
knew the war had become a farce, but I could not stop playing
my role. I knew the border areas, particularly south Armagh,
remained committed to the military struggle, but Belfast's
commitment had almost disappeared – in reality, if not in
appearance. And Belfast was where the real power of the organization resided and where the final decisions would really be
made. Sinn Fein's influence was growing even stronger. If it
remained subordinate to the army then it would lose the credibility it had with the wider community. The needs of a radical
populist party did not sit easily with the needs of the armed
struggle. The IRA could no longer afford any civilian casualties. It had not lost the war, but nor could it win an outright
victory. Military victory could only come about if the Republic
of Ireland rose in total insurrection and seized the north in a
bloody civil war, but there was absolutely no possibility of that
happening. So the IRA's struggle had become pointless: the
only justification for our existence was to protect Catholic areas
from loyalist death squads. We had no right to take offensive
action, and the Irish people had told the IRA in the recent
elections that they had no mandate to continue the war in their

name. The mere 13 per cent vote for Sinn Fein in the north did not give the IRA the justification it needed to continue the war. The nationalist people were saying: call it off.

In the last quarter of 1984, I was finished as an IRA man. My involvement with Sinn Fein and the Nutting Squad had only accelerated the process of my disillusionment. Yet I still could not let go. Why? Was the alternative so difficult to face? I had even begun to question my own Marxist analysis. I had started to ask myself seriously whether I was living in a political fantasy world. I began to think that the republican movement's shift towards political compromise was based on a more perceptive appraisal of reality than my own Revolutionary-Communist-Group-inspired analysis. I could see how the development of Sinn Fein represented in some ways a leap into the real world.

Some days later, Hardbap phoned me late at night to ask me to come immediately to Dundalk to pick up Mooch, as he needed a lift home. I refused. I said: 'I'm not a fucking taxi service,' and I put the phone down.

19

BREAKING POINT

By the end of 1984, I had started to feel real fear. I fought hard to control it, but my nerves had started to fray. I was beginning to feel mentally ill, afflicted by a growing sense of the awfulness of what I had done.

I suspected that the police knew I had been promoted to the Nutting Squad. I could hardly step outside my door without being stopped and searched. I knew I was being watched wherever I went. I worked hard to counter the surveillance, but the price of my vigilance was constant paranoia.

At night, unidentifiable voices would threaten death over the telephone. In recent years, the Crown forces had shot dead several unarmed members of the IRA in shoot-to-kill incidents. There was a new ruthless effectiveness on the part of the state. The intensity of the interest being shown in me filled me with foreboding. I began for the first time to have premonitions of my own death.

I went to Dundalk to meet with Mooch to discuss the setting-up of the security unit's safe house in Newry and to have a preliminary meeting with the three prospective recruits from Banbridge. I waited in the shopping centre for him to arrive. As I waited I watched the shoppers with their children going about their ordinary business. Their faces looked calm and untroubled, absorbed by their innocent routines. I envied them. My wife had had our second child in November, but I had hardly spent any time at home. I just wanted to be human again, if I could.

Mooch arrived. He told me that the Banbridge men had not been able to make the journey, but he said there was now something more important: that the south Armagh IRA leader wanted to see me as a matter of urgency. 'It's about the safe house.' My jaw must have dropped. I said: 'Nobody is supposed to know about this. This was meant to be kept in a tight circle. Now south Armagh knows. Does Hardbap?' Mooch said he did. I asked: 'How many others know? Why don't you put it in *Republican News?*'

The south Armagh man, when we met, came straight to the point. He said that he thought the idea of a security unit safe house in Newry was unrealistic, and anyway, there was no way he was going to allow it. He gave some reasons why, but I knew his real motive was hostility to a perceived encroachment on his patch. He told me again that he wanted me to be a security officer for the border area, not for the whole of the north, as John Joe and Scap wanted. I said that Scap had asked me to prepare the safe house in secret because he thought there was an informer in Dundalk. This suggestion was dismissed: 'If there's an informer here, we'll sort him out ourselves.' I could see that my behaviour was beginning to worry him. He had hoped he could rely on me to put the interests of my own area first, but now I seemed to be moving into Belfast's camp.

Then he changed the subject. He asked me what was going on between me and Hardbap. He said that Hardbap was complaining I wouldn't work with him. He said that he had known many men in the IRA who had hated one or other of their colleagues, but they had always agreed to bury their differences for the common good. The meeting finished with a plea to me to sort this thing out with Hardbap.

I returned home feeling even more disillusioned. I could sympathize with those in south Armagh who felt the need to counter Belfast's growing dominance, but their concerns seemed more like those of medieval warlords fighting a primitive territorial battle.

Christmas brought a shock. My cousin Mickey, although still in his twenties, suffered a heart attack after a heavy drinking session. I drove to the hospital. I took Mickey's girlfriend with me, and we stood by his bed surrounded by family and friends. Mickey was covered with wires; a heart monitor hummed beside him. His eyes flickered open and he saw me. He beckoned to me with his finger. I moved close to him and bent my ear to his mouth. He said: 'Did it go ahead? Was he got?' I realized that he was talking about a part-time UDR soldier that the South Down Command had been hoping to kill on Christmas Eve. I said the operation had been called off. Even on the verge of death, all Mickey could think about was killing.

Scap contacted me in the New Year and we arranged a rendezvous in Belfast. He drove me to Magee's house in Andersonstown. We went in and John Joe was sitting there with rolled-up shirt sleeves. Scap said: 'Tell him about the father of that dead IRA man.' I told John Joe who said: 'If he's just giving low-grade stuff then we'll let him go, but if he's been doing serious stuff then he won't be going home.' I said that I was working on tricking him into going to Dundalk. John Joe said: 'Good. Now tell me what is going on between you and Hardbap?' I decided to forsake my loyalty to the South Down Command by telling Magee what Mooch and Hardbap had been up to: particularly the Newry safe house fiasco.

I started to do more work for the security unit and even less work for Hardbap, although now we tried to be at least civil with each other. My next job in Belfast was to attend an IRA court martial. Scap told me I was going to be one of three judges who would decide the fate of an OC from Fermanagh who had endangered the lives of volunteers by going across the border into Donegal to try to kill a UDR man from his area who was on holiday with his family. He had been instructed by a senior commander not to go ahead with the operation, but he had ignored the order and had gone ahead with the operation. The UDR man noticed that he was under surveillance and had fled the holiday camp before the IRA could strike.

Scap said: 'He's a real arrogant bastard and it's time to get rid of him. He should be dismissed.' But he added that, as an impartial judge, I would have to make up my own mind about the man when I heard the evidence. I said: 'Look, do you want this man dismissed? I'll take your word for it that he's a bastard.' Scap said he wanted me to decide for myself. We met up with another Belfast IRA man who was also going to be a judge. He said to Scap: 'Have you filled in Eamon about this fucker?' I could see this OC was not about to receive the fairest of hearings.

We drove to a secluded bungalow in the Poleglass area, some way off a main road. We sat in a side bedroom with the other judge and talked among ourselves until John Joe walked in, holding a copy of the Green Book. He read out a number of instructions, almost calling us to attention. He asked whether the three judges required to constitute this court martial were present and accounted for. We said we were. A young woman arrived. She was in her late teens, with a clear face and blonde hair. Several garish rings covered her fingers, which were red with the cold. John Joe said that she was the note-taker and that he was the president of the court. Tables and chairs were arranged formally in the room. A small, stocky, serious-looking man with a Tyrone accent entered. He stood to attention. He was the prosecuting counsel. An old man called Liam was the next to arrive. He had neatly-combed grey hair and spectacles and carried himself with dignity. He said he was the convenor of the court martial and it was his duty to swear us in. We, the judges, swore by almighty God not to show fear, favour or affection to the accused but to reach our decision solely on the facts of the case and to dispense justice fairly and impartially. The note-taker and the others took a separate oath.

The court martial was ready to begin, but the accused had not yet arrived. We waited and waited. An hour passed but there was still no sign of the OC. Finally John Joe said that the man obviously was not going to turn up so we would have to try him in his absence. The facts of the case were put to us. We decided unanimously to dismiss him from the IRA. We informed President Magee of our decision. The prosecuting counsel stood stiffly to attention and asked the court formally for its decision. Then we were dismissed. I felt I had taken part in a kangaroo court.

In early February of 1985, the south Armagh Sinn Fein

leader Jim McAllister called me to a meeting at Camlough Sinn Fein office. I suspected it had something to do with my proposed candidature in the coming council elections. I had resolved to tell Jim that I no longer thought I wanted to stand as a Sinn Fein councillor, but I soon discovered that the decision had already been made for me. My encounter with Gerry Adams at Brendan Watters's funeral was still reverberating. The first thing that Jim asked me when I sat down in the office was: 'Did you call Gerry Adams a Sticky?' I could not believe that this was still an issue. I told Jim that my words had been misinterpreted and that, anyway, I had already explained myself to Danny Morrison and Tom Hartley in Belfast. Jim said: 'Well, there are some very angry people in Belfast and it led to an ugly incident only recently.' Jim told me that a delegation from the Newry/south Armagh areas had gone down to Belfast for a meeting. Among the delegation was a small, stocky, bearded man from Newry called Brendan. As the delegation was waiting for the meeting to begin a Belfast man said to Brendan: 'You must be the bastard who called Gerry Adams a Stick.' Brendan, whom I knew, was not the type to take an insult lightly. He denied saying anything of the sort to Adams, and there was almost a fight. Things had only calmed down when they realized that the man was not Eamon Collins.

Jim moved on to the main business. He said it had been decided that I was not an appropriate person to stand as a Sinn Fein candidate because I was a British customs officer. He said that people thought it would be a little strange to have an officer of the Crown representing Sinn Fein. I said I was happy to stand down.

As I drove home, I began to feel angry at this touch of farce. I could no longer give myself any logical reasons for going on: my emotional commitment to the memory of the dead hunger strikers seemed to be about all I could cling on to. I realized how expendable I was. And what about the hunger strikers? Perhaps they had been expendable too.

One Sunday in early February 1985, I had received a phone call in the afternoon. A man with a softly-spoken Ulster accent said: 'Is that Eamon?' I said it was. I did not recognize his voice. He said: 'I've got some information for you.' I was suspicious but I remembered that Mooch had told me to expect a call from 'an insurance guy' who wanted to pass on some intelligence to the IRA. I knew my phone was tapped so I could not ask for his name or where he was telephoning from. I said: 'How did you know to contact me?' He replied that he had been told that I was the man to see about this information. To cover myself, in case the call was being recorded, I said that the only information I wanted to hear concerned the person who had started a recent fire in my father's hay-shed. He said he could tell me. He told me to meet him at noon on the back road to Camlough beside the greyhound track, and said he would be driving a silver Ford Fiesta. I thought, from his car, that he could be the insurance man. I drove to Mooch's to ask if he knew whether the insurance man had a silver Ford Fiesta. He did not know. I left Mooch's home and decided to drive to the rendezvous. As I set off, I decided on a whim that I would pick up Teddy and bring him with me. Teddy agreed to come.

I made my way to the greyhound track. I drove along the back road. As I came to the first crossroads I stopped to give way. I noticed a brown car parked on the opposite side of the road. A casually-dressed man was sitting at the wheel. He had a thick head of wavy black hair and a moustache. He looked directly at me. Suddenly I felt nervous. I knew I was entering into danger: an ambush? Were they going to abduct me? The police? SAS? Loyalist paramilitaries? I drove across the road and up a steep hill. The greyhound track was at the top of the hill. Teddy and I did not speak but we were both keyed up and alert. I knew the man at the crossroads would have radioed ahead by now to say that we were coming. I was glad I had brought Teddy with me: whoever was waiting up the road would not have expected another person in the car. His presence might force them to abandon their plans. As I crossed over the top of the hill I saw a silver Colt Lancer move off from the side of the road just in front of me. I put my foot on the accelerator and came right up behind him. I thought: 'If anything happens now, I'm going to ram this bastard.' I memorized the registration number. As we passed a road on the left I glanced down and saw a lime Vauxhall Cavalier parked at the side. A heavy-set man in his late forties sat at the steering-wheel.

I drove on with the Colt Lancer in front of me. The road was now too narrow for overtaking. Hedges lined it, obscuring us from the view of anyone in nearby farmhouses. We passed a disused cottage with a white Toyota Hiace van parked in front of it. I thought: 'This is a set-up. It's an SAS set-up.' Teddy memorized the registration number of the van. Another moustachioed man sat at the steering-wheel. He gave us a quick glance as we drove past. The car in front began to accelerate. I did the same. Then I spotted a driveway. I braked suddenly, reversed in, and then shot back down the road I had just come up. On a hill running almost parallel to the road I could see the white Hiace van followed by the lime Cavalier. I accelerated and as I turned a corner I saw the brown car that I had seen at the crossroads speeding towards me. I held most of the road and drove at him. He pulled in to let me pass. Then, as I passed, he smiled at me and gave me a wave that was more of a salute than a wave, as if he were saying, 'You've got away this time, but we'll meet again.' I did not acknowledge his wave. I drove on and got clear of the area. Teddy was almost in shock. He said: 'Don't ever ask me to go on something like this again.'

Later that day, I heard from local people that soldiers had been digging themselves in to fields near the greyhound track. On Monday I went in to work and did something very incautious: I put the two registration numbers through the vehicle computer without trying to disguise what I was doing. There was no record of either vehicle. I knew for sure that I had been the target of a military operation. Later that month, the SAS shot dead three IRA men in Strabane.

One night in the last week of February I got a call from Scap. He said it was imperative that I attend a meeting in Dundalk on the following evening. The next day I was babysitting my two-year-old son Tiarnach because my wife was in bed with post-natal depression. My son had a cold. I decided to take him with me to the meeting. I went to the agreed house and found John Joe, Scap, the south Armagh leader, Mooch and Hardbap waiting for me. I apologized for bringing my son but explained there was no one else to look after him as my wife was ill. The woman of the house brought a playpen into the room and I put Tiarnach into it. John Joe said: 'We want to ask you about this situation over the dead IRA man's father.' Hardbap was outraged; it seemed that I had dared to use him as bait to get the suspected informer up to Dundalk. Mooch had obviously told Hardbap that I was trying to trick the man into coming up here by holding out the possibility of a drink with his 'friend'. I could not see what the problem was. If I had asked him merely to go for a drink with me he would have wanted to know why we could not go for a drink in Newry. His handlers would have alerted him to danger even if he were not sharp enough himself to realize what was going on. Using Hardbap's name was the most sensible way of getting him to Dundalk without making him suspicious.

Scap said nothing, even though he had first suggested this ruse. The south Armagh leader said: 'Well, if you'd done it on me I would have had you lifted.' He was saying that he would have had me picked up (and interrogated? and beaten?) if I had used his name to help catch an informer. I asked him what I had done that was so wrong. He said: 'You're compromising Hardbap. You're using that man's name. I'll tell you what, you wouldn't use my name.' I said that Hardbap was living safely on the run in Dundalk; I could not see how I was compromising him. Then suddenly I saw what was really going on: Hardbap did not want the suspected tout brought up for interrogation because he was worried about what the man might say about what Hardbap had let slip on the phone during his friendly conversations. The south Armagh leader was willing to back Hardbap as a way of undermining me, because I had shown myself not to be one of his boys after all. What puzzled me the most was the way John Joe and Scap were not doing anything to protect me. Perhaps the news that I had called Gerry Adams a Stick had reached them too.

My son started crying. I went over to comfort him. Scap said: 'Next time you come up, don't take the child with you. This is serious business.' My son would not stop crying so we all moved into the next room as the woman came in to deal with him. In the next room, I could still hear my baby son

crying. The woman came in and said: 'He won't settle down.'
I went and picked him up and brought him into the meeting,
but my inquisitors had decided to call it a day. John Joe said: 'I
want you and Scap to find another way of getting that man up
here.' I told them about what had happened to me recently.
The south Armagh man said that people had disappeared from
Crossmaglen in the past and he had no doubt that the Brits had
'disappeared' them. I asked what I should do? John Joe asked
me what sort of security I had at my home. I told him that I
did not really have good windows or doors. He told me to get
them installed, and to start checking under my car. Neither of
them seemed particularly concerned that I might have been
killed. I had thought that they might have suggested that I
moved south for a few months, but no: I was on my own.

I strapped my son in the front seat of the car. He slumped
down, and fell asleep almost immediately, exhausted by his
heavy cold. I thought that I should have been at home looking
after him, instead of here with these people. My son needed
me more than the IRA.

I drove home thinking those people represented the Irish
nation's fight for national liberation and what petty bastards
they were. In my anger I thought that we represented nobody
and nothing but ourselves, that we were fighting only for a
twisted version of freedom. The only reason the war was
being fought was to facilitate the petty power plays of people
like Hardbap and the south Armagh leader. My wife was ill in
bed, my son was ill in the car, and I was spending my life running around for people who could not have cared less about
me. I realized that I was the only one out of the group I had
just left who worked for a living except for Scap, who worked
occasionally as a builder. The others relied on the state to pay
for their freedom-fighting. I wanted to live now for my son
and my family. I was going to get out. [I was going to leave the
republican movement behind]. I had fought this so-called just
war for six years and what had I become? A diminished, dehu-
manised being incapable of feeling for my victims, only
capable of feeling for myself and my family. I thought I could
be killed at any time: and so what? Another pointless death to
add to all the other pointless deaths I had been responsible for.

The next day I got a call from Hardbap. He wanted to know whether he could borrow my car for IRA business at the weekend. I said no: I was going to be taking my wife and kids away for a little break. Hardbap said: 'Some things are more important.' I replied: 'No, they aren't.'

20

THE EXPLOSION

I got up around 6 a.m. for my early shift on 28 February 1985. I did not know it was going to be my last day of work for Her Majesty's Customs and Excise.

It was a beautiful winter's morning and I enjoyed the quiet in the house as I set about raking out the fire. I wanted my wife to wake up to warmth when she rose with our baby son, Lorcan, then three months old. My eldest son, Tiarnach, was already walking about, sucking on his dummy. He watched me light the fire.

I thought of the day ahead. I would finish work by two. Then I would go into town to buy a wide-angle lense for my camera, for I was preparing to go on holiday with my old Revolutionary Communist Group mentor – to Vietnam, which had defeated the mightiest empire in the world. It had always been a place that fascinated both of us, and now it seemed a place of refuge. My friend was lending me some of the money to go. I heard Bernie move across the bedroom upstairs to soothe the child and I imagined her taking him to her breast. The night before, she had told me that she was suffering so greatly from post-natal depression that she was thinking of seeking psychiatric help at a specialist hospital in Armagh. Her declaration was a terrible blow. I had seen her looking exhausted and gloomy for several months and yet in my own self-absorbed fear and obsession I had not reached out to her.

I had felt guilty about not being at home often enough to lessen her burdens, but instead of even trying to talk to her, I had buried my guilt and got on with my work for the republican movement. I had watched, like a bystander, as she retreated into a private world of depression: I had hoped – perhaps even expected – that she would find her own route out of her despair.

My mother had a mental breakdown when I was a child, caused by my father's infidelity and cruelty. She had spent time in the same hospital in Armagh that Bernie wanted to go to. She had emerged after weeks of ECG treatment and had continued to be a good mother, but the person we had known had never returned from Armagh.

I had brought myself, my wife and my family to the point of collapse. For Hardbap? For Mooch? For Scap? For Gerry Adams? For all my other comrades who did not care whether my family was ruined or not? The revolution would have to take place without the help of Eamon Collins. Yet even at this point of profound disillusionment, I still doubted my ability to break completely with the IRA. I knew that I had to cut my links with the South Down Command, but perhaps I could continue to help out the south Armagh men, the sort of characters in whose company I could still feel moments of pride. And so I flailed around in my head. Tomorrow, Friday, my day off, I would spend with Bernie and the children. Then, in the evening, I would take Bernie out somewhere nice – she had not been out at all since the baby's birth. It was time my family came first.

My day at work passed uneventfully. I went on a coastal patrol before returning back through the Mourne mountains. The beauty of the countryside revived me slightly, as it always did, and gave me an idea for how I would spend tomorrow with Bernie. In the afternoon I went in to town to buy the lens. When I returned to my car I noticed a police patrol checking vehicles parked along the main street, close to the market entrance. I caught the eye of a grey-haired policeman carrying a Ruger rifle. He stared at me as I drove past.

In the meantime, I knew I could not get out of my commitment to help distribute that week's *Republican News*, which would have arrived in the town by now. I picked up a batch of 350 papers from the home of a Sinn Fein member and drove around dropping off smaller batches with my regular helpers. I drove into Catherine Street and found myself stuck behind a line of traffic. The cars moved slowly down the street past the police station in Corry Square. I watched a patrol of six RUC men walk out from the station and tread briskly but cautiously down the road. There seemed to be a lot of RUC activity in the area: it was as if they had been warned that something was coming their way, but they did not know quite what.

I called on Mooch to drop off another batch of papers. I left his house around six-forty. Mooch walked with me to my car. As I was about to open my car door I heard several explosions in quick succession. The sounds came from the direction of the town centre. I looked at Mooch. He grinned and said: 'There was supposed to be a load of mortars coming in this week sometime.' My only thought was that the police were certain to raid my house that night: I could now be sure of a visit whenever any IRA operation took place in or around Newry.

Darkness had begun to fall. I called at another three houses to leave papers and then I made my way home. As I drove along a hill overlooking the town centre I could see several ambulances threading their way through the traffic, sirens blaring, lights flashing. The whole of the main street seemed to be lit up with flickering red, yellow and blue lights. I felt the adrenaline of fear seeping into my stomach. I knew something really serious had happened.

I sped home and parked my car. Bernie had gone with the children to her mother's for the afternoon. I turned on the radio: the first reports said there had been a mortar attack on the police station in Corry Square; there were several casualties. I was sure the house was going to be raided, but I hoped the police would not arrest me. After all, I had had absolutely nothing to do with the attack. Then I thought for a moment about what I was saying to myself and I began to laugh bitterly at my foolishness. How were the police to know that I had had nothing to do with the attack? I was Newry IRA's Mr Big, as far as they were concerned. Mr Big, indeed: I had never felt so useless and vulnerable. If I were arrested now, I knew it might be enough to trigger a complete breakdown in my wife. What would happen to the children?

Just then, two local lads called at my back door – seventeen-year-old Lawrence O'Keeffe, and his slightly older friend Paul Maguire. They helped me sell *Republican News* around the estate. Neither was in the IRA, and Paul in particular was not a boy who would have been let near a military operation. All they could talk about was the mortar attack. I gave them their bundle of papers and they left the house. Then Bernie came home with the children. I kissed her and asked her how she was. I told her where I had been on patrol that day and said that I wanted us all to spend a day in the countryside tomorrow: 'It'll do us all good.' She said everyone was talking about the attack. Her voice was terribly tense. Then a friend, whose wife worked at the local hospital, called to say that the word was there were nine bodies in the morgue. He asked me if I wanted to stay at his house for the night as he was sure I was about to be arrested. I turned him down. My father was the next visitor. He looked worried. He asked me to stay with him on the farm for a few days. Again I said no.

My father left. We had our tea and I got Tiarnach ready for bed. We had become so close that he refused to go to sleep unless I got into bed beside him and put my arms around him. I changed into my pyjamas and lay down next to him. I was so tired that I almost drifted off to sleep. Shortly after nine, I went downstairs dressed in my pyjamas. Bernie was in the living-room. Paul and Lawrence were there too, their papers sold. They still talked about the rumours of dead RUC men. 'That'll teach them for the three boys in Strabane,' I said, referring to the Provos shot by the SAS a few days previously. I felt nothing for the dead men, neither sympathy nor satisfaction.

Just then the phone rang. It was Hardbap. He said: 'Have you heard the news?' I said I had. He asked me if I knew how many casualties there had been. I said there were nine bodies in the hospital morgue. He said: 'Fuck! Well, don't do the PR on it. Someone else is going to do that. It's a joint one.' He meant that the operation had been carried out with the help of volunteers from south Armagh. I could have guessed: mortars were south Armagh's favourite weapon. Hardbap said: 'We needed this one badly. We've been having a very bad time of it lately.' Then he laughed and said: 'I'll see you in seven days.' He was referring to the seven days of interrogation which he expected were about to come my way. The words had hardly emerged from his mouth when there were several loud bangs on the door. I knew the police had arrived. I said to Hardbap: 'I've got visitors.' He said: 'Oh fuck. You're away. Good luck.' I put the phone down and walked into the living-room where Bernie sat, expressionless. The two boys stood up, terrified. I told them to tell the truth: they were there to pick up news-papers, nothing more.

I opened the front door. A burly policeman with a beard stepped forward and put his hand on my shoulder, saying: 'Eamon Collins, I am arresting you under Section 12 of the Prevention of Terrorism Act.' He walked into the house, fol-lowed by several others, all carrying Ruger rifles. I went upstairs to get dressed. The arresting officer followed me and stood on the landing watching as I put on some clothes. I kissed my sleeping son before leaving the room. The policeman followed me downstairs. He did not say another word. Nor did any of the other policemen. Nine of their colleagues had just died violently. I told Bernie to contact my solicitor and doctor. I kissed her, told her not to worry, then I walked out-side with the arresting officer behind me, his hand still on my shoulder. They were not even bothering to search the house.

The night was damp and heavy. I walked to a grey armoured Land Rover. A few neighbours watched silently as I got into the back. I moved as far in as I could go and took a seat on the left. Several policemen followed me in and sat themselves around me. They did not say a word to me: it was as if they were in a trance.

Lawrence and Paul were led into the vehicle. I felt sick and was appalled to see them. While their presence made it less likely I would be summarily executed by these stunned police-men, they were only here because they had been in my living-room at the wrong time. The Land Rover moved off. Other Land Rovers followed. We drove out on to the Armagh Road into a huge traffic tailback caused by an army checkpoint. The driver put on his siren and other vehicles got out of the way as the Land Rover convoy jumped the queue and was waved on by a Para at the checkpoint. The police just sat there silently staring straight ahead.

The convoy arrived at Gough Barracks. The arresting officer took me out of the Land Rover first and directed me into the reception area. A doctor examined me. I explained to him that I had been on an early shift that day; I also said that my wife was breast-feeding our baby so I had not been sleeping properly for several weeks. Even divulging that amount of information was risky, but I hoped the advantages might outweigh the disadvantages. The doctor gave instructions that I was not to be interviewed beyond 11 p.m. I was taken back into the reception area. A set of steps led upstairs to a door which led to the main block of cells. The prisoners' cells were made of prefabricated materials, presumably to act as a deterrent against mortar attacks. I was put in cell 23. The door slammed shut behind me and I lay down on the single bed, which was chained to the floor.

On the wall above the door was a circular light, controlled from the outside. I tried to sleep. Just as I dozed off, the light which had been so soothingly dim was turned up full. Sleep was impossible. Helicopters hovered outside all night long. I could hear several more prisoners being brought in and placed in cells. After midnight a new policeman came on duty. He wore heavy hobnail boots and stomped up and down past the cells for the rest of the night.

On Friday morning, I was taken for my first interrogation. The following is an account of what I later told the Court at my trial had taken place during my interrogation. There were two interrogators. The first man said he wanted to do everything by the book. He was a meticulous man and would constantly flick imaginary pieces of dandruff from his shoulders. His colleague, who had less exacting standards of personal hygiene, removed his jacket and I noticed large sweat stains under his arms. Both of them talked to me about God. They quoted whole passages from the Bible relating to sin and the fate awaiting sinners. The younger of the pair said that if I was not involved in the mortar attack then I should say so: I did not have to talk about anything else.

The two of them spent more than an hour assuring me that if I could provide an alibi then I could go home and everyone would be happy. They wanted to convince me that they were genuine, decent policemen out to do a job and that they had nothing against me personally. They said the mortar attack was a dastardly deed; someone was responsible for it and that someone would have to be brought to justice. I kept silent, although I had already started to break one of the key anti-interrogation strictures: I was listening to what they were saying. I tried to block their words from entering my mind. I tried to concentrate on a rousing song, a person, an event, a flickering flame, a spot on the wall, but I still found myself listening to them. I listened – and communicated through my eyes and body-language that I was listening – in order to get them to ease off the pressure. They knew I was listening and they did ease off, engaging in long-winded and fairly innocuous speeches. I felt temporarily in control, but I had already made the cardinal error of allowing the interrogators to enter my mind.

I had a different two-man team for my next interrogation. They were conscientious and methodical, and wore expensive but conservative suits. Their approach was simple but penetrating. Would I not answer a few simple questions? Where had I been on Thursday afternoon? What had I been doing on a particular housing estate? He named Mooch's estate. I asked myself how they knew I had been there. Was someone talking already? They would ask questions, then pause for a while. They were relaxed and easy-going and walked about the small interrogation room constantly. They would move from a pause to a sudden movement, and soon I began to find their behaviour disquieting. The taller one would occasionally sit on the table near my chair. He would swing his foot towards my balls in a casual way. I understood the message he was communicating.

The second session came to an end and I was taken back to my cell. It was around 1 p.m. The interrogations had started at nine that morning. I had survived the first four hours – only another six and a half days to go. I had found the first sessions tolerable but I knew they were only preparing the ground for what was to come. I had expected to see the first team again after lunch, but I was wrong. I was taken downstairs to be met by yet a third team. Six detectives, all for me.

The two detectives in the third team were dressed in smart jackets and well-pressed trousers. Their tactics were coarser than the previous team's. A pungent smell of aftershave filled the small interrogation room. They stared at me, radiating hatred. They began to behave like giddy schoolboys, cracking jokes and making continuous derogatory remarks. One of them pulled out a packet of cigarettes and offered me a smoke. Both were watching me closely. Each would laugh at every joke made by the other, then would stop laughing abruptly, lean forward and stare at me. One said: 'A fucker like you ought to be taken out into the yard and shot. I don't know why we waste time on you.' He said he had no doubt that I would not talk, but he told me that whether I talked or not I was going to be charged with murder: 'And that is beyond doubt.'

These men verbalized the tension and anger that seemed to fill every cubic centimetre of Gough Barracks after the death of so many police officers. I thought that a murder charge was the least I could expect. I remembered the story about the IRA prisoner who had been found hanged in his cell at Castlereagh interrogation centre some years before. The inquest had called his death suicide, but no one in the republican movement had believed that. One detective told me that there were several 'Newry boys' lining up to talk to me and before the week was out I would wish I had never been born.

Each interrogation took place in a different room. Changing rooms frequently helped to disorientate prisoners. Although in Gough Barracks most of the interrogation rooms were the same size, several were smaller: a smaller room could create a greater sense of claustrophobia; your interrogators would appear to be almost on top of you. The room I now entered was smaller than any I had been in.

A detective was already waiting in the room. I sat down on the chair on one side of the small table. His colleague sat down on the other side and spread out his long arms. He began shouting at the top of his voice. I could see clearly the furrowed lines in his face. He screamed at me: 'You've been bubbled. There's a man in the IRA and he wants out. He's talking, and he's talking about you.' His young colleague leaned down beside me and shouted in my right ear: 'You murdering dog. You murdering dog. Nine police officers dead and you did it. Nine families without their loved ones and you're responsible.' He continued shouting at such volume that my ears began to ring.

Again I began to participate in my downfall by listening to what they were saying, picking up every word. I wanted to know who, if anyone, was talking. I was allowing them to break the composure and concentration that is necessary to withstand an interrogator's onslaught.

I knew a number of men who had been under pressure from their wives and families to get out of the IRA: which one of them had cracked? I expected them to bring one of my comrades through the door at any moment to point me out. The older man shouted in a mocking voice: 'We only have to be lucky once. You have to be lucky all the time.' His colleague continued to shout: 'You murdering dog. You murdering dog.' The older one kept up his derisory tone: '"That'll teach them for the three boys in Strabane." Heh, heh. You know what we're talking about, you murdering dog, don't you? "That'll teach them for the three boys in Strabane."' I felt myself sinking in my chair. Either Maguire or O'Keeffe was talking. I did not feel angry with them. They were little more than boys, but I should not have allowed myself to worry about them. I knew the interrogators would only use my anxiety to penetrate my psychological defences, but I could not help myself. I was making myself vulnerable: I was becoming open to persuasion and suggestion.

My concern for the two boys, my concern for my wife, and my fears for my own safety were creating a dangerous vulnerability in my mind. But then, just as I was slipping down the slope, I would pull myself back. The aggression of the interrogators would help to remind me who I was. I would say to myself over and over again: 'These fucking Orange bastards. Fucking Orange bastards. Fucking Orange bastards.' I would convince myself that I could survive anything the police threw at me.

One detective went out of the room. After a few minutes he

returned and, grinning, he waved some sheets of paper at me: 'It's all here,' he said. 'The mortar attack, your role in it and what you got Maguire and O'Keeffe to do.' He slid the statement towards me, smirking, watching me closely and keeping one finger on the corner of it. I should have looked away; I should have torn it up; I should not have done what I did – which was to read it.

I saw the name 'Lawrence O'Keeffe' at the top of the first page. I began to read quickly. The statement referred to me asking him to do 'a wee job'. I had taken him into the Sinn Fein centre, brought him upstairs and explained to him that 'a red lorry' would be coming down Francis Street; when he saw the lorry he was to wave at it to indicate there were no police or army about.

It was absurd. There was no way that I or anyone else in the IRA would involve Maguire or O'Keeffe in an operation as important as the mortar attack. A lorry-load of mortars coming in from south Armagh and we would use a couple of kids to scout it down the street on the last important leg of its journey? I felt desperately sorry for O'Keeffe. I wondered what they had done to make him sign, after only one day, a statement which could put him away for life. I felt a terrible burden of responsibility for getting him into this mess. I knew Maguire's statement would be next. The detectives correctly gauged my train of thought: 'You've ruined O'Keeffe's life. He's only seventeen and he's going to get nine life sentences.' They screamed this in my ears over and over again. Then the younger man turned the screw tighter: 'I want to give you my personal guarantee that you're not walking out of here after seven days. You might think you are, but you're not. You're going to be charged with murder, and that is beyond doubt. Keep that in your mind.' I was taken back to my cell.

On the way back I saw a woman doing some photocopying at the machine. She gave me a look of the purest hatred. A group of detectives and uniformed officers stood outside a room opposite the photocopier. As I walked past them they spat abuse at me: 'You bastard . . . you murdering fucker . . . you IRA cunt.' One of them seemed almost intoxicated with rage. He had bloodshot eyes and he swayed on his feet as he cursed me. I felt that I was at the centre of their anguish, the sole focus of their unrestrained hatred, the cause of their understandable grief. It was now almost twenty-four hours since the mortar attack and the atmosphere in Gough Barracks had changed from sullen despair to hate-filled aggression. I felt they were all convinced that I was the man responsible for the deaths of their nine colleagues – a tally which included two women constables. I was frightened for my life; I felt the police officers were moving out of control. I was grateful to reach my cell. The door slammed behind me.

I sat on my bed feeling powerless and terrified. My head felt ready to explode with the pressure. I thought of Maguire and O'Keeffe. I had to do something for them. I could prove they were innocent: I could contradict the time O'Keeffe was supposed to have met me during the day.

The second team came on again. They were angry. They had read O'Keeffe's statement. I had to take a chance. I began to talk. I said it was madness to think that Maguire and O'Keeffe had been involved in the mortar attack: there was not one iota of truth in O'Keeffe's statement and they should discard it. I said that I had not seen the boys in the afternoon, had not been to the Sinn Fein centre and knew nothing about the mortar attack: I had several witnesses who could prove my whereabouts at the crucial times. I drew for them on a sheet of paper my movements during that day: the routes I had taken, the people I had met, the times that I had met them, and what I had seen. They asked me to open up more, to answer more questions. I said that if they had wanted to ask me questions they should have come to my house and spoken to me instead of arresting me and taking me away from my wife and children. I said I would be prepared to answer any question about the mortar attack so long as it was put to me in the company of my solicitor. Then I said I wished to exercise my right to remain silent.

One of the policemen left the room and I could hear a hurried conversation taking place outside. The RUC man came back in, and the interrogation continued, but I would not say any more. I hoped foolishly that they would have the decency to do something about Maguire and O'Keeffe.

The final interrogation of the evening was carried out by the pair who made up the third interrogation team. One kept saying: 'Nine policemen, all tatey bread.' They were both extremely aggressive. One of them said: 'Come on. Open up. You opened up for the other boys so you could lie through your teeth. Open up for us. Why did you open up, you murdering bastard? I know why you talked: because you're fucking guilty. You killed those nine peelers and you know you're going down. That's beyond a doubt.' Far from using my explanation of my whereabouts to release Maguire and O'Keeffe, the police now seemed to want to break me in order to corroborate O'Keeffe's statement and to produce the necessary result: the charging of three members of the IRA team which had killed nine police officers. I realized that as far as they were concerned, Maguire and O'Keeffe were guilty because they were republicans in the company of a known IRA man.

One of my interrogators told me that a friend of one of the dead women would be on duty that night. I was put back in my cell. The light was kept full on all night to ensure another sleepless night. During the night I became desperate to use the toilet outside the cell, even though I was frightened I would meet a friend of one of the dead policewomen. I asked to be let out. As I went into the toilet the door was booted shut with extreme force, seeming to shake the whole structure of the cubicles.

Back in my cell, I could hear Maguire being sick several times. I tried to make contact with him but every time I tried I could hear the slight squeak of rubber-soled boots tiptoeing towards my cell to peer through the peep-hole. I retreated to my bed and lay there, staring at the ceiling. I asked myself what I was doing there. If I had still been as committed to the IRA as I had once been, then I would have found this ordeal bearable, but I knew that all the anti-interrogation techniques in the world could not compensate for my lack of commitment. I knew how vulnerable I was.

On Saturday morning, the first team went at me again. They talked at great length about the statement I had made. They said they had contacted the customs and discovered that I had been lying: I had worked the ten till six shift. Had someone at the customs given them the wrong information or was this simply a tactic to throw me off balance? Both of them continued their practice of bellowing into my ears at close range.

For the rest of the day none of the interrogators let up the pressure. They kept pushing and pulling my chair, telling me to sit up as I was too comfortable. In a later session with the first pair who had interviewed me, the younger cop of the team spent a long time detailing the injuries to civilians as a result of the mortar attack. During all of these interrogations, whenever one of the interrogators spoke directly to me, the other one would leave the room, ostensibly to get a cup of tea. But they would always return after a few minutes and begin their own direct questioning, following logically from what had just gone before. I was sure that when they left the room they would spend time looking through the spy-hole to observe my body language more closely.

The second man of the first team kept returning to his favourite topic – God and the Bible. I continued to give the impression that I was listening to what they were saying and in doing so I distracted them slightly, letting them travel up byways, which afforded me occasional momentary relief. I hoped my behaviour might help steer them away from the real danger zone for me, the weakness that could destroy me: my concern for my wife. I continued to feel terrible about Maguire and O'Keeffe but I felt to some extent that I had done everything I could for them. Now the focus of my concern shifted to Bernie. What if they arrested her too? The thought of her being subjected to this was sickening.

Another detective entered the interrogation room. He said: 'Is this the cunt here? Is this him? Is he talking yet?' He was carrying a copy of the *Irish News*. He opened it up fully for my benefit. I could see the front page photographs of the carnage caused by the mortar attack. They offered me the classic option of pleading guilty to a lesser charge. My role in the attack might have been limited; I could not have known that so many people were going to be killed; there was a way out of it for me. I could simply admit to the lesser charge of 'assisting offenders'. I would end up with a maximum ten-year sentence and probably serve only five. They said: 'Take the soft option.'

I had survived two days of interrogation. I spent the night

thinking about Bernie. On Sunday, during the second interrogation before lunch, I found myself once again with the first pair of interrogators. They were even angrier than before. The younger man spoke through clenched teeth when he was not shouting directly into my ear. He said: 'I'm going to the first of many funerals today. After the funerals I'm going to your house and we are going to turn it upside down. I'm going to arrest your wife and she's coming here for seven days.' I went numb. I felt faint but I dared not move. 'I'm going to arrest her and bring her here. I have more funerals to go to in the evening, but tomorrow I'm coming in here bright and early and guess who is my first interviewee? Your wife. I'm booked in to see her for the first interview, then after that I'm coming straight round to see you.' I could feel his breath on my face. 'And, you know, Eamon, I've got a name for your wife. I'm not going to call her Bernadette . . .'

He asked me why my wife had not telephoned the barracks to find out how I was: 'You've been in here two days.' That was one trick I was not going to fall for: I had been there for three days. They were hoping to disorientate me further, to make me feel that I had lost track of time. 'Wives always ring in each day enquiring about their husbands, but your wife hasn't. Maybe she's horrified at what you've done! Maybe she wants nothing to do with you. Maybe she knows you're a murdering shit.'

If they had taken me out of the interrogation room and brought me to a room where they would have shown me my wife, I would have broken: I would have given them everything they wanted to know. My realization of this fact terrified me: I knew I was no longer an IRA man; I was a husband and father. My family came first. I wanted them more than I wanted a United Socialist Ireland. I was sick of republican clichés. I no longer wanted to play a part in carrying the burden of the centuries of struggle. But I held on and the interrogation ended.

In my cell, I ate my lunch on a paper plate with plastic cutlery. I had not finished when uniformed police officers opened my door and took me down to the cells on the bottom floor. I began to panic. I sat down in my new cell and listened. I could hear a woman sobbing several cells away. The blood rushed to my head and I ran towards the door. I raised my closed fist ready to rap on the door and surrender myself. I heard the slight shuffling sound of a body moving towards my cell. I retreated back to my bed.

I dreaded the next interrogation. I dreaded being told that my wife had been arrested and was now crying her eyes out in a cell only two doors away from mine. I would crack, and I did not want to crack. I did not want to betray my comrades and everything I had fought for over the last six years. I had to find a way of blotting out those sounds. I rapped the door and asked to be taken to the toilet. Once in the toilet, I had a piss and then tore off pieces of toilet paper and put them tightly in my ears. I stuffed my ears full of paper and felt slightly better. It was a desperate, stupid measure but I was so far gone that it seemed a sensible thing to do. I threw cold water over my face and left the toilet.

A detective and two uniformed officers were waiting for me outside. I was told to get up against the wall. They searched me and looked in my ears. 'He's got earrings on,' said one of the uniformed officers. They must have had a secret camera in the toilet. 'You silly fucker,' said the detective. He led me to the interrogation room where one of my tormentors was waiting. He said: 'Get those things out of your ears, you silly cunt, or I'll take them out.'

Within an hour a doctor arrived. I left the interrogation room and had a private consultation with him. He said, half smiling: 'Have you been hearing unpleasant noises?' I said that I had put the paper in my ears because they were sore due to a tooth-ache. 'Putting paper in your ears won't help. It's more likely to damage your ears.' He removed paper from deep inside my ear. I wanted to tell him the real reason for the paper, but I did not trust him. How could I? He was a Protestant; he supplemented his income by working part-time for the police; and he was probably on his way to play a round of golf with the chief constable. He asked me if I had any complaints. I spoke hesitantly. I said: 'Not really, except for the verbal abuse I'm getting.' He said: 'Hmmm. Well, that's near enough a complaint.' I regretted saying anything.

I was taken back and placed in the interrogation cell. A uniformed sergeant appeared a few minutes later. He said: 'You have a complaint to make?' The last thing I was going to do was to give this sergeant details of my complaint. They would use those details to identify my weakness and to break me down further. I did not say anything to him. He left the room, angry that I would not talk to him. One of the smartly-dressed policemen walked in looking dismayed. He accused me of having complained about them. He said: 'Verbal abuse? Verbal abuse is about the only thing we can give you Provie fuckers. I wonder what you'd give me, you Provie bastard, if you were interrogating me in some barn in south Armagh? It wouldn't be verbal abuse, you murdering cunt. No, you'd be taking lumps out of me with an iron bar before you put a hole in my fucking head. That's what you'd do, Eamon. You know it, and I know it.'

I now knew that they knew I was in the Nutting Squad. I thought about what the RUC man was saying. I knew he was right: the IRA would torture a captured member of the Special Branch if he did not speak. Then they would shoot him. A peculiar feeling overcame me. I felt sympathy for him: I did not want to envisage him in that awful situation. I was ashamed that he was right in what he said. I could see that he felt hurt and angry at the loss of his nine comrades, in much the same way I felt when I heard about the deaths of IRA volunteers. The interrogation ended. They had not mentioned my wife. I was taken back to my cell.

For a brief few moments I felt a slight sense of relief, but as soon as I thought of Bernie a crushing emotional impotence gripped me. I knew I would be prepared to betray everybody and everything for her. I lay awake all night, expecting to hear the sobbing woman again. But I heard nothing. When I went to the toilet I noticed something I had not noticed before: a sanitary towel dispenser. I had been put in the women's cell block. In my fevered mind this confirmed that they were preparing to detain my wife.

On Monday morning, I had a visit from my solicitor. A uniformed inspector sat with us, but at least my solicitor was able to inform me that Bernie had not been arrested. I wanted to tell him to go to my wife and tell her that she had to take the children and herself to Dundalk for a few days, but I could not risk saying anything with the inspector there. My solicitor advised me to keep silent and, after only a few minutes, he left.

The interrogations continued with the same intensity. A detective approached me and put his finger on my forehead. He said: 'That's the mark of Cain.' My family and I would be cursed forever as a result of it. He said that others who had received the mark of Cain had lost their children in tragic accidents. The interrogators kept up their shouting, and then suddenly they stopped. The older detective from the first team said that he wanted to apologize for calling me a liar on Friday night. He said that they had checked again with the customs and it appeared that the information I had given them about my working hours was correct. He blamed the customs for giving them the wrong information. He apologized profusely and encouraged me to talk about what I had been doing on the day of the mortar attack. I remained silent. As one man talked quietly to me, the other began shouting in my ear again. He told me that he knew how much I loved my son Tiarnach. He described him as a ball of fluff. He leaned close towards me and said: 'But for this conflict, you and I could be friends!'

I was deeply tired. I had not slept since I had arrived in the barracks. During my next interrogation I was almost talked to sleep. A detective from the third team spent almost an hour talking quietly about a lecture I had given in the Sinn Fein centre about the socialist development of the republican movement. He said how much he would have liked to have been at that lecture. He said he would have liked to have made his feelings known about his own people's role and place in Irish history. He spoke with conviction and erudition. He sounded genuinely hurt that someone like him could be excluded from a discussion of Irish history. In my peculiar emotional state I felt moved by his talk: I loved talking about Irish history and I felt he had an important point to make. He talked intelligently and authoritatively about Lady Gregory and the Irish sagas. He also told me about the serious illness he had suffered recently. I felt sorry for him. I felt sorry too that he felt that republicans were depriving him of his Irishness because of the fact that he was a Protestant. He spoke with such conviction and emotion that I almost found myself reaching over to take his hand, to prove to him that I understood his plight and that I felt for him as another sympathetic human being.

But he himself managed to stop this dangerous drift of sympathy: after an hour of gentle, intelligent persuasion on a topic that was close to my heart, he suddenly swung from soft to hard in an outburst of aggression. He said: 'But you, you cunt, you wouldn't let me be there at that meeting, would you? You would be there to kill me, to murder me, to shoot me. That would be your answer to my questions.' In that moment he put me back on my guard by becoming just another loyalist whom I knew I had to resist. With hindsight, that was always the weakness of the RUC interrogators' way of operating: they would not spend the necessary hours developing a particular sophisticated, perhaps off-beat, line. They were always too ready to return to what they were best at: confrontation and aggression.

On Tuesday morning I felt strangely calm. I had now survived five nights in this interrogation centre: only two more to go after today. Time was running out for the police: I knew that, and they knew that. After the threat of Bernie's arrest had receded I felt more confident in my ability to hold out. I took my ten minutes' exercise in the yard, then showered and changed my clothes. They informed me that O'Keeffe had been charged with murder and was now being held at Crumlin Road Prison in Belfast.

At my first interview of the day, my interrogator sat on the table. He began to turn the key which was to unlock my defence: 'A trip to Vietnam. Ho Chi Minh City, the Perfumed Garden. £1,300, just like that, all paid for. Where did you get the money?' I had dreaded this moment: they had obviously been to my house, turned it upside down, found the travel documents, and arrested my wife. I lost my composure. My head dropped. The policeman grabbed my head in his hands and jerked it up: 'Look at me, Eamon, look at me. I was talking about that Vietnam holiday you won't be going on.' I pushed his hand away and he went to grab me again, but I slid to the floor and lay there. Both of them grabbed me and lifted me up off the floor back on to my chair, where I sat limp. I fell to the floor again. They left me there this time and started to kick my

feet continuously as they walked around me. Then they would
lift up my feet with their feet and drop them to the ground.
They put me back on the chair, where I sat for a minute before
falling again to the floor. One of them stuck his knee in the side
of my head as I went to the ground. They shouted and
screamed at me but I was not listening. I could think only of
my wife. She had been arrested, I was certain. I felt my will to
resist seeping away.

I lay on the floor during the next interrogation. The team
seemed delighted and excited by my behaviour. 'Lying on the
floor, you Provie cunt? This couldn't be better. The cameras
can only partly see you.' The other sneered at me: 'Look at
your clothes. Fucking rags. You haven't even got a suit in your
wardrobe at home. Nothing but fucking rubbish.' He was confirming for me that they had been to my house and arrested my
wife. Others were probably interrogating her now. I felt a sharp
kick on my ankle. One of them got down on the floor beside me
and started to rock me back and forward for several minutes.
'I'd love to give you a good kicking. We're putting you away
whether you talk or not.'

He turned me over. I felt my chest being forced into the
floor. I could hardly breathe. I began to gasp for air. A weight
bounced up and down on my back. He prised his knuckles up
and down my vertebrae. Then, after several minutes of making
it pliable, he forced his finger joints up and down the vertebrae,
causing intense pain. The second man had moved closer. I felt
a hard object on one of my calves pushing into the muscle. I
felt an excruciating pain. My hair was pulled so that my head
was lifted off the ground. My head bounced off the floor. I
screamed in pain. Someone grabbed my left leg and pulled it
up off the ground. It was yanked as far forward as it could go:
'He doesn't like this. He doesn't like this one little bit,' he said,
laughing. This continued for almost two hours. They said they
could do whatever they wanted to do and there was nothing I
could do about it.

I limped back to my cell. I told a uniformed officer that I
wanted to see a doctor. 'Bye,' he said, and slammed the door. I
was taken, almost in a state of shock, to my next interrogation.
Once again I lay on the floor. They told me to get away from

the radiator pipes: they must have assumed that I was going to wrap my arms around them in order to give myself burns which I would later blame them for inflicting. Both of them went berserk, pulling the table across the floor to make space for them to get around me. They both lay on the floor beside me, one at each ear, and began shouting in unison: 'Murdering dog. Murdering dog. You're going away for life, you murdering dog.' They screamed at the tops of their voices for at least half an hour.

Suddenly, as I lay there, I began to feel like a participant in a spectacle from an absurdist play. Everything seemed ludicrous and unreal. I could not go on, could not continue to perform my allotted role. In that moment, as I floated in unreality, I realized that I had lost my will to resist. The wall that I had tried to shore up between myself and my interrogators over the preceding five days collapsed.

I got up off the floor and sat down in the chair. The two of them went silent. I began to smile. I felt a strange compulsion to laugh, but I did not. I knew it was over. They both looked at me.

I said: 'I want to speak to someone in authority.'

21

TALKING TO THE ENEMY

I knew when I sat in that chair and began talking that I was willing to tell the police everything they wanted to know.

As soon as I asked to speak to someone in authority, one of the interrogators left the room and within minutes he came back with a superior officer.

Although most policemen seem to have something in their manner which marks them out as policemen, this man could easily have passed himself off as a successful middle-manager. He sat on a chair close to me without at first saying anything. He folded his arms, crossed his legs and looked at me intently. He said: 'I understand you would like to talk about some matters.'

I told him that I had a lot of information about IRA personnel and operations which I would give but only on condition that I was not charged with anything. I said that I wanted the immunity that others had been given. I explained that O'Keeffe and Maguire were completely innocent and that O'Keeffe would have to have the charges against him dropped if the RUC wanted me to co-operate: I would prove to him that they had no involvement with me in the mortar attack because I had had absolutely nothing to do with it, except for the fact that I had been in a house in Dundalk several months ago when the idea for the attack had first been discussed, and then only casually. (Francie's idea had seemed almost hare-brained then, and no one could have imagined it would be so murderously successful.)

The RUC man was expressionless. He said: 'What have you got to tell me? What have you got to bargain with?'

I gave him a taster, by sketching some of the operations and killings I had helped to organize.

He told the two detectives to leave the room. There was something in the way he treated them which indicated that they were not the sort of people he would choose to socialize with. I found this reassuring. When we were alone, he said that he might want me to go out and continue to operate as a volunteer. He said the situation was completely fluid. For the moment he was going to give me a pseudonym, 'Frank Trainor'. He wanted me to use this name when I talked about all the IRA operations I was involved in. To me this was an indication that I would not be charged with anything and that they would simply use me for information. My mind was so muddled that I was open to this gentle persuasion. After a while I would have believed anything he said for the simple reason that I wanted to believe it.

I spoke at length about Maguire and O'Keeffe. He said that if they were innocent then all charges against them would be dropped. To me this cop seemed to be a decent and fair man. He said that there were a number of people who might want to speak to me, but I was not to speak to them. I assumed he was referring to people from military intelligence. He was going to be the only person looking after my case. I could trust him; he would not let me down. When he had relaxed me further I let him in on my greatest concern. I said that I wanted his assurance that my wife would not be bothered by the police and certainly not arrested. I thought she had been arrested already but I did not want him to know this.

Once I started talking, I crossed over into the enemy camp. Effectively I had become a hesitant convert to the forces of the Crown. Looking back, I realize that the interrogator must ensure that in the prisoner's mind loyalty to his new friends replaces loyalty to his old ones. This smooth operator certainly knew how to create and cement such loyalty.

He asked me if I was hungry, and I said I was. He got the

menu sent down from the police canteen. 'I can recommend the steak. They do it well here,' he said, and I was grateful after five days eating the muck they give prisoners. During my debriefing he ensured that we ate like kings. Later I would remember a line from a song: 'He sold his soul for penny rolls and slabs of hairy bacon.' We had all our meals together and talked on an informal basis about personal things. I felt us becoming friends. Of course I knew I was being manipulated but I allowed it to happen. He was a shrewd professional: he knew he had only a few days to get out of me everything that he needed. For all his suave calm, I could sense that he was a man in a hurry.

The first plan to form in my befuddled mind had been to try to bluff the RUC into thinking that I would become an informer. They would let me out to resume my IRA career, but once they released me I planned to go to the IRA and confess what I had done. I knew that for coming forward I would not be harmed, and I would move to the Irish Republic and start a new life independent of both the IRA and the RUC. But this man was not a fool. He led me by the nose and got me to tell him everything I knew.

Later – after I had admitted to a multiplicity of IRA operations – he let me know that the situation was no longer 'fluid': after consultation with his superiors, they had decided not to release me to become an informer; they thought instead that I had the potential to be a good witness against my former comrades. The only option now open to me was to turn Queen's evidence. I asked him what this would mean. He said that I would have to be charged with several offences, although not murder, but I would be pleasantly surprised by the outcome, and I would have to testify in court. My role in helping the police would be taken into account by the Secretary of State, who would release me after I had served a minimum of three years, maximum five, even though the judge would probably sentence me to several life sentences. He said I would serve my sentence in an open prison where I would have regular access to my wife and children. Then I would be helped financially to start a new life outside Northern Ireland. They would give me a new identity, help me buy a house and find me a job. He was asking me to become a supergrass at a time when the credibility of the supergrass system had already been brought into question. Even international observers had begun to comment disdainfully about the mass show trials in which some of the supergrasses appeared to be little more than ventriloquists' dummies, reciting police suspicions concerning people they wished to remove from circulation. Usually there was no corroborating evidence.

I realized I had played a dangerous game ineptly and I had lost. My new master had me by the balls and I knew it. As this reality sank in, in my desperate and confused state, his offer sounded reasonable. I had been involved in a great many IRA operations which I now regarded as pointless and meaningless. I told myself that I had been exploited by the IRA and that I owed the army nothing. What had I got to lose by turning against it? Yet even as I said that I would be willing to go through with it, I did not really believe that I would have to. I tried to reassure myself that the more I co-operated, the less likely it would be that I would have to become a supergrass.

On that Tuesday night I took Valium to numb myself. I had now been taken into the inner sanctum of Gough Barracks — a specially-constructed bomb-proof bunker deep within the building. I was led through a series of steel gates and doors. Closed-circuit cameras watched our progress. We passed an area surrounded by steel-wire meshes protecting row after row of files, all neatly ordered, numbered and indexed. I assumed they were files on suspects.

They brought me into a large, air-conditioned room. There was a table in the centre of the room and an imposing black chair. On one wall was a portrait of a military figure whom I could not identify, and on other walls were maps of Northern Ireland. I felt I had moved into an alien world. I imagined that this was the room in which the shoot-to-kill operations had been planned. Had I now travelled so far that I could be offered a seat in this nerve centre of the Crown forces?

I sat up with the RUC boss until 4 a.m., talking about everything I had done, and everything I had planned to do in the IRA. A young detective spent part of the time with us. He was in charge of the tape recorder whose spools I would sometimes watch revolving quietly as my words fixed themselves on the tape. I talked until I was exhausted. I could not face going back to my cell. If they had sent me to bed at eleven, I might in the quiet of my cell, have faced the terrifying reality of what I was doing and turned back. But I was frightened to be alone with myself. I stayed up late with my shrewd police mentor every night. And each night I was given two Valium tablets.

My interrogations had in fact only begun. Over the following days, in the skilful hands of my new friend – who indicated that he had dealt with several other republicans in my position – I told them everything.

He showed me large numbers of photographs of IRA suspects. Many of the photos were quite old and had obviously been taken at demonstrations, funerals or celebrations. Some had been taken from army surveillance positions, others from hidden cameras. Many of them were not of a very high quality. For all their manpower, technology and resources, the various branches of the intelligence services did not seem as all-seeing or all-knowing as they were hyped up to be.

I co-operated fully. I could not enjoy what I was doing, but I found myself adopting a pose of almost professional detachment as I looked at the photos.

On Wednesday, he made it clear that he really wanted me to turn Queen's Evidence. He said that the level of operational participation that had existed between me and others was now crucial in deciding my future. He said that the only evidence that would be of any value in court would be my own eyewitness evidence: the times when I had seen people with weapons, the times I had planned terrorist acts, the times I had participated myself in such acts. The more detail I could give, the better the deal I could expect. He said that it was imperative that I did not hold anything back from him: I must be willing to open the closet and bring out all the skeletons. Even if something appeared trivial or unimportant, I had to tell him because I might be holding on to something useful.

I spent hour after hour talking to him. He said he was especially happy to have someone who really understood the nature of the Provisional republican army and its political manifestation, Sinn Fein. This was an area he returned to again and again, questioning me in depth about the workings and development of the movement. His questions were always pointed and analytical. We must have spent days on this subject and he would return to particular areas where my answers had raised other interesting questions.

The RUC man flattered me, saying it made a pleasant change to deal with someone who was intelligent, knowledgeable and capable of understanding complexity: 'You're squeaky clean. You've got a clean record; you've held down a responsible job; you've got a wife and family; you haven't been running around having affairs. You'll have a lot of credibility as a witness.' He said that in the past he had had to deal with a lot of unsavoury characters, such as the INLA supergrass Jackie Grimley. He said that Grimley was a stupid and deeply unpleasant man: 'I got tired of having to answer to his every whim.' He kept reminding me that it was essential I held nothing back. He said that two other supergrasses had held things back to the detriment of everyone: the INLA supergrass Harry Kirkpatrick had reserved information and as a consequence he did not think that all the accomplices who had been charged on his evidence would be convicted ('But don't tell Harry that when you meet him'); and the IRA supergrass Anthony O'Doherty had substantially weakened the case of a man charged with the murder of a Catholic police sergeant by not being detailed enough.

He said that I would make a convincing witness and that I would give some much-needed credibility to a supergrass system which had recently taken a battering.

I made a huge number of verbal admissions and I signed several statements, but I believed I would not be charged with much, certainly not with murder. After all, the IRA supergrass Christopher Black had been granted immunity and I hoped I would get the same treatment. I was being strung along, of course. After days and days of intensive, exhausting discussions, he suddenly told me: 'Prepare yourself. You are going to be charged with murder in a few minutes.' I remonstrated with him: 'But you said I wasn't going to be charged.' He told me not to worry: 'They're only holding charges. We can drop them later on. There's going to be a long drawn-out court procedure.

You won't end up charged with murder at the end of it. You can plead to a lesser charge.'

He saw that I was upset. He said: 'Listen. Trust me. I showed you how much you could trust me. I sat up all night with you. I didn't force you to go back to that cell. I didn't arrest your wife.'

I had gone so far down the road that I had no choice but to trust him. He had become my protector and I would become his loyal grass. After breaking, talking and signing statements, I had become totally dependent upon him. In a peculiar way I began to take on the values, mannerisms and role of the policeman. Of course, no ideological conversion had taken place: I had not become a supporter of a system which I had spent the previous six years fighting, even though in a practical sense I had become its agent. I was simply so morally and emotionally exhausted that I had become like an empty vessel floating in whatever direction my weakness and fear would take me, guided only by the controlling hand of my policeman saviour.

He told me that I would have to confront my former colleagues and identify them in the interrogation centre. The thought sickened me, but I was spurred on by my desperate need for self-preservation. The only cause I had left to fight for was the survival of myself and my family. I had no comrades, no community, no identity. The only light ahead of me was the light of a new beginning. By my act of betrayal, I hoped I could turn my back on the horror I had lived with and created. Of course, I was naïve to believe that this process could be so simple or that an act of betrayal was the best way to expiate the sins of my past. Yet I could not allow myself to stop for a moment, to consider what I was doing. I was in a trap from which my only hope of escape was to co-operate with a man whose murder I would once cheerfully have plotted and who had now become the nearest thing I had to a friend.

I did not go back to my cell until morning. This was the usual pattern of my days with my RUC patron: I would talk until I was utterly exhausted, then I would return to my cell for a few hours of sleep, although I rarely slept for more than an hour at a time.

I told him that an IRA colleague had information about a

pony club in the area of Newcastle, County Down, which was used by senior RUC and military personnel. We had heard that one senior policeman took his disabled child riding at the club. He told me that he took his own son riding, but he did not tell me whether he used that particular club. Once I also told him that I had been targeting a vehicle which I knew to be driven by a detective operating out of Gough Barracks, and he told me that he drove a similar car. And we talked about these things conversationally.

With hindsight, I realize he may have been telling me lies about his personal life in order to make me feel closer to him. However, I think he was sharing aspects of his life as a father and husband because they were important to him and he knew I would appreciate and respect him for his human side. I believed everything he said, which at the very least is a mark of his skill as an interrogator. Even though I knew he was manipulating me, I could not help liking him and trusting him.

He unveiled his strategy so gradually and skilfully that I did not grasp for a long time that he was working to a clear plan. The way he worked was to draw me in and to close down gradually all possible avenues of retreat.

The next day I confronted several of my former associates. The RUC man used it as an important test of my ability to cope as a potential supergrass. He told me that another policeman would be there to observe very closely how I reacted. If I showed hesitation, weakness or fear, I would jeopardize my possible future role. He told me not to underestimate the effect that these confrontations would have on the men. He put his hand on my arm and said: 'Are you going the whole way, Eamon? Have you the balls for it? Now's the time to prove it.'

His own superior accompanied me into each interrogation room and asked me to identify each man as an accomplice. All of my former comrades looked as if they were under great pressure, but I looked each one of them in the eye and said that I identified him as an IRA man. I looked right through them, as if they were not there. I felt nothing – no fear, no shame, nothing. The more senior policeman was delighted at my performance.

That night, my mentor sat up with me again, showing me yet

more photos of suspects. He asked me why I had chosen Vietnam as my holiday destination: 'It's not the sort of place I'd ever want to go to for a holiday.' I explained that I admired the struggle of the Vietnamese against American imperialism. I was also interested in their history, culture and architecture. He said he could see no point in going to a communist country which had been supported by Russia and China, but he cut himself off. He sensed the danger of exposing the lack of common ground between us, and the incongruity between my revolutionary mind-set and my alliance with what only a few days previously I would have regarded as the forces of imperialism.

He explained to me that I was going to Crumlin Road Prison where I would be held on remand in a special annexe with the other supergrasses. I would be given privileges not available to other prisoners.

He then asked me about my wife, how I thought she was likely to react to the news that I was willing to turn Queen's Evidence. In the peculiar state of fantasy and self-delusion in which I was living, I thought my wife would accept what I had done. I said she would realize I had done it for the benefit of our family, that there might be some initial tension but I was sure that I could talk her around. Later that night, he said that my wife was in the barracks and was waiting to see me. He said: 'Eh, I'm a bit worried about how she's going to react when you meet her. She's a very angry young woman.'

I walked into the room where my wife was sitting at a table. She looked bewildered, frightened and sullen. I began talking robotically, outlining the course I had embarked on in an almost matter-of-fact way. She looked at me in horror and dis-belief. She said: 'A supergrass? You mean to tell me you're a *supergrass* now?' The very word had brought bile to her mouth and she spat on the floor in front of me. 'You fucking bastard,' she said. 'If I had a gun, I'd shoot you myself. Now I know why all our friends have been arrested. All our friends. You've ruined our lives. My life and the children's lives have been ruined. Why, why, have you done this?'

I tried to explain, but she would not listen. She said: 'Do you know that your brother Ray has been arrested and I've been arrested by your new 'friends'? Catch yourself on. Only

scum do this and if you do it you'll be scum forever in my
eyes.' I felt myself falling into a void: I was losing the one
thing that now held any meaning for me – my wife and children. I mumbled that she could not have been arrested, but if
she had been then I would get her released immediately. But
why had they arrested Ray? My wife pleaded with me again:
'Catch yourself on! Don't do this. I'm begging you, don't do
this. Try to hold your head up. Be what you were. Have some
pride in yourself. These are not our people and never will be.'
I was so distraught that I had to leave the room. My RUC
man was waiting for me. I said: 'What are you doing? My
wife's been arrested, my younger brother's been arrested. Are
you trying to destroy me?'

He tried to calm me. He said that my wife had not been
arrested: they had only told her she was being arrested in order
to get her to the barracks, as otherwise she would have refused
to come. As for Ray, he claimed that they had received a tip-off
that he had been involved in the mortar attack: 'We had no
choice but to arrest him.' I assured him that Ray had not been
involved in the attack or the IRA: 'Never has and never will.'
He assured me that my brother would be released soon. I said:
'I want my wife to be taken home right now, this minute.' He
wanted to know if I was going through with it, going all the
way. I said I was, but I wanted my wife to go immediately. He
gave me his word she would be released immediately. I went
back in to where Bernie was sitting and told her she was going
home. She said: 'You'll never see me and the children again.
I'm going to divorce you.' She walked out of the room.

I felt there was no way out. What would have happened if I
had told him I was not going to go through with it? My wife
would have been arrested, held and interrogated. My warm
feelings towards the RUC man had been dealt a blow. Even in
my disorientated state, I knew that his explanation for Ray's
arrest was only partly true. They had arrested him in order to
put further pressure on me at a critical moment.

Another senior policeman came to see me to say that their
offer to take my wife and the children somewhere secure away
from Barcroft Park had not gone down well. She had refused,
as the policeman put it, 'to come over to our side'. He asked me

if I thought her refusal would put her in danger from the IRA. Wouldn't the IRA, at the very least, try to use her to get me to retract? I told him I was convinced that the IRA would not harm her: in the community such behaviour would cause outrage, regardless of what I had done, although I agreed that the IRA would probably try to use her to make me think again. However, I told him I was still determined to turn Queen's Evidence. I felt I had no choice.

The most important thing in my mind was to hold on to the only source of security I had – my new relationship with the police. At some stage over the next twelve hours my brother Ray was brought to me. I told him that he was going to be released. I asked him to tell our mother and father not to worry: I did not want them to be upset about what I had done. I was genuinely relieved when he was released.

The RUC manipulator began to consolidate his grip. He told me to prepare for my appearance the next day, Friday, at Banbridge Court where I was to be formally charged with various offences.

Just after breakfast on Friday morning, he spoke to me in one of the interrogation rooms. He said he was still not satisfied that I had not been involved in the mortar attack. He could not believe that I had been at the heart of the IRA's operations in Newry for so many years yet had somehow managed to avoid having anything to do with the IRA's most successful attack on the RUC since the troubles began. I swore to him again that I had had nothing to do with it and I was angry and frightened at the way he doubted me.

He said that he wanted me to explain to his superior officer why I had not had anything to do with the mortar attack. I met the man in the visitors' area. Again I declared my innocence. Why would I admit to all those bombings and killings and then hold back on the mortar attack? I was not going to serve any less time by not admitting to it: the only way I could hope to mitigate my sentence was by telling what I knew. I asked the two of them whether they wanted me to admit to something I had not done? They denied it, but I was not convinced. They must have been aware of how strange it was going to look when O'Keeffe and Maguire appeared in court charged with their part in the massacre – with me named as the person who assigned them their roles – while I was charged with everything other than the mortar attack.

I spent more than an hour persuading them that I had not played a part in it. I was frightened only that their suspicions about my role in the attack would undermine my relationship with my new 'friends'. I could no longer see any wider picture; all I wanted was to be clear of this.

We were standing in the enclosed visiting area. It was a wooden veneer construction between the holding cells and the interrogation rooms on the ground floor. The windows were made of thick-plated tinted glass. The first pair of detectives sat in here on the previous Sunday night watching me walking past on my way to a late-night interrogation by another team. I had noticed one of them laughing as I walked past. The next day during his interrogation he told me why he had been laughing: I had 'marched past like a real wee Provo on parade, wearing black beret and dark glasses'. Now four days later I stood in the same area as a broken, pathetic creature.

By the end of our discussion I think I convinced the senior policeman that I had not been involved in the mortar attack, but I was not sure. It was being held like an axe over my head. They used this threat to squeeze more and more out of me. I was like a hungry little dog with his master. He would appear to hold out little morsels; I would snatch at them and he would withdraw them.

I prepared for my trip to Banbridge. I put on my blue customs anorak and a young policeman approached me. He was softly-spoken and clean-shaven. A very pleasant and friendly young man. He put handcuffs on me, almost apologizing for doing so, and asking me whether they were too tight. He said: 'I want to thank you for what you have done, and all the police in Newry appreciate what you have done. We feel a bit safer now that all those people have been arrested. You're a good man.'

Had he been set up to say that? Was he part of the whole operation? Perhaps he was, but at that time I did not care. His words lifted me out of my despair. They were the first kind words I had heard in a week and they seemed genuine. I walked with three RUC men into the yard and got into an armoured car.

I looked over and saw my ambiguous protector and some other detectives getting into a Fiat 132. The car looked similar to one I had followed in Newry some weeks previously which had contained members of a divisional mobile support unit (the RUC's élite, heavily-armed anti-terrorist unit) from out of town.

We left in a convoy of Land Rovers and drove at speed through Armagh City to Banbridge. The young constable continued to speak to me. Policemen stood at every set of traffic lights, every intersection, every crossroads, all precisely synchronized. The convoy did not have to stop, slow down or give way. Hundreds of policemen must have been involved in putting on what was almost a victory parade for the RUC, a morale booster after the catastrophe of the mortar attack. I looked out and saw RUC men on points duty saluting as we drove past. I was now an ally of this Protestant militia in a Protestant state – a collaborator, a traitor, a tout. The land looked dry and hard. We drove through the little Protestant villages and hamlets – Gilford, Lawrencetown, Waringstown – all named after Cromwellian officers who had been given huge tracts of land in return for services rendered in subduing the natives.

The convoy went round the back of the courthouse, down a street which had been sealed off. The police vehicles came to a halt in a yard and I got out. Around the perimeter fence was a large crowd who screamed and shouted as I was led into the courthouse: 'Bastards . . . murdering scum . . .' I saw a bespectacled man in a long dark coat pressed against the wire. He was banging his hands back and forth. As I looked at him he seemed to try to climb up the fence: 'Burn the IRA bastards . . . Hang the IRA murderers.' I was taken inside the building, into a large room. Standing against one of the walls was the OC of south Armagh. He stood straight-backed and defiant. Against another wall stood young Maguire, trembling and broken. The Armagh man looked at me quickly and I felt a jab of shame. A policeman shouted at him to turn his head: 'Keep looking at the wall.'

Then they took me into the court. I looked around and saw my wife sitting next to my brother John. She looked drained and frightened. I remembered her words the evening before. Her defiance and anger had stunned me but what had really stuck in my mind was the pained statement: 'You've ruined our lives.' I could not take any more. I felt that I had to retract. I looked towards my RUC boss who had a look of disgust and shock on his face. My escort took me back out into the side room where he and one of his men joined me almost immediately. He said: 'He can't go to the supergrass annexe in Crumlin Road now.' The detective put his hand to his chin and looked at his feet. He said: 'He can still go to the annexe. That's where he'll be tonight. He didn't know what he was signing in there. He didn't know what he was doing.' He said hesitantly: 'But he retracted—' The other man cut in: 'He didn't know what he was signing.' He turned to me and said: 'Eamon, you didn't know what you were signing, did you? I guarantee you'll be in the annexe tonight.' They were sure I had not intended to sign away my life for thirty years. They comforted me and reassured me: they would save me from my own weakness.

I was taken out of the court and put back in the armoured car. The convoy set off again, heading for Belfast and the supergrass annexe. The decision had been made for me and there was no turning back.

We drove along the West Link, past the Unity Flats where I had marched many years before. We drove on to the round-about at Carlisle Circus and up the Crumlin Road past the Mater Hospital. I heard the ticking of the indicator as we slowed and prepared to turn into the mock-gothic fortress that loomed up before us: Crumlin Road Prison, linked by a tunnel to the courthouse across the road.

The huge iron gates swung open and the convoy drove into the courtyard. Dirt from the industrial chimneys of Belfast had encrusted itself on the granite and gave the building the air of a grim Victorian factory.

I got out of the car, handcuffed, and looked up at this vision of ugliness. My police escort pulled my hand and led me on.

22

SUPERGRASS

I entered Crumlin Road and found myself in a domed circular space, an expanse full of noise. People shouted, doors banged and boots crashed on polished tiles.

I felt I had stepped back into the nineteenth century. Under the fluorescent lights the screws, the owners of those boots, came towards me. I did not recognize faces: I saw only blobs of white sandwiched between dark uniforms and peaked caps. Sets of keys swung on one side of their bodies; batons on the other.

My escort undid my handcuffs and handed me over to my new masters who handcuffed me again. I followed them across the red circular floor. At various points around the circle, heavy perspex doors opened on to the prison wings, fanning out like the spokes of a wheel. A door took us into a descending corridor. I glimpsed the south Armagh OC and Maguire again.

After a strip-search, we passed through several more doors and entered an air-locked compartment.

It was a square construction, approximately eight foot by eight. The walls were made of bullet-proof perspex. The screws carried out a thorough body search. The door on the other side of the compartment hissed open and I entered a small corridor with several cells opening off it. One screw took off my handcuffs while another gave me blankets, a pillowcase and some sheets. I was shown into a small cell with a bunk bed

and ordered to strip again by screws who carried out yet
another search. As I entered the cell I noticed a little card on
which was written my name and the number 714. The door
slammed shut and I found myself in silence. I was in the
supergrass annexe. But where were the grasses?

The cell felt cold. A bulb burned brightly in the middle of
the ceiling. The whitewashed walls added to the intensity of
the light. I felt that everything I had ever been, every quality I
had ever had, had been sucked out of me. My mind was so
exhausted, my confusion so complete, that I was incapable of
rational thought. Bernie would not yet know that I was back on
track as a supergrass.

I heard men's voices outside. I stood on the end of the bed
and listened out of the window. I was desperate for human
contact. Words came to me: 'Hi. Can you hear us? Hello. Why
are you locked up?' I whispered out: 'Are you talking to me?
Who is it? Who am I speaking to?' I pushed my head out of the
aperture as far as I could. I laid my cheek on the base of the
aperture and crooked my neck. I looked out through rusted
steel bars.

At first I could not hear every word that was spoken. I had
to attune my ears to the hushed sounds. The voices were
coming from the cells on my level. They had to be the voices of
the other grasses. I made out more words: 'Why are you locked
up? Why have we been put in our cells? Why are you not
allowed out to associate?' I whispered back that I didn't know,
that I'd been promised I'd be allowed to associate; maybe they
wanted to see if they could trust me. I asked who they were.

One voice said: 'I'm Harry. Harry Kirkpatrick.' This I knew
was a former member of the INLA. Twenty-seven men were
awaiting trial on his evidence. He had already received five life
sentences after pleading guilty to various murders. Another
man said: 'I'm Budgie Allen.' I had heard about him too: he
was a loyalist, a former member of the Ulster Volunteer Force.
He had received a fourteen-year sentence for attempted
murder and was preparing to give evidence against no less than
forty-seven men.

Both voices sounded welcoming. For a moment I felt a sort
of happiness. We continued to talk. They told me to talk as

quietly as possible so that the prisoners above us would not hear. Apparently the prisoners above were loyalist and republican 'lifers' in their final year of imprisonment: they were 'working out', which meant that each day they were released to go to work and only had to return to prison in the evening. I knew they would pass on anything they overheard to interested parties in our respective communities.

Harry and Budgie told me they were pleased I had come. To them I was a new recruit to the system, living proof that it had not yet been abandoned. I offered them hope as I tapped them for their knowledge. We discussed whether the police would keep to their promise to release us within a few years. A third voice cut in. He introduced himself as Jimmy Crockard. I knew he was another former UVF man. He had pleaded guilty to playing a part in the sectarian murders of two Catholics, as well as many other offences, and was serving a life sentence. He had implicated twenty-nine people, but most of them had walked free only a few weeks before my arrival in the annexe after the judge at their trial had questioned the reliability of Crockard's evidence. It was, needless to say, the first time in my life that I had conversed with loyalist paramilitaries.

Jimmy had a soft voice and the sceptical intelligence of his words was reassuring. He said: 'We are all in the same boat, Eamon. None of us is certain of anything. None of us knows exactly what will happen.'

He said that we all had one thing in common: we broke, we betrayed our comrades, our beliefs and our communities. We no longer had communities that we could return to. He said the safety and security that we once had in our respective ghettos had gone. The peelers might let us down. That was always the possibility, but it was unlikely. There were bigger political forces at work than the peelers. Those forces would make the decisions; be the ones to decide whether we were politically useful. Now, even if they decided that we were not, it was still going to be important for whatever little scenarios they had in mind for the future that we should not be seen to have been used and then abandoned.

There seemed to be complete silence as he spoke. The position of the cell windows with the huge outer wall nearby and the mesh above our heads helped the acoustics. His words were soft and soothing, spoken with conviction and insight, and I clung to every one of them. This man did not even know me: all he needed to know was that I had broken. He knew the pain of embarking on such a course. I could tell it was a pain he continued to feel. After a pause he continued by saying that we had taken a certain route and had to consider all the alternatives. There was nothing for us to turn back to. At the very least, our communities would never treat us the same again; many of our families had suffered because of what we'd done. But they would never understand the choices we faced. Harry said it was time to stop talking: the prisoners above us had gone completely silent and were probably listening.

I lay down in my bunk feeling slightly less desperate and I tried to sleep. I thought about what Jimmy had said. Could we trust the peelers? 'Can we fuck,' I thought. Yet co-operation with them still seemed to be my only hope of freedom, and that was the hope I clung to.

Early next morning the screws gave me breakfast. Before the greasy eggs and bacon had slid to their resting place, the screws put me in handcuffs and led me through the prison. 'You're going to Castlereagh,' one of them said, meaning the interrogation centre in Belfast, which was notorious to all nationalists. They drove me there in an armoured van, the inside divided by a perspex screen.

The interior of Castlereagh reminded me of Gough Barracks. I walked behind a policeman who showed me into a long rectangular room where my disappointed RUC protector was waiting.

He greeted me coldly. He asked me to change my solicitor. 'I cannot tell you what solicitor you should pick but I can give you the list of all solicitors in Northern Ireland and allow you to pick a solicitor of your choice.' He opened a blue softbacked book, and as I looked at the page he ran a finger down it and tapped at a particular name. I read out the name of the solicitor, of whom I had never heard, and looked at him for approval. He smiled. I wanted to help him so he would help me. He said if that was my choice then he would follow my instructions.

I spent the rest of the morning going through piles of hard-backed police ledgers which contained details of every IRA incident in Newry and the surrounding areas over the previous fifteen years. The police wanted me to tell them everything I had heard about every IRA operation that had ever taken place there. It might sound strange but I still felt a peculiar pride as I noticed that effective IRA operations had increased greatly after Brian's arrival and, later, me. Prior to 1979, I could see from the ledgers that IRA operations had consisted largely of ill-conceived and badly-executed strikes with only the occasional success to counterbalance the blunders.

I was told that for the rest of the day I would be confronting several of my former IRA comrades. I felt sick at the thought, but I showed no emotion.

I confronted several people over the next few hours. The most painful confrontation was with Francie. The police took me into his cell. He sat there with his arms folded, tears in his eyes. I noticed that his interrogators had removed the sock and shoe from his right foot – a little taunt to tell him that they knew he had been shot in the foot when Mickey had killed the two policemen at Rostrevor. I felt for Francie, but at the same time I was moving more and more decisively into a new set of allegiances based upon my own fear and vulnerability. I felt already divorced from my former friends and allegiances. I had convinced myself that there was no way back. I felt that even if I stopped helping the police, I had already done terminal damage to my relationship with the IRA. Of all the suspects I confronted, Teddy was the only one who spoke. He said plaintively: 'What have they done to you, Eamon?' I stared through him. A policeman repeated his words, then wrote them down. I was indifferent to Teddy and the others. I feared only for myself. I told myself that they would have to take care of themselves as best they could.

There seemed to be a hot line to Gough Barracks. Throughout the day interrogators would ring asking me to provide additional information about the particular weaknesses of particular suspects. In many instances I did not know what to say; I would suggest exploring the character weaknesses that I had felt in myself. The way that the RUC interrogators used me indicated the relative success of the IRA's anti-interrogation techniques. It seemed clear to me that the RUC really had no answer to the right to remain silent so long as the suspect did keep silent.

I was taken back to prison late that evening. As I went through the seemingly unending series of gates and doors I noticed that the whole prison seemed to be quiet. Even the annexe was silent. As I walked past Harry's cell I noticed his eyes looking at me through the slit in his door. I stopped momentarily and said hello. The screws shouted at me and rushed me to my cell. They asked me what I had said to Kirkpatrick. I said I had merely greeted him, but they told me not to speak to him or to any other prisoner in the annexe until such time as I was given permission to do so. This annoyed me: I had been promised that I would be able to mix with the other prisoners. As soon as I had been locked in my cell, the others were let out of theirs. I could hear them arguing with the screws, asking them why I was not allowed out to mix. The screws said they were only following orders.

I stood by my cell door. Through a small gap in the side I could see Harry. He looked like the newspaper photos I had seen of him – long black hair falling down to his shoulders; his face partially obscured by a manicured Mexican-style moustache. He was leaning against a wall with one of his arms outstretched. He said: 'Are we a danger to that man?' A screw said no. 'Then is he a danger to us?' The screw again said no, but he added that his orders had come 'from the top'. Harry said: 'Well, then, he must be seen as a danger to us and if he's a danger to us he shouldn't be here.' With hindsight, I believe that the police suspected that it was only a matter of time before I retracted again. They were afraid that I would pick up useful information about the other grasses, several of whom were about to have their day in court. There was also another possibility: I might be an IRA man sent in specifically to admit to a series of IRA operations with a view to gaining access to the annexe in order to damage the system or even to kill some of the more important grasses.

The next day, I said that I was upset at being kept in my cell away from the other prisoners. My RUC protector said that there had been a misunderstanding with the prison governor and he would sort it out by Monday.

The RUC man who now controlled my life then began to debrief me even more deeply about every aspect of the IRA's operations. He was particularly interested in how they dealt with informers and he asked me if I had ever shot one. I said no. He discussed Scap and John Joe Magee with me in great detail, spending most of Sunday afternoon on the subject. He took me meticulously through everything I had done in the Nutting Squad. He asked me how Scap and John Joe operated together. What was their personal relationship like? How did they complement each other in interrogations? What were they like as people? What did they get up to in their personal lives? What were their strengths and weaknesses? He was particularly interested in how the IRA tried to prevent infiltration and how they were countering the effects of the supergrasses. Reading between the lines of his questions, I could tell that the RUC feared the IRA regaining the initiative. The police had temporarily destroyed the IRA in Belfast – but they wanted to maintain the upper hand.

The RUC's questions made me see that the RUC did not really understand their republican enemies. For all their intelligence-gathering over the previous sixteen years, for all their touts, for all the thousands of republican suspects they had interrogated, they lacked profound insight into the republican psyche. They grasped aspects of it, often important aspects, and they used those insights to good effect in their own military terms, but that would never be enough. I had decided from my own experience that the IRA could never win. However, my time spent co-operating with the RUC convinced me also that the IRA would never be beaten. The RUC could only ever aspire to maintaining an acceptable level of violence.

But my RUC man would occasionally exhibit a degree of honesty about this reality which I admired. He admitted that, regardless of the damage that I or anyone else did to the IRA, they would always be able to reorganize to fight back, and be there in some form.

Sometimes he would ask me questions which I felt had a direct personal relevance. He asked me whether the IRA would directly target the families of RUC officers. I asked him did he mean would the IRA kill family members who got in the way during an operation to kill an RUC officer. No, he said: he wanted to know whether the Provos would ever turn the families themselves into legitimate targets. I told him I thought they would never do that. The main reason why they would not was because the present-day IRA sought to avoid any operations which had *obviously* sectarian overtones: a policeman could be justified as a legitimate target, his non-combatant Protestant family could not. The IRA – regardless of their public utterances dismissing the condemnations of their behaviour from church and community leaders – tried to act in a way that would avoid severe censure from within the nationalist community; they knew they were operating within a sophisticated set of informal restrictions on their behaviour, no less powerful for being largely unspoken.

He was amazed when I explained to him the IRA's relaxed attitude to membership: volunteers could come and go almost as they pleased. They could go away, take a break, come back eventually or stay away permanently if they so desired. He thought that membership of the IRA was a lifetime allegiance: once a Provo, always a Provo, as if volunteers took a sort of priestly vow on joining.

As well as a home, a job and a new identity (including plastic surgery if I wanted), I was told I would receive a payment of at least £100,000. I did not need any of this: I wanted only my freedom to be with my family. I would make my own way in the world. But my controller said I was entitled to all those things and he would make sure I got them. In the meantime, he asked me if there was anything else I needed. Books, for example?

One of his most interesting questions was: 'If I had unlimited resources to fight the IRA, how would you advise me to use them?' I had a simple answer: 'Support, encourage and make possible at every turn the development of Sinn Fein.' This puzzled him; he thought I was contradicting what I had said earlier. He looked at me suspiciously and said: 'But you said the army was taking over Sinn Fein to ensure it didn't contradict or undermine the precedence of the military struggle.'

I said that he had not quite understood what I was conveying
when I had told him about how I had been sent into Newry
Sinn Fein to take it over on behalf of the army. It wasn't Gerry
Adams or Martin McGuinness who sent me in. It wasn't the
Belfast leadership; it was south Armagh. They and the activists
from a few other hardline border areas could see that the
growth of Sinn Fein was going to mean the end of the IRA in
the long run. They knew that once the republican movement
got sucked into the constitutional political system they would
eventually be waving goodbye to the armed struggle. The
democratic system would be able to accommodate the
Provisional republican movement just as it had done other
republican militants in the past. I pointed to the debate that
was taking place within the republican movement about
whether Sinn Fein should sit in the Irish Parliament: the very
fact that such a debate was taking place at all indicated the
nature of the shift in attitude among the leadership.

Intending to provoke, I said: 'Of course, you know that the
end of the IRA's campaign will mean the end of the RUC's
power too.' I suggested that the RUC's political role in propping up the unionist system depended on the continued
existence of the IRA, and that it wasn't only the south Armagh
IRA which might be interested in keeping the *status quo*.

I returned to the prison that evening, handcuffed again, sitting almost blind in the back of a dark transit van. I walked
again through the unnatural silence of the prison into the
safety and security of the annexe. As soon as I was locked in
my cell, the other prisoners were let out of theirs. They made
their way to my door. I was glad to see them: I was sick of talking about Sinn Fein and the IRA.

Harry and Budgie brought me over sandwiches, tea and the
Sunday newspapers, although everything relating to my case
had been torn out, presumably on the instructions of the
RUC.

Later that morning, I was introduced to my new solicitor in
the conference room. He was a man in his late thirties, blond
hair, silver-framed glasses and the usual Irish solicitor's full-
length black crombie. He did not hold out much hope for me.
I had made statements so I had no case to deny. He suggested

that I continue to co-operate with the police as I had the potential to become a useful Queen's witness. He said that such a course would not necessarily guarantee me anything: I would have to take my chances with the judge.

But his next question threw me. He said: 'Had you any involvement in that mortar attack, because if you had you would be advised by me to get it out into the open. If you can be undermined in any way by any evidence implicating you in the mortar attack, your case could collapse.'

I left the solicitor and was taken to a nearby room where the senior RUC man was on the phone: 'Yes, sir. I know, sir. He says he wasn't involved in the rocket attack on Newry RUC station, sir. He's afraid he'll get thirty rec' [recommended] if he admits to it. I know, sir. Yes, sir. Goodbye, sir.' I could not believe that they still suspected me of involvement, nor did I think that I had been allowed to overhear this conversation by chance.

He turned to me and said: 'There's a problem with your case. My boss still thinks you did the mortar attack.' He was using the mortar attack as the stick to beat me with and I felt the whacks. I could see my hopes disappearing. Perhaps they were only interested in the mortar attack; perhaps they regarded everything else I had given them as of little consequence; perhaps they would prosecute me for everything I had already told them and throw in the mortar attack for good measure.

Yet again, I went methodically over the reasons why I had had nothing to do with the mortar attack. Then I redoubled my efforts to convince him of my complete co-operation; I searched my mind for anything new I could tell him about the IRA. I was so desperate to please that I had no difficulty in fobbing off my mother-in-law and my wife's best friend when they got in to see me in Castlereagh that day. They told me that Bernie did not want me to go through with it. A screw sat in with us, but I would have behaved the same even if he had not been there. I heard later that the women had described me as speaking and behaving like a policeman. They told me that Bernie would not be coming to see me until I had retracted. Behind my façade of detachment I felt a burst of anger: my wife should have been with me, putting me first, not the IRA or the community or anyone else. I felt that she had betrayed me as I had betrayed everyone else. So now we were equal. There was almost no one or nothing from my past which I could hold on to. It's not surprising I gave my visitors the impression of emotionless indifference. Only the RUC could now offer me hope.

That night, for the first time, I was allowed to mix with the other prisoners. Harry and Budgie welcomed me into the group. The three of us went into Harry's cell and talked about the events of the last few days. I could see that they were good friends. Budgie was open and talkative, a bouncy, humorous man, who looked surprisingly young. He said: 'We thought we were the last. We thought the system was finished, but you've made it down here so it's going to be continued. You've given us new hope.'

Budgie told me that the annexe had once been reserved for juvenile offenders, and had been brought back into service for the supergrasses. Harry, the veteran of the system, said the place was a hole but it had been even worse when he had first arrived. The grasses had been kept locked up all day without work. He said there was a conflict of interest between the police and the prison authorities. The RUC wanted to give the grasses special treatment; the screws had wanted to run the prison uniformly, with no privileges for anyone. Harry had united the grasses in protest. At first they pestered their police handlers to change things; then they had engaged in a policy of non-co-operation with both the police and the screws; then finally they had got word to their former republican and loyalist colleagues on the outside that, in return for certain guarantees, they would retract.

The police discovered what was going on and, faced with the total collapse of the supergrass system, had forced the prison authorities to improve conditions in the annexe. Harry had been the prime mover behind the campaign: he had become a sort of trade union representative for the grasses.

I told Harry that I had seen the screws with a small red hardbacked notebook with my name on it. He said: 'The only other people with Red Books are up on the A3 landing in A wing. That's where they keep the really bad boys. You must have been a bad boy.' He told me that he had once had Red Book status, but had got the police to downgrade him. He said I should do the same: 'You're no terrorist danger in here as a grass. It's stupid.'

We talked about the shame of having to face former comrades during confrontations. Just talking to Harry and Budgie about the turmoil in my mind seemed to make my crisis a little more bearable. I told them that I still felt I was a republican, to some extent; that I was trying not to think about the whole mess because I was frightened I would go crazy.

I felt a huge sense of relief to be talking to men who understood my fears and doubts and hopes. Budgie told me that you didn't give up a lifetime of beliefs and betray former comrades and friends overnight without severe self-doubt, that you felt recriminations for a long time. They had all experienced that. But whenever he began to have doubts, he thought of some of the incidents he was involved in and the violence he had witnessed: 'I can tell you, Eamon, they were wrong. I seen one guy, after hours of torture and beatings – a middle-aged Catholic picked up on his way home drunk from the pub – having his head cut off with a garden hoe.'

I remember the way he said it, and his words stuck in my mind. The image revolted me. It reminded me of who I was talking to – Budgie Allen, a former loyalist paramilitary, the sort of man who only a few weeks ago I would have willingly set up for assassination. Yet here in the annexe we were becoming friends and, even allowing for the peculiar circumstances, I felt myself liking him greatly as a human being.

They both told me how their families, and those of the other grasses, had suffered. Some had had to be moved from their homes. Budgie's wife and children had stuck by him. Harry's wife had divorced him, although he was philosophical about it. He said it had happened, it had hurt, but he had got over it and was well on the way to recovery. Budgie told me later that the most grievous blow to Harry had been when the leader of the INLA, Dominic McGlinchey, had a part in the murder of Harry's closest childhood friend, 'Sparky' Barkley. Sparky, also a member of the INLA, had visited Harry several times in

Crumlin Road Prison after Harry had first turned grass, to try
to get him to change his mind. Harry had even been on the
verge of retracting when Sparky's tortured body had been
found dumped in a farmyard. Apparently, the body had been
carried around in the boot of McGlinchey's car for several
days before being dumped. After that incident Harry had
vowed to cause as much damage as possible to the INLA.

On that first night of free association in the annexe, I met all
of the other grasses. It was strange meeting these men about
whom I had read so much. On the outside I had regarded them
as despicable. Now I was one of them. As I sat in Harry's cell,
Tony O'Doherty came in and shook hands with me. I had read
a lot about Tony. In many ways his case was the most peculiar
of all. While in the IRA he had been a police agent, an
informer, and – so it was alleged in court – had started carrying
out robberies for money with the connivance of one of his
Special Branch handlers, who had shared in the profits. When
a Catholic police sergeant had started investigating the pair's
activities, the Special Branch man had allegedly shot him dead.
The Special Branch man was now on remand at Crumlin
Road, charged with murder on Tony's evidence. I heard how
Tony had also at one stage infiltrated the INLA and had been
uncovered as a tout by them. He had narrowly escaped being
executed. He found himself in the back of a car driven by
Dominic McGlinchey. As McGlinchey taunted him, telling
him he was going to be executed. Tony had escaped by pulling
out a small pistol provided by the police which he had hidden
in one of his socks. He was a friendly man, but I could sense
sinister and dangerous depths in him and I did not feel I could
trust him.

Tony brought me into Owen Connolly's cell. Owen was
sitting on his bed. He was a small man, mild-mannered, old
enough to be my grandfather and, like my grandfather, he
had a full head of snow white hair. He was thin and slight,
with bright blue intelligent eyes. Owen had been one of the
IRA's most unusual recruits. He had served in the RAF
during the war and had then worked in the Northern Ireland
civil service for more than thirty years, ending up working in
the heart of unionist supremacy at Stormont Castle. Although

a Catholic, he had lived with his wife and daughter in a respectable middle-class area in Protestant East Belfast. Embittered by his personal experience of discrimination at work, he allowed the Provos to use his home as a safe house. The IRA team which killed the assistant governor of the Maze Prison had stayed in his home. One of the IRA men – a 'red light' – was later stopped at a checkpoint. In his address book the police found Owen's phone number. Owen had agreed to turn Queen's Evidence only to save his wife and daughter from prison.

Despite his years in Belfast, Owen still spoke with the south Armagh brogue of his youth. I told Owen that my mother was a Cumiskey from Crossmaglen. He said he knew the family, although he had been reared closer to Cullyhanna. He told me that he had broken only after seeing his wife and daughter in a distressed state in Castlereagh. He saw co-operation with the police as the only way of freeing them and enabling himself to spend the remaining years of his life with them. I felt very sorry for him. There was a terrible sadness about him.

I also met the man whose words had acted like soothing balm on my first night in the annexe: the former UVF man, Jimmy Crockard. I found him playing chess and shook his hand warmly. Jimmy was a broad, solid man, bearded, wearing metal-framed glasses. Beneath the east Belfast hard man there was a gentleness and warmth which was very easy to like. Jimmy invited me to play chess with him. He was a far better player than me, and he helped me to improve my game. Over the next few days I developed a great respect for Jimmy, even though he horrified me with some of the stories from his UVF past.

While I was with Jimmy, the only other grass whom I had not yet seen, John Gibson, poked his head around the door and said hello. He struck me as a fitness fanatic and, indeed, he spent most of the time training on the multi-gym equipment. He was clean-shaven with cropped hair. He exuded physical energy. I heard that there was tension between Jimmy and John because of a rumour that John, a fellow UVF man, was about to retract. Obviously, if he retracted he would be returned to his former comrades in the rest of the prison. They would debrief him, and would be particularly interested in finding out about Jimmy. Gibson had already received a life sentence for 143 offences, including four sectarian murders. He was supposed to have been a UVF battalion commander in east Belfast. He had implicated more than fifty people.

The more I conversed with these men and discovered how the system worked, the more I began to question my own future as a grass. The other effect of talking to them was that for the first time since I had broken, I began to think clearly. It was as if I were reaching into myself to retrieve some way of acting independently. Even their use of the mortar attack to put pressure on me began to provoke feelings of irritation and exasperation rather than fear. I was beginning slowly to regain some of my confidence. I look back now and realize that I was searching for the courage to retract, although I knew I could never return to the IRA – nor did I want to. I knew that if I had faced up to the reality of my flagging commitment to the republican movement in the first place, I would not have found myself in this claustrophobic bubble of fear.

The morning after my first day of association, the screws unlocked our cells at seven-thirty. People showered and brushed their teeth. Some did their washing and hung it from the overhead rails in the shower-room. I found myself alone with Owen as we shaved. I started speaking to him. He kept glancing over his shoulder as we spoke, checking that we were still alone. I realized that he was eager for company but distrustful of the others, although I was not sure why. Then he said: 'We can't really talk here, Eamon. Come up to my cell later, after work.'

The screws led the workers out of the back of the annexe, through a gate and up a narrow metal staircase, into a large space with very few cells around it. Harry told me that this used to be death row in the days of hanging. He pointed to a partition wall and said that the hanging cell, where the gallows had stood, lay behind it. There was a strange peacefulness and solemnity about the place.

Work for most of us consisted of putting 'Wello' hairbrushes into presentation packages. Jimmy stayed downstairs cleaning the kitchen, while Owen stood apart from us wearing a long, ill-fitting storeman's coat as he used sandpaper to rub down pieces of wood which he then nailed together to make picture frames. His meticulousness fascinated me. He performed each action with precision and diligence, as if he were working with gold and diamonds. Later I brought him over a mug of tea and asked him why he kept his distance from the rest. He said: 'Some people would stoop to any level to save their own skins and curry favour with the police. Some of these people would put away their own mothers and sisters if necessary.' But Owen was honest enough not to delude himself about his own status. He said to me at one point: 'Let's have no illusions. We're all informers here.' I had read enough prison literature to know of the parody of the class system that tended to develop among prisoners. But I was still surprised and amused to find even in this prison within a prison that there were such strange hierarchies.

A screw sat reading a book while we packed brushes. Harry and Budgie laughed and smoked and listened to the radio. When we broke for lunch, I discovered that the grasses cooked for themselves, because food prepared outside the annexe could not be trusted. Jimmy did most of the cooking. His chef's apron was a black bin-liner in which he had cut a hole for his head and two holes at the sides for his arms. That day he served up heaps of boiled rice dotted with currants and covered with chicken curry. He took pride in his cooking and wanted us to enjoy it. 'Is it all right?' he kept asking, a ladle in his hand.

The next day I was returned to Castlereagh. We spent the morning discussing IRA operations that I had been planning. I had accumulated reasonable intelligence on around twenty part-time and full-time members of the Crown forces. The files in my mind on each of them were at various stages of completion, but I knew enough to give the go-ahead for at least five attacks.

I had another court appearance coming up that Friday. I was told it was important that I tell the court that I was no longer being represented by P.J. McGrory. I said that I knew who my new solicitor was. The RUC man congratulated me and said that mine was going to be 'a super case'. He told me that his own superior no longer believed that I had played any part in the mortar attack.

When I returned to prison that evening, the annexe was quiet. I met John Gibson. He was dressed in his gym clothes and was wiping himself down with a towel after his training session. We shook hands and chatted for a while. He said he had had enough of the annexe. He had decided he was going to retract his evidence: 'I can't wait to get out.' I admired his resolution; it underlined my own weakness. He had decided to serve a life sentence rather than continue as a grass.

After tea in the annexe that night, I went to Owen's cell. Owen tended to eat alone in his cell. He had a pair of Adidas trainers for me. He said they would be better for walking around the annexe than the shoes I was wearing. He also gave me apples, oranges and biscuits. We talked again about his former life. He still thought that what we were all doing as grasses was terrible, but he felt that the stance of some of the others, who he thought were brutal and unscrupulous, was even more reprehensible.

On Friday I had my second court appearance, this time in Belfast. I had visitors when I returned to Crumlin Road, my brother John and my sister Alice. They had been in court. John told me that after I had been led away he had gone to confront my new solicitor and had accused him of working for the supergrass system rather than for me. The solicitor said that he would withdraw immediately from my case. John talked to me at length about what I was doing and his words began to hit home. He said that he had spoken to several republicans in Belfast and Dundalk about me. All had said the same thing: retract and all would be forgiven. They understood what I had been through and they bore me no malice: I had broken under pressure from a police force that had just lost nine of its officers. He said that the Sinn Fein councillor Jim McAllister had made several public statements about my case, censuring the RUC, not me, for what had taken place.

Suddenly I could see the way forward with a clarity that had eluded me for two weeks. I felt intense relief that my former comrades could apparently forgive me so easily for what I had done. The conditional and grudging nature of their pardon would become clearer later. What had been keeping me on my current path was my conviction that I had cut myself off completely from my friends, from my family. Now they were saying: we forgive you; retract and return to where you belong. Of course, I knew that I faced a life sentence for retracting. But a life sentence now seemed a small price to pay for being able to expunge the shame and isolation of betrayal, the complete loss of connection with life that the men in the annexe had to accept.

Until that point, my act of betrayal had left me feeling almost a sense of grief. John's assurances made my depression lift. I began talking to him, falteringly. Alice recognized what was taking place. She said: 'He's coming out of it. Good man, Eamon.' Mixing with the other grasses, and having more time to myself to think, had given my weakened mind arguments against continuing to co-operate. Early release from prison would be too high a price to pay. The glimpse of possible forgiveness was enough to swing my mind resolutely behind the idea of retraction, even though I felt bitterly alienated from the IRA. My feelings were personal, no longer political.

I told John and Alice that I wanted to get out of the annexe. They arranged for my solicitor to visit me later that afternoon.

But I had already made my decision. I was not going to remain a supergrass. Later that afternoon the solicitor arrived at the prison to see me.

This man brought with him another affidavit of retraction. I was about to sign but later that day word was smuggled to me that the IRA wanted me to remain in the annexe for another little while in order to find out as much as I could about the other grasses, in particular Harry and Owen. They wanted me to delay signing until Monday. I felt sick at the idea. I had come all this way out of the annexe and now the Provos wanted to prolong the agony by getting me to betray people who in a few days had become my friends. I could not do it, but I was not going to antagonize the IRA by refusing. I told the intermediary that if I stayed I would have to continue talking to the police. He told me to tell them that I needed a break because of exhaustion.

I did as I was told. On Saturday, when I went to Castlereagh, I saw the doctor and told him I was worn out. He agreed that I needed a break. My RUC mentor seemed a little surprised at my exhaustion: I think he must have suspected something, but felt powerless to act. I was sent back to the annexe.

Over the weekend, I told the others that I had asked the peelers for a rest. Harry, sharp as ever, knew somehow that my solicitor had been up to see me. He asked me why. I told him that pressure was being put on me from other sources to retract. I seemed to reassure them that I was still steadfast. During the weekend I spent as much time with them as possible, but I did not pump them for information. I felt angry with the IRA for trying to use me in this way. I told myself that whatever I had gleaned from Harry and the others over the last few days I would pass on, as my offering of repentance, but that was all. And in any case, I saw very little of Harry and Budgie over the weekend.

Attention was distracted from me by the departure of John Gibson. There were no emotional farewells. John had not been particularly popular among the grasses. As he left, Jimmy gave him a threatening scowl. Then he said to me: 'I don't think you're the type of man to go through with this either. You should think seriously of retracting. I don't think this is for you.' I was surprised. Did he suspect something too? I said that I'd signed a great many detailed statements which I'd never be able to beat. Jimmy listened thoughtfully and said: 'Well, there was a boy recently was down here. He retracted and fought the statements and he nearly beat them. Somebody, some day, is going to beat them.'

On Sunday night, I went into Owen's cell. I told him that I had decided to retract and would sign an affidavit the next day. Owen was not surprised: 'You know what is best yourself, Eamon. I'd take the same path if I wasn't such an old man.' I felt a great sympathy for Owen and for his predicament. He was going for trial on Monday. He would plead guilty and would be sentenced to life imprisonment in the space of a few minutes. He would get out after a few years, but I knew he would then spend the rest of his life imprisoned by guilt and fear. In the morning, I made a point of going into the washroom as Owen shaved. I told him to hold his head up high in court. We hugged each other, and I wished him good luck.

My solicitors from McGrory's arrived for me. I signed the affidavit. I felt a mixture of relief and trepidation: relief that I was now free from the control of the police, but fearful of the future, despite my brother's reassuring words. For some reason I expected the prison authorities to know immediately what I had done. But they did not, and I was returned to the annexe. I behaved as if nothing had happened.

Owen returned from court. As expected, he had received a life sentence. The judge called Owen an evil man and accused him of betraying the principles he had once served so well in the RAF.

I told everyone that I had retracted. No one seemed surprised. Suddenly two screws came towards me: 'Get your belongings packed. You're going to B wing now. Why didn't you tell us you'd retracted?' I began to pack, but before I had finished they took me to the governor's office. I told him that I wanted to be put with other republicans. He made me sign a document exonerating the prison of any liability in the event of my being attacked by the IRA within the prison.

As I left the governor's office I met my police mentor. He seemed nervous and excited. He said: 'I knew you were going to do this. Why didn't you talk to me about it before you signed the affidavit?' I shrugged my shoulders. Part of me felt guilty about letting him down. I said: 'I couldn't do this to my children. I don't want them to inherit only this.' He realized that he had lost me: 'Ah well. That's it. Decide in haste, repent at your leisure.'

I returned to the annexe to finish packing. I said goodbye to everyone. Owen embraced me. He had tears in his eyes. I was handcuffed and led out. Owen waved at me continuously. A rat-faced screw shouted at him to get back into his cell. I entered the air-lock for the last time. I heard the hiss as the pistons released the locks and I was led across to B wing. They put me in a cell which contained only a bed, a mattress and a Bible.

Now, about two weeks since I had first broken under interrogation, I was on my way back to the IRA. I felt euphoric, but only because I had freed myself from the control of the police. As I lay on the bed my euphoria gradually dispersed. I was about to mix with republicans again, people with whom I no longer felt any real affinity – including the very people I had betrayed.

23

A SORT OF REPUBLICAN

'I don't know what to do with you, Collins. We haven't decided where to send you yet,' said the senior prison officer who came into my cell.

I was in B wing, which housed the ordinary criminals; the loyalists were in C wing. I wanted to go to A wing to join the republicans, and I told him so. He was surprised: 'Aren't you afraid for your safety?' I said no.

I was not frightened; merely numbed. I tried not to think about my act of betrayal, but there was no escape from the truth: I had gone over to the system and become a supergrass, albeit temporarily. I was still relying on Valium and sleeping tablets to divert the confusion and anguish.

I felt the 'republican family' would regard me as a bastard, a mongrel, a social outcast. I would not be able to draw on the collective strength of the movement because my actions and theirs had destroyed the previous bond of trust. Whenever I remembered what I had done I would feel a sense of mental crisis. I was frightened that insanity beckoned. I tried to fight each dangerous thought by turning my mind to the absurd. I clutched at any pleasant fantasy I could conjure up.

But this retreat into fantasy offered only temporary relief: I knew I would have to face up to reality. Even at this early stage of drugged confusion, I realized that my only way forward was to become my own man. I knew that the battle to achieve independence would have to be fought against both the Provos and the prison system.

In the afternoon a screw came to escort me to A wing. I felt people staring at me as I entered what was to become my home for the next two years. I stood on the ground floor, A1. Prisoners and screws were milling about. Screws shouted orders: 'Yard . . . education . . . so-and-so for a visit.' All of the screws seemed to be wearing shoes with metal tips on the heels. They slid, banged and tap-danced their way around the place, making as much noise as possible. I loathed the screws; over the next two years I saw them sometimes enjoying, and abusing, their power. Occasionally I would come across a decent screw – about one in thirty.

I bowed my head timidly as I entered the wing. I was ashamed at the thought of coming face to face with some of the people I had confronted only the week before. I walked up the stairs to A2; then I walked up a further flight to A3, the top floor, home of the Red Books. I was shown to a cell at the end of A3. The screw told me to leave my things on the bed and to follow him. He took me to the room of the prison officer, the man in charge of the wing. The PO said: 'Give me no trouble, and I'll give you no trouble. He told me that 'the RCs' – this was how the screws referred to republicans – were exercising at present and I could join them in the yard.

I walked out into the yard. The sunlight almost blinded me. The yard was a gaunt patch bounded by three walls and the prison block. Two of the walls were of recent construction, made up of thousands of unplastered concrete blocks; the other wall was ancient and blackened. Perched high on its left-hand side was what looked like a space-age construction – an observation bubble made of tinted bullet-proof glass. Surveillance cameras were dotted all over the walls and on the roof. Rolls of barbed wire snaked across the top of the walls.

Groups of men stood huddled in corners; others walked around in a circle, hands in pockets, heads down, deep in hushed conversation; others played football with a tattered leather ball. I recognised Teddy in one of the groups. I remembered his words when I had confronted him last week: 'What have they done to you, Eamon?'

I walked towards him, but before I reached him I was intercepted by two men. They introduced themselves as Bobby and
Joe. Joe was broad and stocky with a big head set on a thick
neck and massive shoulders. Several of his teeth were missing,
and he had very flushed cheeks. He was wearing Doc Martens,
a green flying jacket and blue Wrangler jeans – an archetypal
Belfast Provie if ever there was one. I found out later that he
came from the notorious Unity Walk flats in West Belfast and
was known as the Hawk. He had never broken under interrogation although he had had countless seven-day detentions.
His catch-phrase was: 'The Hawk from the Walk don't talk.' I
walked around in circles with them. The Hawk did most of the
talking and was very friendly. I liked him immediately,
although in my frame of mind I would have liked anyone who
showed me even the minimum of kindness. I told them that I
had not held anything back from the police: 'I gave them the
heap.' They accepted what I said without condemning me, but
the Hawk said I would have to write down everything for them
on pieces of cigarette paper. However, he said I could wait a
few days until I had settled in to A wing and got my head
together.

After my talk with them I went over to Teddy. I apologized
for what I had done. He nodded. Soon the exercise period
ended. I did not see him again because within the next few
days almost everyone who had been arrested as a result of my
statements walked free. Only a handful who had signed statements themselves remained in custody – Brendan, Joe and a
few other small fry.

All volunteers who broke under interrogation and signed
statements were debriefed by IRA security officers in prison.
Reports were then written up and sent out secretly through
'comms' (notes written in minute handwriting on cigarette
papers, which were then wrapped up into tiny balls , covered
with clingfilm and passed on to visitors – often through a kiss).
These would then be read by security officers outside who
would scrutinize them and ask for more information on specific
points of concern or interest. The Hawk debriefed me and he
sent out his report. A little while later he said he had heard
back from the security unit: the verdict was that I had broken

in a moment of weakness. They did not feel there was any
need for further investigation or recrimination.

The IRA leadership in the prison ('the staff') were very
interested in finding out about the supergrasses. I told them
what little I knew. They tried to get me to use my friendship
with Owen Connolly to arrange a meeting between him and a
republican intermediary, who wanted to discuss a possible
deal with him. I tried, but Owen got wind of what was going
on and refused to meet the man. I refused to try again, to the
annoyance of the IRA. I had already told them that there
was no deal they could offer Owen that would make him
retract his evidence.

The IRA gave permission for the leading INLA man,
Jimmy Brown, to talk to me about the supergrass Harry
Kirkpatrick. I knew as well that my impressions of the loyalist
supergrasses, for what they were worth, were passed on to the
loyalist leadership within the prison. So it was not just within
the annexe that the supergrass system brought together loyalists and republicans. I assumed that the loyalists passed on
information to the IRA that they had gleaned from debriefings
of their own former grasses. On the outside, too, the two sides
co-operated extensively in the campaign to destroy the system.
Of course, this co-operation only went so far because another
way in which the IRA benefitted from the supergrass system
was through picking up a lot of useful intelligence about their
enemies from what was said in court. Indeed, the IRA and
INLA went on to kill quite a few of the loyalists who had been
named by supergrasses, and the loyalists killed several republicans named by IRA turncoats.

There were several other Red Books, including the Hawk,
Jimmy Brown and his INLA colleague Gerard Steenson, nicknamed 'Dr Death' by the tabloids. The Red Books were under
special surveillance. We were moved regularly to new cells and
subjected to continuous strip-searches; screws stood beside us
during visits; we were not allowed to share a cell with another
prisoner; and no more than two of us were allowed out on the
wing at any one time. Everything about us was recorded in
the Red Books which were kept in a little wooden box on the
A3 landing.

At the end of the first week I had my first visit from Bernie. She looked pale and tired. We sat across a table with a screw standing next to us. I held her hand: it felt small, cold and lifeless. At that time I could not envisage Bernie having a life that did not somehow involve me. But we had become strangers: the only things we seemed to have in common were our children. She apologized for the harsh things she had said to me in Gough Barracks. I told her to forget them. I did not tell her that I could not forget them, and – even though her words had been understandable and justifiable – I felt betrayed by her allegiance to the republican movement in that moment of crisis. We hardly talked.

I found her visits extremely painful: they left me feeling desperately insecure. I wondered how long she would stay with me. I began to dread her visits as much as I looked forward to them. After each visit I would lie in my cell examining in minute detail every word she had said, every facial expression, every little movement. It embittered me to learn that the republican movement in Newry had put her on a pedestal for her harsh treatment of me. She was devoting a lot of time to working for Sinn Fein and then, to my horror, spending most of her visits talking to me about 'the movement this' and 'the movement that'. I thought they were using her. And she was allowing herself to be used.

As the weeks and months crawled past in Crumlin Road, I slipped into a deep depression. I did not believe I had a chance of escaping a life sentence. Every morning I would strip to the waist and shave myself while standing beside a line of men similarly stripped with towels around their waists. Through the fog of condensation I would meet the same dead eyes in the mirror and have the same thought: 'This is your life.'

For me, the only person in those early months who shed light into this fog was my solicitor Paddy McGrory. My self-disgust at my own weakness had left me feeling worthless in the company of my fellow republicans. I was sick: sick of myself, sick of the armed struggle which had brought me here, and sick of looking ahead to see only thirty years of imprison-ment. At first I was a shambling, self-pitying wretch, barely capable of rational thought. Paddy helped to restore some

sense of dignity; then, through his efforts to build up a frame-
work for a defence, he enabled me to perceive the faintest,
dimmest glimmer of a chance.

Although I felt shame at what I had done, I resisted – without at first quite realizing what I was doing – the urge to crawl
on my knees in repentance for my sins against 'the republican
family'. I knew that my breaking under interrogation had not
been merely a straightforward response to police pressure. I
knew my collapse had taken place as a result of a long process
of disillusionment. In prison I had the time to consider in
detail all the factors which had brought me down to the lowest
point of my life. By searching through the past I wanted to discover who I now was. Paddy helped me to clarify my thoughts.
He had seen hundreds of republicans who had broken, signed
statements, and then faced up to a future behind bars. He was
case-hardened, as he told me himself, but not cynical.

We discussed his heart condition – he had had a heart attack
in his early forties, just as his career had started to take off –
and I would watch him take his medication in the special cell
reserved for legal visits. I told him about my father's heart
attacks. Paddy would laugh when I described how my father
would follow a strict diet for one week and then rebel the next,
launching himself on an orgy of trifle, downing Scotch by the
bottle, and smoking forty Gold Leaf cigarettes a day. These
discussions about the threat of death allowed us to develop a
bond and moved us on to the more human terrain of fragility
and fear. I detected that Paddy feared death, though probably
no more than the rest of us; his heart attack had merely
reminded him sharply of his mortality. He sat there during
the cold months wearing a camel-coloured crombie coat, similar to my father's. I spoke to him about why I had broken and
discussed how I felt about all the murders I had been involved
in. I told him that the murders were wrong and I had been
wrong. I realized during our talks the subtle part that my conscience had played in the complicated and drawn-out process
which had led to my collapse.

He told me that in the early seventies, when sectarian attacks
had been at their height, he – and many people like him – had
come close to joining the IRA. But he had pulled back because

he believed in the law and he hoped that the state could be reformed by the law. He said he still believed that he had been right to place his faith in the law. He said that the Provos had carried out some dastardly attacks against the very people who were working to make the law a vehicle for delivering impartial justice in society. He mentioned the shooting of Judge Doyle, a Catholic member of the judiciary killed by the IRA.

I started studying again for my Open University degree. This began to provide an important focus in my life, but I still could not get used to the suffocation of prison life. Around nine months into my remand I was sweeping out my cell one day when the INLA leader Ta Power poked his head around the door. He had been on remand for four years on the word of various supergrasses (latterly Harry Kirkpatrick). He asked me if I had settled in. I said: 'No. I'll never settle in. This will never be my life. I'll do all I can to hold on to the life I have outside with my family.' He paused for a second and said: 'This here is your life.'

It took me some time to realize the truth of what Power had said. What he meant was that I had in one sense to let go of my life outside the prison and instead concentrate on creating a fulfilling life for myself within. I had to submit to the change. Life started to become a little easier when I began to establish a prison life with some purpose to it.

I continued to grow away from the republican movement. I did not help myself by making known my criticisms of the armed struggle. In conversation after conversation I would say that, although I thought ours was still a just war, we could not win it using our current strategy and therefore it was wrong to continue. The more independent I became, the more willing I was to express my dissident views. Gerard Steenson warned me once that I was only going to make trouble for myself. Perhaps I should have listened to him, but I had not quite realized how extensive the IRA's intelligence network in prison was. There was a lot of eavesdropping, surveillance and routine observation. Word soon got around that I was a trouble-maker.

It was almost a year before I was arraigned for the preliminary enquiry to decide whether I had a case to answer. As I waited in the downstairs cells prior to entering the court, my

senior RUC man walked in. I had not seen him since my last
day in the supergrass annexe. He had come to read out all the
charges and to hand me my depositions. He sat down at a table
facing me. Another detective hovered in the background, walking to and fro smoking a cheroot. We looked at each other
silently for a few seconds, then he said: 'How are you? Are you
all right?' I paused, not sure whether to say anything, then I
said: 'I'm all right.' That was all I said, except for 'not guilty'
to every charge. There was no bitterness between us. Indeed,
I was surprised at the peculiarly warm feelings I felt towards
him: it was as if there was a bond between us and, in one sense
of course, there was. I had talked to him in those two weeks in
a way that I had not talked to anyone, let alone an RUC man,
before. I found myself wanting to talk to him again. But I
could not. Perhaps the presence of the other detective inhib-
ited me. I knew that they were going to try to nail me in court,
but I did not mind. I did not feel in any way hostile towards
him. He had only been doing his job and, within the bounds of
his job, he had behaved with kindness and decency, more than
was necessary to keep me on side. Now we were just professional enemies again.

In court, I stood in the dock with a few of my former comrades who had been arrested on my word and who had then
gone on to sign statements implicating themselves. The TV
repairman who set up Norman Hanna was one; Joe was
another; Brendan, my fellow customs officer who had helped
set up Toombs, was also charged with murder but he was not
at this arraignment. The only friendly face in the court was
that of my brother John. My wife was not there. I had wanted
more than anything to see her face in that courtroom, but I had
learnt over the course of the year not to expect too much. She
had remained heavily involved in Sinn Fein, partly I suppose
to help expunge the stain of my betrayal. I felt I had lost her,
yet I still loved her and hoped – perhaps fantasized – that she
still loved me. I no longer felt bitter towards her. I felt I
deserved what I had got; I had earned this treatment, just as I
had earned the life sentence that seemed inevitably on its way.
The Provos had got six good years out of me; the state would
get the rest.

Bernie rarely even wrote letters. I wished she could have been there, but she had at least told me in advance that she would not be able to make it. She had typed up a transcript of a memoir written by a former Provo entitled *Newry's Struggle*. As a reward, he was taking her out for a meal that evening. I did not begrudge her the meal. I told myself to accept that she would soon be gone from my life. If I had not lost her yet, then I would at some time in the future when I was serving my life sentence. I was no fool: I knew that most prisoners' wives and girlfriends were fair game for anyone. And the pursuers were usually ex-prisoners, members of Sinn Fein or IRA men. Very comradely behaviour. But how could a prisoner blame his partner? Why should she experience a life sentence of deprivation too? That night, in my cell, I thought about the way in which I had neglected her in order to lavish care and attention on the IRA right from the earliest days of our marriage. I knew I would have to lose her if I received a life sentence.

Soon after the arraignment I talked to Joe in the yard. He told me that he had overheard several members of the IRA staff discussing my case. They had expressed delight that I was likely to get several life sentences; and one of them had even said that if I got off I was going to be shot by the IRA anyway. They had described me as an arrogant little bastard.

I decided to approach the veteran republican Martin Meehan, a fellow Red Book, and a member of the IRA staff. I liked Martin, although I did not really trust him. He was a tough man, although not without flashes of warmth and humanity. He could also be very funny, and his practical jokes often helped to raise morale. I told him what I had heard (although I did not say who told me). I said that I found it strange that members of the staff could gloat over the fact that I was about to be sent down for life. I said that I had done what the IRA had asked me to, and retracted. I asked him to tell me what the score was. He described the possibility of me being shot as 'shit'. He said that I was making a very serious accusation and if it turned out to be unfounded I could be punished physically. I said: 'So I'm being threatened now?' He denied he was threatening me: 'But these sorts of accusations can have very serious implications.' I said that the only reason I was approaching him was because I wanted to clarify that the IRA intended keeping its promise not to harm me. He assured me that the IRA had a policy and they would stick to it. He said: 'As far as I'm concerned, you retracted and that is the end of it. You're an IRA man, a republican, the same as the rest of us.' I appreciated what he said, but he was wrong. I was not the same as the rest of them, and I had become determined to live a life independent of them if I could.

This incident underlined the change that had taken place in attitudes towards me. Things had begun to go downhill after the release of the Hawk, who was a member of the staff but one of my defenders. The prison OC was now Patrick McCotter who did not hide his dislike for me. He did not like the way I had stopped attending the Provos' educational lectures, which I had described incautiously to a number of people as a load of clichéd tripe. But McCotter had power and he began to try to exert it. The first run-in I had with him concerned my preference for staying in my cell during the one-hour exercise period, in order to work on my degree.

McCotter told me that I had no right to choose to stay in my cell: I would have to ask the IRA staff's permission to do so. I felt like telling the petty-minded bureaucrat where to go, but I knew that direct confrontation with the IRA hierarchy would have been very dangerous for my health. So instead I sought to flatter the ego of power: each time I wanted to stay in my cell I went to him first to ask his permission.

At one stage, McCotter accused me of being too compliant with the screws: he had a point, to some extent – I was being a good boy, not getting into any confrontations with the system, because I wanted to finish my OU degree in peace. What McCotter did not realize was that my actions were based on my desire to exercise power for myself. My degree was a symbol of independence. McCotter wanted me to create tension between myself and the screws in order to further the aims of the IRA within the prison, but I had spent enough of my life furthering the aims of the IRA.

My next run-in with the people's army concerned a jacket. I had become friendly with a young Protestant man who was serving a short sentence for some ordinary criminal offence. He was a decent, innocent sort of a lad and he needed a jacket. I gave him mine. McCotter heard about this from one of his spies. He insisted that I get the jacket back and give it to a republican prisoner. I had no choice but to do as I was told.

A loyalist prisoner once asked to join the republicans' 'O' level sociology class: apparently there were not enough loyalist prisoners showing interest to form a class of their own. I was in favour of allowing him to join because I thought it was important that loyalists and republicans met each other. I felt that such encounters would at the very least provoke lively debates about our respective political positions. I also thought they would provide a great opportunity for members of each working-class community to learn about the other (and I once would have despised such meetings). Such encounters might, I felt by then, eventually result in a challenge to the sectarian *status quo*. However, McCotter and his officers rejected the loyalist's request. To me, this rejection was evidence of the IRA's need to keep the two communities polarized in order to justify the continuation of the armed struggle and, ultimately, their own power.

I had gone over to the police and didn't like what I had found. Now I found the Provos aggressive and bigoted too. I found myself in a limbo – of my own making, of course. The prison system tried to destroy you as a free-thinking individual, but the IRA command structure in prison was no less oppressive in the way it demanded a surrender of your will to the needs and commands of 'the movement'. I grew to loathe the words 'the movement'. It was hard to have any sort of conversation without someone parroting 'the movement this' or 'the movement that'. In the IRA's war, I came to see that there was no room for variation, no room for anyone who could think for himself. What the IRA wanted was blind complicity.

I developed friendships with IRA men – some of whom were even on the staff – but I grew to reject the organization's reason for being. Just before my trial, a republican said to me after I had yawned at some war news: 'Don't you worry about the war any more?' I replied: 'If my child needed his nappy changed I'd be more concerned with that than the fucking

war.' My remark must have got back to McCotter because he
later accused me yet again of being 'arrogant'.

And yet right up to my trial I experienced ambivalent feelings towards the armed struggle and the efficacy of political
violence. I felt a personal revulsion against such violence – and
a determination not to engage in it myself in the future – along
with a sense of the futility of the IRA's campaign, but I could
not yet condemn the use of violence in Northern Ireland that
might spring from more truly revolutionary aspirations. I was
still in transition, not quite able to let go the dream of a pure
people's army. It was only after my trial that I fully believed
that, at least in the context of Northern Ireland, political violence from whatever source was unjustifiable.

One morning in January 1987, less than a week before the
start of my trial, I was slopping out when I heard a screw
shout up from the first floor: 'E. Collins for the governor!' I
wondered what the governor wanted with me so early in the
morning. I was escorted through the prison to his office. I
began to feel queasy: this had to be serious. I was shown into
the office. The governor sat behind his desk. He said: 'I have
a bit of bad news for you, Collins. Your father died this
morning. You will of course get an extra half-hour visiting
time. In fact, your brother and wife are here to see you now.
I'm sorry I've had to tell you this. You can go back to your
cell and collect your thoughts.' I was not going to cry in front
of the screws. I tried to remain impassive as I walked back to
my cell. I walked past republican prisoners but said nothing.
This was my father, my grief, my problem, and I would suffer
it alone.

The screws who took me for my visit commiserated with
me. Their kindness did not extend to foregoing the strip-
search on the way through the box. My brother John and
Bernie were waiting for me. John said my father had collapsed
at the funeral of one of his uncles. He had suddenly fallen to
the ground, dead from a heart attack. He had been due to visit
me that day, bringing my son Tiarnach, as he had done every
week throughout my imprisonment. I had enjoyed his visits:
once he had been on the verge of fighting with the screws
when he felt they were cutting short his visiting time.

After the visit I went to the yard. I saw three close prison friends and told them. I did not want the IRA staff to know. That night I stayed awake thinking about my father. When the prison had gone quiet and I could no longer hear the screws prowling about on the landing, I put my head under the blankets and cried quietly. I cried for about ten minutes: it was the first time I had cried since I had been in prison, and I have not cried since.

The next morning I got out of bed. I washed, had breakfast, returned to my cell and started to study. I could not concentrate. I stood up and took the hard mattress from my bed and put it up against the wall. I began punching it hard, again and again, until I built up a sweat. Then I ran on the spot; I did press-ups; I exhausted myself. I thought of my father and my childhood, but stopped myself. Instead, I did what Gerard Steenson had once told me to do in moments of despair. I paced up and down my cell with my eyes closed, thinking only of black. I had done this so many times before over the last two years that I knew exactly when to stop and turn. I could bring the shutters down on my mind at will. After half an hour I could see nothing but blackness.

I was refused compassionate leave to attend my father's funeral.

A few days later, I was eating in the canteen. McCotter came up to me and said: 'I heard your father died. Why didn't you tell any of the staff?' I said that I did not think they would be interested. My action in not telling them had been designed to convey a clear message: 'I don't need you people. I won't share my life with you. I no longer believe in, or support, your ludicrous war. Get off my back.' McCotter looked embarrassed. He said: 'You should have told us.'

I knew he had got the message.

24

BRITISH JUSTICE

I spent almost two years on remand. In January 1987 I entered Crumlin Road Courthouse to begin my defence against five charges of murder and forty-five other serious offences.

Paddy McGrory decided that my best defence, my only defence, was to question the admissibility of the confessions I had made. My defence would be that I had made the statements under duress after being assaulted and subsequently offered inducements, such as a reduced sentence, a new life abroad and money.

In Northern Ireland terrorist offences are tried in so-called Diplock Courts, without juries. A judge sits alone. If a defendant questions the admissibility of statements that are going to be used in his prosecution, then what is known as a Voir Dire hearing takes place before the main trial. This hearing is effectively a trial within the trial in which the judge decides whether statements are admissible. This procedure can take weeks, or even months, as evidence is presented and witnesses are examined and cross-examined.

Paddy said that he had in mind a strategy which he had used successfully before. He said that he had represented a man who was accused of having played a role in a bombing, which he denied. However, he had made other incriminating confessions in custody. The defence team had convinced the judge that the defendant had only signed statements under duress. The statements were deemed inadmissible. However, the accused had admitted during the Voir Dire that he was a member of the IRA, so the judge sentenced him to six years imprisonment for IRA membership. But the House of Lords had overturned this conviction on appeal, ruling that it was permissible to make such an admission within the Voir Dire without it being treated as an admission of guilt.

I asked Paddy if that meant I could tell the full truth in court: if we would be trying to get the case thrown out because of the unlawful means used to obtain my confessions, surely I could still admit that the confessions themselves contained the truth of what I had done? Paddy looked at me as if I was a half-wit. He said: 'And admit to murder?'

'Yes. Why not?'

'Because no one will be there to represent you after you admit that.' He explained that the gravity of such an admission – to multiple murder – would surely undermine the extent of the legal privilege that normally existed for incriminating admissions made during the Voir Dire.

But how on earth was I going to explain away the detailed tape-recorded confessions?

The answer was that I should say I couldn't remember making them. I didn't know what I was admitting to. I was to say that I was in the IRA but that I only acted as a scout; that I didn't really know what I was telling the police.

To McGrory, I said that I supposed it sounded semi-plausible. Inside I felt deeply uncomfortable. I was not sure that I would be able to handle a cross-examination with such a defence. I also felt sick and fearful at the thought of the full extent of my betrayal of the IRA being exposed publicly for all to see. Two years previously I had been a broken man. On top of everything, in the days before the trial I was still feeling grief-stricken at my father's death.

There was another reason why I had hoped the Voir Dire hearing would enable me to admit to the truth contained in my statements. I wanted to be able to confirm that Brendan had been desperate to have the Toombs operation called off and that he had only answered the phone – when Iceman had called to check whether Toombs was there – after I had assured him that the call would only be a test of his commitment.

McGrory was alarmed, yet he was sensitive enough to appreciate my reasons. He pointed out that each defendant in that courtroom would be advised by his own counsel in a particular way to get him off or, at the very least, to secure a deal which would result in a reduced sentence. Paddy said that none of the other defendants would be in the least concerned about me, or anyone else for that matter. He said: 'In that courtroom it's a clear case of "every man for himself". It's imperative that you realize that from now on. They're going to have their own solicitors and experienced counsel to do that for them.'

I had resolved at least to put up a fight, so now I knew I was going to have to fight by lying. I still expected to go down for twenty-five years but I was not going to make it too easy for the system because, regardless of my own natural desire to grasp the only opportunity for freedom, I was still then a sort of IRA man, and I shared every republican's view of the Diplock Courts: they were corrupt institutions, abnormal legal tribunals, and no justice could be expected from them. They seemed to deny any presumption of innocence. The reader should bear this in mind in what follows. I lied, but the presumption was that the game was played that way.

I felt a sense of dread entering the court each day. I had grown apart from the republican movement but that did not mean that I was embracing the Orange State. This was their system, their law, their judiciary, owing allegiance to their Queen – represented on the wall above the judge's head by a plaster coat of arms.

Throughout the trial, I found that they put pressure on me even when I had left the court for the day. Every few days I would be moved to a new cell, while at night the light in my cell would be kept on. I complained frequently, but to no avail. One night I stood on my bed and removed the light bulb. For most of the rest of the night a screw stood by my door shining a torch on me. Visits from loved ones would be cut short.

Each day, before we went into court, I would sit downstairs in a cell with Brendan. Each day, he would follow the same routine: he would dab water on his face and eyes and then ask me to join him in saying the rosary, which I did, just to keep him happy. He told me that he had been writing to a Carmelite nun whose replies were helping him face his ordeal. Each day I kept up his flagging morale by telling him that he had a better case than I had and he would easily win. I lied: I knew he was going down for life, and I was certain that I was too.

I was not prepared for the slowness of court procedure, particularly in the first two months. Witnesses were brought in to detail every incident I was charged with. Sometimes the witnesses were people who had narrowly escaped bombs and bullets. One of the saddest figures was Sammy Hamilton, the housing executive worker and part-time RUC man shot by Seán at close range in a car-park. He was barely able to walk, and he gave evidence wheezing and gasping through damaged lungs. The judge was moved by him, and so was I. He was terrible proof of the waste our campaign had created.

Torpedo-like bomb casings were placed before the judge, as were plastic bags full of sharp metal cuttings, nails, nuts and bolts. The worst piece of theatre arranged by the prosecution was the appearance of a detective from the Gardaí. He said he worked in ballistics. Without warning, he produced from a battered leather satchel a Browning Automatic. He said that the gun had been recovered in the Republic and that ballistics tests had proved it was the weapon used to kill the former UDR man, Norman Hanna, shot by Mickey in front of his wife and child. Hanna's widow was in the courtroom. She broke down in tears and left the court. The judge, Mr Justice Higgins, rounded on the detective with the roar of a lion. He shouted: 'Get that gun out of my court now. Get it out now. Get out of my court before I have you thrown out.' The detective looked puzzled, but he obeyed the command and hurriedly got up to be ushered out of court by a sympathetic RUC man. The prosecution team looked embarrassed, particularly the chief prosecutor.

After two months, it was my turn to appear in the witness box. Paddy had warned me that, once I took the stand, he would not be able to give me any further advice – or even talk to me – until I returned to the dock. The court had filled with detectives, including all my interrogators, there to witness my come-uppance. I looked only at the judge, never at the prosecutor or the police. I gripped the side of the witness box with my right hand as a way of channelling the tension and fear out of my body, enabling me to remain focused and calm. I had got the idea from the story Iceman had once told me about the former British agent the IRA had captured and interrogated in the early seventies. After several weeks his interrogators had noticed that he kept his hands firmly grasping his legs. The poor man had only broken when he had been ordered to loosen his grasp.

My senior counsel stepped forward and took me through what had happened in Gough Barracks and Castlereagh. I detailed everything clearly, precisely and fluently. When my counsel had finished, I could tell the prosecution realized they had a fight on their hands. It was a Friday, and the court was about to go into recess for the weekend. The prosecutor stood up. He said that in my evidence I had claimed that the police had tape-recorded me in the interrogation cells in Gough Barracks. However, he said, there were no electrical power points in any of those cells. He sat down with a smug look on his face.

My counsel returned on Monday with an architect's drawing of Gough Barracks: it clearly showed there were power points in every cell. He then rebuked the prosecutor for making me out to be a liar at the very point when I had been strongest in my evidence.

But over the weekend there had been another important development. I had decided, on my own initiative, in the absence of McGrory, that I would try another defence. I felt that the detailed nature of my statements rendered impossible the defence that I did not know what I was saying to the police. In what I knew he would regard as an act of madness I resolved to admit to making the statements – but with one slight difference: I would say that the person who committed all the terrorist acts mentioned in the statements was my cousin Mickey (who was living safely across the border). I would say that the police had inserted my name in the statements in place of Mickey's. Within the parameters set by that one overarching lie, I would try to tell the truth.

On Monday, I launched this wildly improbable defence and watched the faces of my defence team sag in disbelief. I felt I had probably dug an enormous hole for myself. I did not expect that I might find a way out of it. To a large extent, I did not care. I was going to put up a fight, and that was all that mattered. Over the next week, the prosecuting counsel went through every single statement, asking me after he had recounted each violent incident in detail: 'And who do you say did this?'

'Mickey.'

'Mickey!' he would exclaim. He suggested at one point that if Mickey had committed all of these acts then Mickey must be a psychopath. I hesitated, but I felt boxed in by the question. I did not regard Mickey as a psychopath, but nor did I know what he really was. To have denied the prosecutor's suggestion at that point would have undermined my defence. I said it was reasonable to assume that he was a psychopath.

I explained that I had only been in contact with the IRA with a view to writing a book about them in the future. For that reason, I had accumulated a lot of specialist knowledge, helped by my family connection with a leading IRA member. I could hear whispered laughing from the police. The prosecutor spent the whole of that week trudging through every one of my statements, meticulously and patiently. I knew he was scoring points, but I stuck to my story. He described me as an evil terrorist, a communist insurgent dedicated to worldwide terror – a line fashioned specially for the judge who was known to be a very conservative Catholic.

On Friday, the state's counsel announced that on Monday he would bring into court a number of tape-recordings which would prove both that my statements were true and also that I was a dedicated, ruthless, experienced terrorist of above-average intelligence who had spoken to the police happily and without pressure. He said he would put the lies back in my mouth.

Back on A wing, Martin Meehan asked me how things were going. He would ask the same thing at the end of each day. Perhaps he was genuinely interested, but I suspected that he was only trying to pick up titbits to feed back to John Joe and the boys in Dundalk. He need not have bothered because most days in the court there was a Sinn Fein observer taking notes.

I felt low over the weekend. I was sure I was doomed. However, because the prosecution planned to introduce 'this further evidence', I was allowed a legal visit from Paddy and my barrister, who surprised me by saying that the prosecution had indicated that a deal was on offer. He said that if I pleaded guilty, then they would seek only a life sentence without a recommendation about how long I should serve. I thought about the offer, but I did not find it enticing. I felt sure that for me a life sentence would still mean staying in prison until the war was over and an amnesty was on offer for everyone. And who knew when that might be? I said: 'I'll plead guilty if they drop the murders and offer me twenty years. With remission, I'll serve ten.' My barrister smiled: 'You south Armagh people drive a hard bargain.'

Paddy thought I had held out well against the prosecution's onslaught, but I could tell he thought the tapes would sink me. Paddy and my barrister started talking about John Joe. Paddy said he had represented him in the early seventies when he had got seven and a half years for possession of ammunition. At that time John Joe had also been found in possession of a map of Belfast on which several buildings had been crossed. A number of the buildings had been blown up in the days prior to his arrest. John Joe's defence had been that he was travelling around visiting hotels and buildings of architectural or historical interest. Paddy and the barrister laughed. Paddy said: 'But what was most damaging was a manual he had in his possession which detailed every type of terrorist bomb that had ever been made in explicit, diagrammatic detail. There was even one section detailing how to make explosives out of grass.'

Paddy told me not to be overawed when I heard myself on the tapes. I must hold tight: 'What we really want now is to get those detectives into court and to cross-examine them.' Later that day, my barrister informed me that the prosecution refused to drop the murders, so the deal was off.

I felt nervous as I walked up the stairs into the courtroom on Monday. I sat down and was confronted by several huge loudspeakers which were being tinkered with by a long-haired hi-fi engineer. I looked at the rows of detectives who looked rather smug.

The prosecutor opened by going over my denials of having admitted to being present when Mickey had first tested the Browning Automatic in Dundalk prior to shooting Hanna. Then he played the tape. My voice boomed out, clear and precise, giving detail after minute detail to the police. I described graphically how Mickey had tested the Browning in Seán's presence. I included details of the conversation they had. I could not help smiling. The prosecutor noticed my indiscretion. He stood up and said: 'I do believe he is smiling, your Honour. That is how absurd he believes his own denials are.' I wiped the smile off my face swiftly, but not quite swiftly enough because the judge said: 'Yes, I do believe you're right.' I shook my head vigorously and said: 'I can assure you, your Honour, I am not smiling. I do not think it's funny.'

After the tape had finished, the prosecutor said: 'Only someone who knew guns could give a description like that, Mr Collins. What have you got to say in answer to that?' I said that in Mickey's flat I had seen a hardback illustrated book on guns, which included the Browning; also, I had learned about holding and cocking a weapon from several American police films that I had seen. He bristled: 'I suggest, Mr Collins, that that is a tissue of lies to such an extent that you thought it funny when the lies were put into your own mouth.'

'No, it is the truth.'

'The truth? The truth? Whose voice is on that tape, Mr Collins? Is it yours?'

'Yes, it is.'

'You admit it is your voice, then you must admit the statements are yours and are a true account, otherwise how could you make these tapes which you admit were made with your own mouth and which confirm the statements?'

I replied: 'I made those tapes to impress the police, to ensure my wife would not be arrested and to make sure I got a deal. I was prepared to say anything. I knew about all those operations because Mickey told me. I wasn't involved in any of them.'

The state's lawyer seemed pleased: 'So we're back to Mickey again. Well, let's hear something that introduces people other than Mickey.' He played the story I had heard from Scap about the tout he had shot after telling him he was going home. It was a chilling tale. I knew he was scoring points, but I held on. Every day of that week I had to sit there and listen to tape after tape, admission after admission. Paddy's last words kept me going: 'Hold out. What we want is the detectives in the box.' By Friday, I felt that the prosecutor had hit me with everything he had: there was nothing more to be frightened of.

My cross-examination continued into a third week. I knew my appearance was coming to an end and I looked forward to being released from this endless questioning. I discovered that the prosecutor still had a few tricks up his gown, as the following exchanges, based on notes taken at the time, will show. On my final day in the witness box, he produced my statement about Brendan's involvement in the murder of Toombs. He read it out: 'It says here that your former colleague came to your house begging you to have the operation called off. It also says you convinced him the whole thing was an elaborate test set by your senior IRA colleague, and that you assured him the operation would not take place. Would you agree that that is what is written in this statement?'

'Yes.'

'Good. We also have it on tape. Would you agree with me that if this statement is true, it could probably assist your one-time colleague and friend?'

'Yes.'

'Well, realizing that, are you prepared to admit that this is your statement and is a true account?'

'No.'

'Oh. So you're saying the police made it up; you didn't make it; your mind was so befuddled you had no idea what it contained or what you were doing and it was probably something you learned from Michael Collins?'

'Yes.'

'So you are not prepared to help your former colleague?'

'I'm in no position to do so.'

'Are you saying he never came to your house that night?'

'Yes.'

'He never begged you to have the killing of Toombs called off?'

'No.'

'And you didn't convince him it was only a test?'

'No.'

'And you deny all this, realizing that by so doing you are not helping your former colleague.'

'Yes.'

As McGrory had warned me, it was every man for himself. I still felt sick at not casting a line to Brendan, who was the least guilty of any of us, though he knew what he was doing in helping to set up Toombs.

He asked me whether I had made a deal with the IRA, receiving an amnesty in return for retracting my evidence. I said no. He said that the IRA had asked me to come into court and to make allegations against the police.

'I suggest you have lied and lied to protect yourself from the IRA.'

'No.'

'I suggest you have lied and lied, again and again, because you don't want the IRA to know what is contained in these 1,000 pages of transcripts you gave to the police.' He had his hands on the transcripts. He began patting the huge bundle. There was absolutely nothing in those transcripts that the IRA did not already know, but his suggestion – noted by the Sinn Fein observer – would help in future to make things difficult for me.

At that, he stopped. The court was silent. He looked about him, turned over a few sheaves of paper. The judge asked him if he was finished. He said: 'Yes, your Honour.' I felt a wave of relief. The worst was now over. It was February 10. I had been in the witness box for 14 days since January 22. I went back to the dock and sat down.

It was now the turn of my police interrogators to face a legal grilling. As each of them took the stand I noticed that they all gripped the side of the witness box with their right hands, just as I had done.

The police denied to a man that there had been a hostile

atmosphere in Gough Barracks at the time of my arrest. Despite the mortar attack and the deaths of nine police officers, the atmosphere, they said, was normal – not bad, not mad, not sad, just normal. All of them denied that any bad language, threats or assaults had been used during my interrogation. My counsel asked one of them if there had ever been other complaints of assault made against him. He said that he believed there had been, but he had no idea how many. 'Come, come,' said my counsel, 'you must have some idea. One, two, three, four?' The RUC man maintained that he did not know the figure. My counsel refreshed his memory by informing him that more than a dozen complaints of serious physical assault had been made against him by prisoners in the past. He strenuously denied the truth of all those allegations.

One of the doctors denied that when he had helped me remove the pieces of toilet paper from my ears he had asked me whether I had been hearing unpleasant noises. One of the uniformed policemen denied having had a particular conversation with detectives within my hearing. Unfortunately for him, the detectives had already admitted that they had had such a conversation.

The police argued in court that I was promised nothing: no inducements, no immunity, no deals. They claimed that on the fifth day of my interrogation I had suddenly started talking, and that I had continued talking happily for a period of several hours to my main interrogators about every operation in which I had been involved. According to their account, the senior RUC man who took charge of me had entered the room only after I had unburdened myself completely to his colleagues.

The cross-examination of the police witnesses went on for days. I felt that there were enough discrepancies in their evidence to raise a few doubts in the judge's mind, but still I did not have the slightest hope that such doubts would be enough to outweigh the evidence against me.

I could tell during the trial that Mr Justice Higgins despised me. He would look at me at times as if I were the scum of the earth. I was not surprised, yet as the cross-examination of the police drew to a close I no longer really cared what he thought or what decision he would reach. In the trial I had achieved what I had set out to achieve. I had been a broken man for two years. My first step in prison had been to try to re-establish my identity as an individual; the fight in court was the second step, however strange it may now seem.

It was a Friday. The case was practically over and the prosecutor was summing up, drawing together all the pieces of the jigsaw. I had already heard everything he had to say, and I had fallen into bored inattention. Suddenly Mr Justice Higgins interrupted, jogging me out of my stupor. I sat bolt upright, as if his words carried an electric shock into my body. 'Surely you are not asking me to accept that the police are all white and Collins is all black? Surely you are not asking me to accept that there are no shades of grey on the side of the police evidence to this court?'

'Your Honour—' began the small, plump, bewigged figure of the prosecuting Queen's Counsel. But he was interrupted again by Higgins: 'Even if I do find that Collins is an accomplished liar, that he lied and lied, again and again – which I assuredly will find – do not ask me to accept that it is a simple case of black and white. For it most certainly is not.'

His Honour could not have had a greater impact if he had taken a grenade from under his wig and hurled it at the prosecution team. The court went completely silent. The prosecution team looked tense and gloomy, and seemed to sense the danger, although I knew it was still far from certain that they had lost. I stifled all urges to move or to smile. I kept as still as a statue, a fixed look of impassivity, so that the judge would not detect me taking any satisfaction from the discomfiture of the police and the whole prosecution team. I feared that there was still a strong possibility that the judge would slam shut the mantrap which I felt his words had started to open.

The court was quiet as Higgins prepared to leave. He said he would give his judgement in eight days' time. The screws took me down to my cell. They were quieter than usual: they knew, as I knew, that I suddenly had a chance of freedom.

I felt elated, yet I knew it was too soon. I could still end up in the Maze for the next twenty years. But even that thought no longer frightened me in the way it once had. At least I would go to prison knowing I had escaped into my own head; I knew

I would be able to develop according to my own desires. I would stay with the republican prisoners, but on my own terms, despite the last two years of petty battles with the IRA hierarchy within the prison. I felt enabled to cope with whatever life threw at me, and to that extent I was at peace.

In the last days of the Voir Dire hearing I had returned to A wing at night and sorted out the books and photographs and bits and pieces that I wanted to take with me to the Maze when I received my life sentence. Everything else I had arranged in a pile to be sent back to Bernie.

After a short while, the bolt was again drawn back and the screws came in to escort me back to the main prison through a tunnel that crossed under the Crumlin Road. I had often thought as I walked through this tunnel of the cars, buses and lorries trundling over my head; people going about their ordinary business. However, before we could set off down the tunnel, I heard a voice saying: 'Hold on. Legal visit.' I was escorted back into the legal visits room beneath the court. Paddy McGrory was waiting for me. I was a little surprised. I did not know why he wanted to see me now. 'Hello, Eamon. Sit down there.' He began to talk hesitantly, which was unlike him, I dreaded his awkwardness.

He said: 'I just wanted to speak to you about the possibility of you being acquitted – which is a million-to-one chance, but a chance none the less. Where are you going to live, if such an event takes place?'

I was stumped. After a pause I said: 'Newry, I suppose, or maybe Camlough.'

'Newry,' echoed Paddy, almost sighing. He hesitated again before speaking. In a roundabout, hesitant way he said that he had been speaking to Gerry Adams quite recently and that this present case and its progress happened to come up in the general conversation. He had mentioned the possibility – however slight – of my release. He 'got the impression from him' that 'interested parties' with an axe to grind wouldn't want me back in Newry. Gerry had said, 'South Armagh is a notorious area where they would kill their own granny if they had to.'

His words dazed me. I said: 'But I retracted. Those people, the IRA, made an agreement when I retracted. They told me,

"Retract and you'll be allowed to live as you please. You'll never be harmed." They understand what has happened.'

Paddy shook his head: 'I don't feel that that would be the end result at all. Never in my experience as a lawyer dealing with republicans have I come across such bitterness and jealousy as is directed at you.' He said that there were a number of possible reasons. First, the amount of high-grade information about the IRA which I had passed on. They felt I had done a lot of damage over a wide area, but especially in Belfast, by outlining the divisions, frictions and power struggles within the movement. McGrory continued: 'Also there's the fact that you had a decent job in the Customs and Excise, that you went your own way in prison, finishing your Open University degree, and that you still have a chance of being acquitted after having signed statements naming a lot of people.'

I said: 'Maybe I could live in Belfast.' Paddy said no. I asked him about England. He said I would not be allowed in. I suggested Canada. Paddy said they would not let me in there either. 'I think you should go to somewhere like Waterford in the Republic and lead a very quiet life.'

I went back through the tunnel in a world of my own. I reached the search boxes. I did not even see the screws. I handed over my shoes, socks, trousers, vest and shirt. I dropped my underpants and shook my penis to show that I was not hiding anything. I went to my cell, then went straight out to the canteen for my tea: dried-out peas, crisped-out fish, spongy potatoes, followed by cardboard cake with watery custard.

Perhaps I had been too honest in prison about the changes in my thinking. Perhaps I should have followed Steenson's advice and kept my mouth shut about the doubts I had concerning the armed struggle. I had said, perhaps once too often, that the continuation of the conflict was only hurting our own people and that the public had neither the will nor the stomach for the fight anymore – if indeed they ever had. Without explicitly rejecting the republican movement, I had made plain my independence from it. That was what annoyed them: they could have forgiven my fall from grace if I had returned to them on my knees, repentant and offering to start anew as a born-again republican.

Meehan and the IRA staff had obviously been getting information because they said occasionally that they had heard that
I had a good chance of release. That evening I did not have to
seek out Meehan. He came to me to ask his usual question:
'Well, how was it today?' I moved over to the record-player.
Confidential conversations usually took place close to the
record-player so that the music would render ineffective the
listening devices which we assumed were dotted around the
place. I told him what Paddy had said.

I said: 'Look, I've kept my side of the bargain and now I'm
faced with Christ knows what if I get out. Perhaps they're
going to shoot me.' Meehan said I had nothing to worry about.
I did not know whether to believe him. I was not convinced he
knew – or would have any influence over – what was being
planned for me.

It was a long eight days. I felt unsettled and anxious, but I
was strong enough mentally to decide one thing: if I got out I
would be returning to Newry. I would not be running anywhere, and certainly not to Waterford. I went to mass on
Sunday and took the prayer sheet back to my cell with me. I
had not prayed in two years – apart from saying the rosary
with Brendan – but as I waited for Wednesday I read all the
prayers every morning. I prayed to get out of this prison and
away from these people with whom I no longer had anything in
common. My actions were rather bizarre because I could not
believe in God.

On Wednesday, I got up earlier than normal and paced
around my cell, waiting to be taken through the tunnel. I did
not say goodbye to anyone: I did not want to be that presump-
tuous. The screws came to handcuff me. Normally I kept them
waiting for a few minutes while I readied myself, but that day
I was eager to go. I walked along briskly, so briskly in fact that
one of the screws shouted: 'Slow down. You weren't in such a
hurry any other morning.' I arrived at my holding cell and the
handcuffs were taken off. I debated whether to bring my coat
with me up to the court, but decided not to. In two hours I
would know my fate. I do remember taking a vow never to
engage in violence again if I was released.

I walked up the stairs and into the court. It was emptier

than usual. Only my wife sat in the public gallery. There was
no sign of the Sinn Fein observer. Even the chief prosecutor
had decided to stay away, and had left his stand-in. I noticed
my former RUC master looking dejected. Paddy sat motion-
less. The judge entered, wearing his long black coat.

'All rise.' I rose and sat down again. I felt almost faint as he
began to speak. He was speaking clearly but I could not quite
make out what he was saying. I heard him say that he thought
I had lied repeatedly in the witness box. But as he moved
methodically towards the conclusion I heard words which conveyed that he was not going to accept the admissibility of my
statements.

His actual words, taken from the transcript of his ruling,
were: 'On the evidence before me I am not satisfied that
Collins was not assaulted and I find that the Crown has failed
to exclude the reasonable possibility that Collins was assaulted
in such a way as to constitute inhuman or degrading treatment. I cannot say that I am satisfied beyond reasonable doubt
that the admissions made by Collins to the police were not
induced by inhuman or degrading treatment. In reaching this
conclusion I have given full weight to my grave reservations
about the truthfulness of Collins's evidence.

'Accordingly I have excluded all the admissions, verbal and
written under section 8(2) of the Northern Ireland
(Emergency Provisions) Act 1978.

'The decision under section 8(2) must be based solely on
how the admissions are proved to have been obtained and not
on whether they or any of them are true. I repeat what Lord
Lowry, the Lord Chief Justice, observed in "Regina versus
Hetherington" at page 16: ". . . in certain respects our criminal
law demands that not only the evidence but the means of
obtaining it shall be above suspicion."'

The words took an age to sink in. My barrister asked the
judge whether I was free to go. Mr Justice Higgins asked the
prosecution whether they had any other matters to raise with
me. They said no. The judge said I was free to go.

I could not believe what I was hearing. I went downstairs for
my coat which I put on in the cell. A screw closed the door
behind me. I said: 'What's up? I've been released.' He told me

to wait until the judge had finished talking. I waited for ten seconds then I thought: 'What am I doing waiting here? These people have been telling me what to do for two years.' I shouted: 'Open that fucking door. I'm a free man.' He opened the door and I ran upstairs and out of the court.

In the court hall I found Paddy McGrory and his son Barra. My wife came down the stairs. I hugged her. I could see RUC people rushing about. Some of them looked at me. They were urgently trying to discover whether there was anything they could hold me on. Paddy said: 'If you're arrested and held for seven days, remain silent for all seven days as you did during your first five in 1985.' I said goodbye and walked out to the car-park with Bernie. On the way out, I met Brendan's father. We shook hands. I told him what he wanted to hear, which was that Brendan would soon be out with me. But I knew he would be staying behind.

As we drove towards Newry, I felt euphoric. I remembered a story told to me in prison by an INLA man about one of his comrades called Bobby. The police had stopped Bobby with his family on his way to Belfast International Airport. He had been named as an accomplice by Harry Kirkpatrick. Bobby said to the police: 'I'm going to the Costa del Sol in an hour.' The peeler had looked at him and said: 'No, Bobby. You're going to the Costa del Crum.'

I laughed as I waved goodbye to Costa del Crum.

25

THEIR JUSTICE AND OURS

At first after the trial, I felt numb. Then a different feeling hit me. Prior to joining the IRA I had somehow believed in the system, only to have that belief destroyed both by the brutality of the British Army and my own corrosive revolutionary hatred. I had lost so much of what was moral and good in my fight against oppression that I had been left without faith in any defensible aspect of civilization. Even though my disillusionment with the armed struggle had contributed to my decision to confess everything to the police, I had still spent the last two years in prison wondering whether I was right to reject political violence. During my two years on remand awaiting trial I had told my fellow IRA prisoners of my doubts about the validity of the campaign. I knew the armed struggle was wrong, yet so was the daily oppression of nationalist people. I had felt confused and lost. I had tried to find a justification for abandoning political violence, yet the state seemed to exist to inflict political violence on nationalists.

But the judge's words had sent a real shock through my body. I felt peculiarly emotional about them. The law, that part of the system at least, had revealed its genuine dignity: there could be such a thing as the impartial application of the rule of law. This judge had brought to life for me, even though he loathed the IRA, principles which were important boundaries between civilization and barbarism. The implied judgement on what I had been doing for the past six years was one that I absorbed, and the contrast with our revolutionary justice was extreme. All the judge was upholding was the principle of law that demanded that the means of obtaining evidence should be above suspicion. What he was saying was that in his eyes, the prosecution had failed to exclude the reasonable possibility that I had been treated in such a way as to constitute inhuman or degrading treatment. So even though he suspected I was as guilty as hell, he was willing to let me walk free on grounds that many people would have regarded as a technicality, a foolish abstraction.

Mr Justice Higgins had only needed a reasonable doubt about the behaviour of the police. I remembered what I had learned as a law student at Queen's University. 'Reasonable' had to be measured according to what the ordinary man would consider 'reasonable', and the measure of the 'reasonable man' was to be found on the 'Clapham omnibus'. What a quaint, yet powerful idea of reasonableness. In reality, of course, what an impartial judge would regard as the reasonable feelings of the man on the Clapham omnibus tended to bear little relation to what a genuine ordinary man would regard as reasonable. The man on the Clapham omnibus would probably have liked to have seen me hung, drawn and quartered, with my entrails fed to rabid dogs, and my head stuck on a pike for public edification. Yet now this civilized idea, this majestic abstraction, had set me free.

When the reality had sunk in, I knew I really could abandon violence because the system, for all its manifest injustices, carried within itself the possibility of justice. When British justice worked, when it operated impartially according to its highest principles, it could still represent the highest achievement of a civilized society. I felt that the mental struggles I had undergone over the last few years had been vindicated in the most bizarre way. Mr Justice Higgins had upheld the rule of law; and thereby made it transcend the subordinate role which the police and army had assigned it. The law had a potential as a weapon for true justice, not merely as an instrument which the Protestant ruling class could use to crush the rights of the Catholic community. I could feel nothing but admiration for this judge who, on such a fragile legal abstraction, had set free a man from an organization which even during the trial had tried to murder him by firing a rocket at his home.

My happiness and the clarity that came from the extraordinary outcome of my trial did not last long.

I hardly expected a warm welcome from my former comrades. I had talked, and I had not shown them respect, but all I had wanted was for them to honour the agreement they had made with me two years ago. I did not care if they despised me for what I had done: I just wanted to be left alone to get on with my life. But Paddy had alerted me to the likelihood that some people were looking for revenge.

Bernie drove straight to my mother's house. She entered the house first and went into the bedroom where my mother lay. I waited outside the door. My mother said: 'Is it bad news, Bernie?' Then I walked inside. My mother started to cry. I went over to her bed and hugged her. We talked briefly, but I did not stay long. I wanted to meet my son Tiarnach coming from nursery school.

I waited for him as he walked up the path. I ran to him and picked him up. I felt on the verge of tears as I held him: it was the happiest moment of my life.

As I walked my son back home, I met a Sinn Fein woman I knew. I said hello, but she ignored me. She had never been in the IRA, and my actions had in no way harmed her, but she was my first encounter with the unforgiving face of the republican movement. In later years, when I had got used to this treatment, one fact would amuse me: the republicans who tended to ostracize me publicly were often those who had played no part at all in the armed struggle.

I found it difficult to acclimatize to the outside world. At first I felt a stranger in my own home, and I detected a certain coldness in Bernie. She was genuinely pleased to have me back, but at times I felt we were strangers. During my time in prison, I had discussed with her why I had broken, but I felt that she could never quite understand what had happened. Once she had said to me sadly: 'I thought you were invincible.'

I withdrew into myself. News came through that Brendan had received a life sentence for his minor role in the killing of

Toombs; the man I call Joe had already received twelve years; the TV repairman received a suspended sentence for passing on information; a year earlier, and not on my evidence, O'Keeffe received five years for his supposed role in the mortar attack, but Maguire, who made similar confessions, was acquitted. A few other small fry on the peripheries of the IRA whom I had named also received sentences. Everyone else, all the major players, had either remained silent during their seven days or gone on the run. In prison, the INLA man Gerard Steenson had said to me: 'Don't feel guilty about those people who signed statements. Get on with your life.' I tried to follow his advice, but I continued to feel bad about those who had been sent down, especially Brendan, even though I told myself that ultimately it was their own signed statements which had put them away.

After the sentences were handed out, I began to receive threatening phone calls from cranks and drunks. I recognized the voice of one caller: he was a former republican who had himself received a punishment beating from the IRA after he had made derogatory comments about the Provos at a disco in Dundalk. A victim looking for a scapegoat.

Bernie encouraged me to go out. In those first few days of freedom I met a veteran republican called Stephen. He shook my hand and wished me well, saying that what had happened to me could have happened to anyone. I began to feel that perhaps things would be all right after all.

Then I met the RUC, or rather they made a point of meeting me. They stopped my car constantly and searched me. They would pull the car apart and give me a lot of verbal abuse. On one occasion, I had a heated exchange with an RUC man: he came towards me threateningly, poised to bring his rifle butt down on my head, but he stopped himself. Each time I was stopped – and they seemed to be showing me more attention now that I was out of the IRA than they did when I was in it – at least one RUC man would say smugly that he knew I would be going to Dundalk soon to be dealt with by the IRA and that I would not be coming back. This thought seemed to please them, as if they were relying on their greatest enemies to administer justice.

In those first few days, a British Army foot patrol also
stopped near my house. A well-spoken officer knocked on my
door and asked me how I was. He said: 'I hear you might be
going somewhere soon.' He reminded me that I was still a
British citizen who had the right to the protection afforded to
all by Her Majesty's armed forces and that I should not hesi-
tate to contact them in the event of the arrival of any unwanted
visitors. I had to smile. Of course he was mocking me, but at
the same time his point was not lost on me: if the IRA did
come for me, then my only hope would be for the Crown forces
to intercept them.

As a treat, my wife took me away to Dublin for the weekend,
but I did not enjoy myself. The city was playing host to a
rugby weekend, and it took us ages of trudging around in order
to find a hotel. I felt disconcerted by the busyness of the place
and the crowds of people milling around. Over the weekend I
discussed my future with Bernie. I said that now I had a degree
I would like to apply to teacher-training college: I wanted to
become a history teacher. In the meantime I needed to earn
some money.

When we came home on Sunday night, there was a message.
The IRA had phoned my mother-in-law's looking for me. The
caller was Mooch. I felt ill. My sense of dread had been justified. I knew that the call was the start of something.

At her next Sinn Fein meeting, Bernie spoke to an IRA
intermediary. He told her that I was to go to Dundalk at the
weekend. He wanted me to check in to the Imperial Hotel: I
had to be prepared to stay a few nights. They wanted to talk to
me about a few things. I could not see why they needed me to
check in to a hotel: Dundalk is only thirteen miles from Newry.
The only explanation was that they were launching 'a full-
scale investigation'. Bernie said that she had received an
assurance that I would come to no harm. I asked her if she
believed them. She said she did, but she was still involved in
Sinn Fein and had a confidence in the honour of the republican movement which I no longer shared. The very words
'republican movement' turned my stomach. But, more perti-
nently, I knew enough about the workings of the Nutting
Squad to know that I could be walking into a trap.

My wife and I checked in to the Imperial Hotel. We had
been told to be in the lounge for seven o'clock. We sat down
and were about to order a drink when I noticed at the end of
the very long bar the unmistakeable shapes of Mooch and
Teddy sitting hunched over half-finished pints of beer. Mooch
walked over to us. He dispensed with pleasantries and began
giving orders. I was to go to 'Number 40' where my 'debriefing' would take place. He turned to Bernie and said that orders
had come from Belfast that she was not to discuss any Sinn
Fein business in front of me. I told him not to worry, that
Bernie didn't discuss Sinn Fein with me because it was an
irrelevance to me. He walked away.

I went on my own to Number 40 at the agreed time. I had
been there many times before. A man told me to sit in the
living-room. After a short while, Mooch arrived and told me to
go with him. We walked out of the house in silence. The street
was deserted. We walked together along the wet pavement and
crossed the road to a recently-renovated one-up-one-down
house. These houses had once been homes to the unskilled
workers of the factories and the docks. Now they were popular
with down-at-heel Provos on the run. I asked Mooch if I was
going to be shot. Mooch said: 'You wouldn't have come up
here if you believed you were going to be shot.' That was not
quite true: if I was sure I was going to be shot, then of course
I would not have come. But I was not sure of anything.

I walked into a dingy living-room. On a sideboard was one
of those cheap radio/tape-recorders. There was a small two-
seater settee and two wooden armchairs. I sat down on one of
them. The house reeked of cheapness and frugality. I suspected that a single man lived here; there were certainly no
female touches. I waited for a few minutes, then I heard the
sound of people entering through the front door. My cousin
Mickey came in to the living-room, followed by Mooch and
Teddy. No one said anything to me, but Mickey's eyes glared
hostility. The three of them squeezed together on the two-
seater settee. Mercifully, Hardbap would not be coming
because he was serving a short sentence for being found in
possession of a stolen van. But I knew the team for the evening
was not yet complete. There was a knock on the front door.

Mooch got up to answer it. He came back with John Joe Magee, chief executioner and witchfinder general. His face was a little flabbier, but apart from that he looked much the same as when I had last seen him.

John Joe sat down and said hello to me. He asked me how I was. He told me I had nothing to fear, regardless of what I might have heard. 'You know you have an amnesty.' He asked me if I minded whether he taped the proceedings. I said I did not. He knew that this request would trigger other fears: normally people were only tape-recorded when they had confessed to being informers and were about to be shot. However, he did not turn on the tape-recorder.

He said they were honourable men and would keep to their agreement. All he wanted to do was to tie up some loose ends and to go through what I had told the police. I said that I had covered that ground fully when I was debriefed in prison; also, the whole story had just come out in court. What more was there to say? John Joe said that as far as he was concerned there were still questions to be answered. He proceeded to go through the whole story from the very beginning. The time passed slowly. Friendly moments were interspersed with insulting and snide comments.

At one point he asked me: 'Did you call Mickey a psychopath during your trial?' I looked over at Mickey. He was glaring at me, his eyes cold and expressionless. I felt both embarrassed and afraid but I explained the context in which I had said he was a psychopath. I said that after days of cross-examination the prosecutor had boxed me in to a corner: he had said that if Mickey was responsible for everything I said he was responsible for, then would I not agree that he had to be a psychopath. After hesitation I had agreed that it was reasonable to assume that he was, but I had only done so in order to preserve my hard-fought defence. I hoped I had at least half-convinced Mickey.

John Joe moved on to another subject. He said that Scap had been supposed to be there that night too, 'but he didn't feel he could contain himself'. I said brightly he should have come as I would have been happy to see him again.

John Joe then asked me whether I had good security at

home. I said I did not have any. He had a conversation with
Mooch about British soldiers who had been seen hiding in
fields close to my house. John Joe said he was worried they
might assassinate me using captured IRA guns so that they
could blame the killing on the Provos. I knew he was trying to
scare me: by ostensibly warning me about lurking Brits he was
really saying that IRA bullets might still end up in me, regardless of the amnesty. Whatever else that could be said about the
Brits, I knew that by this stage in the conflict they had assumed
a certain professional detachment: once a target had been
neutralized – once someone was no longer a player – he would
be left alone, no matter what he might have done in the past.
Of course, the locally-recruited forces were different. The
UDR-man-by-day-UVF-man-by-night types might have
conceivably mounted an operation against me, but the Brits
were too professional to seek petty vengeance; it was a pity
that my former comrades did not adopt the same standards.
John Joe succeeded only in underlining for me that my most
deadly enemies at the moment belonged to the IRA.

He said: 'You became very bitter towards the republican
movement when you were in prison.' I did not deny it. He
seemed to know a lot about things I had said and done in
prison – he even referred to a song I had sung in the canteen
once. I knew I had been under surveillance in prison; I had not
realized the extent of it.

Then I was told that I would have to write down everything I told the police. I could not believe it: how many more
times did they have to hear this story?

Magee assured me again that they would honour the
amnesty. However, he said there were three conditions attached
to it.

'First, you must give an honest account of all you told the
police. Second, you must come and meet the IRA at any time
or place they choose. Third, you must move your home if so
requested, to anywhere the IRA orders you to go.'

I wondered whether I would have retracted if I had known
such conditions were attached. What worried me was the real
meaning behind them: I felt they were a means to provide the
IRA ultimately with an excuse to shoot me or, at the very least,

to send me into exile. John Joe ended the debriefing abruptly.
He said it would resume in the morning. I walked back alone to
the hotel.

I spent a sleepless night with Bernie. In the morning Teddy
came and drove me to the debriefing house. I sat there for
almost an hour before Magee arrived. I had told him the night
before that I had written some notes for my defence team which
I thought might span a lot of the ground he wanted me to cover.
He took me up on that. He told me to get hold of them from my
solicitor and leave them in Dundalk. 'There's no hurry,' he
said. 'Anytime within the next four weeks or so will be fine.'
He said I could also use the next month to write up the other
material he had asked for. At that, he said I could go on my way.
I was agitated, uneasy and fearful: this was far from over.

Within a month I had asked Bernie to deliver a set of my
typed-up defence notes. I also discovered to my horror that
during my trial the IRA had asked Bernie to see if she could
get the '1,000 pages of transcripts' of my police interrogations,
which had been referred to by the prosecution. Without telling
me what she was doing, she had approached Paddy McGrory.
Paddy had told her that he did not have the transcripts, but
that even if he had he would not have given them to her. I was
angry that she did not seem to believe that she had done anything dangerous.

Shortly afterwards, I got a call asking me to go to Number
40, the security unit's house. When I arrived I found Mooch
and Teddy waiting for me. Mooch held out my notes and said:
'These are of no fucking use to us. These are your official
defence notes. What we want are written notes by you of what
you touted to the peelers.'

He said he wanted the notes delivered within forty-eight
hours, otherwise he would have me dragged out of my home
and taken to Dundalk, where they would batter out of me whatever they wanted. He said: 'Is that clear?' I said yes. He said:
'You're not an IRA volunteer. You're a tout, and I want you to
get on your bike, get back home, and write down everything and
everybody you touted about on paper and get it up here. Now
off you go.' Mooch had always known that I regarded him as a
low-life and now was his chance for vengeance.

·   I returned home feeling more angry than scared. I sat down and wrote late into the night. I started by mentioning every name I had given the police and then I proceeded to write about all the operations I had worked on. The notes took me several days, and even then they did not touch on everything I had told the police concerning other subjects. I decided that I would take the first batch to Dundalk. I photocopied them: I would give the IRA the photocopy. I wanted to create a little insecurity in their minds. Had I left the original with a solicitor, priest or journalist?

I set off for Dundalk with my wife and two children in the car. I did not enjoy the drive, although it was a clear spring morning and the scenery was so beautiful. On each side of the road, thousands of green pine trees blanketed the land for several miles. On other days like this I could remember feeling overcome with the power of life. But today I could think only of death – other people's deaths and my own.

Close to this border road, the IRA had shot dead the informer Maurice Gilvarry. He had given the information which had led to three IRA men being killed in an ambush by the SAS in north Belfast. I had talked to the man who claimed to have shot him. Gilvarry's head had been wrapped in a black bin-liner to contain the blood shed by the executioner's bullet.

My wife trusted my former comrades, she believed them when they told her that there was nothing sinister afoot. They had assured her that they wanted only to debrief me further about what I had told the police. But I knew more than my wife about the sort of people she was putting her trust in.

We crossed the border into the Republic of Ireland. We left a heavy-hedged side road and joined the main road which took us into Dundalk. After a few minutes of driving we had arrived at the street with the safe house. It was very quiet. I parked near Number 40. My wife stayed in the car with the two children. She said she would drive me home later.

I got out and walked across the street to the other mean house where my first debriefing session had taken place. I knocked on the door and was let into the narrow hallway. I handed over the notes to Mooch and was told to go upstairs. I walked up, followed by a young IRA volunteer whom I had worked with in the past. I entered the front bedroom which contained a double bed and a few pieces of cheap furniture. The IRA man directed me to a door at the other side of the room. The room beyond was only half the size of the first. It felt very cold. There was an old mattress lying in the middle of the floor, and bits and pieces of junk about the place. There were no chairs, so I sat on the floor near the window. The man who had showed me upstairs stayed in the other room. He left the door of my room open, then sat on the bed and started to read a magazine. He had matured a little since I had last seen him, but he still had a boyish look and a seemingly fixed smile. Although only a kid when I first met him – he was only in his early twenties now – I had used him to drive getaway cars after murders and bombings. He had always performed well.

This room was different from the rest of the house: everywhere else seemed clean and tidy, if poor. This room was in a mess: a junk room, I thought. I turned to thinking about an article I had read recently in the *Irish News* about the murder by the IRA of a Belfast taxi-driver. He had been asked to come to Dundalk on suspicion of working for the police. He had been allowed to go back to Belfast after initial questioning but later the IRA asked him to return to Dundalk for further enquiries. What the taxi-driver had not realized was that the IRA had already decided to kill him, although at that time they had probably not got all the information they needed. Perhaps they wanted to watch him meet his police handlers one last time. These tactics bore all the hallmarks of John Joe: allow your suspect to feel he can trust the interrogators; make him think you are honourable; then prove your honourable intentions by letting him return home. In this way you soften him up, put him off his guard, lull him into a false sense of security. The taxi-driver was playing a role in his own murder. It did not matter that the poor bastard was an alcoholic, vulnerable and weak, with six children.

They had taken him to what Father Faul, the Dungannon priest, had called a 'death house', specially equipped as a torture centre, where they had half-drowned him, given him electric shocks, and then shot him. At one time I would not have believed that article. Now, in a way, it made sense to have a house set aside for interrogation and torture. In my time I had only come across safe houses lived in by ordinary families, who would allow their bedrooms to be darkened and used for most of the day by the IRA. Downstairs, the children would sit watching television, or doing their homework, or getting their tea. Upstairs, the IRA would be having a chat with some unfortunate individual. But this house felt different.

I realized suddenly that the junk had a purpose. Near the old double mattress in front of me, there were a few old blankets and a number of ties lying beside them. I reached over and picked up two of the ties. They were torn in places, stretched, and had obviously been knotted. I felt my whole body go limp: it was as if any strength I had was draining out of me. I felt utterly helpless. My mind began to race ahead into all sorts of horrors, but I tried to remain calm. 'I must not panic. I must not panic,' I told myself over and over again. I turned to the window, and my terror increased as I examined it. It was fitted with very thick glass set in a double-glazed aluminium frame. There was no catch, no division on the window where it could be opened; it was all one piece. I looked at my young companion. What he was doing on the bed was guarding me, that was what he was doing. Although I had not been 'arrested', like an informer, I was scared, frightened of the power these people had. I realized that I was probably in the death house.

I glanced quickly at my guard. When he was 17 I had welcomed him into my home, made a bed up for him in our back room, watched him as he taught my wife how to play chess, fried bacon and sausages for him, made sure he was taken out of Newry safely after operations. Now he was guarding me.

A radio was playing downstairs. I could hear a woman walking towards the house: I assumed it was a woman because I could hear the clip-clopping of sandals or clogs. I did not dare to look out the window as I was directly in my guard's line of vision. The woman walked with a slow, laboured gait, indicating she was of heavy build. There was a knock on the door, and I heard the voice of a woman say, 'Well, all right,' which was a typical greeting in Northern Ireland, but more common in Belfast. I had learned in prison that a woman was now OC of the South Down Command. Was this woman who had just arrived the new OC? I could hear her talking downstairs, but the radio ensured that I could not distinguish what was being said.

Outside in the street, I saw Teddy speaking to my wife. She had discovered that our car had a flat tyre, and maybe he was offering to change it. I saw him unlock the wheel and go to the boot for the spare. What in fact he was doing, as I later discovered, was telling her as he worked that they might have to keep 'this man' overnight, and would she mind? She said it would be all right. No problem, as though she had a choice.

I felt completely alone. I could feel the chill of this room even more. There was a very strong smell of stale sweat. Someone had spent a considerable time in this room, had sweated a great deal, had been frightened, so much that he had sweated absolute terror. I thought that this must be the sweat of the taxi-driver. I am not a superstitious man, and I am sceptical of most things, but in that room, on that evening, I sensed that man's death in the smell of sweat lingering in my nostrils.

Nothing I could say or write could enlighten the IRA any further. They already knew what I had told the police, and they had known that in full two years ago. This situation was not about the need for them to know, it was about authority, control, the giving and taking of orders. I had to be categorized, boxed, compartmentalized, stereotyped as a tout, informer, supergrass, an enemy of the republican movement. I had to be debased as a human being, to have my character expunged. If they could not do this to me then their whole position in the community, the illusion that they had a policy that was justifiable, and a strategy that was achievable, was put into question. I was living proof that their analysis was seriously flawed: British justice had given me justice.

The street was so very quiet, save for the sound of the tyre being changed. I could see a wide blue sky, washed clothes blowing on a line, the sunlight. I could hear someone else arriving downstairs. There was the sound of a rubber-soled working man's boot as he entered the hall, stopped at the inner door, and was met by other voices. A chair was screaked along the floor to provide a seat for the new arrival.

I heard every sound as the wheel was changed on the car. I

heard the nuts being loosened, squeaking for lack of oil. I heard Teddy puff and pant, straining on the wheel brace as the nuts gave way. I could hear a grating noise as the spare tyre was lifted out of the boot. There was the whirr of the jack raising the car and lowering it, making the car body groan. Then a final clanking sound as the wheel-brace and the jack were thrown into the boot. I could hear a few laughs, keys in the ignition, the old car jumping to life and driving off.

I wished I was with Bernie and the children in that car instead of sitting here. Downstairs, I heard the voice of the latest man to arrive. He had a deep south Armagh accent. I could not hear what he was saying because of interference from the radio, but he spoke without interruption. He was laying down the law, telling them all how it was going to be. He spoke with authority. He was in control, and the others would obviously do as they were told.

Seconds seemed like minutes. I looked at the sealed window again. No wonder the room smelled so badly of sweat: it had never been properly lived in, it had never been part of normal living. This room was a tomb. Suddenly I could hear movement downstairs. Two people left the house. Hurried footsteps – doors banged, cars drove off. I did not look out or move.

Then I could hear the radio being turned off. Briefly there was silence. A voice shouted up: 'Come downstairs.' My guard rose, languid and cool, and motioned me to move. I got up to go.

I met Mooch at the bottom of the stairs. He said that they would read the notes and get back in touch with me. In the meantime, he wanted me to write up the rest of them. He said I could go.

I realized that they were not going to kill me: this whole charade was a piece of theatre, a little bit of vengeance to make up for their loss of face, an exercise in humiliation for someone they could not get the go-ahead to kill. I realized also that although they were probably going to let me live, they were not going to let me live in Newry.

On the way home with my wife, I decided that in the next batch of notes I would tell my former comrades a few home truths. I started writing them as soon as I got back to Newry. I began to explain fully why I had become disillusioned. I listed the killings that should never have happened, the executions that should not have been carried out, the mistakes that had been made. I detailed what I had told the police about the power struggles within the IRA, the role of Belfast in these struggles, and the shifting balance of power within the movement. I also mentioned the examples of corruption I had encountered. I knew these notes would enrage them, but I did not care. I suspected they were going to send me into exile anyway, so I wanted to give them a little kick as I went on my way. I delivered the notes and waited for their response.

Within days, I was summoned back to Dundalk. This time I took the train. Teddy met me at the station and drove me to Mickey's house. I was taken upstairs to a bedroom where I sat on the bed. I heard Teddy downstairs saying: 'Will I bring that man up a cup of tea?' This suggestion did not meet with the approval of my cousin: 'Fuck the cunt,' he said. He had become an IRA zombie: any sparks of goodness and decency had long ago been extinguished, and the vacuum had been filled with an unthinking brutal commitment. The needs of the IRA were the touchstone of his morality. We were linked by blood but that no longer mattered to Mickey, except in the sense that he felt our kinship tainted him. When I had looked into his cold eyes on that first night in Dundalk I had seen only hate: I knew he would have been delighted to receive the order to execute me.

I sat in that room for three hours. Then I heard people arriving. Feet trod on the stairs and the door was opened. Teddy entered, followed by Mooch and Mickey, who was holding a baby. John Joe strolled in behind them. He was in a rage. He laid into me verbally right away: 'What you've written is a load of fucking shit.' He reiterated the conditions of my amnesty and then said that he wanted me to write out everything again. He raised his voice: 'You're giving us fuck all; we're giving you your life.' He ranted on for another short while: 'When we snap our fingers, you're to be here. I don't care what time it is or where you have to go, you're to be here. Do you understand? Unless you're having a fucking heart attack.' I nodded. I did not say anything. He turned around and left the room. I said to Mickey: 'Is that your wee lad?' He did not say anything.

I left the house, but as I walked down the path Mickey called me back. He said that my handwriting in the second batch of papers had been atrocious: 'You better start improving it when you write the other stuff.' Teddy did not offer me a lift back to the station. I walked the two miles. IRA men drove past me at various stages of my walk, presumably to frighten me. I kept walking. I wondered how much more of this humiliation I would have to take. I felt worse than I had even in the darkest days in prison. I had no one to talk to: even my wife seemed to feel that it was nothing less than I deserved, and she was continuing to devote a lot of her time to Sinn Fein.

Since I was sure that the IRA were going to send me into exile, then and there I determined that I was not going to return to Dundalk. Nor was I going to write anything else for them.

I told Bernie that I thought they were going to send me into exile. She did not say much. She was getting ready to go out to a Sinn Fein meeting. I said: 'Do you understand what I'm saying? Why are you working for them when they're going to send me into exile?' She did not say anything. I said: 'I don't want you to go to that meeting tonight. You should be here with me and the children.' She ignored me and started to move towards the door. I slapped her around the face, not a hard slap, it was more of a flick with my fingers. I had never hit her before and I have never hit her since. She looked stunned. She ran out of the house and slammed the door.

I sat downstairs with the children for a while and then I put them to bed. Lorcan still liked me to sleep with him to help him get off to sleep. I got into bed with him and dozed. After a few hours I heard the door opening downstairs. I heard Bernie rushing up the stairs. She threw open the door and ran over to me. She lifted her fist and was about to hit me, then she saw Lorcan sleeping beside me. She stopped herself. She did not say anything, just turned on her heel and walked out. She slept that night in the spare bedroom.

Within a week Teddy and Mooch began ringing me. I kept

telling them that I was not available to go to Dundalk. They began ringing me every other hour. Finally I unplugged the phone. The next day I plugged it back in. Teddy got through to me: I gave him another excuse. He said: 'You're some boy. You're some boy.' There was silence, then he rang off. They even sent a car to my house to give me a lift. I sent the taxi-driver away.

One Sunday morning, there was a rap on my front door. I looked through the spy-hole and saw a man I did not recognize. I opened the door. As soon as I opened it, John Joe Magee stepped out from the side and entered. There were two other men with him. All three trooped in. John Joe said: 'We need to talk to you for a minute, somewhere private.' I took them upstairs into my bedroom. His two companions sat on the side of my bed; John Joe at the foot. He asked me to sit down. I remained standing: I was not going to be told what to do in my own house.

He said: 'This is like the mountain coming to Mohammed instead of Mohammed coming to the mountain.' Then he said: 'What you wrote in those notes is nothing but a load of shit. You must write them out again.' I said: 'No. Those notes were true and accurate and I'm not writing them again.' His face flushed: 'They were shit, and it is a condition of your amnesty that you have to satisfy us that all you wrote is a true and frank account of what was said to the peelers; and as yet I'm not sat-isfied.' He began to list the amnesty conditions again, counting them on his fingers. He came to the last condition which said I had to move wherever the IRA told me to move. I interrupted him: 'I'm not moving my home for anyone.' I did not have to repeat my words. Either I had said what he had wanted to hear or my words had so stunned him that he began to lose control.

'Right,' he said, 'no one is to contact this man again, not by phone, not personally, nothing. From here on in, no contact at all. Do you men hear that?' They muttered yes. Then he got up off the bed. 'Right, let's go.' The other two left the room first. John Joe turned to me and said: 'Maybe you think we're the boy scouts?' I said that I had been in the IRA long enough to know that we were anything but the boy scouts. I followed him down the stairs. The others opened the front door and started walking down the path. When they were out of earshot, John Joe turned to me again and said: 'Put it another way: you're an embarrassment we can't afford to have.' With that he walked off.

I waited three weeks for them to deliver the sentence of exile. On 7 July 1987 an IRA messenger came to my door and handed me a brown envelope. He said he was giving it to me on behalf of the republican movement. I knew him slightly: he had joined the IRA while I was in prison. He was a well-known local thug whose chief claim to fame was that he had once – prior to becoming a revolutionary – burnt down the caravan of a man who was passing through Newry while raising money for charity.

Inside the envelope was a badly-typed note giving me seven days to leave 'the war zone'. After that date I would be executed at their convenience if I remained in Newry. The note said that I had to live in the Republic of Ireland 'south of Drogheda'.

I laughed bitterly at this final indignity – having to receive my expulsion notice from a criminal-turned-revolutionary who had probably been sleeping off hangovers when I had been risking my life and taking the lives of others for the republican 'movement'.

I left the war zone one day after the deadline: a final small act of defiance.

26

MYSELF ALONE

My expulsion order did at least help to end my wife's involvement with Sinn Fein. She was devastated by the news; and in
a way it brought us closer than we had been since I had
returned home from prison. I realized that she had been maintaining her commitment to Sinn Fein partly in the hope of
ensuring that no harm came to me. When they sent me into
exile she cut all links with the republican movement.

I felt intense anger at the IRA's treatment of me, although
there was an element of relief: they had done the worst that
they were going to do for the moment, and I was still alive. I
knew that if Mickey had had the final say, I would have ended
up on a border road with a black bin-liner for a shroud. I could
not help thinking of Mickey's English mother, and his own
upbringing in England: the vicious zealot was nothing more
than an adoptive nationalist trying to be more Irish than the
Irish themselves.

I hated the idea of having to leave my family, but I knew if
I stayed I would be providing the IRA with the excuse they
needed to kill me. I discussed the future with Bernie, and we
agreed that I should get completely out of the country for a few
months. I decided to go to the United States, where I had
some friends who would put me up for a while and perhaps
help me find temporary work.

I travelled to Shannon Airport near Limerick in order to get the transatlantic flight. As I browsed through the Duty Free shop I picked up a national tabloid newspaper. Inside was a story with the headline: 'Grass on run for his life.' I walked away, furious and humiliated. The Provos' publicity machine had obviously gone into action to explain why someone who had been given one of their amnesties was being sent into exile.

In the Newry Sinn Fein newsletter they branded me an informer. I remembered John Joe's final words to me: 'You're an embarrassment we can't afford to have.' Yet as I walked towards the plane my anger gave way to a feeling of despair.

I was not even sure they would let me into the United States. I had visions of being held in some detention centre and then deported. When I landed, I was questioned by FBI men, who warned me not to get involved in any republican activities in the US. This was a bit ritualistic, because one of them met me outside the airport building and tried to recruit me 'to keep my eyes open' in the Irish community in New York. He gave me a lift to the other terminal for my connecting flight to Rochester. During the short ride, I told him I had never been an informer and had no intention of starting now.

He asked me if I knew a guy called Martin Meehan, 'a little bald guy with a beard'. I said I had met him in prison. He said that he had once arrested Martin in New York. He said: 'He had a scar on the back of his head, like a horseshoe, where the Paras cracked his head with a rifle.' I laughed: Martin showed everyone that scar. He said he had tried to recruit Martin who had refused, telling him that the cause of republicanism was 'in the blood'.

We reached the terminal building. I took my luggage from the boot of the car. He gave me his card and we shook hands. I walked off to get my connecting flight. I never spoke to him again.

I stayed in Rochester, New York State. All around me was a new society and culture, yet in my mind I remained in Northern Ireland. I could not relax or concentrate. I thought constantly of Bernie and the kids. Bernie was pregnant again. My friends tried to bring me out of myself by taking me on tourist trips. I remember visiting the Great Lakes; I stared out across that vast expanse of water and saw only the Irish border country. After three weeks I had had enough. I decided to return to Ireland, but not to the so-called war zone. I went to Dublin.

I needed very little to live on, but had to have something to live on, so I put as much brass in my neck as I could manage and asked for my old Customs job back – from an organization whose staff I had helped to murder and whose warehouses I had helped destroy. The Provos' publicity about my exile notice, in which they effectively said I had been one of them, didn't help my case. While my application was being considered, my union paid emergency hardship money of £50 a week. After a few months they rejected my application but, just prior to my expulsion, I had lodged a case for unfair dismissal. I continued with the industrial tribunal case until the Secretary of State, Tom King, issued a Public Interest Immunity Certificate stopping proceedings.

I arrived in Dublin and found a squat in the run-down working-class area of Ballymun. I was told about the many empty flats in the stark tower blocks that littered the area's bleak landscape. A friend helped me choose a flat and I moved in with little more than a sleeping-bag.

On my first night in that dank flat I slept on the floor. I was thirty-two years old and I realized I had gone down about as far as I had ever imagined I would go. I felt the lure of self-pity, but I resisted, most of the time. I spent the night thinking about the past and the future, and in the morning I felt strangely invigorated. I realized, at the very least, that I had the greatest degree of independence I had experienced for many years. I also had my wife and two children – with another one on the way. I was going to fight back for myself and my family. I felt like an outcast, alienated from my community, and partly from myself. But that was the way it was. I would have to live with my status. Perhaps I could even use the knowledge my status gave me to help others.

In the late seventies, I had read about a priest in Dublin who worked with young homeless people and drug addicts. At the time I had toyed with the idea of going to work for him voluntarily, but instead I had got a job and joined the IRA. While in prison, I had come across another article about this priest,

Father Peter McVerry. Now I decided to seek him out to see if he needed help. I knew he had an office in one of the other Ballymun tower blocks.

I liked Peter immediately. I felt I was in the presence of a very special man. He was tall with a pleasant face and a genuine smile. He spoke softly, and he was intelligent and polite. He was patient with me but I could tell he was in a hurry. That same sense of quiet urgency never left him throughout the three years I worked for him. He dressed plainly and modestly. He had a remarkably thick head of hair, indeed, I discovered later that the boys referred affectionately to him as 'Hedge'. I respected him tremendously for his work agitating and lobbying on behalf of the Dublin poor.

In his presence I felt I could be completely honest. I told him about my past as an IRA man and how I had ended up in Dublin. I said that I had been thinking that my future might be as a worker in adult and community education, so I offered to work for him voluntarily to help build up experience which would enable me to rebuild my life. He also represented, for me, the path of changing society through peaceful means. He asked me a few questions, and then said that he could offer me work for two nights a week, keeping an eye on boys at one of his hostels. I agreed readily.

I signed on at the dole office. Over the next few weeks I worked for Peter and enrolled for a diploma in adult and community education at Maynooth College, just outside Dublin. In the meantime, I also tried to make my squat more habitable. Bernie brought me a camp-bed, an electric kettle and a mobile stove. In the first week, junkies tried to smash my front door open, but the six-inch nails I had battered into it helped to keep them at bay.

Even the poverty I had witnessed in the ghetto areas of Belfast had not prepared me for the grim concrete towers of Ballymun. I experienced a loneliness and isolation in that flat which was more oppressive than any I had experienced in prison. I could understand how some men wanted to return to prison after their release. At least in prison you have company and a few friends. And I would often experience a sense of rage at the IRA. What embittered me most was that there was no appeal against their sentence; but their kind of justice does not need or want legal safeguards.

My work with Peter helped to ease the depression that would often threaten to engulf me. I was working with young men who were far worse off than me: many of them were mentally disturbed and had come from families in which appalling cruelty had been inflicted on them, both by their parents and also by the institutions that were supposed to protect them. I found common ground with those damaged children: I could understand the brutalized, desensitized mental worlds in which they lived.

During that first year in Dublin, I thought a lot about the IRA's campaign. I asked myself whether I would have remained in the Provos if they had welcomed me back and forgiven me unquestioningly after I had broken. I could honestly say to myself that I would not have gone back to any form of military activity. Yet if they had treated me decently, I know I would initially have retained some respect for them. So in a way I am thankful for their behaviour, because it sent me further along the path of asking questions about the whole nature of republicanism and political violence which perhaps I would not have asked so searchingly if I'd been allowed to stay in republican Newry. As it was, the IRA convinced me in a very personal way over many years that they could never win anything, certainly not the hearts and minds of the whole Irish people.

However, no one ceases to be a revolutionary nationalist overnight. For several years after I emerged from prison I still had ambivalent feelings towards the IRA tradition. Sometimes I would surprise myself with the strength of sympathy I felt for my former comrades. I remember feeling an incredible visceral rage when the SAS shot dead three unarmed IRA members in Gibraltar in 1988. Rationally, I could not properly explain where my feelings came from. After all, I believed that the armed struggle was pointless and I accepted that in war combatants ran the risk of being killed. But emotionally I wanted to attend those funerals and – if I am honest – I wanted to see the IRA hit back.

And then, almost within days, I saw one of the results of the

IRA hitting back. The loyalist Michael Stone attacked mourners at the funeral of the Gibraltar three, killing another three people, one of whom was an IRA volunteer. At that volunteer's funeral three days later the nervous crowd thought they had foiled another loyalist attack when they dragged two armed suspects out of a car. The two men turned out to be undercover members of the British Army. The soldiers, who themselves had resisted firing their Browning pistols into the crowd when surrounded, were then brutally beaten and shot dead with their own weapons, their bodies left half-naked on waste ground.

I watched part of the incident on television and I felt sickened and horrified by the images. A hovering helicopter had filmed the whole thing, giving the killings a sad impersonal inevitability and pointlessness. The murders reminded me of what I would have to defend morally if I gave even conditional support to the IRA. The killing of those corporals was morally indefensible. I felt that, even in the IRA's purely pragmatic terms, those men should not have been killed: what a tremendous propaganda coup it would have been for the republican movement if those men had been released as a gesture of humanitarian goodwill. Instead, they were lynched on camera, and enormous worldwide damage was done to the legitimacy of the nationalist cause and to the reputation of the Catholic population generally.

In those early years after leaving Crumlin Road, a part of me missed being in the IRA. I had spent six years leading an action-packed existence, living each day with the excitement of feeling I was playing a part in taking on the Orange State. At the very least, such activity gave a strange edge to my life: I lived each day in a heightened state of alertness. Everything I did, however trivial, could seem meaningful. Life outside the IRA could often feel terribly mundane. It has taken me many years to appreciate and enjoy the mundane pleasures and challenges of everyday life.

The former INLA (and later IPLO) leaders Jimmy Brown and Gerard Steenson told me in prison that I would eventually snap out of what they described as my 'alienation' from my revolutionary self. In 1988, Jimmy came to see me in Dublin (Gerard had been killed in an internal feud the previous year,

not long after his release from prison). He felt that the IRA, led
by Belfast, were moving towards calling the war off. He even
suggested that they were setting up their own hardline volunteers to be assassinated by the Brits.

He asked me to join the IPLO. I suppose he thought I still
shared some version of their Marxist analysis, and in prison he
had treated me like a human being, but I turned down his
offer. I said I could not see how the killing of one more soldier
or policeman or loyalist paramilitary would further the cause of
a united socialist republic. I said I was interested in struggling
against injustice and inequality but I felt that the work I was
doing in Dublin was of more use than the taking of life. He was
disappointed in me, but we parted on good terms.

When I first lived in Dublin, Bernie would come to visit me
every weekend, bringing the children and some new piece of
second-hand furniture to help me make my squat more comfortable. One Sunday her car started to play up. I decided – as
she was heavily pregnant – that I would drive her back to
Newry so that I would be able to deal with any breakdown. We
drove late at night and took the back roads into Barcroft Park.
I knew I was taking a risk, but I could not let Bernie drive back
on her own. The next day she drove me to the railway station
so I could travel back to Dublin. I stood on the windswept
platform in the pouring rain, a hood pulled up over my head. I
had crossed a threshold: I was starting the return journey.

I started to travel home regularly at weekends. I would
always travel at night. Usually, I took the train to Dundalk. On
the journey I would never sit in a carriage; I would always
stand outside in the corridor by an open window, often pushing
my head out into the wind. I did this partly for security reasons
but partly also because I felt such a social outcast that I no
longer felt comfortable with other people.

Bernie would wait for me in the station car-park. She would
take the back roads through south Armagh to our home. I
would stay for the whole weekend, not daring to step outside
the house. We had to tell the two young boys not to say a word
to anyone about my visits. We would keep the blind closed in
the kitchen, and the heavy mahogany security doors we had
installed would be locked. At night we shut the security gate at

the bottom of the stairs. I also kept a baton by my side at all times. Whenever anyone rang on the doorbell I would step back into the kitchen until I had seen who it was. I became paranoid, but my paranoia was based on a very real threat. It would only take one person, one vindictive person, to spot me and to inform the IRA that I was ignoring their diktat.

Then, at the end of the weekend, Bernie would drive me back to the station. I felt most vulnerable waiting for the train. Indeed, I lived in fear of being recognized on the platform, but I think I was only spotted once. After about two years of these trips I had got a little cocky and had dropped my guard slightly: normally I stood at the far end of the platform with my coat collar turned up high. I tried to avoid people. But one night I did not follow my usual precautions and just as the train was about to arrive I looked up to see a friend of Mickey's staring straight into my eyes. My heart jumped. I knew she would report me to Mickey so I stopped going home for several weeks until I felt it was safer to resume my journeys.

I hated returning to Dublin on my own. I would feel a terrible emptiness on the journey back to my squat. As the years passed, this feeling only got worse. I went through a period when I kept getting the urge to break down and cry. I missed my wife and children; I missed my father; I missed them all the time. But I fought my urges to cry: I feared that if I cried I might trigger a mental collapse, and then I would be truly lost.

During that first year in Dublin, I studied during the day and worked occasionally for Peter at night. One day after I came out of the dole office, I found a member of the Irish Special Branch waiting for me. He said he had called at my flat several times but had not found me in: he wanted to search the place. He followed me back to the flat. He was surprised at my few possessions. He did not take long to turn the place over. As he went about his business he said: 'Jesus, boy, you did the Provos some harm, didn't ye.' I said nothing.

It was not a serious search. Obviously he had just wanted to let me know that the Special Branch knew where I was and were keeping an eye on me, just in case I was thinking of trying to rehabilitate myself in republican circles by doing a bit of IRA work in Dublin.

I had not seen the last of my new friend. Sometime later I
called to see my former OC, Seán, who was also in exile. He
was friendly and welcoming: he did not look down on me for
having broken under interrogation, and I appreciated this.
When I left his house I found the Special Branch man waiting
for me around the back. He said: 'Are you in visiting your
friend Seán? Are you planning something?' I said that neither
of us had anything to do with the IRA. I claimed that I was
trying to get Seán to come over to do a bit of work for the
priest. The Branch man said: 'Jesus, you're well trained, boy.'

I finished my diploma at Maynooth and Peter McVerry took
me on as a full-time worker. I started taking some of the boys
away for trips into the countryside at weekends. One time I
hired a car and took three boys down to the Cork area. Not
long into the journey, I noticed that I was being followed by a
sleek car containing four men wearing suits. They looked like
Italian mafiosi. They were certainly too smartly dressed to be
Provos, so I assumed they had to be Special Branch. They followed the car for several hours before disappearing. When I
got back to Dublin, Peter told me that he had received a call
from the police asking what I was doing driving three lads
around Cork. Peter had explained the innocent purpose of my
trip. The police must have assumed that I was taking the boys
to an IRA training camp.

Once I was earning money again, I decided to take Bernie
on holiday for a week. We wanted to go to Mullaghmore in the
north-western county of Sligo. This posed a problem: my exile
notice had said that if I intended staying in Ireland I would
have to live south of Drogheda. What I needed to know was
whether this line of territorial exclusion extended right across
the country, cutting Ireland into two neat halves, or whether it
only went halfway across, stopping beneath the westernmost
part of Northern Ireland, creating merely a rectangle of exclusion, which would leave me free to travel into places like
Donegal and Sligo.

Bernie decided to seek clarification from the IRA. She made
an appointment to see Teddy, who now lived in Dundalk. As
soon as she walked into his house he asked her: 'Are you
wired?' Bernie told him to catch himself on. Teddy said, in

response to Bernie's question of geography, that he assumed that the line ran straight across the country. Bernie said it was absurd: what was going on in Donegal, Sligo, Mayo or Leitrim which I could have any influence over? Teddy said they were all war zones, all part of the theatre of war. Obviously the IRA had placed most of Ireland on a war footing, even if they had not told the people who lived there. We decided to take our holiday in Sligo anyway.

After three years in Dublin, I became obsessed by the desire to return home permanently. I applied for, and was offered, a job as a youth tutor and community education organizer at the Ulster People's College in Belfast.

Bernie decided to see if she could get my exile notice lifted officially. She went to Belfast to see the senior Sinn Fein figure, Joe Austin. He told Bernie that he had never had a problem with me. He said he had not been aware that I had been branded as an informer but he had heard that 'some people' had a problem with me.

In 1988 I had been approached by a television producer, Stephen Scott, who worked for Thames Television's 'This Week' programme. He had heard about my case and was keen to make a film about me. At that time I was tempted, but for various reasons, including considerations about my personal safety, I turned him down. However, I knew that the IRA knew about the television producer.

Austin indicated that if I had been returning home at weekends, and no one was bothering me, then perhaps I could consider that it was safe to return home permanently. He said that so long as I was prepared to keep my head down, then he was sure that the IRA would probably let sleeping dogs lie. Reading between the lines – as one always has to do when analyzing anything said by republican spokesmen – I felt he was saying that the IRA would grudgingly let me live at home so long as I did not go telling tales to anyone. This compromise was to their advantage: they would not have to officially withdraw the exile notice – which would have meant a public climb-down – yet they would keep me feeling insecure and at the same time ensure that I did not make a documentary or write a book.

I took the chance, and returned to live in my home. During

the week I travelled to Belfast to work. At weekends I did leave
my house, but I tended to be careful about where I went and I
tried to keep a low profile. No one bothered me.

I worked in the Ulster People's College for eighteen months.
The college was sited in a middle-class area close to the Malone
Road. The neutrality of its location encouraged people from
both sides of the community to use it. The college existed to
promote reconciliation and radical grassroots politics through
a process of community education. Although some of my colleagues knew about my background, I kept pretty quiet about
my past and lived in fear that it would surface. After a while I
began to become aware of the existence of hardline loyalist
elements within the college. My period there coincided with an
increase in the number of sectarian murders by loyalist paramilitaries in Belfast, and I began to feel anxious about my
personal safety.

I could easily, from terrible familiarity with the methods,
work out the best way of killing someone like me. I identified
my routines and changed them. I started to vary my routes into
work; I made sure I never arrived at the same time; and in
every other area I removed any element of predictability in my
behaviour. It was a frightening and chastening experience to
put myself in the role of the hunted after spending so many
years as the hunter.

However, I enjoyed my work at the college. It gave me the
freedom to explore areas that interested me. In particular I
began to explore the history and culture of Protestantism
within Northern Ireland. One of my projects was to start up a
summer school dedicated to studying the life and work of the
radical Presbyterian writer and campaigner Robert Lynd, who
had supported the idea of a United Ireland.

One of the people I met was the legendary Catholic priest
Des Wilson. I admired him greatly for his work as a radical
man of peace and I spent many hours talking to him about the
nature of the conflict. I discussed with him an idea I had had
for a Ph.D. I thought it would be interesting to examine the
way in which prisoners' education in the H-Blocks had influenced and effected social movements on the outside. Des
helped me develop my ideas.

I knew I would need the co-operation of the republican movement in getting access to former and current prisoners, but Sinn Fein, in the person of Tom Hartley, one of Gerry Adams' key lieutenants, shut that door in my face. Hartley threw me out of a Sinn Fein POW department office. I felt angry and humiliated, but also endangered. What would happen now? Would they enforce my exile notice again? Then I experienced a surge of defiance: I was not going to spend the rest of my life running away from them.

As part of my work I had to go out to visit a variety of community projects in the city. This was how I met the former UVF leader, the notorious Gusty Spence. In 1991, I dropped in to the Shankill Road Resource Centre. I had used a former member of the UDA to get me a guarantee that I would not be harmed. I had to wait to see Spence: when I arrived he was talking to a group of people from the south of Ireland who were on a fact-finding mission to the north. I saw Spence sitting on a high chair with his arms folded, wearing a white, open-necked shirt. The group of southerners were hanging on his every word.

For a moment I felt ashamed, not only of myself but of them also. What were we all doing here talking to this grandfather of sectarian murder? Spence had served a life sentence for the killing of a teenage Catholic barman back in 1966; two other Catholics had been wounded at the same time. All of them had been targeted for no other reason than that they were Catholics.

I felt an overpowering sense of nausea. For an instant I could only see before me a deadly enemy of my people. Suddenly I was filled with a killing rage, all the old anger coming back. I felt I ought to have been moving towards him holding a revolver, firing bullet after bullet into his body, instead of standing there waiting to be ushered into his presence.

But the feeling passed and my rage subsided. I knew that murder was the logical outcome of that rage, and murder would not solve anything. In that moment, I realized how far I had travelled in my life.

After the southerners left, I shook hands with Spence. He took me into a back room where we discussed the conflict. He was an articulate and intelligent speaker and I listened carefully to what he had to say. At times he spoke with violence and aggression; and I could detect that same rage that had just overtaken me. I realized that he had not moved that far forward in his thinking since 1966, but he had moved, and I had moved, and that was important.

After eighteen months at the Ulster People's College, I began to look elsewhere for a better-paid job. However, the world of community education within Northern Ireland is relatively small: there are only so many jobs in the field. After a while I realized that everyone seemed to know everyone else. And those who were in a position to offer jobs had all got to know about my past. I was told this by a member of the Workers' Education Association after I had applied for a job with them, which I had failed to get, even though my qualifications had seemed ideal. He said that he thought I would have real difficulty in getting another, more senior job in Northern Ireland because people would not want to work with someone who might be a target for either republican or loyalist bullets. Potential colleagues would be worried about the possibility of being caught in crossfire.

My contract with the college came to an end in 1992 and I found myself on the dole. I spent six months claiming benefit and looking around for work. I found myself in the ironic position of having to seek work away from home. This was how I ended up spending two years of self-imposed exile in Scotland. I got a job as a senior community education worker in a deprived area of Edinburgh. I did not want to leave my family again, but I now had four children and I could not accept the idea of bringing them up on state benefit.

Before I left for Scotland, the IPLO leader Jimmy Brown came to see me again, in August 1992. I had grown more and more detached from my republican past, and I had come to regard the idea of a socialist republic as fantasy. I had spent many years working with drug addicts and I did not like the fact that his organization (which was undergoing one of its periodic feuds) was clearly involved in the drugs trade. Jimmy did not deny that the IPLO were dealing in drugs but, with impressive circumlocution, he insisted that the end justified the means. And for Jimmy the end was to raise funds to build a strong revolutionary organization, which he was confident he was in the throes of doing.

Again he asked me to join the IPLO. Again I turned him down. I told him that the only organization I wanted to be a part of was my family. I told him that he should forget about the revolution too: I said he would be better off spending time with his child. I could see in his eyes that he looked at me with pity: he lamented what he regarded as the waste of a revolutionary. I never saw him again. Within a week of our meeting, he was shot in the head several times at close range by one of his former comrades. Within a few months, the IRA had moved ruthlessly to crush the remnants of his organization.

I enjoyed Edinburgh so much that I seriously considered moving my family there. I spent two years sorting out a community centre where no one else had appeared to want to work. Members of the community would wander in with machetes and knives. The previous manager had been threatened with a baseball bat. Most of the community which the centre was meant to serve had been barred from using it. I helped to make the place safer by employing a janitor who was a former boxer. For special events I also employed two former Paras as bouncers. Within a year the centre was thriving.

I came to realize a fact which initially shocked me: I felt more at ease in Scotland than in the Republic of Ireland. Culturally, I was closer to the Scots – who shared strong roots with most Ulster Protestants – than I was to my so-called kith and kin in the south of Ireland. I had a simple, almost laughably ironic, realization: I had more in common with Ulster Protestants than with southern Catholics.

I travelled over regularly to see my family, but after two years the separation from them had become unbearable. I decided to return to Northern Ireland. In 1994, I managed to get a job running a youth club in Armagh.

My new job was a lot quieter, but I found some similar problems. As in Edinburgh, I found that small groups had begun to run the place into decline. I saw my task as opening the centre up to the whole community and I succeeded in packing the place out with people who had formerly been excluded.

I used my knowledge of the bureaucracy to secure funding for several new projects.

I felt more relaxed back at home. My 'case' had been pretty much forgotten with the passage of the years, as happens in this strange corner of Ireland where people have to learn not to enquire too closely about the past. I began to walk about Newry freely once again.

I came to own the old family farm in Camlough where I was brought up. My grandfather had rebuilt the place after the war, but no one has lived there for more than a decade and it has fallen into dereliction. The fields are full of rushes, the drains are all astray, and the fences lie broken. Several years ago vandals got in and smashed the house to pieces. They did a far more thorough job than the Paras had managed back in 1974. I boarded the house up, but I noticed recently that kids had found a way in and had daubed graffiti all over the walls.

I like walking around the fields where my father and I calved so many cows and heifers. Often when I am there, I remember my father. I can see him wandering around, clutching a black-thorn stick, threatening officials from the Ministry of Agriculture. One time he lost his driving licence after being found guilty of driving with a little too much alcohol in his blood. He started travelling everywhere in a horse-drawn cart, sometimes stopping at petrol stations to get water for the horse. On his trips he would wear a huge top hat that I presume had been passed down from his grandfather. My mother would pretend she was embarrassed, but she used to laugh secretly at his antics. She worried what the neighbours would think. My father did not care what people said: 'Fuck them all,' he would reply, and off the horse would trot, with my father holding the reins.

I want to restore the farm while keeping the good features from its past. I want to see my children there, laughing and playing. The anger and hatred this place has seen may in time be forgotten, if not forgiven. I do not want much else more.

Acknowledgements

I wish to publicly acknowledge the people who helped me during what was a difficult but interesting journey, rebuilding my life from 1985 to the present.

Crumlin Road Prison 1985-87

These men treated me as a fellow human being in prison: friendship can transcend politics in a hard place. Aiden Grew, 'Ducksy' Doherty, Stephen Donnelly, William McGuinness, Seamus Shannon, Gerry Loughlin, 'Crisp' McWilliams, Paul Donnelly, and the following who are now dead: Gerard Steenson, Martin O'Prey, Jimmy Brown, Thomas Power. Nick Scott, education officer, and the Belfast Open University staff who did everything to assist me in completing my first degree on remand.

The late Paddy McGrory, a great criminal lawyer and Irishman. Also his son Barra McGrory.

Dublin 1987-90

Father Peter McClerry, Father Michael Sweetman, Brendan Corce, Sister Sandra McSheffney, Sister Kay Barry, Lily Murphy, Dr. Tom Collins, Shea Hurley. Not forgetting Jason, Paddy, Coso, Kieran, Eddie – homeless youth of Dublin, now dead.

Jim Canning of Dungannon provided a welcome life-raft when I was forced into exile.

Belfast 1990-92

Professor Tom Lovett, Dr. Jude Collins, Deidre Rice, Father Des Wilson, Rita Duffy, Andrew Boyd, Paddy Scott, Robert Greacen, Robert Ballagh, John O'Connell Cosh and John Kelly Lurgan.

Edinburgh 1992-94

Christine Machary, Mike Rosendale, John Player, Gerry White, John Haywood, Gerri Kirkwood, Hamish Murphy, Brian Greatorix. Very special thanks to Vernon Galloway and Myra; Derek Suttie; also Scott, Will, Billy, Laura, Mike, Rab, Mac, Allison, Adrian and Flo.

Keady 1994-5

Terry Pattison, Charlie Fanning, Greg, Paul and all the Pattisons.

Aran Islands
Fr. Dara Molloy, Tess Harper.

Mater Hospital, Dublin
Cardiologists Dr. McCann and Dr. Sugrue; surgeon Dr. Hurley. A
special thanks to all the doctors and nurses in Sacred Heart Ward, St.
Cecilia's and St. Theresa's who did so much for me.
   My late friend in hospital Joe Croley, a wonderfully funny man and
a great 'Dub'.

Family
I owe my brothers John and Bernard and my sister Alice a special
debt of gratitude. But for John's dogged tenacity and Bernard's per-
severance I would have had little strength to return from the abyss.
They showed great courage and generosity.
   My late father Brian, although ill, never missed a visit with my son
Tiárnach to whom he showed great love. My mother as always never
let me down and still sustains me whenever I need support; a woman
of tremendous dignity and simplicity of character.
   My wife's family for the much needed help and support during the
last fifteen years.

London
Jason McCue and Brian Hepworth from Henry Hepworth Solicitors.
   To all at Granta, especially Neil Belton for having the courage to
grasp this book and to follow it through with such professionalism
and sense of purpose to the end. And to Frances Coady for supporting him.

Newry
Jan, Allison, Paula, Pauline and Julie.